We, the People of the States of Bharat

'Given the ethnic, linguistic and religious mosaic that constitutes India, a study of identity politics demanding recognition and representation as states and related configurations within the Indian Union, in a democratic framework, is a daunting challenge. Sanjeev Chopra addresses that challenge admirably and painstakingly analyses the changing maps, nomenclature and the concomitant politics of give and take. The result is a masterpiece of a compendium which will prove to be seminal and a standard reference on this subject.'

– **Dr Ishtiaq Ahmed**, Professor Emeritus, political science, Stockholm University and honorary senior fellow, Institute of South Asian Studies, National University of Singapore

'Excellent work. The author's style of narrating the political, social and economic factors leading to realignment of the borders of all Indian states, a continuing exercise of the executive, displays his vast and deep reading, spanning from Gibbon to papers produced by young probationers of IAS as well as his ability to make this somewhat documentary type of a subject matter a compulsory read.'

– **G. Balachandran,** former IAS officer and adviser, Tamil chairs in Harvard, Toronto and Houston Universities

'Geography – mountains, rivers, oceans – play an important role in the destiny of nations. For example, all great ancient civilizations, such as the Indian, Chinese, Egyptian, Persian, came up on the banks of major rivers. Boundaries of civilizations are also decided largely by its geographical features. Equally important factors in deciding boundaries are language, culture, political aspiration and religion. Sanjeev Chopra's book emphasizes and elaborately explains the relevance of these factors and how they shaped the internal boundaries of our states. It is a very well-researched and scholarly work, with a brilliant exposition on how the states of the Indian Union were formed and continue to evolve since our independence in 1947. The language is lucid and the narration is engaging. It is a book meant for scholars and laypersons alike and a must for your personal library.'

– **P.K. Basu**, author, columnist and former member of the
Central Administrative Tribunal and the Academic
Council of Visva-Bharati

'Dr Sanjeev Chopra has written this remarkable history of India's unification – from a motley assembly of disparate, incoherent princely states to a functioning democracy, a constitutional republic, a stable nation. It is a profound work of painstaking scholarship. Only somebody with his deep insight into governance in India, across sectors and geographies, could have analysed the myriad related events so comprehensively from a political, administrative and international perspective. A must-read for all public administrators, political analysts and aspirants.'

– **Raghav Chandra**, author, educator, commentator, ex-
secretary to Government of India and director, Bhopal Literature
and Art Festival

'The States Reorganisation Act, 1956, acknowledges the fact that the formation of the states of India prior to 1956 was a result of historical accidents and circumstances. Dr Chopra's book, however, takes us before 1956 and then beyond 1956. He has brought out the little-known aspects of the Roy–Sinha proposals, about the probable merger of West Bengal and Bihar in 1954. This book is a work of painstaking research and hard work. It is a major work on our contemporary history and politics, written in elegant prose, which makes it an interesting read.

'With this book, Dr Sanjeev Chopra has contributed to our understanding and scholarship on the leadership in the states, for hitherto, the focus was always on the political contest for Delhi whereas history was being made elsewhere: in Sikkim, Punjab, Assam, Uttarakhand and Telangana, to name a few.'

– **Justice Sudhanshu Dhulia**, Supreme Court of India

'How India won independence is a well-known story about which there is very little contestation. But how India created its states is a story that is playing out in multiple ways even today. Former IAS officer Sanjeev Chopra looks at how the map changed from 1947 to 2019, when the last change was made in the Jammu, Kashmir and Ladakh region.

'State formation was a complex and protracted exercise full of fault lines and eggshells – princely states, language chauvinism, ethnic and tribal pride, Sikkim merger and foreign territories. The author dusts and pulls out many fascinating details from the archives – the debate around the various proposed names for United Provinces – Awadh, Brij Koshal, Aryavarta, Bhagirath Pradesh, Nava Hindu, Ram Krishna Prant, Bharat Khand; the making and unmaking of Assam; and how Tibet appeared, disappeared and reappeared in the map of India between 1950 and 1960 is itself a telling example about Nehru's dilemma. Imagining India through its states is a study of aspirations, assertions and adjustments, he writes insightfully.'

— **Shekhar Gupta**, editor-in-chief, The Print

'Scholar-administrator Sanjeev Chopra has dug deep into the vast repository of archival material on the formation of states. His own experiences in Kalimpong, Cooch Behar and the newly created state of Uttarakhand are also reflected in this timely treatise on mapping the states of India.'

— **Parameswaran Iyer**, CEO, NITI Aayog

'Having known Sanjeev as a fine administrator for over three decades, I am delighted to see that he has now taken up the task of looking at the administrative and political history of India from the perspective of maps and state boundaries.

'He is a master raconteur, and the book will be a very useful addition to the personal collection of all those who wish to get a perspective on how India has evolved, and continues to do so, for as has been said – there are no full stops in history!'

— **Bhaskar Khulbe**, former secretary and adviser to
Prime Minister Narendra Modi

'I am delighted that the maps produced by the Survey of India have resulted in this magnum opus on the history of our country based on the changes in political cartography. I compliment Dr Chopra for giving the Survey of India the acknowledgment it deserves for its quiet, but painstaking work.'

— **Lt Gen. Girish Kumar**, Vishisht Seva Medal awardee and
former surveyor general of India

'Maps both reflect and influence how a nation regards itself. Original, unique, even unprecedented, in its method of understanding the evolution of the republic, Sanjeev Chopra recounts the political reimagining of post-independence India through its changing maps. Looking especially at the progress of state formation and changing contours of Indian federalism, this remarkable book gives voice to India's cartographic re-imagination.'

– **Makarand R. Paranjape**, professor of English, Jawaharlal Nehru University and former director, Indian Institute of Advanced Studies, Shimla

'This is a masterful work on boundaries and belonging. Chopra presents a granular vision of India's diversity in its cartographic details. His understanding of how imaginary lines make for citizen aspirations is very engaging. Written in a lucid style, this is a must read.'

– **Dr Manisha Priyam**, professor, National Institute for Educational Planning and Administration, New Delhi

'Sanjeev Chopra has fine-tuned his rich administrative experience with the mining of a vast historical record to provide an animated and gripping account of modern India's political cartography. History, ethnicity, political expediency and linguistic nationalism all come together in this fine study of how the constituent units of India's federation came to be and how they continue to evolve.'

– **T.C.A. Raghavan**, historian, columnist and former diplomat

'The redrawing of borders after World War I in Europe and the Middle East have been the subject of mighty tomes. The partition of British India has also led to similar works. Yet, the redrawing of borders within India and the creation of new states since 1947 has largely escaped attention not only of journalists but also of scholars. Sanjeev Chopra paints with a broad yet delicate brush how these developments have changed this seventy-five-year-old nation.

'One such delicate observation by Chopra is about the 2019 abolition of Article 370 and Article 35A that gave special status to the state of Jammu and Kashmir. He reveals that Ladakh had sought to attach itself to the Lahaul–Spiti area of the then Punjab state, which included modern-day Himachal Pradesh and Haryana, as early as 1948. He also points out that the focus has almost entirely been on Kashmir Valley while 'the views, interests and concerns of people inhabiting the frontier regions of Ladakh, Chitral, Gilgit, Baltistan and Tibet have been peripheral to the discourse''. To this day, India claims 78,114 square kilometres held by Pakistan and 42,735 by China.

'Chopra's book not only dives into details but also examines fundamentals of state formation. Starting off by examining the visions of Gandhi, Nehru, Patel and Ambedkar for India, the author goes on to examine the formation of different states such as the linguistic states of south India and the more recent states of Chhattisgarh, Uttarakhand and Jharkhand. His last chapter examines the formation of Telangana, the second state for Telugu speakers. Full of colourful vignettes and trenchant analysis, Chopra has penned a masterpiece that should be read by politicians, government officials, foreign diplomats, academics, journalists and citizens to get a better understanding of this great nation of ours.'

– **Atul Singh,** founder, CEO and editor-in-chief, Fair Observer

'Packed with insights, this is a compelling and deft narrative of the refashioning of internal borders that has shaped Hindustan/Bharat/India since independence.'

— **Manreet Sodhi Someshwar**, award-winning author of
The Radiance of a Thousand Suns

'The internal geometry of India in 2022 has practically no resemblance to the geometry of the former India as it looked under the British rule. Indeed, even the very first internal boundary map of the independent Republic of India has little similarity to the latest official internal boundary map of current India, reflecting the establishment of Ladakh and Jammu and Kashmir as Union Territories in 2019.

'While there has been considerable general discussion, as well as scholarly explorations, behind the reasons that led to formation of specific states, the analysis has been conducted more as independent case studies. No one has imagined and comprehensively discussed the evolution of India's internal state boundaries and in turn told a story of the making of India.

'A remarkable balance of nuances and insights relating to specific case studies, alongside the extensive coverage of boundary changes that occurred across the length and breadth of India, is skilfully accomplished through identifying how certain critical political and cultural issues of the time were "resolved", leaving behind a geographical imprint. Dr Chopra avoids the seductive trap of editorializing on whether a particular representation of India was right or wrong, and disciplines himself in presenting documented facts and evidence with a scholarly interpretation of what they meant at that time. This aspect of his book is most refreshing and a rare trait, especially in today's time.

'*We, the People of Bharat* will appeal to the uninitiated as well as the initiated. Specifically, it is an ideal book for undergraduate- and graduate-level courses focused on the story of independent India, both in terms of content as well as the uniquely interdisciplinary perspective he brings to this discussion. In short, this book is a tour de force. It is not simply a story of the making of India in the past tense, but with his incredibly lucid style of narration, Dr Chopra makes it clear that it is a story of *India in making*.'

– Professor S.V. Subramanian, professor of Population Health and Geography, Harvard University

We, the People of the People of the States of Bharat

The Making and Remaking of India's Internal Boundaries

Sanjeev Chopra

HarperCollins *Publishers* India

First published in hardback in India by HarperCollins *Publishers* 2022
4th Floor, Tower A, Building No. 10, Phase II, DLF Cyber City,
Gurugram, Haryana – 122002
www.harpercollins.co.in

2 4 6 8 10 9 7 5 3 1

P-ISBN: 978-93-5629-142-3
E-ISBN: 978-93-5629-166-9

Typeset in 11.5/15.2 Bembo Std at
Manipal Technologies Limited, Manipal

Printed and bound at
Thomson Press (India) Ltd.

For Bijli, who lights the path,
And Bannu, who walks ahead: so I do not stumble

CONTENTS

CONTENTS

PROLOGUE

I was an eleven-year-old during the India–Pakistan War of 1971. My father was, at the time, the staff officer to the highly decorated Ashwini Kumar, Indian Police, Padma Shri, inspector general, Border Security Force (BSF). We were then staying in the Punjab Armed Police Lines, BSF campus, in Jalandhar cantonment. I could see and hear the movements of BSF troops to the border. The 'sense of war' came from the sirens renting the air, blackouts at night, deep trenches in public places and drills at school. In addition to trenches for emergency use during the air raid warnings, we were also privileged to have a protective bunker in our backyard. And though the situation did not arise where we had to use it to take cover, it became a favourite spot for playing hide and seek, for reading books (under torchlight), and generally to show off to cousins and friends who did not have an armed forces background.

Every evening, I would walk with my father to the Control Room to see the map of the India–Pakistan border. The 'Out of Bounds' board outside made the entry to the room quite wondersome. I could see the maps with different coloured tapes and marker pins. The area where the Indian forces had moved ahead was marked with an arrow. Understanding strategic acronyms like CBJ (Chhamb Jaurian) and DBN (Dera Baba Nanak) made me feel like I was in the possession of some secret knowledge. Mr Kumar was a versatile personality, as fond of reading as he was of sports and music, and indulgent towards children. He would answer my various questions and give me sweets from JB Mangalam confectionary, as I recall very fondly. The officers would continue their conversations while I sat in the background, happy to flip through magazines such as *The Illustrated Weekly*, *Dharamyug* and *Filmfare*.

Maps continued to fascinate me through my school and college days: one probable reason was that one could score cent per cent in the section on maps if one knew the direction and flow of the rivers, the location of the mountain peaks and the capitals of different states. On joining the Indian Administrative Service (IAS) in 1985, the map of an assigned subdivision or district also kept me in touch with maps. But it was during my posting in Cooch Behar as an additional district magistrate in 1990–91, when the district administration was asked to prepare the background papers and maps with regard to the transfer of Teen Bigha to Bangladesh, that the issue of enclaves and exclaves made me personally aware of how borders and boundaries impacted lives of people. Not only did we have enclaves between India and Bangladesh, but we also had some villages in Cooch Behar which could (then) be reached only through the Dhubri district of Assam. The administrative construct of Cooch Behar always struck me as very odd – Mekhliganj, for example, was next to Jalpaiguri, just about 35 km away but administered from Cooch Behar, which is 110 km away. But this is not specific to Cooch Behar or West Bengal. Throughout the country, examples abound of subdivisions and tehsils which are geographically distant to their own district headquarters but proximate to another district within the same state. Thus, in Punjab we have Phagwara subdivision of Kapurthala that can be reached only after crossing the entire length of Jalandhar district. We have Rishikesh as a part of Dehradun, rather than Haridwar which is closer, and the Kempty Falls tehsil of Tehri can be reached only after crossing Mussoorie which falls in the jurisdiction of Dehradun.

While these issues were always there in the back of my mind, I did not get down to writing about them because they were more in the nature of irritants, rather than real roadblocks. Why was the convenience of citizens not the overriding factor in determination of boundaries? This is closely linked to how borders and boundaries are drawn, and though one was aware of what the Survey of India did, the circumstances that led to those changes was known only in a general sense. In the course of curating Valley of Words, a literature and arts festival based out of the Doon Valley, I had been reading books across various genres including *Durand's Curse*, by Rajiv Dogra, and that led me to ponder over the impact which people like Durand, Radcliffe and McMahon left on the subcontinent. Another book that I had just finished reviewing was Hindol Sengupta's *The Man Who Saved India*, a biography of Sardar Patel. This book highlighted Patel's role in the making of India – both on account of his commitment to a strong and merit-based civil services, as well as his decisive actions in integrating the 562 princely states into the Union of India. In September 2019, I had been invited to speak on this subject at the Indian Institute of Advanced Studies, Shimla. A visit to the Statue of Unity on the occasion of the launch of Aarambh (the common foundation course for the civil services) in October 2019 led me to the exhibition in which many legal documents, such as the Instruments of Accession and Merger Agreements, were on display, along with the handwritten letters exchanged between Patel and some of the princely rulers.

Various strands of thought thus started coming together when I accompanied a batch of IAS officers to their briefing and field study on survey techniques at the Survey of India campus sometime in February 2020, just a few weeks before Covid-enforced solitude gave some of us the rare opportunity to read, reflect and write about issues. The young officers were being briefed about satellite imaging, aerial drones and precision mapping; it was certainly a long way from our times when we had to look at Gunter's chain and theodolite instruments to 'survey and settle' the land. However, my attention veered to the display of the maps of India – starting from the map of India in 1799 – when Warren Hastings was the governor general and the organization was still called the Survey Office of Bengal. I saw the map of India published immediately after Independence in 1947, when states were still called provinces, the first map of the Republic of India in 1950, and the maps published in the years when new states were formed. The latest map was the one in which the Union Territories (UTs) of Ladakh and Jammu and Kashmir (J&K) had been created.

My research has drawn primarily from secondary sources, journals and newspaper articles and government reports that were available at the Gandhi Smriti Library at the Lal Bahadur Shastri National Academy of Administration – which is a repository of nearly two lakh books.

I found a great ally in Lt Gen. Girish Kumar, the then surveyor general, and his team of officers. The surveyor general's office is a very interesting organization under the ministry of science and technology, which draws its officers from both the military and civilian side – and the tools, techniques and processes employed by them in the making of maps is the subject of an altogether different study. My purpose was to access all the maps printed by them from 1947 to 2019 and study the changes during that period. I got the prints of the maps in my study at Him Shikhar – the director's official residence – as well as in the Gyanlok section of the Gandhi Smriti Library. I also asked Dr Sivaprasad Senapati, our principal library and information officer (PLIO), to start looking for books on the formation of states in India. From the beginning of March 2000 to August 2021, I have been to this library at least three times a week, if not more, trying to immerse myself into the story of how each state got its border, or its new name or status. While the exhaustive bibliography and endnotes will go into details, here I will only mention those books and articles which have impacted the way my thoughts have been shaped and conditioned. We are at a point in history where more material can be accessed than ever before, and the expert will always be able to point out additional facts that may have been missed out while discussing each state. But this is a book on how boundaries were shaped, not about any specific state as such. The readings which I went through week after week as I sat down to write my column on 'Mapping the Indian States' for *Millennium Post*, that has serialized this from March 2020 onwards, have been listed.

I started this project with a re-reading of my personal copies of V.P. Menon's seminal works, *The Transfer of Power* and *The Story of the Integration of Indian States,* gifted to me by Chandan Ghosh, the law officer attached to the ministry of tourism in West Bengal when I was holding additional charge of the department. Menon's books are a treasure trove for anyone looking at the factual documentation of official India from 1946 to 1950 – the four years which saw India emerge as a modern nation-state with some kind of uniformity in administration. Asha Sarangi's introductory essay to *The Story of the Integration of Indian States* gives an excellent account of the work done by the ministry of states in getting the rulers of princely states to sign the Merger Agreements. This book also documents the contribution of the Praja Mandal volunteers in expediating this process.

The Academy had brought out a special edition of *The Administrator* on the Sardar, with focus on the civil services and the integration of states in the Indian Union. The special issue, edited by Bindu Katikithala, had articles from Rajmohan Gandhi, Shakti Sinha, Ratika Gaur, Hindol Sengupta, Sanjay Joshi, K. Srinivas, Rajnikant Puranik and Shirin Mehta. A new biography of V.P. Menon by his grandniece Narayani Basu brings to light the deep personal bond and rapport shared between the Sardar and Menon, as well as the latter's photographic memory and ability to connect the dots.

The fascinating story of how India chose to call itself Bharat is covered in the sixth volume of Constituent Assembly debates. A recent book by M.A. Asif, *The Loss of Hindustan: The Invention of India*, throws light on the contest of names for India. This has also been discussed at length by Catherine Clementin-Ojha in her paper, 'India, That Is Bharat …: One Country, Two Names'.

Barbara N. Ramusack's *The Indian Princes and their States* and the *Princes of India in the Twilight of the Empire* makes the counterpoint to the popular narrative of *Maharaja* and *Maharani* by Diwan Jarmani Dass in which the ruling princes were caricatured as oriental despots and stooges of the Empire. She brings empirical evidence to show that many of them were consummate politicians who exercised a considerable degree of independence and autonomy until the sudden disintegration of the Empire. The Congress party had been ambivalent in their approach to them, though the Muslim League and the Hindu Mahasabha were keen to project them as the natural leaders of their respective communities. Ramusack's books cover a broad temporal span – many of these states were in existence long before the East India Company took on a governance role – and show how the Indian states were both victims and beneficiaries of a system in which 'order, hierarchy and stability' became an end in themselves. The princes also played their role as patrons of arts, sports, education and religion. In, *A Princely Affair*, Yaqoob Khan Bangash tells the story of accession and integration of nine states to

Pakistan. The life, times and legend of one of the most well-travelled maharajas of India, the Francophile Maharaja HH Jagatjit Singh of Kapurthala, is brought out in *Prince, Patron and Patriarch* by his grandson Brigadier HH Sukhjit Singh and Cynthia Meera Fredrick.

With regard to the formation of borders of states, I have made extensive use of the 'State Papers' submitted by the officer trainees to the Academy. Year after year, officers assigned to a state are expected to write a paper covering different aspects of the political geography, demography, natural resources, river water projects, etc. and the key features of these submissions are presented before the Planning Commission and the NITI Aayog. These were supplemented by inputs from reports in the *Economic Weekly*, the precursor journal to *Economic and Political Weekly*. JSTOR's search engine came in very handy for each of the state-specific chapters, as well. Thus for Jammu and Kashmir, I consulted the journal articles of Adarsh Sein Anand, Shailendra Singh Jamwal, Jagmohan, B.G. Verghese, Ayesha Jalal, Ashutosh Varshney and Louise Tillin, besides books like M.J. Akbar's *Kashmir, Behind the Vale*, Wajahat Habibullah's *My Kashmir: The Dying of Light* and P.C. Dogra's *1947 Kashmir Invasion: Why Stalemate?*. I also had the benefit of discussions on the Kashmir issue from the sessions held at Military History and Strategy verticals in Valley of Words and JCM sessions at the Academy, especially those with Lt Gen. Ata Hasnain, Shiv Kunal Verma and Lt. Gen P.J.S. Pannu, and the extensive readings on the subject in *Fair Observer* curated by its intrepid editor, Atul Singh. Ambassador P. Stobdan's writings have helped me understand the Ladakhi perspective on the creation of the new Union Territory.

With regard to the Hyderabad and Telangana chapters, in addition to Menon's detailed description for Hyderabad, I have based the chapters on the books of Gautam Pingle and Narendra Luther, besides journal articles by Ian Copland, Taraknath Das,

Nani Gopal Chaudhuri, Rasheedudin Khan, Sunil Purushottam and A.G. Noorani.

The States Reorganization Commission (SRC) report itself makes for fascinating reading. This 267-page report is easily downloadable, and is, in many ways, the 'foundational report', and a fine example of erudition, scholarship and reasoned reflection. Dr B.R. Ambedkar's thoughts on linguistic states as well as his representations to the Linguistic Reorganization Commission (LRC) and SRC, and his comments on the SRC report are prescient. The SRC report was commented upon very extensively, and the search engines show Satish Kumar Arora's article 'The Reorganization of the Indian States' in the *Far Eastern Survey* (February 1956) on the top. This is indeed a well-researched article, which not only gave me a sense of perspective, but also led me to understand the position of the Congress on linguistic states. This, together with Marshall Windmiller's account on 'Linguistic Regionalism in India in Public Affairs' (December 1954), helped set the context.

Three books stand out for their conceptual clarity on the language debate in the '50s. These include Robert D. King's *Nehru and the Language Politics of India, India: The Most Dangerous Decade* by Selig Harrison and Paul Brass's *Language, Religion and Politics in North India*. How language politics panned out in the south is best brought out by Rajmohan Gandhi in his work *Modern South India*. With regard to the making of linguistic states in the south, the writings of J. Balan, V.B. Ganesan, C.T. Kurien, E. Raghavan, E.R. Manor, Janaki Nair and F. Perlin provided both the facts and different perspectives on the issue.

The chapter on the frontiers of Assam is based on the works of B.G. Verghese, Sanjoy Hazarika, Yasmin Saikia, Udayon Misra, V.S. Jaffa, H.K. Barpujari, Rajen Saikia, Subir Bhaumick, Verrier Elwin, V.K. Sarin, Nandita Haksar, Mahender P. Lama and Nari

Rustomji, among others. The ministry of home affairs reports, proceedings of the All Party Hill Leaders' Conference (APHLC) and the parliamentary debates when each of the states and UTs was formed also made for good background reading.

Nitish Sengupta's *Bengal Divided: The Unmaking of a Nation, 1905–1971,* supplemented with *Bengal Divided: Hindu Communalism and Partition, 1932–1947* by Joya Chatterjee and Semanti Ghosh's *Different Nationalisms* as well as the debates on the Roy–Sinha proposals in the *Economic Weekly, The Statesman* and *The Times of India* and the Calcutta High Court judgment in the Hem Chandra Roy case provided the material for the chapter on Roy–Sinha proposals. This aspect has still not received the attention of scholars, and it is my hope that it will become the subject of further academic exploration.

The Foreign and Commonwealth Office (FCO) records on the integration of French and Portuguese territories give an idea of how the Cold War and the politics of NATO delayed the merger of the Goanese territories with India. The collected works of Dr T.B. Cunha, P.D. Gaitonde and Dr Ram Manohar Lohia give an insight into the struggle for integration. Shailendra Nath Sen's book on Chandannagore and Akhila Yechury's paper on the integration of French territories into India were the basis for this chapter.

With regard to Chhattisgarh, the material was drawn from the writings of Dharmendra Kumar, Ish Narayan Mishra, Louise Tillin, Anil Nauriyal, Rajat Kujur and Dietmar Rothermund, as well as, Nandini Sundar. This was supplemented by my conversations with Maninder Kaur Dwivedi, a senior civil servant from the state. I would like to specially place on record Mishra's article, for it highlights the role played by the Gandhian-Marxist Shankar Guha Niyogi in creating the 'Chhattisgarhi identity', in much the same way as A.K. Roy did for Jharkhand. That these two mass leaders with a Marxist perspective could not work with the 'ideologically inflexible CPI and CPM' is yet another area that needs to be probed.

Just when statehood for Jharkhand was announced A.K. Roy wrote his article 'Jharkhand: From Separation to Liberation' for the *Economic and Political Weekly*. This was reinforced along with the writings of Ashutosh Kumar, Anuradha Rai, Akhtar Majeed, Vijai Prakash Sharma, Siuli Mukherjee, Ram Dayal Munda and writings on and by Jaipal Singh Munda. The material on Uttarakhand, the third state formed in 2000, is very extensive, especially because almost every book and article on the state is part of the Uttarakhand state file. The writings of R.S. Tolia, Ramachandra Guha, Shekhar Pathak, Emma Mawdsley, Pampa Mukherjee, Antje Linkenbach and M.P. Dubey, as well as conversations with Chandi Prasad Bhatt, Sunder Lal Bahuguna, Indu Kumar Pandey and Dr R.S. Dobhal were an extremely valuable resource.

Harjot Oberoi's book on the construction of religious boundaries, *Culture, Identity and Diversity in the Sikh Tradition*, provides the backdrop to the assertion for the Gurumukhi script, as well as the demand for a separate Sikh state, and later Punjabi Suba. Baldev Raj Nayar's *Minority Politics in Punjab* and Jyotirindra Das Gupta's book, *Language Conflict and National Development*, explain the Hindi–Punjabi struggle in post-independent India with special focus on the Sachar Formula (after the name of the then chief minister of Punjab, Bhim Sen Sachar) which could have formed the basis of a solution, but it was the intransigence of the Hindi press in Jalandhar which finally paved the way for the making of Haryana and Himachal Pradesh. I must refer here to *Hindus and the Punjabi State* by Om Prakash Kohal of the All India Hindu Mahasabha – an out-of-print book which I came across in the Gyanlok collection, which argues that Hindus of Punjab ought to own, accept and celebrate Gurumukhi as their own, and that it was a language in its own right, and not a dialect of Hindi. Gulshan Rai and M.S. Ahluwalia's books on Haryana and Himachal bring together empirical data as well as the submissions made to the SRC by the proponents of these states. The editorial comments of *Economic Weekly* and *The Tribune* also came in handy.

The chapter on Orissa draws from the report of the Simon Commission – which must get the credit for having carved out the linguistic states of Orissa, Bihar and Sindh, while accepting the principle that revenue, judicial and administrative work is best done in the language of daily discourse. The memorandum submitted to the Government of India justifying a separate state can be traced to 'The Oriya Movement: Being a Demand for United Orissa' by two anonymous BA students, but we know that the publisher was H.H. Panda, BA, secretary of the Oriya Samaj of Ganjam. Scholarly articles by Pritipuspa Mishra, Kamalakanta Roul, G.N. Dash, Mamata Dash and Biswamoy Pati and writings by and on Madhusudan Das, Gopabandhu Das, Biswanath Das and Hare Krishna Mahtab gave me the confidence to write 'Utkal Bande Janani' and narrate the story of the state.

One must admit candidly that most of the material researched has been in English, though one is aware that when it came to the reorganization of the country on linguistic lines, the material in Indian languages must be substantial. I leave it to the next generation of historians to probe this further. Each one of our states, and the political and social leaders at the helm, have lost out to the New Delhi–centred narrative which has privileged prime ministers and their colleagues in key ministries like foreign affairs, home, defence and finance. Therefore, little is known about the ministers who shaped our policies on a host of subjects – from health and education to agriculture and social justice. This gap needs to be addressed – and writings by and on leaders like on Partap Singh Kairon, B.C. Roy, S. Nijalingappa, Devaraj Urs, Hare Krishna Mahtab and K. Kamaraj who stood their ground when it came to the central leadership of the Congress are important to any study of this kind.

Perspectives

In any work of this magnitude, generalizations and broad propositions have to be offered – and this is certainly not a substitute for specialized writings on any particular aspect: scholars on Sikkim or Punjab or Gujarat, for example, will obviously have a better grasp on the subject. It is also not a substitute for those wanting to study any state, region or linguistic aspiration in greater detail, or for an academic audience. But the Sikkim example will show how perspectives are shaped by those who write them: the first book on the subject was Sunanda K. Datta-Ray's *Smash and Grab*. He wrote it from the perspective of his good friend, the Chogyal, and took a view that big brother India had forcefully dominated a hapless and helpless Himalayan kingdom. B.S. Das's *The Sikkim Saga* takes an entirely different view. It gives the viewpoint of the administrator – how the Chogyal and his 'coterie' brought this upon themselves because they refused to share power with the majority community: the Nepalis. Andrew Duff builds his story on the letters written by the Scottish missionaries who ran the local school and were part of the charmed circle of the Chogyal and Gyalmo. His take is more nuanced than the first two books, because he wrote this after three decades of the merger. G.B.S. Sidhu's book, *Sikkim: The Dawn of Democracy*, is from the view of the Research and Analysis Wing (R&AW) – and he is candid in stating that this has been done to rescue the reputation of the first CM, Kazi Lhendup Dorjee, who was at the receiving end in many narratives on Sikkim. A recent book on the subject by IFS officer P.M.S. Malik brings in the Chinese angle and portrays Sikkim as a pawn in the power game between India and China. Needless to say, there is an element of truth in all these narratives, but an author has to take a view: mine has been conditioned by the fact that the first few years of my service in the IAS were spent in Kalimpong (infamously called the 'nest of spies') where my wife Rashmi and I had the privilege of being hosted both by the Queen Mother of Bhutan as well as the Kazi Saheb and Kazini Eliza Maria Dorjee and Tashi Pempa Hishey whose family controlled the India–Tibet trade when Kalimpong was the last outpost on the Indian side, before all trade stopped in the aftermath of the 1962 war with China.

As mentioned earlier, I have greatly benefitted from the declassification of records of the FCO of the UK. Week after week, the high commissioner of the UK to New Delhi as well as his deputies in Mumbai, Kolkata and Chennai would send their reports, along with newspaper cuttings from the prominent English-language papers – mainly *The Statesman*, *The Times of India*, *The Hindu*, *The Indian Express* and *Hindustan Times* for the foreign office mandarins in the UK. One read and understood how the UK foreign office tried to protect the interests of the mining industry, tea plantations and the agency houses as well as their interface with the Union and state governments. Whether or not one agrees with their viewpoint, one has to agree that the record-keeping and classification are quite meticulous. While we do have a lot of material in our archives, we need to document and classify it better, and make it more accessible.

The focus of this study is on boundaries of states as well as their nomenclatures. Naturally, all changes in the lines are impacted by politics – and personalities. To the extent that an event influences the border distribution, it is within the scope of this study; otherwise, even if the event is in itself very significant, it is not covered. Thus, the discussion on the Dixon plan regarding the boundaries of J&K is part of the study, but the breakdown in the Nehru–Sheikh Abdullah relationship, as well as the latter's subsequent arrest is not. The biggest challenge in a study like this is to draw the line on what does not directly impact borders.

Are there lessons from this study? Yes. First and foremost is the fact that while the notion of identity is certainly fluid, there are certain binding elements that prevent it from meandering too far away from the accepted course. Language is usually a force which brings people together – but in the case of Punjabi, the script became the divisive bone of contention. Second, there is a considerable difference in the way pan-India parties and regional (state-based) parties look at issues. Third, political parties also change their perspectives with time. Fourth, migration affects demography, and demography has a direct bearing on electoral politics. Fifth, there is a gap between what the national political leadership of a party may want and what the ground-level workers do. Sixth, the opposition to an idea can come from the most unexpected quarters. Seventh, the English language press, the Hindi newspapers and the regional newspapers have different points of view on most issues. Even the coverage varies. Eighth, every story has multiple perspectives – which is highlighted from the Sikkim example. Ninth, while seven decades is a long time in the history of an individual, for a nation, history spans centuries; and from a civilizational perspective, one looks at millennia.

Last, but not the least, history is written by its victors, or are close to those who have power. There is an irreverent limerick in Amit Ranjan's biography of John Lang, the first two lines of which are:

History is fickle,
In what it decides to pickle…

From the meta narratives that I have read and enjoyed – Ved Vyasa's Mahabharata to Edward Gibbon's *Decline and Fall of the Roman Empire*, Francis Fukuyama's *End of History* and Yuval Noah Harari's *Homo Deus* – it is clear that no dynasty or group can stay in power forever. Power creates its own contradictions, 'hubris' is inevitable, and the quest for control is always couched in a grand narrative of cultural/civilizational identity, or sustainable development, or of a 'golden past' whose revival will be the silver bullet to all current and future problems.

With this rather long prologue/monologue, let us move on to the story of how India continues to redefine itself. Let me also mention that like India itself, this is a work in progress, and as new scholarship brings hitherto hidden facts to light, new findings will be incorporated – for history is always in the making!

1

MAPS AND MILESTONES

The Marking of Internal Boundaries in India

We, the People

The Preamble to our Constitution clearly states that 'We, the People' have constituted India into a 'Sovereign, Socialist, and Secular Democratic Republic'.[1] The first three articles[2] define the name and the territory of the Union. As India, that is Bharat,[3] is a union of states, it is clear that the constituents of the quasi-federal Republic of India can also redefine the internal boundaries of the nation. This option has been exercised by the people of India fairly frequently – but there is a context, and many subtexts, in most of the cases. For, while the procedural aspects outlining the making of a new state, or the alteration of boundaries, or change of nomenclature, have been clearly laid down, there tends to be a strong political component to every change in the boundary or nomenclature which is reflected on the maps printed by the Survey of India.[4]

Given that the nine provinces[5] of British India (as the states were then called), as well as all the 562 princely states,[6] are not reflected on the map of India in the seventy-fifth year of independence

1

speaks volumes about the nation's ability to negotiate its political and administrative boundaries with its citizens. Reimagining India through its constituent units – the states – has been marked by aspirations, assertions and adjustments of almost every ethnic, linguistic and regional group. Perhaps no other country in the world has been witness to such a large-scale readjustment of internal boundaries. While some changes have taken place on account of administrative requirements, especially during the first three years when India was making the transition from the Dominion of India to the Republic of Bharat, most other changes in the internal boundaries have been brought about by strong movements of linguistic and/or ethnic groups seeking their place in the state and federal polity.[7] In fact, one can argue that the right to assert a community's voice and identity, take control of the budget[8] and natural resources, provide employment and patronage, have been the driving forces of many a movement.

Interestingly, all the four leaders who imagined India in their own ways – the Mahatma who wanted a minimalist state,[9] Babasaheb who strongly believed in state intervention for social justice,[10] Nehru who believed in centralized planning, and the Sardar who prioritized governance and national integrity above all – were unanimous in their belief that acceptance of linguistic states would strengthen, rather than weaken, the unity and integrity of the country. It is true that in the immediate aftermath of Independence, both Patel and Nehru felt it prudent to first ensure a modicum of stability in the newly divided country before raking up regional issues. However, there was never any doubt about the long-term vision in this regard. The Congress had established its own units on linguistic lines from 1918[11] and, therefore, expecting the constituent units of the nation to be organized on a similar basis was quite logical.

From the Dominion of India to the Republic of Bharat: The Maps of 1947 and 1950

The first thirty months of India's tryst with integration of the princely states within the new administrative and political architecture of the country is a marvel by itself. Many Churchillians thought that Independence was the beginning of the end, for they believed that India was only a geographical aggregation rather than a civilizational entity.

The near-smooth transition from a dominion to a republic is actually a grateful nation's tribute to Sardar Patel and V.P. Menon. While Hindol Sengupta does talk of Patel as *The Man Who Saved India*, the role of his able and trustworthy lieutenant V.P. Menon cannot be underestimated.[12] While the Sardar laid down the broad policy, the responsibility of drafting the Instruments of Accession, and ensuring that all the princely states signed on the dotted line – both for the Instrument of Accession, as well as the Agreement on Merger – fell on Menon, who also ensured that India chose to call itself the 'Dominion of India'[13] instead of the 'Dominion of Hindustan',[14] as preferred by an important section of the British establishment. The Dominion of India thus became the natural 'successor state' to British India – else Pakistan could have staked a claim in the territories held by Portugal and France, especially in pockets that had substantial Muslim populations. Menon thus showed a rare insight by insisting on India, rather than Hindustan, as the chosen name for his nation. Even our Constitution says, 'India that is Bharat', thereby reinforcing the primacy of India as the name of our country.

It is true that the Chamber of Princes,[15] and some of the larger princely states, did want to assert their 'independence', and collectively they could have posed a challenge, for they occupied roughly two-thirds of the country's area and 48 per cent of its population.[16] However, they were hopelessly disunited, lived in a world which was frozen in time, and most importantly, were no match to the movements for popular democracy in their states. Moreover, the imperial power which had propped them for over a century was no longer willing to offer anything beyond platitudes.

From the time of Subhas Bose's presidency,[17] the Congress had taken the view that the states were an integral part of India, and that the Praja Mandal or the All-India State Peoples' Movement had to be supported, though they were reluctant to openly declare their support against the Indian princes. This was more 'tactical' as it was clear that once the British paramountcy lapsed, the princely states would collapse like a house of cards. The Government of India Act of 1935[18] did not make any express commitment to the princely states, and while the British did encourage the states to contribute liberally to the war effort, they were not making any commitments on behalf of the Crown. One must not forget that over fifty of these states had well-trained standing armies and that many troops had seen action in the World Wars. Although, in retrospect, it appears that their internal prejudices and differences were superficial, the fact of the matter is that 'this is what defined their lives' (table of precedence, gun salutes and personal entitlements),[19] and they were willing to commit the resources of their state to achieve these distinctions.

Some individual officers of the Indian Civil Service (ICS), especially those on secondment to the political service, working as residents in the princely states and in the political department, had developed a very good rapport with the individual states. But that was never looked at approvingly by the viceroy's office or the secretary of state, and as also by Patel and Menon. The inclusion of the representatives of princely states in the Constituent Assembly was a masterstroke: the princely states could not complain that they had not been consulted in the new governance architecture, and all their assertions and claims were responded to with flourish and finesse. Although, as a matter of principle, the representatives of the states had to be 'elected', in many instances they were nominees of the princes, and some like C.S. Guha represented more than one state, like both Manipur and Tripura, in this instance. Be that as it may, the map of 1950 was quite different from that of 1947, and though there were variations between the states under governors and states under *raj pramukhs*, the map becomes more recognizable when seen with the present states and UTs.

'Raj Bhasha Hindi' – 1952: The First Hindi Map of Independent India

The first Hindi map of India was published in 1952.[20] With that, the Hindi-speaking states of Rajasthan, Uttar Pradesh, Madhya Pradesh and Bihar created the so called Hindi Heartland. Six decades later, three new states – Uttaranchal (now Uttarakhand), Chhattisgarh and Jharkhand were created to meet the development aspirations of these sub regions. But even before that, Haryana and Himachal Pradesh had been carved out of Punjab as Hindi-speaking states in 1966 and 1971 respectively. Together with the National Capital Territory (NCT) of Delhi, Hindi is the official *lingua franca* in the contiguous territory of the states Haryana, Himachal Pradesh, Uttar Pradesh, Uttarakhand, Rajasthan, Madhya Pradesh, Chhattisgarh, Bihar and Jharkhand, making it the largest geography and demography in the Indian Union. The more the Hindi enthusiasts propagated Hindi, the greater resistance it faced, not only from the four southern states, but also from those whose mother tongue was Assamese, Bengali, Marathi, Punjabi, Gujarati and so on. In 1965, when the fifteen-year period for the use of English as an official language for the Union was coming to an end, Prime Minister Lal Bahadur Shastri was compelled to give an assurance that English would continue to be an associate official language[21] till such time as there was a consensus on the issue. The language issue resurfaces every now and then, especially before elections and whenever there is a change in the education policy.

The Appearance of China and the Disappearance of Tibet[22]

This was also the first map on which China is shown as our neighbour. Prior to this, India's northern border was marked as Tibet or 'undefined territory'. In this map, both Tibet and China are marked; but by 1956, Tibet disappeared from our cartographical imagination, and we were all parroting '*Hindi–Chini Bhai Bhai*', oblivious to the Chinese interpretation of the McMahon line, which we claim as our boundary demarcation. Tibet finally makes a comeback in 1959 – but the point to note is that for five years Indian maps did not acknowledge its existence. Thanks to the intrepid Major Bob Khating[23] of the Indian Frontier Administrative Service (IFAS), the monastery of Tawang (then in North-East Frontier Agency [NEFA], now Arunachal) was firmly in Indian hands from 1952. Else, the escape of His Holiness the fourteenth Dalai Lama to India may have been extremely problematic.

1953: The Andhra State and the SRC

The fast unto death of Potti Sriramulu in 1952 led to the immediate announcement of Andhra State by separating Telugu-speaking districts from the erstwhile state of Madras. It also highlighted the fact that the driving factors for political mobilization in India had changed forever after the attainment of independence. While the Congress continued to be the dominant political party, they had to resort to 'back-seat driving' and questionable nominations, as, for example, that of C. Rajagopalachari[24] to the Legislative Council of Madras. Having spent the last few years of his political career as a governor and governor general, Rajagopalachari could not fathom the popular upsurge in the Telugu-speaking areas and his attempts to woo the Tamil constituency by shifting the course of the waters of the Krishna river for the Krishna–Pennar project made him a suspect in the eyes of the Telugus, and his education and language policy made all the non-Brahmin parties resent him for being a stooge of the Congress high command. Incidentally, Rajagopalachari changed his views on the language policy many times, and he made many opportunistic alliances in the course of his political career.

The announcement of the SRC put on hold linguistic agitations in most parts of the country, except Bombay and Punjab. This 267-page report,[25] including the dissenting notes, is one of the most read and quoted reports in the country.

The SRC was led by Justice Fazal Ali and included K.M. Panikkar and H.N. Kunzru, the only person known to have refused the Bharat Ratna as he had opposed it in the debates of the Constituent Assembly. The SRC travelled extensively across the country, received over 1.5 lakh documents, besides being greeted by demonstrations and counter-demonstrations for the making of new states or the retention of old boundaries. The government accepted many of its recommendations even though the SRC itself was not unanimous on several counts. The principle followed was that if two members agreed on a suggestion, it was accepted.

1956: The Foundational Map of India

One would not be far off the mark to say that this was indeed the foundational map of India, because with the exception of Bombay, Madras, Mysore and Jammu and Kashmir, the names of all the erstwhile British provinces and princely states were obliterated from the political map of India (in terms of state boundaries). But even while the names of Mysore and Madras were retained, they were now linguistically aligned as Kannada- and Tamil-speaking territories. Later, their names would also reflect the privileged status of Kannada in Karnataka and of Tamil in Tamil Nadu. Bombay remained a bilingual state, along with Punjab, but the Malayalam-speaking people got Kerala. Both Bombay and Punjab would be divided later in 1960 and 1966 respectively.

The linguistic states of north and central India included Madhya Pradesh cobbled out of the Central Provinces with the addition of the Hindi-speaking states of Madhya Bharat, Vindhya Pradesh and Bhopal; Rajasthan which now included Matsya Pradesh, Rajputana and Ajmer; Uttar Pradesh; and Bihar.[26] Although the Roy–Sinha proposals[27] for the merger of West Bengal and Bihar did not materialize on account of vehement opposition from both states, territorial adjustments were made between the two states to ensure the geographical continuity of West Bengal.

This also marked the end of an era for *maharaj pramukhs*, raj pramukhs and *jyestha* and *kanistha up raj pramukhs*. The artificial distinction between Part A, B and C states also disappeared. It was also clear that the SRC was looking at a minimum size and administrative viability: thus it proposed the merger of the Union Territory of Himachal with Punjab, and of Manipur and Tripura with Assam. Later events would show that the SRC could not fathom the political depth and vigour of these ethnic and linguistic sentiments.

The End of Bilingualism

The 1956 Accord was unacceptable to both Gujarat and Maharashtra, as well as to those who were promoting Bombay as a Union Territory, and the three Congress PCCs (Gujarat, Maharashtra and Bombay) were at daggers drawn. The Congress high command could not withstand the pressure, and after serial losses in all elections – Municipal and Zila Panchayat, State Legislature and the Union Parliament – the state was bifurcated into Gujarat and Maharashtra with Bombay remaining in Maharashtra. Once that happened, there was no logical argument to refuse Punjabi Suba[28] except that as a border state, Punjab needed to be a geographically strong and compact area. The full support that the Akalis[29] gave to the 1962 and, especially, the 1965 wars tilted national opinion in favour of the strong and sturdy Punjabis, and Indira Gandhi announced the new states of Punjab and Haryana in 1966. Within five years, Himachal too received statehood.

Integration of Foreign Territories

By December 1961, Goa, the last of the foreign territories under Portugal, was integrated into India after a military operation which lasted less than twenty-eight hours. India had been trying to integrate Goa through the United Nations (UN), the Non-Aligned Movement (NAM) and other diplomatic routes for over a decade. At the same time, Portugal tried to leverage its membership of the North Atlantic Treaty Organization (NATO) and its centuries-old treaty with Great Britain. Portugal also introduced the concept of pluricentralism[30] wherein Goa was declared an integral part of Portugal, and given representation in the Senate and Parliament of Portugal. It also tried to problematize the issue as one of loss of face for Christ, and tried to get the Vatican and the Pope involved. However, this did not cut much ice as the local Christian converts too had witnessed first-hand discrimination. The rejection of the Portuguese overtures was clear when the overwhelming majority refused to participate in the elections conducted under the auspices of the Lisbon regime. Prior to this, Dadra and Nagar Haveli as well as Daman and Diu had been liberated by the local people themselves.

In contrast to the intransigence of the Portuguese authorities, the negotiations with the French were on an even keel. Of course, Chandannagore merged itself into the Hooghly district of West Bengal without reference to any political negotiation between Indian and France, and even the Mahatma and the Congress were concerned with such direct assertions of authority. With respect to Pondicherry, there were interesting twists and turns. There was some talk of the region joining the proposed Dravidisthan, but on the whole, and certainly in comparison with Goa, the transfer of territories was quite smooth. However, it was only in 2014 that the Foreign Jurisdiction Act was repealed when the Parliament was informed that there was no need or rationale for the existence of this Act.

1963: The Creation of Nagaland and the Dismemberment of Assam

The creation of Nagaland is an important landmark in the history of our nation. Thus began the process of establishment of small states that were not likely to be viable without the support of the Union government. The political arguments prevailed over the administrative, and it was an effort to arrest the underground movement by giving political space to all those who sought greater association with the Indian Union. The linguistic ferment in Assam had raised the apprehensions of all the non-Assamese-speaking tribes in the states, and the growing refrain was that while they were happy to be part of the Union of India, they wanted 'out' from Assam. The current picture of the North-east is certainly very different from what it was in the aftermath of the SRC report. The establishment of additional states and Union Territories in the erstwhile territory of Assam (Meghalaya, Mizoram, Manipur, Tripura and Arunachal) has been a positive step, though the linguistic and ethnic diversity of the region is so great that innovative alternatives like Territorial Councils and support to language and culture councils have to be considered.

There are, of course, aspirations which are still to be resolved: the Gorkhas and the Bodos[31] being the ones who have created headlines in the past. The issues there include the fact that the ethnic/linguistic group in question is not in a numerical majority, even in the districts/areas claimed for the state or UT. Thus, the Gorkhas and the Bodos are not in a majority even in the districts of Darjeeling or Kokrajhar respectively. These aspirations have to be met, but it is also becoming clearer that the grant of statehood/UT status is not the panacea for all issues on development and identity. The settlement with Brus after nearly two decades of internal displacement in Tripura augurs well. It also shows that when there is political determination, contentious issues too can be resolved.

1975: The Merger of Sikkim

The two-phase merger of Sikkim to India, first as an Associate State and then as an integral part of the country, called for two amendments to the Constitution. In the first instance, the 35th Amendment laid down the set of conditions that made Sikkim an Associate State, with the addition of Article 2A. Later under the 36th Amendment, Sikkim became a full-fledged state of the Indian Union by inclusion of its name in the first schedule of the Constitution.

The analysis on Sikkim is based on four very different versions of events that took place in Sikkim from 1947 to 1975: elaborating the version of the Chogyal;[32] the narrative from the point of view of the Scottish missionaries; the views of an administrator; and one written to defend the reputation of Kazi Lhendup Dorjee,[33] the first chief minister who played a lead role in ushering democracy and full alignment with India.

The Maharaja of Sikkim had been the vice chair of the Chamber of Princes and, thus, at par with other states (unlike Nepal and Bhutan). Additionally, there was a popular upsurge for merger with India in 1947 as the majority of the population of Gorkha descent did not have the same political, social and economic opportunities as the ruling clans of the Bhutias and the Lepchas.[34] In fact, the position of the tiller of the land was worse than that of serfs.

However, in stark contrast to his behaviour and attitude towards most other nawabs and princes, Prime Minister Nehru indulged the Maharaja, and even conferred the title of Chogyal and Gyalmo on him and his wife. Rather than place the affairs of Sikkim under the ministry of states, and then with the MHA, Sikkim was placed under the ministry of external affairs (MEA) which was directly under Nehru. He also preferred to place IFAS, rather than IAS and IPS officers in Sikkim, which further gave the reigning dynasty the feeling that glory was more than a reflection. The Chogyal's marriage to the American Hope Cooke gave him international media exposure, but the ground under his feet was slipping.[35]

2000: Statehood with Bipartisan Consensus

The formation of Jharkhand, Chhattisgarh and Uttaranchal (now Uttarakhand) in November of 2000 marked a new phase of bipartisan consensus (and political maturity). While the latent demand for a separate identity had been seen in all the three states even prior to Independence, the agitation was more pronounced in the hill districts of UP because of the fear of loss of jobs and entitlements in the region on account of the Mandal Commission's recommendation with regard to 27 per cent reservation for the

Other Backward Classes (OBCs). The population of the hill districts was skewed in favour of Thakurs, Brahmins, Scheduled Castes (SCs) and Scheduled Tribes (STs); there were hardly any OBCs. While these districts were at the forefront of the agitation, the final territorial configuration included Udham Singh Nagar and Haridwar where the OBC population was fairly significant. Incidentally, both Jharkhand and Chhattisgarh had large tribal populations, but they had ceased to be tribal majority districts at the time of their formation. With the exception of the Jharkhand Mukti Morcha, the regional outfits have not been able to make any mark in the electoral politics of the three new states.

2014: Telangana

The acceptance of Telangana marks the beginning of a new trend: the exceptionalism of Hindi to the 'one language one state' formula has been called to question. Demands for a separate state for Vidarbha, North Bengal, North Karnataka (among others), and some sort of parity among states will gain strength. Telangana and Andhra Pradesh appear to be in a competitive mode and the one-upmanship may actually spur growth in both the states. While Telugu will dominate the political discourse in both the states, Urdu too gets a privileged position in Telangana, especially in Hyderabad, and many a government signboard reflects that change.

The initial reluctance of the Bharatiya Janata Party (BJP) and its predecessor party, the Jan Sangh, to accept smaller states on the basis of ethnic and linguistic considerations has given way to a more pragmatic acceptance of newer states to match the development aspirations. The dispute over Hyderabad was intense, and though there was an attempt at making it a Union Territory, two factors were against it. One, the acrimonious experience of Chandigarh, as also the lack of territorial contiguity. Meanwhile, Andhra's proposed capital city, Amravati, also got into a major controversy with questions being raised about the costs and viability, and the proposal to have the centres of executive, legislature and judiciary at three distinct locations of Visakhapatnam, Amaravati, Kurnool.

2019: The Union Territories of Ladakh and Jammu and Kashmir

The last major change in the cartographic imagination of the country was the formation of the Union Territories of Ladakh and J&K[36] on 5 August 2019 and the abolition of those provisions of Article 370 and 35A that conferred a special status to the state and the Permanent Residents, besides allowing it to have its own flag. This change also shows the large extent of the area under Ladakh which is now the 'crest' of India. In terms of area, Ladakh is larger than J&K, but like Arunachal, the population is sparse, and has a common border with the Tibetan region. The Ladakh Buddhist Association (LBA) was quite profuse in thanking the Union government, and recalled that even in 1948 it had sought to attach itself to the Lahaul–Spiti area of the erstwhile Punjab states. The fact that both Jammu and Kashmir regions have been kept together as a UT, and the possibility of grant of statehood has not been ruled out, opens several options. The successful conduct of District Development Council (DDC) elections in 2021, which saw participation and electoral victory of candidates from parties across the political spectrum – from the BJP to People's Alliance for Gupkar Declaration (PAGD) comprising seven parties, including the National Conference (NC), Peoples Democratic Party (PDP), Peoples Conference (PC), the Communist Party of India (Marxist) (CPM), Jammu Kashmir People's Movement (JKPM), the newly formed Apni Party and Jammu and Kashmir National Panthers Party, besides the Indian National Congress (INC) and independents, is a good marker for the restoration of democratic engagement. While the PAGD were way ahead of the BJP in terms of the number of seats, the latter polled nearly one lakh votes more than the PAGD in an election that saw an overall turnout of more than 50 per cent.[37] What is even more significant is that no established political party called for a boycott of the elections, and no questions were raised by any observer with regard to the fairness in the conduct of elections by the State Election Commission. It may be mentioned that prior to this, the provisions of the 73rd Constitutional Amendment, which confer statuary status to panchayats, were not applicable in the state. These elections, therefore, signal the return to normalcy after several decades of global terrorism aided and abetted by the Pakistan Army.[38]

Capital Disputes

There have been disputes over capital cities as well: Chennai was claimed by both Andhra Pradesh and Madras, and as a compromise settlement, Andhra Pradesh got Tirupati and Chennai was retained as the capital of Madras. M. Karunanidhi wanted to shift the capital to Madurai as an assertion of Tamil identity and pride, but the moment was lost. Chandigarh had been planned as the capital of the bilingual states of Punjab and Haryana, and Punjab has never given up the demand for its incorporation. However, the growth of Sahibzada Ajit Singh (SAS) Nagar in Punjab and Panchkula in Haryana have created a vibrant tri-city and, over time, the demand has lost its force, especially as the residents of Chandigarh prefer the status quo. Meanwhile, Hyderabad became the centre point of protest when Telangana was carved out of Andhra Pradesh, and though there was a possibility of making it a UT as well as the joint capital of both the states, the city was finally settled with Telangana. Incidentally, Dr Ambedkar had proposed Hyderabad as the winter capital of India to ensure that the southern states too felt that the 'capital' was close to them.[39] The possibility of Bombay as a UT received consideration at the highest levels in the late '50s, but the idea was rejected largely on account of vehement opposition from the powerful Maratha lobby. Incidentally, the proposition of Calcutta as an independent port city, directly under the Crown, much like Hong Kong, was proposed by the expat population, and though it was rejected by Mountbatten, the governor of Bengal did regard an element of merit in it. The demand for statehood for Delhi, with the inclusion of some neighbouring districts of Haryana, Rajasthan and UP, has been made from time to time, but it has never gained popular currency.

Asymmetries and Implications

There is the vital question of asymmetry of population, territory and political power among states in the democratic system, and the perpetual dominance of UP in India is often questioned, especially by regional political parties, which have also raised the issue of delimitation of parliamentary constituencies on the basis of population. After taking a look at the SRC recommendations, Dr Ambedkar had commented that this marked 'the balkanization of the South, and the consolidation of the Hindi speaking [north]'. This comment was made when states like Nagaland were not on the political firmament!

The political consensus of 1976 about a freeze on parliamentary constituencies for twenty-five years was extended in 2001,[40] and will probably pass political muster in 2026. But, given the very different demographic and economic growth profile of states, the issue will come to the fore in the coming decades. Internal migration and rapid urbanization with cities as the new centres of economic growth will also mark a shift in political and economic power from the rural to the urban. However, as long as the territorial integrity of India that is Bharat is not called into question, all other adjustments are possible. The first seventy-five years have shown that India can and has reimagined itself, and also that there are no full stops or final lines in its political geography.

That there are innovative ways of accommodating political, cultural and linguistic aspirations outside of the political maps is also an emergent possibility. All one can say is that countries that are nimble and flexible about their internal boundaries and political institutions will fare better in a world in which aspirations are always a step ahead of the extant arrangements.

2

1947: THE FIRST MAP OF INDEPENDENT INDIA

Is the whole a sum of its parts? Or can one get a better understanding of the constituent parts if one understands the larger picture? In a larger jigsaw puzzle, which is not necessarily a square/rectangle, do the parts which make the notional centre have more privilege than those which constitute the boundaries? In any case, can you complete the jigsaw without stitching together all the parts?

When one looks at the map of India and its constituent units, one is struck by the fact that every state and Union Territory, including Lakshadweep and the islands in Andaman and Nicobar, have seen a change in nomenclature, or status, or territorial adjustments after 1947. While territorial changes are major markers on the cartographical map, the change of status – from a chief commissioner's province to a Union Territory, and then a full-fledged state – also has major implications for the political system. The change of name of a constituent unit is an exercise of political assertion. It is not possible without the invocation of Article 3[1] of the Constitution, and the passage of resolution(s) in the State Assembly and the Parliament.

Although one is stretching the analogy to the limits of one's imagination, how different is the whole when all connected parts have been altered, not once, but in several cases, many times over? Like in the case of the ship of Theseus,[2] are we talking of the same ship or a different ship?

From the publication of the first map in 1947,[3] when India was still a dominion with nine provinces and 562 princely states, there have been more than a hundred iterations till the 2019 edition. Unlike altering other sovereign symbols like flags, stamps, coinage and currency notes, realignment of maps is keenly contested as they have a direct bearing on the ground, and each change is a mark of political assertion – both at the state and the central level.

In any case, the very first demarcation of boundaries of the Dominion of India was marked by unprecedented bloodshed, rape, assault, violence and wanton destruction of life, limb and property. The task of boundary demarcation was entrusted to Sir Cyril Radcliffe,[4] and his dilemma and predilection is well described in this extract from Auden's poem:

> *Unbiased at least he was when he arrived on his mission*
> *Having never set eyes on this land he was called to partition*
> *Between two peoples fanatically at odds,*
> *With their different diets and incompatible gods.*
> *'Time,' they had briefed him in London, 'is short. It's too late*
> *For mutual reconciliation or rational debate:*
> *The only solution now lies in separation.*
>
> 'Partition', W.H. Auden[5]

The first map of independent India,[6] showing 'Provinces, States and Districts' was based on borders demarcated by Radcliffe and members of his commission. These included Justices C.C. Biswas, B.K. Mukherji, Abu Saleh Mohamed Akram and S.A. Rahman for the Bengal Boundary Commission. The members of the Punjab Commission were Justices Mehr Chand Mahajan, Teja Singh, Din Mohamed and Muhammad Munir.

'Curiously enough, Radcliffe did not attend the public sittings of the commission when the councils representing the parties argued their case. The judges heard the case without the chairman of the commission being present. Some parts of the proceedings of the Bench, or at best, their summaries, were flown from Lahore to Delhi for the chairman. [M.C.] Setalvad, who later became India's first Attorney General, considered the whole procedure "strange and almost farcical". He wrote, "the person whose decision was to be the award was not to have the counsel putting forward arguments on different sides, but he was to decide on a record of these arguments at a place far away from actual scene". When Setalvad pointed out the "procedural ridiculousness" of the course adopted, Radcliffe replied that "as the Award was to be completed before 15 August, he had no time to hear the parties." Setalvad said that he would have preferred to appear as a Counsel before him than the judges. Justice Munir's disappointment is evident in his comment: "The members of the Commission were reduced to the position of the Advocate".[7]

Radcliffe had completed the task by 12 August 1947, but Viceroy Mountbatten[8] urged that the declaration be deferred to the 17 August. The charitable explanation for this is that he did not want violence to mar the Independence Day celebrations in both the new dominions. The harsher opinion is that the responsibility of violence would now lie on the new governments, thereby absolving the Crown of any direct responsibility, which in turn would lend credibility to Churchill's view that Indians were not fit to rule themselves.[9]

The first map of independent India shows how the British left the two dominions and the 571 princely states (562 in India and 9 that aligned with Pakistan) on 15 August 1947.[10]

The nine provinces of India included East Punjab, United Provinces, Bihar, Orissa, West Bengal, Assam, Central Provinces, Madras and Bombay. Besides, the 'seven state unions' were Punjab states, Rajputana, states of Western India, Deccan states, states of eastern India and Madras states. With the exception of the three twenty-one gun salute states[11] of Mysore, Jammu and Kashmir[12] (including Gilgit agency) and Hyderabad, most other princely states, including the two twenty-one gun salute states of Baroda and Gwalior, were merged with the neighbouring state/union of states. These included Bhopal, Indore and Udaipur – which were nineteen-gun salute states – with twenty-one gun salutes to mark a local distinction. This sevenfold grouping of princely states is interesting, for it ceases to exist on the next map, and is probably based on the administrative construct of the ministry of states to facilitate the process of getting the Instruments of Accession[13] signed.

East Punjab and 'Punjab states'

This part of the subcontinent bore the maximum brunt of Partition. Starting 3 June 1947, the date of announcement of the Indian Independence Act, the next six months saw between 500,000–800,000 deaths, grievous injuries, displacement of around ten million people, besides loss of property for many thousands. Far worse was the rape, abduction, murder and honour killings/ suicides of at least a hundred thousand young women. 'Men of all three communities delighted in their momentary sense of power over vulnerable women: such was the courage of these citizens of newly independent states.'[14]

Ishtiaq Ahmed calls it 'the first case of ethnic cleansing in the Punjab … at the end of 1947 all traces of a Muslim presence in the Indian East Punjab were wiped out, except for some Muslims remaining in the tiny princely state of Malerkotla'. Likewise, in West Punjab, Hindus and Sikhs became conspicuous by their absence.

It must be noted that unlike their cadre-based organizations in other parts of the country, neither the Congress nor the Muslim League were deeply entrenched in the politics of Punjab. It was the Unionist Party which brought together the landed interests among the three major communities – Hindu, Muslim, Sikh – that held power. In fact, in Punjab, the Congress was pitted against the 'landholders' for the Punjab Land Alienation Act. The Punjab Land Alienation Act of 1900 restricted the purchase of land to designated 'agricultural castes' only. As early as 1924, Lala Lajpat Rai and other leaders of the Congress were keen on the division of the Punjab and Bengal into two parts. The idea behind the partition of the Muslim majority provinces was to 'make majority rule effective in the contiguous areas, to the extent possible'. For Ayesha Jalal 'it was not a prelude to the partition of India: it was a laboured attempt to forestall such a possibility'.[15] As in the rest of the country, the electorate was restricted to the landed and professional classes: just about 12 per cent of the Sikhs and Hindus and 10 per cent of Muslims participated in the elections held under the GoI Act of 1935, when the Unionist Party came to power. But by 1945, the Unionist Party lost ground to the Muslim League, and the 1945–46 elections saw the Muslim League emerge as the largest party. But the Congress, Unionists and Akalis cobbled a coalition ministry under Khizir Hayat Tiwana. This hardened the attitude of the Muslim League in the Punjab, who were taking their orders from the Muslim League headquarters in Bombay. That was also the time when Master Tara Singh of the Akali Dal placed the demand for a Sikh state – a demand which Jinnah did not pay much heed to. Be that as it may, as Ishtiaq Ahmed writes, 'On June 3, the Partition Plan was announced which required the Punjab and Bengal assemblies to vote on whether they wanted to keep their provinces united or partitioned. Both assemblies voted in favour of partitioning their provinces.'

Thus East Punjab was created with the districts of Amritsar, Gurdaspur, Ferozepur, Jullundur, Ludhiana, Hoshiarpur, Ambala, Karnal, Rohtak, Gurgaon, Faridabad and Kangra. Simla was the capital of East Punjab, though some departments had shifted to Hoshiarpur, Jullundur and Ambala as well. It did not include the princely states of the Punjab which were merged into the Patiala and East Punjab States Union (PEPSU).

As indicated in the 1947 map, with the exception of Bahawalpur and Khairpur which went to Pakistan, the states of Patiala, Nabha, Kapurthala, Malerkotla, Faridkot, Jind, as well as the hill states of Mandi, Suket, Bilaspur, Basahar, Sirmaur and Tehri Garhwal (which came under the Punjab Hill Agency from 1937) were now placed under the category of Punjab states. In addition to the prominent states that found a spot on the map, other smaller states like Nalagarh, Baghal, Mailog, Dhami, Bhajji, Keonthal, Kumharsain, Balsan, Jubbal, Tharoch, Baghat, Kalsia, Dujana and Loharu were relegated to a place in the footnotes. The boundaries of Punjab and Punjab states often crossed each other. Thus Kapurthala state was two islands in the district of Jullundur, and Kangra could be reached only by crossing several hill states. It may also be mentioned that in the erstwhile Political Department, there were two separate agencies to handle the Punjab states (most of which were salute states) and the Punjab Hill states (a majority of which were non-salute states).

The Constituent Assembly renamed East Punjab as Punjab, although West Bengal continued to be called by the same name. Gopi Chand Bhargava of the Congress party became the first chief minister of a Congress–Akali coalition ministry which faced not just the challenge of rehabilitation, but also the brunt of an agitation from Master Tara Singh for a separate autonomous area for the Sikhs.

United Provinces

United Provinces (UP) was one of the largest and more important provinces of British India and subsequently independent India. The veteran Congress leader G.B. Pant had been appointed the premier of the state after the elections held under the GoI Act of 1935. He served on the post till 1939, when all Congress ministers resigned after the British Raj committed India to the Second World War of its own accord.

When fresh elections were held to the provincial legislatures in 1945–46, the Indian National Congress won a majority and Pant was once again appointed the premier. Thus, unlike Punjab, there was continuity and less disruption in the administration of this province, which included nine divisions with forty-eight districts. It roughly corresponded to the combined regions of the present-day Indian states of Uttar Pradesh and Uttarakhand.

Following Independence in 1947, the princely states of Rampur, Benares and Tehri-Garhwal were merged into the United Provinces. On 25 January 1950, this unit was renamed as Uttar Pradesh. The nine divisions of the province included Meerut comprising the districts of Meerut, Dehradun, Saharanpur, Muzaffarnagar, Bulandshahr and Aligarh. Agra division had Muttra (Mathura), Agra, Farrukhabad, Mainpuri, Etawah and Etah, while Bijnor, Moradabad, Budaun, Bareilly, Shahjahanpur and Pilibhit fell in the Rohilkhand division.

Allahabad was not just a divisional headquarter, but also the seat of the high court. It had the privilege of being the capital of British India for one day in 1858. This was when the East India Company handed over the reins of the government to the Crown. Allahabad division included Cawnpore (Kanpur), Fatehpur, Banda, Allahabad, Hamirpur, Jhansi and Jalaun.

Lucknow was chosen as the capital of the state in 1921. This division included Unao (Unnao), Rae Bareli, Hardoi, Sitapur, Lakhimpur Kheri. The adjoining Gorakhpur division had Azamgarh, Gorakhpur and Basti. Mirzapur, Benares, Jaunpur, Ghazipur and Ballia fell in the Benares division, and the Faizabad division included Faizabad, Bahraich, Gonda, Sultanpur, Bara Banki, Partapgarh. Kumaun division had the three hill districts of Almora, Nainital and Garhwal. If Dehradun were to be added to these districts, it would roughly correspond to today's Uttarakhand.

Rajputana

United Provinces, together with Central Provinces and Bombay, shared the border with Rajputana. The latter grouping included Bikaner, Jaisalmer, Jodhpur (Mewar), Jaipur, Alwar, Bharatpur and Dholpur, among others, and all the states under the Matsya union and the Rajasthan union. The Rajasthan union included Alwar, Banswara, Bharatpur, Bikaner, Bundi, Dholpur, Dungarpur, Jaipur, Jaisalmer, Jhalawar, Jodhpur, Karauli, Kishangarh, Kotah, Kushalgarh, Sardargarh (formerly Lawa), Thikana in Udaipur, Mewar, Patan, Pratapgarh, Shekhawati, Shahpura, Sirohi Tonk. Most of these states would later become Rajasthan. In fact, in this large territory, the only area directly under British rule was Ajmer. From 1878, the region had been constituted as a chief commissioner's province, known as Ajmer–Merwara.

Bihar

The province of Bihar was created in 1936 by the partition of Bihar and Orissa province.[16] The first premier of the state was Sri Krishna Sinha of the Congress, and he was at the helm from 1937 to his death in 1961, except for the brief interlude during the period of the Second World War. Thus he presided over the transition of the state from the Raj to the dominion to the republic. A strong advocate of agrarian reforms, he played a crucial role in the abolition of the zamindari system. A polymath and a voracious reader, he donated his personal collection of seventeen thousand books to the public library in Munger which is now named after him.

Bihar comprised three distinct regions: Magadh, Mithila and Bhojpur, each with its own unique features. The state included the districts of Saran, Champaran, Muzaffarpur, Darbhanga, Bhagalpur, Purnea, Santal Parganas, Manbhum, Singhbhum, Hazaribagh, Ranchi, Palamu, Gaya, Patna, Shahabad, but did not include Kharsawan and Saraikela which were princely states under the Orissa states agency. Some territorial adjustments were made in 1956, but there was no significant change in the boundary till the formation of Jharkhand in 2000. Patna was the capital city, and though there was migration of Bihar Muslims to East Bengal, compared to other parts of the country, the administration held its ground, and in the early '50s, the doyen of public administration, Professor Paul H. Appleby, acknowledged Bihar as one of the best administered states in the country: an exemplar to others.[17]

Orissa

The new province of Orissa with the districts of Balasore, Cuttack, Puri, Ganjam, Koraput and Sambalpur came into existence on a linguistic basis in April 1936 by the partitioning of the short-lived Bihar and Orissa province. Prior to the formation of the state, large tracts of the state were in Ganjam and the Vizagapatam district of Madras province. As the Congress initially refused to form a ministry, Krushna Chandra Gajapati, the ruler of Paralakhemundi, was appointed as the first premier on 1 April 1936. He made way for Biswanath Das of the Congress, who resigned with all other

Congress chief ministers when British India joined the Second World War without any consultation with the Congress, which had popularly elected ministries in most of the states. In the 1945–46 elections, the Congress again scored a majority and Hare Krishna Mahtab was elected as the chief minister; he continued in office till 1950. He played a crucial role in shaping the boundaries of the present state of Orissa.

However, the territorial contiguity and the administrative apparatus was jeopardized due to the interposition of twenty-six princely states within the boundary of the state, thereby making it virtually impossible for any administration to enforce regulations – from excise to rations, or even for relief and rehabilitation works. This was further complicated by some of the Orissa and Chhattisgarh states forming their own Eastern States union without any consultation with, or authorization from, the state ministry. Fortuitously, the two biggest states – Mayurbhanj in Orissa and Bastar in Chhattisgarh – had not joined this union, and there was no 'popular representation' from any of the constituent units, and the demand for responsible government under the banner of Praja Mandal was gaining ground. The union's strategy of putting down dissent by the use of Pathans and Ghurkhas was counterproductive, and soon two of the states, Dhenkenal and Nilgiri, had to be brought under the control of the provincial government of Orissa. As such on 20 November 1947 the Eastern States union was derecognized, and a decision was taken to merge all the Orissa states with the province of Orissa and the Chhattisgarh states with the Central Provinces.

West Bengal

The refusal of the Congress to form a ministry in 1937 saw a coalition ministry of the Krishak Praja Party, the Bengal provincial Muslim League and several independents. A.K. Fazlul Haq became the first premier of the state, but when he joined the viceroy's Defence Council, along with the premier of Punjab, Sir Sikander Hayat Khan (of the Unionist Party), Jinnah asked his supporters to withdraw their support. However, Haq continued to hold office with the support from Shyama Prasad Mookerjee, the leader of the Hindu Mahasabha. From 1943, Sir Khwaja Nazimuddin led the Muslim League government. But it lost popular support because of rising food prices and the Bengal famine. After a stint of Governor's Rule, the 1945–46 elections saw the centre-left faction of the Bengal Muslim League led by H.S. Suhrawardy at the helm. Though his frosty relations with Jinnah affected his ambitions of achieving a United Bengal, both wanted Calcutta for East Bengal. In fact, when Jinnah learnt that Calcutta was going to India, he lost interest in the issue. Having the state without its commercial hub was an anathema to him.

The West Bengal Legislative Assembly met on 20 June 1947. At the preliminary joint meeting, it was decided by 120 votes to 90 that the province, if united, should join the new constituent assembly (Pakistan). At a separate meeting of legislators from West Bengal, it was decided by 58 votes to 21 that the province should be partitioned, and that West Bengal should join the existing Constituent Assembly. Likewise, in a separate meeting of the legislators from East Bengal, the view was that the state should not be divided; but in the event of a partition, it should join the Constituent Assembly of Pakistan. The idea of an independent Bengal, which had been doing the rounds till the second week of June 1947, was not put to vote. P.C. Ghosh and Khwaja Nazimuddin were elected to take over as the chief ministers of West and East Bengal respectively. They issued a joint appeal to all Bengalis to desist from violence and accept the final recommendations of the Boundary Commission without bitterness and rancour.

In many ways, the division was on the lines of the 1905 partition of the state. On 6 July 1947, the region of Sylhet in Assam voted in a referendum to join East Bengal. As per the Annexure to the Indian Independence Act, Murshidabad, Nadia and Malda were Muslim majority districts, and were assigned to East Bengal. This was later rectified on 18 August. This is also the reason why in some parts of West Bengal, Independence Day is celebrated twice over. For the second time on 18 August, when the tricolour flew in these districts for the first time.

The province of West Bengal then consisted of Midnapore, Bankura, Burdwan, Murshidabad, Malda, West Dinajpur, Darjeeling, Jalpaiguri, Chandernagore (Hooghly), Twenty-four Parganas, Howrah, Calcutta, Hooghly, Nabadwip (Nadia). One must mention here that the size of the districts was quite substantial. What is important to note is that Cooch Behar and Purulia were still not part of West Bengal, and there was no territorial continuity between West Dinajpur and Jalpaiguri. It was only in 1956 that a narrow strip of land (Islampur) was transferred from Purnea to West Dinajpur district. The Bengali-speaking subdivision of Purulia too was added to West Bengal in 1956 from Manbhum district.

Assam

Assam had been created in 1912 by the partition of East Bengal and the Assam province. With Shillong as the capital city, the province included Goalpara, Kamrup, Garo Hills, Darang, Lakhimpur, Sadiya Frontier Tract, Naga Hills, Cachar, Tribal territory, Nowgong, Sylhet, Sibsagar, Lakhimpur and Lushai Hills. Although population density in the hill districts was not very high, in terms of area, Assam was one of the largest and most ethnically, culturally and linguistically diverse areas of British India. Large tracts were brought under tea plantations and tribals from Bihar, Orissa, Central Provinces and Berar came to work in the labour-intensive industry. While Ahoms and Assamese-speaking people dominated Brahmaputra Valley and the surrounding districts, their dominance was resented by everyone else in that area (Naga, Mizo, Khasi, Garo et al.). Although Shillong was part of Khasi and Jaintia Hills, it served as the capital of Assam. However, Tripura and Manipur were part of the Eastern States. Given the large tribal population, the governor of the state had special responsibilities. Assam had to lose Sylhet district to East Bengal when the majority Muslim population opted for Pakistan.

In the 1945–46 elections, the Congress won sixty-one of the one hundred and eight seats, and Gopinath Bordoloi was unanimously elected as the chief minister. He continued to hold office till his death in August 1950. This was a crucial period for Assam, as together with Tripura and West Bengal, it received lakhs of Hindu refugees from East Pakistan. Bordoloi was also the chairman of the North-East Frontier Tribal Areas and the sub-committee of Assam Excluded and Partially Excluded Areas as the special nominee of the Government of India.

Eastern States

Eastern States is perhaps geographically the most widespread category; starting with Surguja, Jashpur, Udaipur, Gangpur, Kanker, Bastar, Khairagarh, Nandgaon in the Central Provinces, it stretched towards the east to include Cooch Behar and Tripura. Incidentally, Manipur and Khasi Hills are not shown as part of 'Eastern States' – perhaps an indicator of their independent and direct relationship with the Union government. The list also included Kharsawan, Saraikela, Nilgiri, Pal Lahara, Talcher, Hindol, Athgarh, Manipur, Sikkim, Kalahandi, Patna, Sonepur, Baudh, Rairakhol, Bamra, Keonjhar, Mayurbharj, Borai, Raigarh, Korea and Changbhakar,

Kawardha, Sarangarh, Nayagarh, Athmallik, Tigiria, Baramba, Narsinghpur and Daspalla.

Central Provinces (CP) and Berar

The province formed by the merger of Berar with the Central Provinces existed from 1903 to 1950. Berar was the territory leased by the British from the Hyderabad state for an annual payment of Rs 25 lakh. The Central Provinces comprised nineteenth-century British conquests from both the Mughals and Marathas, and covered much of present-day Chhattisgarh with substantial parts of Madhya Pradesh and Maharashtra. After the defeat of the Marathas in the Third Anglo-Maratha War, the territories north of the Satpura Range, Sagar and Damoh, came under the control of the British. Nagpur was annexed to the Empire in 1853 after the demise of Raghoji III of Nagpur under the Doctrine of Lapse.

In one of the first instances of the Empire acknowledging linguistic affinity as an element of administrative reorganization, Sambalpur along with the princely states of Bamra, Rairakhol, Sonpur, Patna and Kalahandi, were transferred from CP and Berar to Bengal, while the Hindi-speaking Chota Nagpur states of Chang Bhakar, Korea, Surguja, Udaipur and Jashpur were transferred from Bengal to CP and Berar in October 1905.

As the name suggests, the landlocked province was situated in the central peninsular India and comprised mountain ranges, plateaus and river valleys. The northernmost portion of the state extended onto the Bundelkhand upland, whose northward-flowing rivers are tributaries of the Yamuna and Ganges. The Vindhya Range ran east to west, forming the watershed between the Ganga–Yamuna basin and the Narmada river basin. The region was linguistically quite diverse and comprised four divisions: Nerbudda (Narmada), Jubbulpore, Nagpur and Chhattisgarh. The prominent districts shown on the map included Nimar, Hoshangabad, Saugar, Jubbulpore, Mandla, Bilaspur, Raipur, Drug, Chanda, Wardha, Nagpur, Yeotmal, Akola, Buldhana, Amravati, Betul, Chhindwara, Balaghat and Bhandara. Administratively, it shared its borders on north and northeast with the Central India Agency, including the Bundelkhand and Baghelkhand regions, and along the northern edge by the United Provinces. On the west, it bordered the princely states of Bhopal, Indore and the Khandesh district of Bombay Presidency. Hyderabad state lay to the south, and on the east, it shared its boundary with Orissa, Bengal Presidency and the Eastern States Agency.

From the beginning of the twentieth century, the Congress party was a strong force to reckon with in the state, and the pre-eminent position of Ravi Shankar Shukla was well established. After the 1946 elections, Congress again emerged as the majority party and Shukla became the premier of the state for the second time. Along with Hare Krishna Mahtab, he urged Patel to integrate the princely order with democratic India as he had been closely associated with the All-India States People's Conference, and knew of their fragile internal governance.

Central Indian States

These included all the thirty-five states of Bundelkhand and Baghelkhand that were organized as the Vindhya Pradesh, as well as the twenty-five states that were later constituted as Madhya Bharat. Of these sixty states, only twenty-five had a salute status. These varied in size and importance from Gwalior, Indore and Bhopal on the one end to Nagod and Maihar on the other end of the spectrum.

We first come to the constituent states of Vindhya, of which Rewa was the most prominent. The only other state with some significance was Orchha with a revenue of just above Rs 25 lakh. Fifteen of the Bundelkhand states had an area of less than fifty square miles, and two of those were less than ten miles each. These were actually large feudal estates rather than states, but the British gave them ostentatious titles to ensure their absolute fidelity and loyalty. Most of them claimed Rajput descent and wanted to be part of Rajputana, but as Rajputana was already too large, they were clubbed with a short-lived constellation of states called Vindhya. Meanwhile, a difficult conciliation between Gwalior and Indore was brought about in the Madhya Bharat union, which also includes Dhar, Dewas Senior and Dewas Junior, besides Datia, Ratlam, Ajaigarh, Alirajpur, Baoni, Barwani, Bijawar, Charkhari, Jhabua, Rajgarh, Sailana, Samthar, Baraunda and Khilcipur, along with, as mentioned earlier, Nagod and Maihar.

Madras

Most of southern India was a part of this presidency, including the whole of the Indian state of Tamil Nadu and parts of Andhra Pradesh, Kerala, Karnataka, Telangana, Odisha and the Union Territory of Lakshadweep. The city of Madras was the winter capital of the presidency and Ootacamund or Ooty was the summer capital. Madras shared its borders with Mysore on the northwest, Cochin on the southwest and Hyderabad on the north. Some parts were flanked by the Konkan region of Bombay Presidency, Central Provinces and Berar. The Oriya-speaking parts were separated from Madras when Orissa was formed in 1936.

In 1937, the Indian National Congress was elected to power for the first time and Chakravarti Rajagopalachari became the premier. He successfully enacted the Temple Entry Authorization and Indemnity Act[18] and introduced both prohibition and sales taxes in the Madras Presidency. But he faced major opposition to the imposition of Hindi as a compulsory subject in educational institutions. The Hindi order was withdrawn when he resigned along with others in the Congress party against the unilateral decision of the viceroy to commit India to the Second World War.

After the end of the Second World War, the Indian National Congress re-entered politics and, in the absence of any serious opposition, it easily won the 1946 election. Tanguturi Prakasam was then elected as chief minister with the support of Kumaraswami Kamaraj and served for eleven months. He was succeeded by O.P. Ramaswamy Reddiyar, who became the first chief minister of Madras state when India gained independence on 15 August 1947. The Madras Presidency became the Madras state in independent India.

All the four south Indian languages – Tamil, Telugu, Kannada and Malayalam – were spoken by the residents of this province, which followed the Ryotwari system of land revenue administration. It included Vizagapatam, East Godavari, Yanam, West Godavari, Kistna (or Krishna), Guntur, Nellore, Kurnool, Cuddapah, Chittoor, Chingleput, Madras, North Arcot, South Arcot, Salem, Trichinopoly, Tanjore, Ramnad, Tinnevelly, Madeva, Coimbatore, Malabar, Coorg, Kanara and Bellary. Later, each of these districts was to be divided into two to three, or even four, districts.

Madras States

Madras states included the two prominent states of Travancore and Cochin as well as the smaller states of Sandur, Banganpallie and Pudukkottai. Within the princely state of Cochin there was the coastal city of Cochin – a British territory – which served as the administrative headquarters for the Laccadive and Minicoy islands in the Arabian Sea.

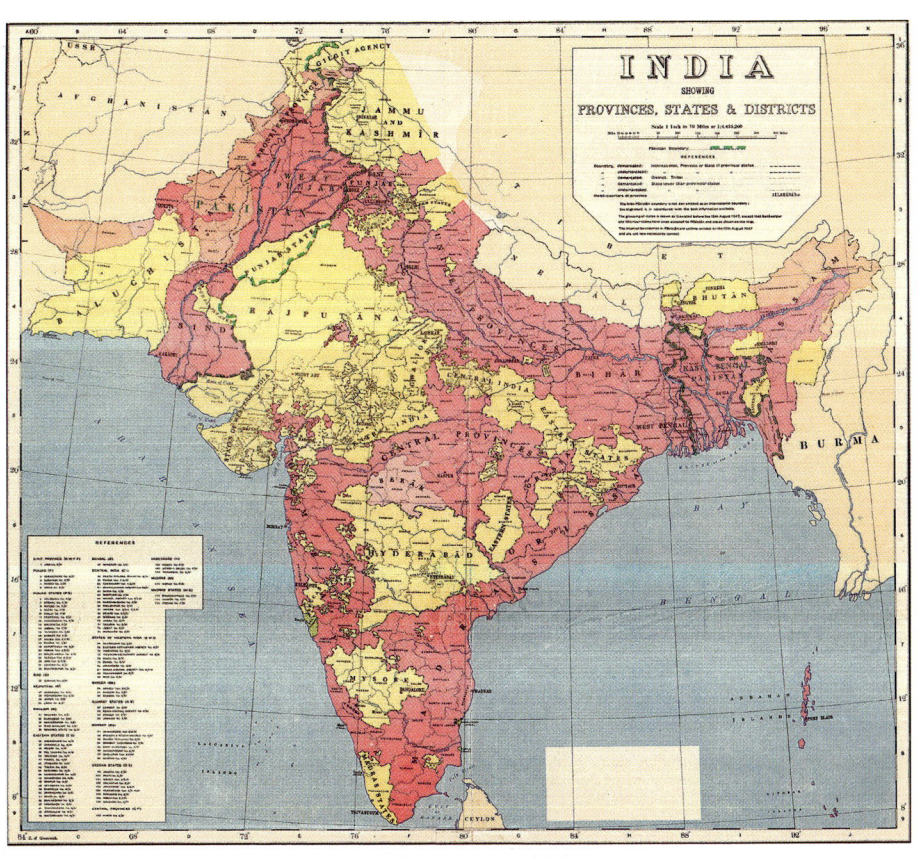

1947 – The Dominion of India

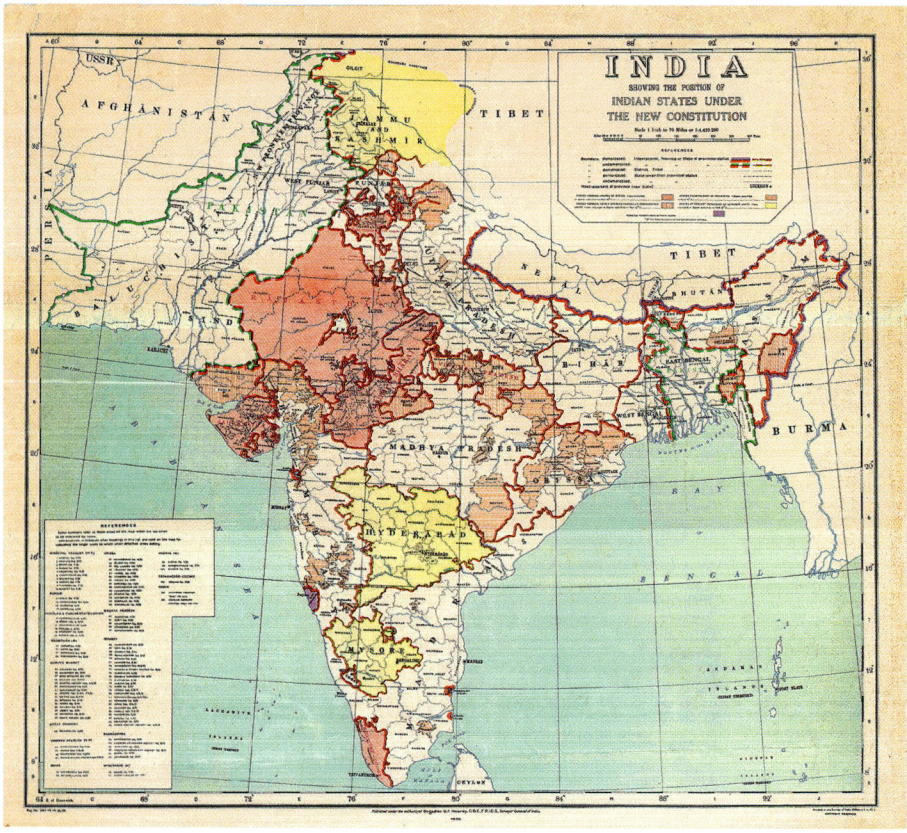

1950 – The Republic of India

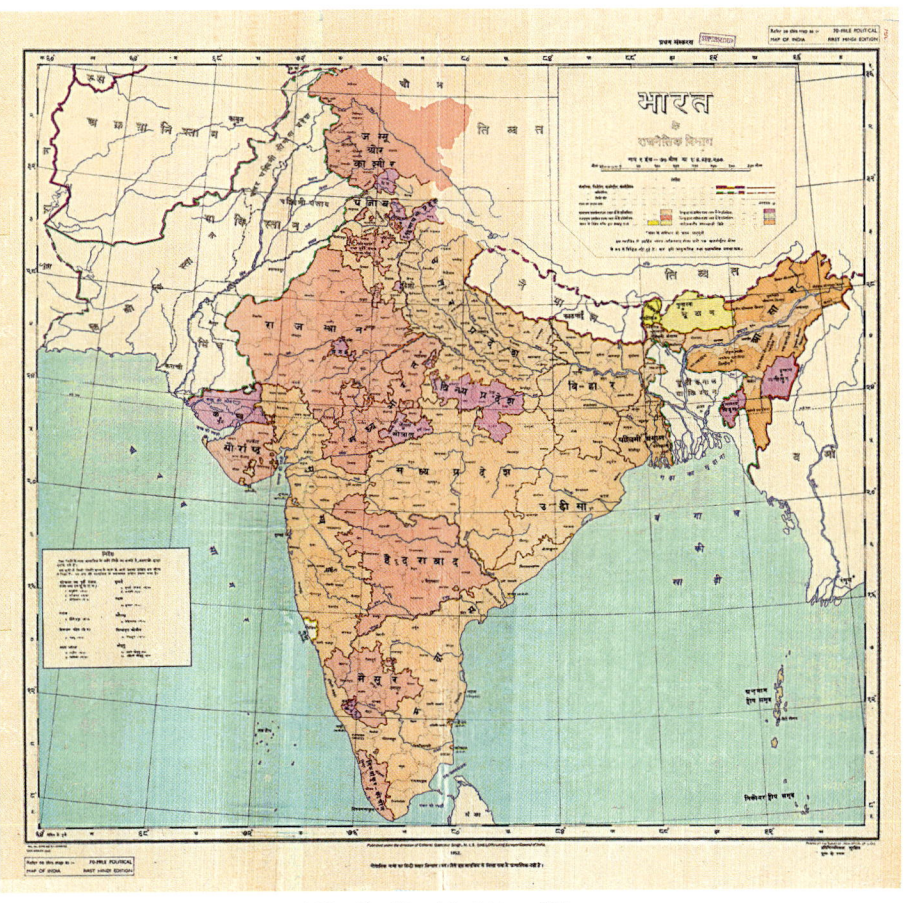

1952 – The First Hindi Map of Bharat

1954 – The First Linguistic State of India – Andhra State

Bombay

As per the Government of India Act, 1935, Bombay Presidency was reorganized into the provinces of Bombay and Sindh. In the 1937 elections, the Indian National Congress won the elections in Bombay but declined to form the government. Sir Dhanjishah Cooper cobbled a coalition comprising Jamnadas Mehta of the Lokashahi Swarajya Paksha (Democratic Swarajya Party), Sir Siddappa T. Kambli of the Non-Brahmin Party and Hoosenally Rahimtoola of the Muslim League. However, the Cooper ministry did not last long and a Congress ministry under B.G. Kher was sworn in. As in other states, Kher resigned in 1939, but was re-elected when the Indian National Congress re-entered politics and won the 1946 election. Kher continued as the chief minister of the state until 1952.

The Bombay Presidency was bounded on the north by Baluchistan, Punjab and Rajputana; on the east by Indore, the Central Provinces and Hyderabad; on the south by Madras and Mysore; and on the west by the Arabian Sea. Within these limits were the Portuguese settlements of Goa, Daman and Diu. It included Kaira, Ahmadabad, Broach and Panch Mahals, Daman, Bombay Suburban, East Khandesh, West Khandesh, Nasik, Sholapur, Bijapur, Dharwar, Belgaum, Ratnagiri, Satara, Poona, Kolaba, Thana, Surat.

The British provinces had been established purely on administrative grounds, and as all official discourse was in the English language, the linguistic affiliations of people did not count for much. However, for the record, Bombay was a multi-lingual state, and the prominent languages included Kutchi in Kutch, Gujarati and Hindustani in Gujarat, Marathi in Thana and the central division, Gujarati and Marathi in Khandesh, and Marathi and Kannada in the southern division. There were also Bhil (120,000) and Gipsy (30,000) dialects. English too held sway amongst the large expat and the Anglo-Indian populations of Bombay.

States of Western India

The 217 states of western India included the salute states of the erstwhile Eastern Kathiawad and Western Kathiawad besides Cutch (Kutch). Cutch was the largest as well as the most prominent salute state, and enjoyed the status of a seventeen-gun salute. The important ones included the states of Bhavnagar with a hereditary salute of thirteen guns (fifteen guns local), Dhrangadhra, also with a salute of thirteen guns, and the nine-gun salute states of Limbdi, Palitana and Wadhwan. The Western Kathiawar agency had the three thirteen-gun salute states of Junagadh, Nawanagar and Porbandar, and the first two also had the privilege of a fifteen-gun local and personal salute. Gondal, Morvi and Wankaner were hereditary eleven-gun salute states, and Dhrol and Rajkot, whose rulers were called Thakore Sahebs, were nine-gun salute states.

Deccan States

Then there is a category called the Deccan states which were seventeen in number, the most prominent amongst them being Kolhapur – but they were a diverse group. There were the Maratha rulers of Akkalkot, Jath, Mudhol, Phaltan and Sawantwadi. Aundh and Bhor were ruled by Brahmins, and then there were the Patwardhan states of Sangli, Wadi and Ramdurg. Janjira and Savanur had Muslim rulers – the former were of East African origin and the latter from the Miyana tribe of the Pathans. One marvels at this diversity (and acceptance) of rulership! It also included Bhora, Jamkhandi, Kurandwad, Ramdurg, Miraj and Phaltan.

Integrating the Princely States with India

This was a real challenge, for in the last decade of the Raj, an attempt was made to develop a direct connect between the princely states and the Crown, represented by the Viceroy. With the introduction of the 1935 Government of India Act, the provincial governments were popularly elected and the Raj did not want the princes to be influenced by provincial governments under any circumstances whatsoever. It is not that all the princes of India were on the same page – though they did have a Chamber of Princes as a representative body, their internal differences were quite marked. As a matter of fact, after the Imperial Proclamation of 1858 which did away with the Doctrine of Lapse, the British made every effort to humour the princes by offering them all the trappings of power and status – from honorary ranks in the army to titles like Knight Commander (KCIE), Companion (CIE), Member of the Order of the British Empire (MBE). But most of all, the British offered them gun salutes which determined their ranking and precedence in the Imperial hierarchy.

According to the White Paper published by the States Department,[19] 'The accession of the states to the Dominion of India was a momentous event in India's history. For over half a century, the states had been a sealed book so far as the leaders of the public opinion in British India were concerned. There were not a few who nursed the hope that, overwhelmed by the combined weight of the partition and the disruption of the states, the Government of India would go under. In the context of these heavy odds and handicaps, the consummation of the idea of a federal India comprising both the Provinces and the States was not a mean achievement. For the first time, after hundreds of years, India became welded into a Constitutional entity.'

This task was entrusted to the ministry of states, which came into existence on 5 July 1947 with Sardar Patel as the minister and V.P. Menon as the secretary. They were given the difficult mandate of dealing with the unprecedented situation of an impending lapse of paramountcy.[20] Although, in some ways, it was a successor to the erstwhile Political Department which handled the relationship between the states and the Empire, the objectives were entirely different. For the Political Department, the 'so-called internal autonomy of the states provided a convenient device for the maintenance of the feudal structure in the states as a bulwark against the movement of democracy from percolating in their domains'.[21] The states had continued to dot the political map of India as disruptive patches, retarding the political and economic integration of the life of its people. In less than two months, the Interim Government had to negotiate with 562 states, covering over 48 per cent of the area and a population of ninety-eight million, and ranging in importance from Hyderabad on the one hand to estates comprising a few acres in Kathiawar on the other. As we shall see later, this was done by either merging them with the existing provinces or constituting them into unions of states under the raj pramukhs.

Foreign Territories

The first map of India also showed the territories of India under foreign jurisdiction. The French had Pondicherry on the west coast, a small territory called Yanam in the erstwhile East Godavari district and Chandannagore in the Hooghly district of West Bengal. Portugal had Goa on the west coast as well as Dadra and Nagar Haveli comprising two separate geographical entities: Nagar Haveli wedged between Maharashtra and Gujarat, and, one mile to the northwest, the smaller enclave of Dadra, which was surrounded by Gujarat. As in the case of the princely states, these foreign administrators exercised their power only with the implicit backing and support of the British government, who had their own diplomatic agendas in the context of England's relationship with Portugal and France. The Congress had already set up state units in Goa and Pondicherry to lead the freedom movement there, though both Nehru and Gandhi were clear that the return of these foreign territories should be by mutual consent – which worked well in the case of French territories, but not so in the case of the Portuguese. This integration was completed only in December 1961, but it took another five decades before the Foreign Jurisdiction Act[22] was finally repealed in 2014.

3

RIYASAT E JAMMU WA KASHMIR WA LADAKH WA TIBET HA

The challenge in writing about Jammu and Kashmir is not shortage of material or sources: it is sifting the grain from the chaff. So much has been written about the state from so many different perspectives so many times that almost anything that one says about J&K is going to be contested. It includes the controversial '&', for J&K became one political/administrative unit only after the Anglo–Sikh War of 1846.[1] Prior to this, both Jammu and Kashmir had their own independent existence. One must also point out that the name that the state gave to itself was *Riyasat e Jammu wa Kashmir wa Ladakh wa Tibet ha* (Kingdom of Jammu, Kashmir, Ladakh and Tibet).[2] It is also true that the greatest focus and contestation has been on the Kashmir Valley, and other regions, including Jammu, have not had their fair share of discourse. By extension, the views, concerns and interests of people inhabiting the frontier regions of Ladakh,[3] Chitral,[4] Gilgit,[5] Baltistan[6] and Tibet[7] have been peripheral to the discussions.

However, if we were to talk about this physically contiguous region, one has to start with the oldest extant calendar anywhere in the world – the Saptrishi calendar, now in its 5097th edition! According to *Rajatarangini*,[8] a history of Kashmir by Kalhana (twelfth century),[9] Kashmir derives its name from Rishi Kashyap[10] who established a vale by creating twelve streams (Varaha Mula, now Baramullah). The settlement was called Kashyap-pura and identified as Kasperia by Ptolemy,[11] Kaspatyros by Herodotus[12] and Kaspapapyros[13] by Hecacateus[14] and Stephanus of Byzantium.[15] Etymologically, Jammu is derived from Jambupura,[16] the settlement on the banks of river Tawi established by Raja Jambulochan[17] in fourteenth BCE or perhaps earlier, from Jambudwip,[18] the continent in which 'Bharat' is situated. Jammu was always with the Dogras, either directly or within the overlordship of Delhi or the Suba of Punjab. Kashmir became part of the Mughal Empire under Akbar from 1586, though the Sufi tradition of Islam was brought in by Nund Rishi[19] or Sheikh Noor-ud-Din Noorani two centuries earlier.

The Dogra tryst with Kashmir started in 1819 when Maharaja Ranjeet Singh defeated the Durrani Afghans[20] to lay claim on the state. The credit for the territorial expansion of the state into Ladakh in 1834, and Gilgit Baltistan in 1839, goes to General Zorawar Singh,[21] the Wazir of Kishtwar under the Dogras who owed their allegiance to the Khalsa Raj.[22] Ladakh was an independent state, but ecclesiastically part of His Holiness the Dalai Lama's sphere of Tibetan Buddhism. Zorawar Singh later led a successful campaign to Gilgit–Baltistan in 1839/40, and expanded his rule over Yasin, Humza, Darel, Chilas, Chitral and Nagar as well. He also led a daring campaign to Tibet in 1841; even though he was not successful, his gallantry and valour was such that even the Tibetans erected a memorial in honour of their adversary.

Meanwhile, after the Anglo-Sikh War of 1846, Dogra Raja Gulab Singh,[23] an erstwhile general and confidant of Maharaja Ranjeet Singh, purchased the 'kingdom' for a sum of 75 lakh Nanak Shahi rupees.[24] The British had three objectives: to 'weaken the Sikhs' after their defeat at Sobraon, create a buffer between themselves and Russia on the one hand and China on the other, and recover the expenditure incurred during the War.

This then was the origin of the strategically located Riyasat e Jammu wa Kashmir wa Ladakh wa Tibet ha in which Tibet lay on the east, the Sinkiang province of China to the northeast, Afghanistan on the northwest and the Russian Turkestan just a few miles across. All the political upheavals since then can be traced to 'a sale deed' signed just after the First Anglo-Sikh War (1845–46).

Having paid 75 lakh rupees for Kashmir, the Dogras' first objective was to extract this amount from their new subjects. Their approach was not that of a benevolent sovereign but a rentier owner – everybody and everything was taxed. This included artisans and craftsmen who led a hand-to-mouth existence. Their tax dragnet did not even spare carpenters, boatmen, butchers, bakers or prostitutes. A contemporary observer, Robert Thorpe,[25] writing in the 1860s said, 'towards the people of Cashmere[26] we have committed a wanton outrage, a gross injustice and an act of tyrannical oppression which violates every human and honorable sentiment …'[27]

With regard to state appointments, all high offices in the state were filled mostly by Dogras followed by Punjabis and some Kashmiri Pandits. However, there were positive externalities as well. Thanks to the spread of compulsory education called 'Zabran' the light of literacy spread to all corners across the state. Among those who attended the compulsory classes was a young boy, Abdullah, born on 5 December 1905, eleven days after the death of his father, Sheikh Mohammed Ibrahim, in Sour village on the outskirts of Srinagar. Even though his childhood was mired in poverty, he matriculated and studied at Shri Pratap College, Srinagar, Prince of Wales College in Jammu, Islamic College, Lahore and Aligarh Muslim University (AMU)[28] where he studied chemistry. It was at AMU that his skills as an organizer and orator first came to the fore. Meanwhile, within the state, resentment against jobs for outsiders was on the rise, and from 1927, the Maharaja was compelled to offer preference to state subjects, or *mulkis*. To address the grievances and resentment of the Kashmiri Muslims, the Maharaja was forced to set up an inquiry commission under the chairmanship of Sir B.J. Glancy,[29] which recommended that Muslims should be given more representation in the services, and that an Assembly should be established in the state. In 1934, Maharaja Hari Singh did establish a Legislative Assembly called the Praja Sabha. However, contrary to the recommendations of the commission, the elected legislators did not have a majority in the Assembly, the legislative powers were restricted and the Council of Ministers was appointed by and were responsible to the Maharaja. Rejecting the Assembly, Sheikh Abdullah said on 29 January 1934, 'The people of this country did not spill blood for such a mock show ... what hopes can the people of this country have in this kind of a representative Assembly in which the dead weight of the officials and nominated majority will always be ready to crush the popular voice.'[30]

Parallels can easily be drawn between Hyderabad and J&K – both were twenty-one-gun salute states, with a large territory and population. Both refused to sign the Instrument of Accession before 15 August 1947 and harboured illusions of sovereignty. Both were amongst the richest of the Indian princely states, but at a personal level, the Nizam and the Maharaja were considered 'stingy' due to being quite parsimonious in their approach to expenditure.

While the Nizam had leased out Berar to the British, the Maharaja had leased out Gilgit–Baltistan. Both denied representation and participation to the majority population (Hindus in the case of

Hyderabad and Muslims in the case of J&K). Both faced popular movements against their rule – the Congress, Arya Samaj and the Communists led protests against the Nizam and the National Conference and Muslim Conference against the Maharaja. The press attaché to Mountbatten, Alan Campbell-Johnson, was asked by the former to visit both the states as his special representative to bring conciliation between the states and the dominion. Most interestingly, Jinnah was not comfortable either with the Nizam or with Sheikh Abdullah, for he felt that his 'sole spokesman' status could be challenged. In both states, the mulkis or local residents started an agitation seeking reservation in government jobs for locals. The Congress and the RSS[31] both wielded considerable influence though neither had a strong organizational presence. In Hyderabad, the Congress piggybacked on the Arya Samaj, and in J&K, they found their 'soulmate' in Sheikh Abdullah. Both states saw a rapid 'turnover' of the prime ministers – as they were responsible only to the whims of the princely rulers rather than to the popularly elected Assembly.

By 1935, Sheikh Abdullah had established himself as the undisputed leader of Kashmir and the head of the All J&K Muslim Conference.[32] However, it must be placed on record that while he held complete sway over the Kashmiri Muslims, his influence in Jammu, Ladakh and the frontier regions was negligible. Meanwhile, the Congress made overtures to him, and his interactions with Saifuddin Kitchlew, Nehru, Badshah Khan and Mahatma Gandhi convinced him that the J&K Muslim Conference should be made more inclusive and secular. In 1938, Sheikh Abdullah moved a resolution in the working committee of the Muslim Conference to change its name from Muslim Conference to J&K National Conference (NC) and open its doors to Hindus and Sikhs. The flag of the party was changed from the 'green with a white crescent' to the 'red with a white plough'. However even though minority leaders like Budh Singh[33] and Pandit Prem Bazaz[34] joined the NC, it could never really expand its base beyond the Valley. But thanks to the Congress, the Sheikh and his party got a national platform. In 1939, the Sheikh attended the Tripuri (Jabalpur)[35] session of the Congress, and was also asked to chair the session on the problems faced by people under states (*riyasats*). Later, he became the president of the All India States Peoples Conference.[36]

Sheikh's proximity to the Congress upset the plans of Jinnah and the Muslim League who were banking on the Muslims of Kashmir to back their demand for Pakistan. The Muslim League always liked to highlight that Sir Mohammed Iqbal,[37] the other prominent Kashmiri, was backing the demand for Pakistan, but the Sheikh was both secular and democratic. When Jinnah visited the state in 1944 and advised the Muslims of the state to organize themselves under the banner of the Muslim League, he met with stiff resistance. So much so that the only public meeting which Jinnah attended broke up amidst shouts of 'Go Back Jinnah'. It is on record that Jinnah had to be escorted to a place of safety by the state police. However, he did succeed in reviving the Muslim Conference under Ghulam Mohammad Abbas.[38] But the party faced a profound dilemma. While it was virulent in its opposition to the secularism of the National Conference, it also realized that its arch rival Sheikh was indispensable to its goal – the integration of Kashmir into Pakistan.

In May 1946, Sheikh Abdullah launched the Quit Kashmir agitation[39] against Maharaja Hari Singh and was arrested and sentenced to three years imprisonment but released after sixteen months in September 1947, thanks to the intervention of Nehru and Gandhi. Incidentally, the Muslim Conference leader, Ghulam Abbas, also appealed to the Maharaja to release Sheikh and he too was promptly arrested.

Thus, on the eve of Indian independence the two political organizations in Kashmir – the National Conference and the Muslim Conference – were led by Muslims, had a largely Muslim support base and both their leaders were behind bars. To achieve anything substantial the two parties had to come together, but repeated attempts to reconcile Sheikh Abdullah with Jinnah failed because both men were conscious of their own positions and importance and could not bring themselves to make the first move.

Meanwhile, it was becoming clear to the rulers of the princely states that Britain was likely to renege on their commitments to them, because after the Second World War, they simply did not have the financial or military muscle to make good their promises. The larger states – Travancore, Hyderabad and J&K – started looking at 'independence' as a possible option. However, they had limited exposure to the actual grind of politics – for their internal autonomy had been guaranteed by the Raj and they lived in their own world of gun salutes, shikar parties and ceremonial pomp with limited understanding of what their subjects really wanted. Their Prime Ministers too were not masters of political acumen for they owed their positions on account of their personal loyalty to the Maharaja and were, at the same time, perpetrators and victims of the court politics where rival factions were keen on consolidating their power, rather than further the interests of the state. In Jammu and Kashmir, Maharaja Hari Singh felt that he could perhaps manoeuvre an independent kingdom for himself, and he instructed his Prime Minister Ram Chandra Kak to bide time. Disliking the idea of becoming a part of India, which was being democratized, or of Pakistan which was Islamic, Hari Singh saw the independence of Jammu and Kashmir as an alternative and viable option, and Kak fuelled Hari Singh's desires, making him believe that Jammu and Kashmir could be an independent country.

This was also the time when an occultist by the name of Swami Sant Dev[40] made his appearance in the court of Hari Singh and began to exercise considerable influence. He was described as the Rasputin[41] of the court of Kashmir on account of his proximity to Maharani Tara Devi, the fourth and last wife of Hari Singh. Kak had reservations about the Swami, but in the power tussle between the Swami and the Prime Minster, the round was won by the Swami, and Ram Chandra Kak was dismissed unceremoniously (and arrested on 11 August 1947). Before Kak lost favour with his Maharaja, both were clearly united in their antipathy to the Congress and the Sheikh, and held parleys with Jinnah who offered a blank cheque to them, as indeed to other princely rulers of the border states (Jodhpur, Jaisalmer) in his bid to expand the territorial boundaries of Pakistan. Kak was the fall guy, and it suited all the parties – the Congress, the Sheikh and the Maharaja – to apply the 'traitor' tag to him. In his memoirs, Kak describes the role played by the Indian National Congress in the affairs of Jammu and Kashmir from 1938, including the propping up of Sheikh to counterbalance the influence of the Maharaja. He felt that the Sheikh's influence was limited to the Kashmiri Muslims of the Valley, but he donned a larger-than-life image because of his association with the Congress.

Jinnah and his team had been more than willing to cut a deal with the Maharaja, which excluded the Congress and Sheikh. In July 1947, Mohammad Ali Jinnah wrote to the Maharaja promising every possible favourable treatment, followed by the lobbying of the state's Prime Minister by leaders of Jinnah's Muslim League party. The Maharaja was promised complete internal autonomy within his state – which included an Assembly with a majority of nominated officials – for Jinnah was not exactly a paragon or patron saint of democratic virtues. However, to the credit of the Maharaja, he resisted all these tempting offers and also politely declined Jinnah's request to visit the state as a private citizen for medical recuperation, for he knew that Jinnah's presence in the state could be a spur for the Muslim Conference to brew fresh trouble.

On 11 August 1947, Major General Janak Singh Katoch,[42] CIE, was brought out of retirement from Himachal and made the Prime Minister. During his brief premiership of less than three months, he signed the Standstill Agreement with Pakistan, but could not anticipate the political volatility on ground with Hindu and Sikh refugees pouring into Jammu; the unprecedented communal violence in Jammu, Poonch and Mirpur; the relinquishment of Gilgit by the British; and the failure of the state troops to prevent the chain of violence against Muslims in Jammu and Poonch, and Hindus and Muslims in Muzaffarabad. The arrest of Ram Chandra Kak – with whom the Jinnah emissaries had opened a dialogue – was a signal that that the option of a merger with Pakistan could now be ruled out.

As such, the Muslim League raised the banner of revolt in Poonch, Mirpur and Muzaffarabad by encouraging disaffection and unrest on account of disruption in supplies of food and fuel. By the second week of September, Pakistan PM, Liaquat Ali Khan,[43] was egged on by Colonel Akbar Khan,[44] Sardar Shaukat Hayat Khan[45] and Muslim League officials in the North-West Frontier Province to organize a large-scale invasion of Kashmir by Pathan tribesmen. With Sardar Ibrahim, a Muslim Conference leader, at the forefront, they took control of most of the western parts of the state by 22 October; on 24 October, they formed a provisional Azad Kashmir.

The Maharaja's troops could not withstand the tribal militia attack in September for three reasons: they were heavily outnumbered, they faced desertions and there was no leadership or clarity among the troops. The Maharaja made an urgent plea to Delhi for military assistance, reiterating the point that he had been keen on accession from late July, and certainly after the deposition of Ram Chandra Kak.[46] However, Nehru wanted that the accession should be endorsed by Sheikh Abdullah as well – although there was absolutely no legal requirement for that. This critical delay cost India quite dearly. Justice Mehr Chand Mahajan,[47] the Maharaja's nominee for his next Prime Minister, had visited Nehru and Sardar Patel in Delhi on 19 September 1947, requesting essential supplies that had been blockaded by Pakistan since the beginning of September. On this trip, Mahajan conveyed the Maharaja's willingness to accede to India. Nehru, however, placed the release of Sheikh Abdullah from prison and the latter's endorsement as conditions precedent for the acceptance. The Maharaja released Sheikh Abdullah on 29 September.

Even after that, there was a delay of nearly four weeks. If Patel had had his way, the accession could have been signed by late September and the Indian Army could have stepped in to ensure law and order. This has been clearly explained in a recent book by P.C. Dogra.[48] He goes so far as to say that only when the Sheikh gave the green signal to Nehru on 24 October was the Instrument of Accession signed by Maharaja Hari Singh on 26 October and accepted by Mountbatten on the subsequent day. Unlike the other 560 Instruments of Accession signed till that date, this one made an exception – with the proviso that it would be submitted to a 'reference to the people' after the state was cleared of the invaders, since 'only the people, not the Maharaja, could decide where Kashmiris wanted to live'. This was against the accepted 'legal position' as sovereignty had been reverted to the rulers after the Indian Independence Act of 1947.

This was a major strategic victory for the Sheikh who exploited it to the hilt in the years to come. In a carefully drafted statement, the National Conference leader Syed Mir Qasim said,[49] 'India now had the "legal" as well as "moral" justification to send in the army through the Maharaja's accession and the people's support of it.'

However the press attaché to Mountbatten, Campbell-Johnson, gives a different version.[50] 'It is probable that nothing short of a full scale tribal invasion to the gates of his capital would have induced the hesitating Maharaja to accede at all.' Irrespective of who or why, on 24 October 1947, Maharaja Hari Singh wired India for military help to defend Srinagar, and sent Mahajan to plead his case. In the capital, Sheikh Abdullah too urged his good friend Nehru to send troops to push back the invaders. India decided to help, but only on the condition that Maharaja Hari Singh sign the Instrument of Accession, which he did two days later on 26 October.

The Indian troops, who were airlifted in the early hours of 27 October, secured the Srinagar airport. They had seen action in Kohima and Imphal, theatres of the second world war, and could accomplish their mission quite comfortably.

However, when the Indian Army was on the offensive and well on its way to capturing Muzaffarabad, Delhi suggested ceasefire, and Pakistan was more than happy to accept the offer – for India was in a position of dominance, and Pakistan would have lost the whole of Kashmir. Perhaps, as pointed out by Thomas Christopher,[51] Sheikh Abdullah never wanted India to capture the territory over which he had little influence. Therefore, after securing the towns of Poonch and Rajouri which had substantial Sikh and Hindu populations, as well as the strategic town of Kargil, the Indian Army was instructed to advance no further. The reasons were never shared with the field commanders: they were simply told that it would be difficult to arrange fuel, food, ammunition and supplies in the coming winter months. From the point of view of India, it was a strategic blunder, but Mountbatten and the British commanders – General Roy Bucher of India and General Douglas Gracey of Pakistan – were keen that troops who had faced action together in the Second World War should not be training guns at each other. It must be mentioned here that Governor General Mountbatten flew to Lahore on 1 November 1947 for a conference with Muhammad Ali Jinnah and proposed that in all the princely states where the ruler did not accede to a dominion corresponding to the majority population (which would have included Junagadh, Hyderabad, as well as Kashmir), the accession should be decided by an impartial referendum, but the offer was rejected by Jinnah.

Meanwhile, on 1 January 1948, India took the dispute to the UN for both Nehru and Mountbatten thought that the global opinion would firmly be on their side. Nehru was probably basking in the glory of the successful Asian Relations Conference[52] held in New Delhi in 1947 in which twenty-eight Asian countries had participated. Despite Jinnah's call to the Muslim countries to boycott this largely 'Hindu Congress' event, most countries in Asia including Turkey, Iraq, Malaysia, Kazakhstan – just to name a few – participated. However, the UN practised realpolitik and by 1948 every dispute in the world was looked at from the prism of the Cold War,[53] and Pakistan was able to project itself as Islamic and anti-communist, as against India's professed socialism and secularism. Moreover, Pakistan swore by the Commonwealth,[54] while India was just about giving its nudging approval. Nehru was also surprised by the very effective and articulate defence of Pakistan by their foreign minister, Zafarullah Khan.[55]

From the Indian side, the best orator was Sheikh Abdullah. Speaking at the UN Security Council on 5 February 1948 he said,[56] 'The (tribal) raiders came to our land, massacred thousands of people – mostly Hindus and Sikhs, but Muslims, too – abducted thousands of girls, Hindus, Sikhs and Muslims alike, looted our property and almost reached the gates of our summer capital, Srinagar ... there is no way we can trust the raiders and their backers (Pakistan army).' The Sheikh went to the extent of saying that the UN-sponsored plebiscite was irrelevant, for 'the accession of the state to the Union of India was the prerogative of the Constituent Assembly of J&K'.

The reference to the UN led to a stalemate. The UN Security Council called for an immediate ceasefire on both sides, and directed Pakistan to withdraw tribesmen and Pakistani nationals not normally resident therein. It also asked Government of India to reduce its forces to minimum strength, to create favourable circumstances for holding a plebiscite 'on the question of Accession of the state to India or Pakistan'. However, it took exactly one year to give effect to the ceasefire – it was only on the first day of January 1949 that the agreement was signed by General Roy Bucher on behalf of India and General Gracey on behalf of Pakistan.

This was followed up by the Karachi Agreement of July 1949; a ceasefire line to be supervised by UN military observers under the auspices of United Nations Commission for India and Pakistan (UNCIP)[57] was accepted by both the countries. At the Shimla Agreement of 1972,[58] India and Pakistan signed an agreement to resolve their differences bilaterally, without any external reference and defining a Line of Control in Kashmir which, with minor deviations, followed the same course as the ceasefire line established by the Karachi Agreement in 1949. Although the UNMOGIP[59] continues to exist, and India provides necessary security, transport and other services to the mission, no complaints are lodged with it from India's side.

There had been a ray of hope for a settlement in 1950, when Owen Dixon,[60] an Australian jurist chosen by the United Nations to mediate between India and Pakistan on the J&K issue, tried to settle the issue after his field level observations in all the regions of the state. The Dixon plan assigned Ladakh to India and northern areas and Pakistan-Occupied Kashmir to Pakistan, besides splitting Jammu between the two countries. It proposed a plebiscite in the Kashmir Valley. In many ways, this reflected ground position as half of Poonch, Mirpur and Muzaffarabad were in PoJK. According to Dixon, there was no need to go in for a plebiscite for the entire state, because of the clear demographic divide along geographical lines.

As things stand today, India claims that the entire Jammu and Kashmir and Ladakh including Gilgit–Baltistan and Askai Chin are an integral part of India by the virtue of legal, complete and irrevocable accession of Jammu and Kashmir to the Union of India in 1947. India asserts right and legal authority over the 2,22,236 sq. km that was held by the Maharaja. This was first stated by Nehru in the Parliament on 28 March 1951 and reiterated by Amit Shah in the Lok Sabha on 5 August 2019, while moving the resolution revoking Article 370. The effective Line of Control (LoC) with Pakistan and the Line of Actual Control (LAC) with China leaves 78,114 sq. km with Pakistan and 42,735 sq. km with China. This includes the 5180 sq. km of the Gilgit–Baltistan territory ceded by Pakistan to China illegally under the March 1963 Sino-Pak Boundary Agreement.

India's claims over Gilgit–Baltistan, Ladakh and Aksai Chin stem from the conquests of the Dogra general Zorawar Singh who expanded the frontiers of the Khalsa Raj towards Ladakh and Tibet, and Gilgit came under the control of the Dogra general in 1840. The 1842 Treaty of Chushul states:[61]

We have agreed that we have no ill-feelings because of the past war. The two kings will henceforth remain friends forever. The relationship between Maharaja Gulab Singh of J&K and the Lama Guru of Lhasa (Dalai Lama) is now established. The Maharaja Sahib, with God (Kunchok) as his witness, promises to recognize ancient boundaries which should be looked after by each side without resorting to warfare. When the descendants of the early kings, who fled from Ladakh to Tibet, now return they will not be stopped by Shri Maharaja. Trade between Ladakh and Tibet will continue as usual. Tibetan Govt. traders coming into Ladakh will receive free transport and accommodations as before, and the Ladakhi envoy will, in turn, receive the same facilities in Lhasa. The Ladakhis take an oath before God that they will not intrigue or create new troubles in Tibetan territory. We have agreed, with God as witness, that Shri Maharaja Sahib and the Lama Guru of Lhasa will live together as members of the same household. We have written the above on the second of Assura, Sambhat 1899 (17 September 1842).

As mentioned earlier the British assumed paramountcy over the state which meant that defence, external affairs and communications were under the direct control of the British. Moreover, given the strategic location of this region, the Indian government created a Gilgit Agency in 1889, for the British to secure the region as a buffer from the Russians. As a result of this Great Game, the British fear of Russian activities in Chinese Sinkiang was increasing. In 1935 the Gilgit Agency was expanded by Maharaja Hari Singh leasing the Gilgit *wazarat* to the Government of India for a period of sixty years and for an amount of Rs 75,000 per annum. This gave the British political agent complete control over Gilgit–Baltistan. However, two weeks before Independence, viz on 14 August, the British cancelled the lease agreement, and the region reverted to the Maharaja of Jammu and Kashmir who then appointed Brigadier Ghansar Singh as the governor of Gilgit.

By November of that year, Gilgit Scouts, a paramilitary force comprising trained locals but commanded by British officers to guard Gilgit, ostensibly on behalf of the ruler of Kashmir, mutinied against the Maharaja under the leadership of its commander, Major William Alexander Brown. Major Brown was later decorated with the MBE and the Sitara-e-Pakistan, which goes on to show that all his actions had the tacit approval of the British commander-in-chief of the Pakistan Army. Under 'Operation Datta Khel' the Gilgit Scouts surrounded the Gilgit Residency and took Brigadier

Ghansar Singh and Wazir-i-wazarat Sehdev Singh Chib along with their families and staff into protective custody. Brown then requested for troops to be sent to the Gilgit Agency from Pakistan and established a de facto military administration and thwarted plans by a large section of his contingent to set up an independent republic called Gilgit–Astor. On 2 November, he hoisted the Pakistan flag over the capital residency and announced the accession of the Gilgit Agency to Pakistan. Brown remained in command of the Gilgit Scouts until 12 January 1948, when he was replaced by Major (later Brigadier) Aslam Khan.

With the ceasefire between India and Pakistan coming into effect on 1 January 1949, a de facto boundary did come into existence. However, with regard to the Ladakh–Tibet frontier, when Mao became the great helmsman in China he took the view that Tibet was never a competent political entity in so far as its external boundaries were concerned and made it clear that he neither accepted the Treaty of Chushul nor the McMahon line. This is contested by Ramachandra Guha[62] when he comments that prior to Mao's interpretation, no official Chinese maps showed Aksai Chin as part of China. In fact, the Sinkiang (Xinjiang) map of the 1930s showed the Kunlun (the mountains) rather than the Karakoram (range) as the customary boundary – which had been the Indian claim all along. Claude Apri believes that the Chinese planned aggression beyond the western boundary of Tibet – which had been taken over by the communist regime in 1950 – through a network of three roads to be built under military supervision passing through Aksai Chin including one which connected Holtan in Xinjiang to Lhasa in Tibet.[63]

Chinese military first made its appearance in northwestern Tibet – that is, east of Ladakh-Aksai Chin – in 1951 and even as Nehru was chanting 'Hindi–Chini Bhai Bhai', deep incisions were being made in Askai Chin; in 1958, then Foreign Secretary Subimal Dutt gave the official confirmation that there was 'little doubt that the newly constructed 1,200 kilometre road passes through Aksai Chin'. In 1962, Chinese troops were stopped by the Indian soldiers near the present-day LAC in Ladakh, and in 1963, Pakistan gifted another 5000 sq. km of territory to China, thereby laying the foundations of the China–Pakistan Economic Corridor (CPEC).

4

THE NIZAM AND HIS
FIRMANS

As the only 'His Exalted Highness'[1] in the British Empire, the Nizam of Hyderabad Osman Ali Khan certainly regarded himself as the ruler of the 'first state in the princely order' in India. The British definitely gave him the impression that he was – for they called on him to assume the mantle of leadership amongst Indian Muslims and issue a *firman*[2] encouraging Muslim soldiers to join the British forces against the Ottoman Emperor[3] who was regarded as the Khalifa[4] of the Muslim world. They conferred upon him the title of 'Faithful Ally of the British Government' as well. However, the Nizam also encouraged a section of the Khalifists to project him as the figure of religious and political authority, well beyond the state of Hyderabad. From 1924, he also subscribed to funds for the maintenance of the deposed Khalifa and, in 1931, he strengthened his ties with the deposed Ottoman ruler, Abdulmejid II, by marrying his sons to the latter's daughter and niece – the marriage was brokered by none other than Maulana Shaukat Ali.[5]

Even though the Muslim population in Hyderabad was just around 12.8 per cent, they comprised the entire military and police establishment as well as administrative elite. The Nizam's patronage of Islamic scholarship, funding of the AMU as well as the passage money of hundreds of Hajj pilgrims from across India, made him a leading name on the Islamic firmament. He established the Osmania University[6] in Hyderabad as the 'trans-regional Urdusphere that connected Muslim intellectuals of Aligarh,[7] Deoband,[8] Lucknow and Hyderabad with their counterparts in Cairo, Kabul and Istanbul'.[9] Therefore, Jinnah was never really comfortable with the Nizam, for if anyone could challenge his status at the 'Sole Spokesman for Indian Muslims', it was the Nizam of Hyderabad. In fact, an influential section of the Jamiat-ul-Ulema[10] passed a resolution in 1940 calling for the 'formation of an Independent Muslim state comprising Eastern Afghanistan, tribal territory, the Frontier Province, Punjab, Sindh Baluchistan to be placed under the Nizam of Hyderabad'.[11] Prior to that, in 1939, two Aligarh professors had suggested dividing India into four independent sovereign states: Pakistan, Bengal, Hindustan and Hyderabad which may agree to confederate. The point to note is that Hyderabad was in the mindspace of the politically conscious Islamists, and all this must have given the Nizam the impression that he held many aces up his sleeve in the post-1947 political configuration, which is what led him to issue the firman on 11 June 1947 that Hyderabad would neither accede to India nor Pakistan.

Hyderabad's geographical position was both its strength and weakness. Together with Berar, which had been leased to the Union government in perpetuity, it was surrounded by Central Provinces in the north, Bombay in the west and Madras in the east and the south. With its population (sixteen million), revenue (Rs 26 crore) and size (82,000 square miles), it was the premier state in the country with its own coinage, paper currency and stamps. However, for all the additional frills and titles that the British conferred on the Nizam, it was not treated any differently than any other Indian state. Lord Hardinge[12] and Lord Reading[13] had been quite 'curt and cut' in their response to the Nizam, and had reminded him on more than one occasion that the paramount power was supreme, not just on treaties and precedent, but independently of them as well. Viceroy Reading emphatically refuted the Nizam's claim that there had ever been any equality between the governments of Great Britain and Hyderabad, and that the Nizam did not stand in a category separate from the rulers of other states. Perhaps, he could not read the writing on the wall, for even after the promulgation of the Indian Independence Act, he issued a statement protesting against 'the way in which my state (Hyderabad) is being abandoned by its old ally, the British government and the ties which have bound me in loyal devotion to the King Emperor are being severed'.[14]

The Nizam also sent a delegation to meet Mountbatten and seek clarity on three points: retrocession of Berar to the Nizam; the grant of dominion status; but if that was not possible, the terms of accession to the Indian Union. With regard to the first, Mountbatten pointed out that from 1935, no change in existing administrative arrangements was possible without consulting the people through their representatives or a referendum – and in such an event, Berar would prefer to remain with Central Provinces than with Hyderabad. With regard to dominion status, the position was reiterated; and with regard to the accession, it was clarified that only three subjects – defence, external affairs and communications – would be handled by the new dominion government of India, for which Hyderabad would not have to bear any expenses. It was in this meeting that the Nizam's delegation raised the possibility of joining the Dominion of Pakistan. The Nizam was trying to bargain hard, but it must be mentioned that Pakistan under Jinnah was never keen on the accession of Hyderabad for two reasons – it was a predominantly Hindu majority state and, more importantly, the Nizam was the only one who could emerge as an alternate power centre to Jinnah.

Language, Religion, Ideology and Power: Competing Interests in Hyderabad

Lest one gather the impression that Hyderabad was all about the Nizam and his firmans, it must be placed on record that the nationalist, linguistic, ethnic and communal ferment that was brewing in the rest of the country was impacting this princely state as well. Mahatma Gandhi had returned from South Africa to India in 1915, and starting with the Champaran Satyagraha in 1917, he transformed the Congress from a debating club to champions of a mass movement, and took up issues that affected the everyday lives of people – from the Champaran Satyagraha[15] to the support for the Khilafat Movement.[16] Satyagraha emerged as a popular technique: 'a weapon of the weak against the mighty state'. From 1921, the Congress decided that its own internal organization would be based on the 'linguistic principle'. The Sindhi, Marathi, Gujarati, Oriya and Kannada circles were formed, and inculcating pride in one's own language became a badge of honour. In this context, the refusal to allow a resolution in Telugu at the Nizam's Social Reforms Conference in Hyderabad in November 1921 led to the formation of Andhra Jana Sangham[17] with twelve members. Andhra Jana Sangham organized the first conference with over a hundred delegates in February 1922 with K.V.R. Reddy[18] as the chairman and Hanumantha Rao[19] as the secretary. Within two years, fifty branches had been established in the Telangana region. It started having regular conferences, but in 1930 it morphed into the Andhra Mahasabha.[20] The focus shifted to economic and social reforms, abolition of untouchability, and security of land tenure.

However, in the subsequent decades, ideological differences within the Andhra Mahasabha led to a split with one faction merging with the Congress and the other with the Communist Party of India.

If the Andhra Mahasabha was focused on Telugu language and social reform, the Arya Samaj[21] movement took on the Majlis-e-Ittehadul Muslimeen party and its attempts at proselytization, allegedly with implicit support from the Nizam. The Arya Samaj pointed to Mafusa and Gayar Mafusa, the two firmans issued in the Fasli year 1339 (corresponding to 1929 CE). These related to 'protection against eviction of Muslim landowners' and 'permission to Muslims to take over the mortgaged lands of the Hindus'.

Founded in Gujarat by Dayanand Saraswati,[22] the Arya Samaj was most active and influential in Punjab and Hyderabad – regions where the Hindus were in a minority – and facing the intellectual, scriptural and cultural onslaught of the Muslims, including conversions of the peasantry and artisan classes to Islam. Before the establishment of the Samaj, there was hardly any resistance to conversion, and once converted there was no way of getting re-acceptance into the Hindu fold. Swami Dayanand Saraswati introduced the concept of Shudhi[23] – or purification for return to the fold of Hinduism.

Arya Samaj had major ideological differences with the Hindu Mahasabha,[24] which followed the Sanatana Dharma[25] and was not as vigorously opposed to the caste system as the Arya Samaj. But when it came to opposing proselytization, the two groups came together. Of course, the Arya Samaj had the upper edge, for it actively sought out recent converts and got them back to the larger Hindu pantheon. The Arya Samaj received a fillip with the election of Chief Justice Pandit Keshav Rao Koratkar[26] as the president of the Hyderabad branch of Arya Samaj in 1905. Over the next three decades, the Arya Samaj had 250 branches in the state, twenty of which were located in the twin cities of Hyderabad and Secunderabad.

The elections held under the GoI Act 1935 (albeit on a limited mandate)[27] saw the Congress emerging as the ruling party in all the three provinces surrounding Hyderabad. In February 1938, the Indian National Congress passed the Haripura Resolution[28] declaring that the princely states were 'an integral part of India', and that it stood for 'the same political, social and economic freedom in the States as in the rest of India'. This announcement spurred the formation of the Hyderabad State Congress, and an enthusiastic drive to enrol members was started. By July 1938, the committee claimed to have enrolled 1200 primary members and called upon both Hindus and Muslims of the state to 'shed mutual distrust'[29] and join the 'cause of responsible government under the aegis of the Asaf Jahi dynasty'.[30] However, despite their protestations of loyalty, the Nizam felt threatened, promulgated a new Public Safety Act in 1938,[31] and declared the Hyderabad State Congress as unlawful. Meanwhile, the communal situation remained tense, and hoping to capitalize on the communal tensions that had been on the boil since early that year, the Arya Samaj announced a Satyagraha on 24 October 1938. Perhaps, to not be outdone, the activists of the Hyderabad State Congress formed a 'Committee of Action' and also announced their satyagraha for the same day. In effect, it became a common call against the Nizam by all the three organizations: the Arya Samaj, the Hindu Mahasabha and the Congress. But the Congress high command did not appreciate this local arrangement, and relied on the report of Padmaja Naidu[32] to Gandhi in which she castigated the State Congress for lacking unity and cohesion and for being 'communal'. On 24 December 1938, the State Congress suspended the agitation after 300 activists had courted arrest, but the Arya Samaj and the Hindu Mahasabha continued their agitation well into the '40s The leaders of the Hyderabad Congress did launch a non-violent campaign of civil disobedience – a satyagraha – for civil rights, representative democracy alongside the Quit India movement led by the Indian National Congress in 1942, but the political mobilization among the Hindus in the state centred around the Arya Samaj and the Hindu Mahasabha.

However, it would not be correct to portray this struggle in the context of Hindu–Muslim binary alone. There were many other contestations – within Hindus, among the Telugu, Kannada and Maratha speakers, between the Brahmins and the rest, as also between the Arya Samaj, the Hindu Mahasabha and the Congress. The Muslims too were divided with tensions among the Mulkis and the non-Mulkis, and the Rizvi and anti-Rizvi factions.[33] With the announcement of the Indian Independence Act, the Congress and the Arya Samaj started the 'Join Indian Union' movement, which was of course resisted by the Ittehad[34] and the Razakars.[35]

The Nizam's writ no longer ran beyond Hyderabad city and the surrounding villages. The stage was set for Operation Polo.[36]

From Nizam to Raj Pramukh

Just before Independence, the Political Department of the Raj had prepared the draft of the Standstill Agreement[37] which 'provided that all extant administrative arrangements of common concern that existed between the "Crown" and the signatory state would continue unaltered between the signatory Dominion (India or Pakistan) until new arrangements were made'. From a juristic point of view, it was different from the Instrument of Accession (IoA) prepared by the States Department (under Patel and Nehru) because the IoA involved the surrender of sovereignty in the three specified subjects of defence, external affairs and communications. Hyderabad was unique in the sense that it wanted a Special Standstill Agreement and that too without signing the Instrument of Accession.

This was also a period of intense political rivalry and struggle within the ruling clique in Hyderabad state. The Ittehad-ul Muslimeen and Kasim Rizvi became the Nizam's key advisers, and they eased out the constitutional adviser Sir Walter Monckton[38] as well as the Nawab of Chhatri[39] from the Nizam's Executive Council. The position was filled by a prominent Hyderabadi businessman, Liak Ali.

By November, the Nizam had confirmed to Mountbatten that he would not accede to Pakistan. As such an exception was made in the case, and India agreed to sign the Standstill Agreement for a period of one year without the Instrument of Accession. However, even before the ink was dry on the Standstill Agreement, two ordinances issued by the Nizam's government – the first declaring that Indian currency would no longer be legal tender in Hyderabad, and then banning exports of precious metals from Hyderabad to India – went against the letter and spirt of the Standstill Agreement. Hyderabad also offered a loan of Rs 20 crore to Pakistan in the form of Government of India securities, and appointed a Public Relations Officer in Pakistan, besides declaring their intent to extend such appointments in other countries as well. From the provocative speeches of Kasim Rizvi and the activities of Razakars, only two conclusions could be drawn: either the Nizam was unable to enforce his control over them or he was unwilling to assert his authority, but in both cases, it left the overwhelming majority of his subjects (including Muslims who disagreed with Ittehad-ul Muslimeen) absolutely terrified. While the Nizam always committed that he would disband the Razakars, as a matter of fact they tied up with communist insurgents to carry out their loot and plunder.

Even though Mountbatten tried his best to ensure an honourable settlement between Hyderabad and the States Department, his efforts came to naught. Before his departure from India in June 1948, he sent his trusted aide and press attaché Alan Campbell-Johnson to meet the Nizam, study the situation and report to him.

After meeting the Nizam and the key players in his establishment–Liak Ali, Kasim Rizvi and El Aldroos (the army commander)–Campbell-Johnson concluded that 'the Nizam was the key man in the situation and that, with regard to the main issue of relations with the Indian Union, nothing was being done without his approval'.[40] He further reported that the Nizam was in a mood of 'aggressive fatalism'.

After Mountbatten's departure, attitude stiffened on both sides, and the margin for the 'faithful ally of the British' was no longer available to Hyderabad. Meanwhile, reports of the gun-running by one Sidney Cotton[41] from the airfield in Karachi, the resignation of the Hindu members of the Nizam's council, their insistence on taking up the matter of Hyderabad in the UN and with the USA, led Governor General Rajagopalachari, Prime Minister Nehru and Deputy Prime Minster Sardar Patel to the firm decision that time had come for military intervention.

The 108-hour military operation led by General J.N. Chaudhari, code-named Operation Polo, commenced on 15 September 1948 and ended on the morning of 18 September with El Aldroos laying his arms. Although this was followed by a general clamour for deposing the Nizam, he had changed his stripes after the meek surrender of his army commander El Aldroos. The Nizam issued a firman on 19 September 'investing full executive authority with power to issue regulations having the force of law' to General J.N. Chaudhari.[42] This was reiterated by another firman of 9 August 1949, which enabled the merger of jagir lands with state lands, and finally on 1 December, by the third firman, the administration was transferred to the chief minister of Hyderabad, the first incumbent being M.K.Vellodi[43] of the ICS, and four members of the Hyderabad Congress joined his council. At the commencement of the Constitution, Hyderabad was integrated into India as a Part B state, with the Nizam of Hyderabad as the first raj pramukh.

5

INDIA AS A REPUBLIC!

The most significant change in the map of India from 1947 to 1950 was the one that reflected the transition of the country from a dominion to a republic. While the masthead on the map of the Indian dominion had classified the territory of India into provinces, states and districts, the map under the republic only mentioned states within the new Constitution. From a cartographic perspective, the biggest change was the disappearance of the 562 princely states from the map of India.

It is true that Jammu and Kashmir, Mysore and Hyderabad still retain their names on the map, but these along with PEPSU,[1] Madhya Bharat, Saurashtra, Rajasthan and Travancore– Cochin were states under raj pramukhs[2] appointed by the President of India, and collectively called Part B states to distinguish them from the former provinces of British India which were known as the Part A states.

In fact, the states ministry acted post-haste to settle the privy purses and get the rulers or regents (if the prince was a minor) to sign the Merger Agreements. It must be mentioned here that the two documents – Instrument of Accession and Merger Agreements – were quite different. The Instrument of Accession was signed on, before or immediately after Independence and traces its origin to the Government of India Act of 1935 to enable the rulers of the princely states to cede the three subjects – defence, external affairs and communications – to the Government of India. This is because the 1935 Act had envisioned a loose federation in which the princely states would participate. However, with the onset of the Second World War, the salience of the freedom movement and the assertion of Congress after the Haripura session[3] (under the presidency of Subhas Bose) that the 'princely states' too were an inalienable part of India, the idea lost steam. In fact, analysts like Barbara Ramusack argue that the princely states were virtually abandoned by the Raj.[4]

~

With the passage of the Indian Independence Act of 1947 on 3 June 1947, the British government announced its plan for the transfer of power to the dominions of India and Pakistan. Meanwhile, Article 5 of the Indian Independence Act defined the territory and extent of India to include the British Indian provinces (governor's provinces) administrative areas under chief commissioners; the princely states which had signed the Instrument of Accession; and other such territories as were accepted by the dominion to be included in the territory of India. However, it soon became clear that such a loose integration would not work, and that the Government of India would have to step in to ensure that there was some parity between the administration of the provinces and the princely states, many of which were so small and insignificant that they could not even manage a police station and a mofussil court. This led to the ministry of states offering Merger Agreements with the states, which inter alia sought the transfer of full and exclusive authority and jurisdiction in relation to the governance of the states to the Government of India. While there were minor variations in the

Merger Agreements to suit individual states, the pith and substance were five key provisions. These included the ruler ceding to the government of the dominion complete civil, revenue, police and criminal jurisdiction and powers. In lieu, thereof, the ruler was granted a privy purse[5] based on the income of the state as well as additional privileges including exemption from wealth tax, income tax and municipal taxes on privy purses and his private properties. In addition to the recognition of the ruler and his right to succession as per tradition, the *rajmata*, *yuvraj* and *yuvrani* were also recognized. The Merger Agreement was signed with the neighbouring province or the union of states with the secretary of States Department V.P. Menon being the signatory witness.

~

The first person who raised the issue of integrating the princely states with the existing provinces was Hare Krishna Mahtab, the premier of Orissa (as chief ministers were called in 1946). After taking over the administration of the state on 23 April 1946, he argued that considering the geographical, linguistic and ethnological affinity of the states with the rest of the province, it was desirable that there should be a common administration for both the states and the province. However, largely under the influence of the British resident for the eastern states, the rulers rejected his appeal, and thirty-nine of them established the 'Eastern Union',[6] with an elaborate secretariat and police organization. It was fortuitous that the two most important states (Mayurbhanj in Orissa and Bastar in Chhattisgarh) refused to be a part of this arrangement, which was basically a trade union of princes without any popular support. In fact, immediately after the establishment of the ministry of states, Mahtab submitted a memorandum to Sardar Patel in which he indicated the administrative difficulties that would be faced if the princely states were allowed to retain their internal autonomy – for many of the rulers were plainly irresponsible, and did not make any distinction between their personal entitlement and the welfare of the state. Based on Mahtab's feedback, the ministry of states refused to accept this union under the leadership of the Raja of Patna (Orissa). Meanwhile, as popular agitations, starting with Nilgiri, made it difficult for the princely states to continue their administration, Mahtab sought and received permission from the Government of India to take over the administration of the recalcitrant princely states. Patel came to Cuttack, held a separate meeting with the rulers of salute and non-salute states, and nudged them to agree for a merger in lieu of privy purses and personal entitlements. In fact, these negotiations set up the process for integration of other princely states with the neighbouring provinces.

~

Soon thereafter, 216 states were amalgamated with the neighbouring provinces of Assam, Bihar, Bombay, Madhya Pradesh (formerly Central Provinces and Berar), Madras, Orissa, Punjab, Uttar Pradesh (formerly the United Provinces) and West Bengal – Part A states – and another 275 with Part B states. The rest, including Bhopal, Bilaspur, Himachal Pradesh (the erstwhile Punjab Hill states), Cutch, Manipur, Tripura and Vindhya Pradesh (Bundelkhand and Baghelkhand states), along with Ajmer Merwara, Coorg and Delhi (areas directly administered by the British) were constituted as Part C states. These momentous changes were comparatively easier to implement under the Government of India Act 1935, which remained the constitutional law of India till 26 January 1950. This Act gave an overwhelming power and authority to the central government to bring about territorial adjustments. The principle followed for the merger of a princely state was to look at the ethnic/ linguistic affiliation of the majority population. Thus Loharu, Pataudi and Dujana were merged with Punjab, rather than with PEPSU.

But there were controversies as well. Cooch Behar was claimed by both West Bengal and Assam. This was an interesting case because while the state was ethnically aligned to Assam, in the immediate aftermath of Partition, the large influx of Hindu population from East Bengal changed the demographic composition of Cooch Behar. As such, there was a popular movement in Cooch Behar, as well as in West Bengal, for its merger with the latter, and B.C. Roy[7] put his political prestige at stake on this issue.

Pending a decision, Cooch Behar was made into a chief commissioner's province. It may be mentioned here that several princely states sought the status of a chief commissioner's province as an interim arrangement, and the policy of the states ministry was that if such symbolic gestures eased the transition, there was no harm in allowing these concessions.

Meanwhile, a popular agitation in the non-Oriya-speaking states of Seraikella and Khargawan saw these states being transferred to Bihar. In addition to these, all the twelve non-salute states affiliated to the Bihar states agency – Mohrampur, Darbhanga, Ramgarh, Ranka, Jagdishpur, Dumraon, Dighwara, Tajpur, Banaili, Kahra, Bhour and Chanaur were also integrated with Bihar.

Madhya Pradesh (the erstwhile Central Provinces and Berar) saw the addition of Bastar, Changbhakar, Chhuikhadan, Jashpur, Kankar, Kawardha, Khairagarh, Korea, Nandgaon, Raigarh, Sakti, Sarangarh, Surguja, Udaipur and Makrai. This was a largely tribal belt and, as such, was under the Fifth Schedule of the Constitution. The governor of Madhya Pradesh was given special responsibilities for the care and protection of the tribal population of this region.

As mentioned earlier, although PEPSU had been established for the princely states of Punjab, three small states of Loharu (in present-day Bhiwani), Dujana (in present-day Jhajjar) and Pataudi (in present-day Gurugram) were merged into Punjab, whose frontiers then extended right up to Delhi and Rajasthan. Of these,

Loharu was a nine-gun salute state, and the family was linked by blood or marriage to personalities like Mirza Ghalib (son-in-law of the brother of the first Nawab, Ahmad Baksh Khan) besides Sir Sayyad Ahmad Khan and Dr Fakhruddin Ali Ahmad, whose mother came from the Loharu family. Although the Nawab of Dujana signed the Instrument of Accession with India, most members of the family left for Pakistan, and the lands and properties were settled with the Punjabis who migrated from West Punjab. Pataudi was a non-salute state belonging to the family of India's famous cricketer Mansur Ali Khan Pataudi. The rulers of Dujana, Loharu and Pataudi were related to each other, and all three had their havelis in Old Delhi. The reason they were not merged with PEPSU was that they had little in common with the predominantly Sikh Misals[8] that constituted PEPSU.

The states that merged with Madras included Pudukkottai, Banganpalle and Sandur. Pudukkottai was a seventeen-gun salute state under Thodaiman Raja Rajagopala, the ninth and the last descendant of his dynasty. With an area of 1170 square miles and a population of a little less than half a million, Pudukkottai had been well administered by the likes of Sir A. Seshiah Shastry, and was also home to the family of Nattukotai Chettiars, the hereditary bankers and financiers of south India. The privy purses and properties were settled after discussions with the government of Madras. Much smaller than Pudukkottai was Banganpalle, a nine-gun salute state of Shia Muslims, and was one of the last to join the Indian Union in February 1948. With an area of 275 square miles, and a population of about forty thousand only, it was originally a jagir of Bijapur, but was fortified by the descendants of Faiz Ali Khan. Banganpalle came under British protection from 1832, and was placed under the Madras Presidency for purposes of control and supervision. After the merger, it was made part of Kurnool district.

The smallest of the states that merged with Madras was the Maratha state of Sandur, with an area of 169 square miles and a population of just about sixteen thousand. It had been a British protectorate from 1818, and as in the case of Banganpalle and Pudukkottai, was managed by the Madras Presidency. The Raja had acceded to the Indian Union on 10 August 1947, but the merger with Madras took place in 1949. In 1956, after the linguistic reorganization of states, Sandur became part of Bellary district of Mysore. Its last ruler, Maharaja Srimant Yeshwantrao Hindurao Gharpade, was a keen wildlife enthusiast.

~

The merger of the twenty-one-gun salute state of Baroda as well as that of Kolhapur marked the end of resistance of the other Deccan states to amalgamation with Bombay. Besides Kolhapur, a hereditary nineteen-gun salute state, there were seventeen other states which formed scattered islands in the politically conscious province of Bombay, and some like Kolhapur, Aundh and Phaltan were quite progressive with regard to education and removal of untouchability. The rulers of the Deccan state were quite diverse in their origin: thus Alakot, Jath, Mudhol, Phaltan and Sawantwadi were Marathas, and their ancestors had carved out the kingdoms when the Peshwas[9] were losing their control. Then there were the Brahmin kingdoms of Aundh and Bhor who owed their existence to a gift by the Maratha ruler of Satara. The Patwardhan Brahmins who were in the service of the Peshwas held the states of Sangli, Wadi, Ramdurg, Jamkhandi, Miraj Senior, Miraj Junior, Khurundwad Senior and Khurundwad Junior. There were two Muslim rulers as well – Janjira was ruled by the warrior tribe of East Africa and Savanur belonged to the Miyana tribe of the Pathans.

However, while the Deccan rulers had their internal differences, especially with regard to status, they were all quite keen to come together for negotiating the terms of their accession to India as well as the possibility of forming a union amongst themselves. As early as July 1946, led by the Raja of Phaltan, they met Gandhi and Nehru, with the latter advising them to first grant responsible government. K.M. Munshi and Kamalnayan Bajaj were drafted to negotiate with the princes, but only eight of the seventeen agreed to join the union with the Raja of Aundh as the raj pramukh and Raja of Bhor as the up raj pramukh. However, as none of the salute states joined the union, it did not gather steam, and by October 1947, the rulers of Jamkhandi, Jath and Akkalkot said that they wanted their states to merge with Bombay. Aundh, which had been in the forefront of the move to form a union now proposed a plebiscite, but this was rejected – both from the point of view of its practicality as well as from the point of view of creating a precedence. At this juncture, the spokesperson of the Deccan States union wanted that the union should merge with Bombay. But the ministry of states took the view that as the union had not been formally recognized, and did not include some of the key stakeholders, each of the individual states would have to sign the Merger Agreement. The anti-Brahmin riots that broke out in Kolhapur and Ramdurg in the aftermath of the assassination of Mahatma Gandhi also necessitated the intervention of the provincial government of Bombay to restore the rule of law. Likewise, Janjira, a small maritime state, was already under the administration of Bombay, and the ruler agreed to the merger – for he was now assured of a privy purse! Thus on 8 March 1948, Bombay added 7815 square miles of territory, a population of nearly seventeen lakh and an annual revenue of Rs 1.42 crore.

After the death of the Maharaja Sir Rajaram Chhatrapati (Saha ji) in 1940, and later of his six-year-old adoptive successor, the Political Department had recognized the adoption of Vikramsinha Rao of Dewas Senior as Saha ji, but the succession was disputed by the dowager queen. After rioting broke out in January 1948, an administrator was appointed by the Government of India. Meanwhile, the fourteen-salute states, along with seventeen non-salute states and 191 non-jurisdictional states of Kathiawar had agreed to form a union, which was subsequently called the Saurashtra union. Although the Kathiawar region was linguistically aligned to Gujarat, it had a distinct peninsular geography and was different from the Gujarat states. It was first inclined to form a union under the leadership of Baroda, but on account of the lack of foresight of its ruler, Maharaja Sir Pratap Singh, who was whimsical, unpopular and unethical, the opportunity was missed. Rather than lead the union, as in the case of PEPSU (for Baroda was the only state to have a twenty-one-gun salute status in the region), he refused to see the writing on the wall. Moreover, he was at odds with the popular ministry under Dr Jivraj Mehta, and was also accused of overdrawing his authorized allowance, besides diverting state resources for his personal use. Worse, he alienated Sardar Patel by his supercilious attitude when he was asked to extend his support to stem the administrative chaos in Junagadh – the Nawab of Junagadh had fled to Pakistan after hastily announcing the merger of his predominantly Hindu state with Pakistan. When Pratap Singh wrote to the Sardar that he should be recognized as the King of Saurashtra and Gujarat, he was snubbed, and told that his help was not required. It is necessary to give a brief background to this, for he gradually lost the support of practically everyone.

Before leaving for England in May 1948, Maharaja Pratap Singh wrote off a loan of Rs 220 lakh to himself, and also drew another Rs 105 lakh from the treasury towards the future marriage expenses of his daughters. Mehta called a special meeting of the Baroda Legislative Assembly, which then questioned 'his fitness to rule', asked him to abdicate in favour of his son, and also sought a special audit of the finances of the state for which a senior officer of the Indian Audits and Accounts Service was deputed. Several serious anomalies, including the misappropriation of Rs 6 crore and unauthorized withdrawal of state jewels, including the diamond necklace with the priceless stones Star of South, Eugene and Shahee Akbar, which had been sent to England, were reported. The states ministry now came to the conclusion that it was not possible for Baroda to retain its 'independence' and that it had to be merged with Bombay. Towards the end, the Maharaja pleaded that he should be allowed to make the announcement of the merger, and it was done by him on 31 January 1949.

The state's administration was taken over by Bombay on 1 May 1949. However, he took the leadership of an informal rulers union in Bombay in January 1951 and started touring states under the pretext of shikar, but really to foment unrest amongst the former royals, for which he received support from the likes of the ruler of Jodhpur. This had to be nipped in the bud, and within April of the same year, a presidential proclamation was issued under Article 366 (2) 'derecognizing' him as the ruler of Baroda, and the mantle was passed on to his son Yuvraj Fateh Singh.

With Baroda unable to provide the leadership to seventeen jurisdictional and 127 semi- and non-jurisdictional states, it was clear that there were limited options for them. None of these states was large enough, and, moreover, their territories were interspersed and interlocked with Baroda, as well as the Ahmedabad and Kaira districts of Bombay. Although they covered an extensive area, nearly 12,000 square miles, the population was just over twenty-one lakh, and the annual revenue was less than a crore and a half. Most of the rulers of the jurisdictional states were Rajputs belonging to the Solanki, Chauhan, Waghela, Sisodia, Parmar and Gohel clans. States under Muslim rulers included Balasinor, Cambay, Sachin and Radhanpur.

The first informal meeting between the states ministry, represented by V.P. Menon, and the rulers of Gujarat was held at the Bombay residence of the Maharaja of Rajpipla in March 1948. They were still hopeful that Baroda may agree to lead the union, but on getting a negative reply, they tried to get concessions similar to the ones granted to Kathiawar (Saurashtra). Rajpipla of the Gohil Rajput dynasty, which lay between Narmada and Tapti, was second in size, resources and population only to Baroda, and assumed the leadership of the Gujarat states. Rajpipla had had a Legislative Assembly from 1932, and its ruler, Maharaja Vijaysinhji was a keen rider, sportsperson, motoring and aviation enthusiast. He had established an airport in 1922, which thanks to the proximity of the site to Sardar Patel Statue of Unity, is being revived after nearly a century. After three days of intense discussions with the rulers of the other states, the Rajpipla ruler issued a statement, which read:[10]

> We have the pleasure to inform you that, as rulers of the Gujarat states, we believe our mother country, and particularly Gujarat looks up to us to make all the sacrifices in the wider interests of India as a whole. We therefore, have cheerfully responded to the call of duty and decided to take the first step in forming the province of Mahagujarat[11] by integrating our states with the province of Bombay. We invoke God's blessings on our decision.

In this he was supported by all the other rulers, including the Babi dynasts of Radhanpur and Balasinor, who though related to Junagadh did not hesitate to sign both the Instrument of Accession and Merger Agreement with India. Balasinor, a nine-gun salute state, became famous in the '80s on account of the discovery of the remains of dinosaurs. Radhanpur was an eleven-gun salute state under Nawab Murtaza Khan. Although efforts were carried out to make them follow the Junagadh example, they stood firm in their commitment to India. Another Shia Muslim state which readily followed the Rajpipla lead was Cambay, a nine-gun salute state, which had lost its importance as a maritime city to Surat on account of the silting of its harbour.

Then there was Bansda, whose ruler was a naturalist as well as a nationalist. Thanks to the efforts of its ruler, the Vansda National Park came into existence and conservation efforts received a fillip in the region. It was he who offered Subhas Bose the presidential cart driven by fifty-one bullocks on the occasion of the Haripura Congress in 1936. The eleven-gun salute Khichi Chauhan dynasty of Chhota Udaipur claimed to be the direct descendants of Prithvi Raj Chauhan, and the state had been at the forefront of spreading a communications network, postal system, educational institutions, ginning factories and waterworks. Dharampur was another progressive state of Sisodia Rajputs.[12] It was a flourishing centre of trade with leading Jain and Parsi traders settling there. The prince Mohan Dev ji was a patron saint of the arts – and was well-versed in both Indian and Western classical music. Lunawada, named after the famous Shiv temple of Luneshwar Maharaj, was under the Solankis, and the ruler, Virbhadra Ranjitsinhji, was an active participant in the Chamber of Princes. Sachin was a predominantly Hindu state, but the rulers were Sunni Muslims of the Siddi (Abyssinian) descent, designated as Nawabs, given a nine-gun salute status, and authorized a cavalry, as well as the right to issue stamps and currency notes. After signing the Instrument of Accession and the Merger Agreement, Sachin became part of Surat district of Bombay. Santrampur (Sant), ruled by Rajput Parmars who enjoyed an eleven-gun local salute status, is situated at the intersection of the states of Madhya Pradesh, Rajasthan and Gujarat. Bordering Santrampur was the state of Idar, which had the legendary Lt. General Sir Pratap Singh, one of India's most highly decorated army officers, as its ruler till he abdicated in favour of his nephew and adopted son Daulat Singh, whose son Himmat Singh signed both the Instrument of Accession and Merger Agreement with Bombay. The royal families of Idar and

Jodhpur were connected by blood, and both families sent officers to overseas campaigns. Vijayanagar was ruled by the Bhils, who were given the title of Rao, and was merged with Sabarkantha district, then in Bombay state. Jambughodha was ruled by Thakur Sahebs of the Kshatriya (Parmar) Koli clan, and although it was a very small state of just 140 square miles and a population of less than fifteen thousand, it had been exempted from the attachment scheme. The state joined Bombay, a few months later than the rest. Its merger took place in June 1948. Palanpur too had been founded by the Parmars, ruled by the Chauhans, but from the fourteenth century it came under the Pathans after one of the forbears married the foster sister of Akbar, and received the governorship as part of the dowry. The Nawabs of Palanpur were known for the eclectic choice of marriage partners, as well as for public monuments – Kirti Stambh, Mansarovar lake, Balarama palace, King George Club and Jahanara Bagh (for Nawab Taley Muhammed Khan's Australian wife Joan Fakiner).

Surgana state was also ruled by the Kshatriya Kolis who held the title of Deshmukh. After signing the Merger Agreement of his state with Bombay, the last ruler, Dhairyashil Rao, served as a member of the Rajya Sabha twice – first from 1952 to 1958, and, more significantly, also from 1972 to 1978 after the abolition of privy purses. It may also be added that the administration of the 127 non-jurisdictional and semi-jurisdiction states had already been taken over by the Government of India on the basis of the amalgamation scheme of the erstwhile Political Department as early as 1935.

~

We now come to the Part C states for which specific provisions for administration were laid down in Part VIII of the Constitution. Vindhya Pradesh is a unique example of a Part B state under a raj pramukh with such intense bickering that it had to be brought directly under the administration of a chief commissioner, and governed as a Part C state. However, the chief commissioners faced a challenge from the leadership of the erstwhile Praja Mandals who were aggrieved that unlike their counterparts in Part A and Part B states, they were denied their legitimate role in deciding the political destiny of their states.

Y.S. Parmar from Himachal, Chaudhary Brahm Prakash from Delhi and S.N. Shukla from Vindhya Pradesh were in the forefront of the demand for responsible and elected legislatures. It led to the passage of the Governance of Part C States Act of 1951, and each of them got a chief minister, albeit with limited powers. Vindhya Pradesh and Himachal were also elevated to the status of Lt Governor's provinces.

It must be mentioned that there was not much in common among the Part C states, except that on account of their strategic importance, historical circumstance, or on the request of their rulers, these states were accorded this status. However, it was quite clear from the very beginning that this was an interim arrangement. In fact, popular movements in many of these states were supportive of merger with the neighbouring province. In the first elections held in Ajmer Merwara, Haribhau Upadhaya from the Congress led the popular ministry winning twenty of the thirty seats, and pressed for land reforms legislation, besides campaigning for merger with the neighbouring state of Rajasthan. Elections in Bhopal saw the rise of Shankar Dayal Sharma, who was then the youngest chief minister in the country, and later became the President of India. Sharma had been at the forefront of the popular agitation against the Nawab of Bhopal for his failure to sign the Instrument of Accession with India, and had been arrested and detained for over eight months. Bilaspur was allowed to retain its identity for the Bhakra Nangal project lay in this state, and was soon to be submerged in the dam area. As such, the ruler M.S. Himmat Singhji's request to be allowed to be the first chief commissioner was accepted. It was merged into Himachal in 1954. As mentioned earlier, Himachal Pradesh saw the emergence of Y.S. Parmar as a popular leader who was always at odds with the chief commissioner. The chief commissioner there was E.P. Moon, formerly of the ICS and the author of *Divide and Quit*, an account which castigated Mountbatten and the British Raj for their complete abdication of responsibility. E.P. Moon's proximity to Rajkumari Amrit Kaur, then the Union health minister and a confidante of Nehru, was irksome to Chief Minister Parmar.

Cutch,[13] Tripura and Manipur were border states, and hence considered to be very sensitive. Cutch was indeed one of the largest states of western India, with an area of 8461 square miles, a population of nearly five lakh and a revenue of Rs 80 lakh. Menon writes 'though Kutch was linguistically and culturally a part of Kathiawar, there were good reasons why we should keep the state directly under our control for some time to come, particularly as with partition, Kutch had become a frontier state with Pakistan'.[14] Another important consideration was the direct involvement of the Centre in the establishment of the Kandla port, which required the building of a railway network and resettlement colonies for the Sindhis who had moved to India. A former Praja Mandal leader and activist, Seth Rajmal Shah, was the chief minister of the state till its eventual merger with Bombay after the SRC recommendations in 1956.

With the creation of East Bengal, Tripura was virtually isolated from India, and its extensive zamindari of 600 square miles was left in East Pakistan. As the Maharaja was a minor, the Merger Agreement was signed by his mother, the daughter of the Maharaja of Panna, who was the Regent. Its capital Agartala, as well as other important places in the state, lay in the narrow belt of land adjoining East Pakistan, with which it shared a 700-mile border. Tripura also shared a common border with Assam, but till that time, there was no road link with Assam, and all supplies had to be airlifted from Calcutta. The Tripura Access Road to be built at a cost of one crore rupees was therefore the foremost priority, and given the strategic importance of the state, it was made into a Part C. While the state had a chief commissioner, there was an advisory council, the most prominent member of which was Sachindra Lal Singh, who subsequently became the first chief minister of Tripura when it became a Union Territory in 1963.

Manipur was also an underdeveloped border state with an area of 8628 square miles of which just about 7 square miles were in the valley, and the rest of the territory was in the hills. The ruling Meitei family had converted to Vaishnavism during the eighteenth century and adopted titles like Maharaja, Shrijut, Manipureshwar. The hill tribes fell into two distinct categories – the Kukis and the Nagas. It was bounded on the north by the Naga district of Assam, on the east by Burma (as Myanmar was then called), on the south by Burma and Lushai Hills (Mizoram) and on the west by the Cachar district. After the controversial Merger Agreement signed by Maharaja Bodhchandra Singh, it became a chief commissioner's province, with the erstwhile Diwan of Manipur Rawal Amar Singh as the first chief commissioner. However, a movement against the lack of representation in state administration was led by Rishang Keishing, then a young socialist leader. As a member of Parliament from 1952 from the state, he kept trying to narrow down the apparently irreconcilable differences between the Meiteis of the Imphal Valley and the Nagas and Kukis of the hills.

Then there was Vindhya Pradesh, which from its very inception was mired in controversies and corruption. The administration of most of the states in Bundelkhand and Baghelkhand was nothing more than the court politics and intrigues of the rulers without any element of public participation. In fact, there was a strong move to dismember the union and split the constituent units between United Provinces and Central Provinces, but this was not resorted to on account of the impact it may have had on the other unions.

The states ministry also felt that 'if the British had managed to keep over five hundred states for over a century, surely they could retain six unions of states for at least a decade!'[15] Therefore, the decision was taken to convert this union into a Part C state – even though it had the size (24,598 square miles), the population (35,69,455) and an annual revenue of Rs 2,43,30,734 to function as a Part B state. There was an element of urgency as after the promulgation of the Constitution, the process of changing the territory/status would require a constitutional amendment. The first chief commissioner of Vindhya Pradesh was N.B. Bonerji of the ICS, and after the first general elections, S.N. Shukla of the Congress became the first chief minister.

With regard to Coorg, it was a territory directly governed by the British from the year 1843. There was a strong movement for its merger with the Kannada-speaking areas, but the countermovement of retaining its independent identity was also quite pronounced. Known for its picturesque settings, coffee plantations and as the birthplace of Generals K.M. Cariappa and K.S. Thimayya, Coorg elected pro-merger Congress leader C.M. Poonacha as the first chief minister.

Last, but not the least in the list of Part C states was Delhi which was also the seat of political power and the national capital. Chaudhary Brahm Prakash became the chief minister of Delhi at the young age of thirty-four. While he did make a strong pitch for enhanced powers for the Legislative Assembly of Delhi, the Union government did not want to give up powers over land and law and order. This was because in the immediate aftermath of Partition, it was felt that Delhi deserved special consideration, and also that the investments required to create India's first city would be far beyond the reach of the Delhi government which, at that time, did not have a strong industrial or commercial base.

6

THE FIRST HINDI MAP
OF INDIA

The first Hindi map of independent India was published in 1952, and the masthead read: *Bharat ke Rajnaitik Vibhag* or India's Political Map. This was published by Col. Gambhir Singh, MIS[1] (India), in his capacity as the officiating Surveyor General of India. Apart from the fact that Bombay was written as Mumbai, Trivandrum as Tiruvankur and Laccadive, Minicoy and Amindivi islands as Lakshadweep, without any formal notification regarding the change of those names, there was no difference in the internal border markings or in the classification of states from the map of 1950, which has already been discussed at length.

However, the one major change that took place along the external border was the acknowledgement of Cheen (China) as our neighbour for the first time. This was a significant departure from the British policy of always describing Tibet as the country on our northern border. Prior to this, the vast Himalayan stretch bordering Ladakh, Himachal, Garhwal (UP), Nepal, Sikkim, Assam (including the Saadiya frontier, which later became NEFA[2] and finally Arunachal) and Bhutan was shown as Tibet. In the 1950 map, the area adjacent to Gilgit-Baltistan was shown as 'boundary undefined'. However, in the 1952 map, this area was marked as China, but Tibet continued to be shown quite prominently. The only physical feature in Tibet identified on the map was Tsangpo (the Tibetan name for Brahmaputra). Incidentally, by 1956, Tibet disappeared from the official map of India, and the entire stretch was shown as China. This depiction continued in the map of 1958, but by 1960, Tibet reappeared as an autonomous region of China.

As in the map of 1950, classification of states under governors (Part A), states under raj pramukhs (Part B), Union Territories under lieutenant governors (Part C) and chief commissioners under the Union government (Part D) was continued in 1952. It also carried the usual disclaimers regarding the India–Pakistan boundary being indicative, and not an international boundary.

As this was the first Hindi map of independent India, let us discuss the Hindi-speaking regions: Uttar Pradesh, Rajasthan, Bihar, Madhya Pradesh, Madhya Bharat, Vindhya Pradesh and Bhopal. The last four entities were merged in Madhya Pradesh in 1956. Incidentally, with the exception of Rajasthan, all the other states were again divided in 2000, with Uttaranchal (later Uttarakhand) being carved out of UP, Jharkhand from Bihar and Chhattisgarh from MP. This chapter will also cover Saurashtra, for the other Part B states are covered in detail later: PEPSU in the discussion on the linguistic reorganization of Punjab; Mysore in the making of Karnataka; Hyderabad in the formation of Andhra Pradesh and, later Telangana; and Travancore–Cochin in the unification of Kerala. The formation of the UTs of J&K and Ladakh is also described in detail when we look at the last major reorganization of the map of the country in 2019.

～

Let us first look at UP which is now called Uttar Pradesh (earlier United Provinces), with its capital at Lucknow. Since 1902, the province had been known as the United Provinces of Agra and Oudh. In 1937, this extended nomenclature was shortened to the United Provinces or UP. Although the high court continued at Allahabad, the provincial capital was shifted to Lucknow in 1937 – perhaps the increasing national consciousness in Allahabad led the provincial government to shift its base to the less politically inclined city with a greater focus on cultural refinements, cuisine and the arts. Interestingly, in the map of 1947, Allahabad was marked out as the capital of UP, but in the 1950 map, the correction had been made.

Unlike Punjab and Bengal, this state did not endure a division of its territory during Partition or suffer the horrific violence that many other parts of north India experienced. Its metamorphosis in the late 1940s and the early 1950s was nonetheless profound. It is true that there was an exodus of several Muslim families including government employees and professionals, and many Punjabi families came to settle in Kanpur, Allahabad and towns like Dehradun, Ghaziabad, Saharanpur and Meerut. However, the numbers were not significant enough for the creation of a Rehabilitation Department as in West Bengal and East Punjab. However, the social fabric of the state had been deeply affected by communal incidents across the country. By this time, the territory of UP also included the erstwhile princely states of Tehri Garhwal, Benares and Rampur.

While there was a general consensus that United Provinces held no meaning in independent India, a consensus on the new name was not easy. As Kudasiya writes, 'Place names can be deeply symbolic and serve as an ideological device to imprint a culturally constructed identity on a given physical space. They provide an intersection between hegemonic ideological structures and spatial practices of everyday life. They connect physical territory to a history and a commemorative past. In post-colonial UP, place names became an important aspect of the post-colonial order.'[3] Meanwhile, the names of most rivers and towns were changed and the prominent amendments included Ganga for the Ganges, Mathura for Muttra. Jumna became Yamuna and Gumti became Gomti. Similarly, Ayodhya, Kanpur, Faizabad and Unnao also got new spellings. The *National Herald* called it 'Indianisation or nationalisation' of place names.

A few days after Independence, a debate started in the UP Legislative Assembly over the question of a 'suitable name' for the province. On 11 September 1947, Chandra Bhal, a Congress member of the Legislative Council (MLC), rose to move a motion for changing UP's name: 'We are witnessing a new birth. I think we should have a new and suitable name. After the birth, the most important ceremony is the *"naam karan"* everywhere and I think we should signal this birth of a new age and a new life in our people by having a really good name for our province ... The name of Oudh can be extended to the whole province. Oudh is an old name, the kingdom of Rama, which would be acceptable to all communities and parties and it is true that today that name is confined to only two divisions comprising 12 districts. But in history expansions have taken place.'[4] Education Minister Sampurnanand disagreed vehemently. He pointed out the difficulties in adopting Oudh as the new name. 'Braj Basi (the residents of Braj) cannot accept Oudh as our province and the people at Kashi and Mathura also cannot accept Oudh as its name.' In doing so, he highlighted the distinct cultural regions existing within the province. Chandra Bhal clarified that Oudh was merely an example. Other possible names could be 'Aryavarta' or even 'Hindustan'. He also suggested that 'United Provinces' could be retained as it could be rendered in any language according to the speaker's choice. It could be Samyukta Prant in Hindi, or Munalik Mutahdda in Urdu, or United Provinces in

English. Speaker after speaker rose to argue that United Provinces as a colonial appellation was unsuitable, as the people of the province simply did not identify with it. They could not be expected to feel patriotic about such a name for it did not reflect their local identity.

Soon the debate seemed to settle over 'Aryavarta'. Speaking in support of this, legislator Pandit Badri Dutt Pande said: 'When Aryans came here, they called it Aryavarta or the abode of Aryans. I think this is the original name. The Aryans came here and settled and they wrote these wonderful books, the Vedas, the Darshans and other systems of philosophy. Let it be called Aryavarta.' However, a consensus could not be reached. There were twenty possible names, which included (in alphabetical order): Aryavarta, Aryavarta Pradesh, Avadh, Bharat Khand, Brij Koshal, Brahmavarta Prant, Bhagirath Pradesh, Brahmadesh, Hindustan, Himalaya Koshlam, Himalaya Pradesh, Krishna Kushal Province, Madhyadesh, Naimisharanya Pradesh, Nava Hindu, Ram Krishna Prant, Rama Krishna Pradesh and Uttarakhand.

There were many 'letters to the editor' in newspapers like *The Pioneer*, *National Herald*, *The Leader* and *Swatantra Bharat*, among others, giving forceful arguments for one or the other name. The G.B. Pant Cabinet decided to defer the decision as tempers were frayed. However, the decision could not have been postponed forever, as by October 1949 the Constituent Assembly wanted to finalize the names of the constituent units of the Union of India. As the matter continued to be contentious, Dr Rajendra Prasad felt that rather than debating the issue in the Constituent Assembly, it was best left to the state governments to finalize the name of the province.

While Education Minister Sampurnanand was firmly in favour of Aryavarta, which apparently coincided with the majority view of the Cabinet and the State Legislature, it was decided to refer the matter to the Provincial Congress Committee. In the committee also, an overwhelming number of members supported this name. Apart from Sampurnanand, the name was also endorsed by G.B. Pant, Govind Sahai, A.G. Kher, P.D. Tandon and Charan Singh. This, however, did not find favour with the Congress high command, and Pant had to retract the proposal as the name was not 'acceptable to other parts of the country'. The feeling outside of the province was that names like Aryavarta or Hindustan signified not merely UP but the whole of India. Constituent Assembly (CA) member from Central Provinces and Berar, R.K. Sidhwa, complained that UP (United Provinces) looked upon itself as the super-most province of India. Meanwhile, Pant also agreed that names like Hind, Hindustan or Aryavarta will not be pressed for again. This was how Uttar Pradesh, a name that was not even put up for consideration, became the new name of the state.

The three erstwhile princely states that were integrated into UP included Rampur, Tehri Garhwal and Benares. With an area of 900 square miles and a population of five lakh, Rampur was the last signpost of the Rohilla power. Under the rulership of the enlightened Sir Saiyad Raza Ali Khan Bahadur, it became the first state under a Muslim ruler of significance to openly accept the accession to India. His request that as an interim measure the state should be first made a chief commissioner's province was accepted. Incidentally, the Oriental Library of Rampur has a fine collection of over twelve thousand rare manuscripts and a wonderful collection of Mughal miniatures. Meanwhile, Benaras (area 875 square miles and a population of four lakh) had also agreed to the merger with UP. With respect to Tehri Garhwal, given its contiguity to both Himachal Pradesh and UP, an option was available especially because it had been clubbed under Punjab states in the aftermath of Independence. Finally, the decision to merge it with UP was taken because Pauri Garhwal and Kumaon were with UP. The state had been founded in 688 CE by Raja Kanak Pal, and the current ruler was the fifty-ninth direct descendant in the male line.

~

As far as Bihar is concerned, the boundaries of the erstwhile state were not affected except for the addition of the princely states of Kharsawan and Seraikella from Orissa. As the majority population there was non-Oriya-speaking, a popular movement wanted Kharsawan and Seraikella to be part of the Hindi-speaking state of Bihar. In addition to these, all the twelve non-salute states affiliated to the Bihar states agency — Mohrampur, Darbhanga, Ramgarh, Ranka, Jagdishpur, Dumraon, Dinghwara, Tajpur, Banaili, Kahra, Bhour and Chanour — were also integrated with Bihar. However, unlike in the case of salute states that had specific civil, revenue and judicial jurisdictions, the non-salute states were basically large zamindaris — and they were easily integrated with the state administration. Of those, Darbhanga[5] needs to be singled out, for unlike other zamindaris which basically depended on intermediaries to collect revenue and manage the estates, Darbhanga had established its own administrative apparatus to manage its extensive estates spread over the six districts of Saran, Muzaffarpur, Darbhanga, Monghyr, Bhagalpur and Purnea. The Raja of Darbhanga had a chief manager to whom fifteen circle managers reported, and G.P. Danby, a former indigo planter, held the position for over two decades. A total of three thousand people ensured that the 4500 villages in the zamindari with an extensive holding of over 2400 square miles was effectively managed. However, the stirrings of the freedom movement and peasant consciousness were seen in Darbhanga as well, and Swami Vidyanand in the '20s and Swami Sahajanand, a decade later, mobilized the tenants to seek security of tenure and press for better wages for the landless workers.

Although the British allowed these large zamindars to use titles like Raja and Maharaja, and also allowed them the privilege of sitting in the same enclosures as the rulers of salute states on ceremonial occasions, the fact was that they were large landowners who had to seek redressal for non-payment of rent and other land-related matters from the local deputy commissioner, a clear indication that they were not really independent. These included the zamindars/rajas of Bettiah with an area of 1800 square miles, Jharia, whose main income came from mining its coal reserves, Hathuwa and Sonbarsa with their famous Durga Pujas, as well as Jagdishpur, Tekari and Dumraon. Palamu district had the six zamindaris of Chaupir, Ladigarh, Ranka, Nagaruntari, Vishranpur and Navajaipur.

With the abolition of zamindari, they were to lose their lands and earnings, though in the first decade of Independence, they continued to exercise extensive political clout. The Raja of Darbhanga, Kameshwar Singh Gautam Bahadur, was also the head of the All-India Landlords Association, and had successfully got the Bihar management of Estates and Tenures Act declared *ultra vires* of the Constitution by the Patna High Court. This was one of the factors that led Nehru to move the first amendment to the Constitution which curbed freedom of speech, enabled caste-based reservation, circumscribed the right to property and validated the abolition of the zamindari system, besides drawing up a schedule of laws immune to judicial challenge.

Kameshwar Singh was elected as member of Parliament (Rajya Sabha) from the Jharkhand Party twice – first in 1952, and then in 1958, and was a member of Rajya Sabha till his death in 1962.

~

When India became independent on 15 August 1947, Ravi Shankar Shukla was at the helm in Central Provinces and Berar. The Legislative Assembly decided to give Central Provinces and Berar a new identity – Madhya Pradesh – which was a literal translation of Central India. Even when Madhya Bharat, Bhopal and the Hindi-speaking parts of Vindhya were merged into the state (post 1956), the name was retained. Nagpur was the capital of Madhya Pradesh till 1956, when the Marathi-speaking areas of Vindhya Pradesh and Berar were transferred to the bilingual (Marathi–Gujarati speaking) state of Bombay. While Shukla was from the Chhattisgarh region, he and his family held complete sway over the politics of Madhya Pradesh, and his influence extended to Madhya Bharat and Bhopal, and Vindhya Pradesh as well.

Although the three nine-gun salute states of Kalahandi, Patna and Sonepur which had been attached to the province were transferred to Orissa, Madhya Pradesh got Bastar, Chhuikhadan, Kanker, Nandgaon, Kawardha, Udaipur, Surguja, Sarangarh, Raigarh, Patnagarh (Patna), Korea, Khairagarh, Jashpur, Udaipur and Sakti. When Chhattisgarh was carved out of MP, all these became part of the new state.

Of these, Bastar was the largest. With an area of 15,029 square miles and a population of five lakh, it was the largest district of the largest state in the country. This was in direct contrast with Sakti, which had an area of 138 square miles and a population of just about four thousand in 1941. As mineral reserves were discovered in Bastar, its importance grew, and the Nizam of Hyderabad tried to lease out large territories from the Maharaja of Bastar. Thanks to the timely intervention of the ministry of states, this was thwarted in time. Chhuikhadan was under the control of the Bairagi sect (ruled by Rituparna Kishore Das) and Nandgaon under the Mahants (ruled by Mahant Raja Digvijay Das) – unique examples of fused spiritual and temporal authority. These were all non-salute states with limited jurisdictions, and their integration was not a problem as the erstwhile rulers were quite happy to settle for privy purses. However, the ex-royals continued to play an active role in the politics of the state (and the Centre). These included the Bhanjdeo family of Bastar, the Deos of Sarguja, the Singhs of Sarangarh, the Singhdeos of Korea and Judeos from Jashpur as well as the Singhs of Khairagarh. However, lack of communication and transport infrastructure made it easier for left-wing extremism to spread in the region. MP was already one of the largest states in the country, and by 1956, it became even larger with the merger of Bhopal, Vindhya Pradesh and Madhya Bharat.

Madhya Bharat, the popular name for the union of Gwalior, Indore and Malwa, was the largest Part B state, comprising an area of 47,000 square miles, a population of seven million and a revenue of Rs 8 crore. It had been formed after federating twenty-five states of central India and, except for a small portion, the entire region was part of the Malwa plateau. However, getting the two leading states Gwalior (a twenty-one-gun salute state) and Indore (a nineteen-gun salute state) with a history of hostility for two centuries into the union was a Herculean task. Gwalior was the first of the twenty-one-gun salute states to agree to integration, and its ruler, Sir George Jivaji Rao Scindia, had transferred power to an interim government of popular representatives, who were also authorized to draw up a new Constitution. The state had cash reserves as well as investment and reserve funds totalling to over Rs 20 crore. As his 'state' was a viable force by itself, merging it with another entity was contrary to the assurances given both by Governor General Mountbatten as well as the ministry of states. Gwalior's traditional rival Indore was equally reluctant, for it was clear that in any scheme of 'merger' Gwalior would always have the edge because of its size, status, revenue and standing with the ministry of states.

It must be mentioned here that the Maharaja of Indore, Sir Yeshwant Rao Holkar, had been snubbed by the Political

Department after he wrote to the President of the USA during the Second World War stressing the imperative need of satisfying the nationalist demands in India. His only concern was that following the Indore tradition to having women at the helm (Devi Ahilyabai), his only daughter Usha Devi should be recognized as the heir. Indore was keen that instead of one union comprising all the states of Malwa, two unions, one each around Gwalior and Indore, should be created. The popular ministries in both the states were also in favour of two unions. However, it was felt that given the longer-term vison of having fewer but viable states, it was better to get all the states in the region together. Else there would be jostling between the two to add smaller states to their respective unions. What finally settled the issue was a lucrative nudge: offering the position of lifelong raj pramukh to the ruler of Gwalior, and senior up raj pramukh to the ruler of Indore, and a consolidated amount of Rs 2.5 lakh over and above the privy purse for holding these 'august offices'. Another issue was regarding the role of the up raj pramukh – for, in every other state, the provision was that the up raj pramukh would function when the raj pramukh was indisposed, or absent from the state. To satisfy Indore, a special clause was added: 'The Rajpramukh may from time to time consult the Senior Vice President (Up Rajpramukh) in important matters connected with the administration of the United State.'[6] To get the other states on board, two positions of junior raj pramukhs (by election) were offered to the rest of the states.

These included the states of Dhar and Dewas, both with Parmar Rajput rulers – in the case of Dewas, two brothers had divided the state between themselves as Dewas Senior and Dewas Junior. Then there were Ratlam, Alirajpur, Barwani, Jhabua, Khilchipur, Narsinghar, Sailana, Sitamu, Jobat, Kathiwara, Mathwar, Rajgarh, Nimkhera, Jamnia and Piploda. These states were all paying their tribute either to the Scindias or the Holkars, but the British gave them all their 'independent status' which served the dual purpose of reducing the strength of these two power centres, besides making them totally beholden to the Raj. There were in addition to these Rajput states, four Muslim states of Jaora, Kurwai, Mohammadgarh and Pathari. Pathari was related to Dost Mohammad, the founder of Bhopal, and the others claimed Afghan ancestry. However, most of the states comprised blocks of territories separated by intervening states creating a veritable mosaic which was difficult to administer or develop. This was yet another reason why it was felt that one union would be better than two unions.

Interestingly, with regard to the setting up of a seventy-five-member Interim Legislature and Constituent Assembly, there was a general agreement that based on the population of the states, forty would be elected from Gwalior, fifteen from Indore and twenty by an electoral college from all the other states.

The union was inaugurated by Prime Minister Nehru on 28 May 1948, who also resolved the 'capital issue' by declaring Indore as the summer capital and Gwalior as the winter capital with the caveat that as Gwalior was much bigger than Indore, the duration for Gwalior as the capital city would be six and a half months!

~

The peninsula of Saurashtra situated at the northern end of the country's western seaboard comprised the fourteen salute states of Junagadh, Nawanagar, Bhavnagar, Dhrangadhra, Porbandar, Morvi, Gondal, Jafrabad, Wankaner, Palitana, Dhrol, Limbdi, Rajkot and Wadhwan, besides seventeen non-salute states, and another 191 small states, exercising varying degrees of jurisdiction. The area was a little over 22,000 square miles with a population of nearly four million.

However, this does not reflect the actual picture on the ground. This is best captured by this quote from *The Tribune* (July 1939):

'As many as forty-six states have an area of two or less than two miles. Eight of them, namely Bodanoness, Gandhol, Morchopra, Panchabda, Samadhiala, Chabbadia, Sanala, Satanomess and 'Vangadhra are just over half a mile each. Yet none of these is the smallest state in Kathiawar. That distinction goes to Vajanoness which has an area of 0.29 square mile, a population of just above two hundred, and an annual income of Rs 500/a year.'

The administration was further complicated by the fact that many of these states had 'enclaves' outside their individual boundaries, with states like Nawanagar, Gondal and Junagadh having nine, eighteen and twenty-four separate areas of territory. The Department of States calculated that the map of Kathiawar could be divided into 860 different jurisdictions. Not only was internal trade hampered, smugglers and anti-social elements could easily slip into other jurisdictions to circumvent the law. Four years before Independence, under the attachment scheme, the Political Department had joined the very small states with the neighbouring states – but after the lapse of Paramountcy and the Indian Independence Act, in a fairly irresponsible step, the Political Department retroceded the Crown jurisdiction, even over railway lands. The States Department moved in post haste, and appointed M.N. Buch as the Regional Commissioner for Kathiawar who began exercising all the powers that the Crown's representative had in the past.

Reference must be made here about the strength of the Kathiawar Rajakeeya Parishad (KRP), which was not only active on the political and social fronts, but thanks to its close association with both Mahatma Gandhi and Sardar Patel, was also organized and disciplined. Following the transfer of power, there was a wave of agitation all over Kathiawar for a responsible government, and the states really did not have the wherewithal to manage the law-and-order situation, which was aggravated by Partition-related events, especially the influx of refugees from Sindh and the Junagadh imbroglio. Moreover, unlike in the past, when popular movements were put down with assistance of the British, now the KRP had support from across the country, especially the Congress workers in the neighbouring districts. Also, the States Department was clear that in the long run, the only option was a responsible government – though there were three distinct views on how that should pan out.

One option – in fact the easiest – was to merge all the states, both jurisdictional and non-jurisdictional, with the neighbouring province of Bombay. Another option was to limit the attachment to the smaller (non-jurisdictional states) only, and encourage the four prominent ones – Bhavnagar, Nawanagar, Junagadh and Dhrangadhra – to act as 'magnet states'. But this too would not have ensured the establishment of a modern administration with separate legislatures, executive and judiciary for each of the four units. Hence, the option of organizing all the Kathiawar states into one unit gained currency – as for historical reasons as well, the entire region had been identified as Saurashtra.

The first step in that direction was taken on 15 January 1948, when Sardar Patel inaugurated the transition of power from the ruler of Bhavnagar in the presence of U.N. Dhebar, Balwant Rai Mehta and V.P. Menon. Later, the Sardar addressed all the Kathiawar rulers at Rajkot, where he hinted that 'while little pools of water tend to become stagnant and useless, but that if they were joined together to form a big lake, the atmosphere is cooled, and there is universal benefit'. In a subsequent meeting with Menon, the states ministry made its views quite clear. 'It is not possible for the 222 states of Kathiawar to continue their separate existence under modern conditions for much longer. The extinction of separate existence of States may not be palatable, but unless something is done in good time to stabilise the situation in Kathiawar, the march of events may bring about more unpalatable results.'[7] One may, therefore, say that even as the states ministry was quite clear about what it wanted, it was trying to build a consensus on this issue, and the name of the Mahatma was also liberally invoked.

Shortly thereafter, the Maharaja of Dhrangadhra came out in open support of the Kathiawar union, and the Jam Saheb of Nawanagar was quietly told to acquiesce and become the raj pramukh of the proposed union or face the consequences of merger with Bombay. Jam Saheb Maharaja Digvijay Sinhji, the nephew of the famous cricketer Ranjitsinhji, seized the opportunity, and addressed all the Kathiawar princes and informed them of the need to preserve the identity of Kathiawar. As the ruler of Junagadh had already fled for Pakistan, the popular mood after the plebiscite was to join the Kathiawar union.

The inauguration of the United States of Kathiawar was done by Sardar Patel on 15 February 1948, and in his speech, the Jam Saheb said, 'It is not as if we were tired monarchs who were fanned to rest, or bullied into submission. We have by our own volition pooled our sovereignties and covenanted to create this new state, the United States of Kathiawar so that the unity of India is more fully achieved.'[8]

In January 1950, before the adoption of the Indian Constitution, it was decided that the union would be called Saurashtra, and that the Constituent Assembly of Saurashtra, together with the raj pramukh (Jam Saheb) should form the Interim Legislature of the state.

~

Last, but not the least, the 1952 map is significant for it marks the first appearance of China (as Cheen in Hindi) on any map of India. As the successor state to British India, the Dominion, and then the Republic of India, took the view that the treaties,

precedents and conventions with regard to the McMahon Line as
the effective boundary between India and Tibet should be regarded
as axiomatic. However, this perception was not shared by China,
which was not party to the Anglo-Tibet Agreement of 1914. This
agreement gave India exclusive access to trading posts like Gyantse,
Gartok and Yatung. The agreement confirmed the freedom that
Tibet enjoyed in its foreign relations to the extent that weak
central governments in China left Tibet to its own devices. All maps
published by the Surveyor General of India till 1952 showed Tibet
as our northern neighbour, and there was no reference whatsoever
to China on any Indian map. Meanwhile, it's also important to
place on record that India's post-1947 relations with Tibet were
temporarily overshadowed by Tibetan unwillingness to recognize
our independence, as mentioned by Claude Apri,[9] on the grounds
that India needed to respect Tibetan claims to some territories south
of the McMahon line around Darjeeling, Kalimpong and Tawang.

However, though we inherited the border, we lost track of the
realpolitik. Rather than make a clear assessment about the nature
of the new regime in China, our ambassador to Beijing, K.M.
Panikkar (later a member of the SRC), and Prime Minister Nehru
continued to look at China through an ideological prism. In 1948,
Panikkar wrote to Nehru[10] that the newly victorious communist
government in Peking (as Beijing was then called) headed by Mao
Zedong is likely to 'take a forward policy' with respect to Tibet.
He averred that an independent Tibet would actually work to
India's benefit, and that it would be 'be useful to recall that Chinese
sovereignty over Tibet has not been recognized by us'. Panikkar
dutifully reflected this posture until August 1950 when, in an aide
memoire submitted to the Chinese government, he inexplicably
described Tibet's status as 'autonomy within the framework of
Chinese sovereignty'.

This unanticipated concession caused a raging debate in India's ministry of external affairs but it was not clear as to why and how such a fundamental shift in stance came about. Consternation in the ministry led Secretary-General Girija Shankar Bajpai hasten to explain on 31 October 1950 that Panikkar's use of the word 'framework' signified Tibetan autonomy within Chinese suzerainty and that Chinese 'sovereignty' over Tibet was 'qualified by complete autonomy' for Tibet. Pursuant to Bajpai's note, Sardar Patel wrote to Nehru 'warning that China's forcible occupation of Tibet was only the beginning of India's troubles with China'.[11] However, given his perilous health and preoccupation with many other matters, including the integration of Indian states, Nehru's view prevailed and India took the position that China indeed exercised some 'suzerain' powers over Tibet.

For Nehru, recognition of Tibetan autonomy had to be balanced with the then surge of Indian friendship for China. He also had to be cognizant of India's involvement in global issues that made its trustful relations with China important. Nehru was also led to believe that Tibetan autonomy would not be undermined by China's occupation, for even the Communist Party of China (CPC) recognized Tibetans as a separate nationality.

Be that as it may, China made its appearance for the first time on the first Hindi map of India published in 1952. However, by 1956, Tibet disappeared from India's cartographic imagination, till it made its reappearance in 1959. But by then the romance of 'Hindi–Chini Bhai Bhai' had turned irretrievably sour!

7

THE ANDHRA STATE AND THE SRC

Contesting Boundaries of Madras

While the first Hindi map of India was celebrated in the Hindi heartland,[1] it met with resistance in south India, especially in the Madras Secretariat where many of the (non-Brahmin) junior functionaries were swayed by E.V.R. Periyar's argument that this was a sure sign of imposition of Hindi hegemony by the duopoly of Brahmins and Baniyas to whom power had been transferred by the British in 1947.

In any case, the lines which defined Madras in the maps of 1950 and 1952 were fiercely contested by the Telugu-speaking population of eleven districts – Anantapur, Chittoor, Cuddapah, Godavari, East Godavari, Guntur, Kistna, Kurnool, Nellore, Srikakulam, Vizagapatam. They felt aggrieved that both the Linguistic Provinces Commission (LPC)[2] and the Jawaharlal Nehru, Vallabhbhai Patel and B. Pattabhi Sitaramayya (JVP) committee[3] had departed from the established policy of the Congress with regard to linguistic states. In fact, as late as 1946, Sitaramayya had been actively engaged in the campaign for the Telugu-speaking state of Andhra and had also extended support to the section of Andhra Mahasabha which had merged with the Hyderabad Congress. When the LPC was appointed, Sitaramayya was the president of the Congress, and expectations regarding the formation of Andhra were naturally quite high.

The LPC had been constituted in November 1947, not by the government, but by the Constituent Assembly which appointed the Allahabad High Court judge S.K. Dhar[4] to head it. The Dhar Commission (as it was popularly called) was empowered 'not only to enquire into the desirability of creating new provinces, but to also report on fixing their boundaries, and assessing the financial, economic, administrative and other consequences in the provinces of Andhra, Kerala, Karnataka and Maharashtra and the adjoining territories'.

However, the commission received representations from across all linguistic groups, including those which were not in the provinces mentioned in the Terms of Reference. The commission's report acknowledged the fact that 'the formation of linguistic provinces has been an article of faith in the current political thought of the country during the last thirty years and has received the support of the Congress and the blessings of Mahatma Gandhi'. With regards to the theory and practise of Congress forming its own units on linguistic basis (Oriya, Gujarati, Marathi, Telugu, Tamil), the report said 'freedom has come to us in a way unforeseen, and unthought-of, and has brought in its train problems and dangers never dreamt of. In view of the dangers which now surround our country and in the circumstances that now exist, the Congress stands relieved of all its past commitments, and it is its right as also its duty to come to a fresh decision on the subject in the light of the present circumstances, the homogeneity of language alone cannot be a decisive factor'.

The committee accepted the fact that the existing provinces were 'administrative units of British Imperialism, not designed to work as democratic institutions', and could do with more scientific and rational planning. 'In determining the boundaries of provinces, the emphasis should be primarily on administrative convenience, and the Telugu homogeneity of language will enter into consideration only on this count, and not by its own independent force.' In rejecting the demands for linguistic reorganization of states, it said 'this enquiry has been an eye opener to us. The work of sixty years of Indian National Congress was standing before us, face to face with centuries old India of narrow loyalties, petty jealousies, and ignorant prejudices engaged in a mortal conflict, and we were simply horrified to see how thin the ice was on which we were skating.'

As such, in the December of 1948, it concluded that 'no new provinces should be formed for the present. All things considered, the consideration of linguistic provinces should be postponed for ten years.'

Robert D. King[5] in his book *Nehru and the Language Politics of India* suggests that the report was strongly influenced (if not actually written) by Nehru himself. While the report may have given satisfaction to the government, the reaction of those hoping for reorganization of states on linguistic lines, including the Congress supporters in the Telugu-speaking areas of Madras, was extremely negative. The Congress party had to then set up a committee under Nehru himself, with the other members being Deputy PM Vallabhbhai Patel and Congress President Pattabhi Sitaramayya, on whose insistence the Congress had established the Andhra Circle in 1918. The JVP committee was at pains to explain the non-acceptance of the Andhra demand, for the eleven Telugu-speaking districts of Madras fulfilled each of the five criterion – geographical continuity, financial self-sufficiency, administrative convenience, capacity for future development and a large measure of agreement within its borders, and amongst the people speaking the same language – with regard to its formation laid down by the commission. The JVP, however, left the possibility of reconsideration of the demand later.

~

The Telugu Ire against Nehru

But this did not address the Telugu angst, and their ire was specifically directed against Nehru himself, for he had made an exception for Andhra in his address to the Constituent Assembly. While on 8 November 1949 he had emphasized that there were many 'more engaging issues' than the formation of provinces on linguistic factors alone, on 27 November[6] he said, 'The demand for the province of Andhra, which, if I may say so, is a perfectly legitimate demand (and) raises relatively few difficulties. It can be included among the provinces in the Constitution, and this decision can be implemented soon after the new Constitution is adopted.'

However, on 24 January 1950, two days before the inauguration of the Constitution, Nehru backtracked at the last minute, mentioning 'outstanding difficulties and unresolved questions that had to be settled'. It was easy to understand that the outstanding difficulty was Governor General C. Rajagopalachari, and the unresolved question was the fate of Madras as both Tamils and Telugus had taken a hardline position in this regard. In local parlance, Madras was called Chennai after a Telugu goddess: and if there was a spiritual city that Tamilians identified with, it was Madurai. But C. Rajagopalachari was quite firm on Madras city being a part of Madras state instead of Andhra, and he carried a lot of weight with the High Command.

The infighting among the Congress politicians of Madras saw a rapid succession of chief ministers from 1946 to 1952. Tanguturi Prakasam,[7] or 'Andhra Kesari', held office from April 1946 to March 1947, and after being relieved from Madras, largely on the insistence of C. Rajagopalachari, Gandhi and Nehru, he turned his attention to Hyderabad and its Telugu-speaking majority. He was instrumental in establishing the Hyderabad State Praja Party[8] and was a votary of Vishalandhra[9] – the coming together of all the Telugu-speaking areas of Hyderabad and Madras.

~

The Hunger Strikes for Andhra

During the short tenure of Tanguturi Prakasam's successor O.P. Ramaswamy Reddiyar,[10] Madras was struggling through a period of severe food shortage. While there was some respite from the Telugu agitation, in 1951, the Gandhian leader Swami Sitaram (Gollapudi Sitaram Shastry)[11] undertook a fast unto death for a linguistic state of Telugu-speaking people, which unnerved the then chief minister, P.S. Kumaraswamy Raja,[12] who sought the intervention of Vinoba Bhave to persuade Swami Sitaram to break his fast after thirty-five days. Meanwhile, the Partition Committee set up under the chairmanship of Chief Minister Raja with Tanguturi Prakasam representing the Andhras could not come to a settlement. However, in the 1952 assembly elections, the Congress received a major electoral reverse, winning only 152 seats, as against 164 of the United Democratic Front (UDF), which was led by Tanguturi Prakasam. In the Telugu-speaking districts, the Congress could only secure 43 of the 140 seats. However, in an arbitrary and unethical move, the then governor of Madras, Sri Prakasa,[13] first nominated C. Rajagopalachari to the Legislative Council, and then invited him to head the Congress ministry which did not have a clear majority. C. Rajagopalachari was not popular with K. Kamaraj who held sway over the Congress organization, and was specially resented by the Telugus, for he was identified as the 'outstanding difficulty' to the formation of Andhra. He had been the premier (1937–39) and later the first governor of Bengal and the first Indian governor general of India. He was also Nehru's choice for being India's first President, but Rajendra Prasad had the support of Sardar Patel and the Congress.

C. Rajagopalachari's second term as premier of Madras was even more controversial than his first term, when he tried to make Hindi compulsory in Madras. This time, he annoyed the Tamilians by introducing the 'hereditary education policy' that was perceived to be a ploy to perpetuate the caste system, and the Telugus rose in revolt when he tried to divert the waters of Krishna river for the Krishna–Pennar project. The A.N. Khosla[14] expert committee appointed by the Union government categorically rejected the project, and instead advised Nandikonda, the site of the present-day Nagarjuna Sagar, as the alternate site (which fell in Andhra).

This provoked further distrust and Potti Sriramulu,[15] another self-effacing Gandhian, began his 'fast-unto-death' in October 1952 and breathed his last on 15 December. This led to another bout of violent agitations, and within days (19 December) the Prime Minister was compelled to announce the formation of Andhra state, but excluding the Madras city, which was keenly contested by the Tamilians. Tanguturi Prakasam became the first chief minister of Andhra state – the precursor to Andhra Pradesh in 1953.

Even though Hyderabad state got a popular government in 1952 under Dr Burgulla Ramakrishna Rao,[16] a distinguished man of letters, the three linguistic groups – Marathi, Kannada and Telugu – were all pulling the state in different directions. However, Nehru was in favour of a composite Hyderabad, and in his monthly despatch (2 October 1952) to his chief ministers he wrote,[17] 'Then there is the cry for a division of Hyderabad on a linguistic basis. For my part, I am entirely opposed to this. If it is accepted, I am sure it would retard progress in Hyderabad for many long years and would create all manner of problems and upset that balance of south India … All our Five-Year Plans and the like will have to be put on the shelf till some new equilibrium is reached.' He felt that such a move would be injurious to Hyderabad and would upset the whole structure of south India.

Dr Burgulla Rao did initiate the process of land reforms and introduction of Telugu in the Telangana areas, but there was no organic unity in the state. The urban Hyderabadis started a 'Mulki' agitation[18] seeking a reservation of jobs for native residents and looked to the Nizam for help and support. But even though he was the titular head of the state as its raj pramukh from 1950 to 1956, he had little moral or political authority over the situation.

Therefore, despite what Nehru wanted, Hyderabad ceased to exist as a state from 1956 when its Marathi-speaking region was merged with Bombay, Kannada-speaking region with Mysore, and Telugu-speaking region with Andhra state.

~

This was just one of the many 'map altering' recommendations of the SRC which had been notified after the death of Potti Sriramulu and the formation of the Andhra State. The three-member commission had Dr Fazal Ali[19] as the chairman and included H.N. Kunzru[20] and K.M. Panikkar.[21] The report that it presented is till date one of the most-read government reports, the others being the Shah Commission of Enquiry and the Mandal Commission reports.

Fazal Ali was then the governor of Orissa, and later of Assam; Kunzru had been a member of the Constituent Assembly, and is the only person ever to have declined Bharat Ratna[22] as a matter of principle (for he had opposed it in the Constituent Assembly); and Panikkar was an editor, diplomat, scholar, statesman and Parliamentarian.

This 267-page report, including the dissenting notes by the chairman and K.M. Panikkar makes for fascinating reading. The commission adopted the report when two of the three members agreed on the substantive issue in question. About the Telugu-speaking areas of Hyderabad and Andhra state, the SRC felt that not only were the two regions far apart in economic development, but Telangana was also the hinterland to Bombay, and Andhra to Madras. The land tenure and revenue systems differed widely due to over a century of different kinds of administrations. As such, the SRC recommended that the unification of the Telugu-speaking areas of Hyderabad and Andhra should be deferred by at least five years. However, this was not accepted by the Union government as it thought that a united, bigger and robust Andhra would be powerful enough to address the communist insurrection in both Hyderabad and Andhra state.

To quote the SRC report, 'One of the principal causes of opposition to Vishalandhra also seems to be the apprehension felt by the educationally backward people of Telangana that they may be swamped and exploited by the more advanced people of coastal areas.'

As a via media, a Gentlemen's Agreement was signed between the leaders of Andhra and Telangana that included a 60:40 ratio in the Cabinet; the reservation of the post of deputy chief minister if the chief minister was from Andhra; establishment of a Telangana Regional Council; and reservation of posts in public services for the Mulkis (erstwhile residents of Hyderabad). In pursuance of this agreement, the Public Employment (Requirement as to Residence) Act was passed in 1957.

Meanwhile, the fears of the SRC were not unfounded. The coastal region was quite happy to have Hyderabad as the capital, but as their domination in the Congress party and government was quite pronounced, the terms of the Gentleman's Agreement were ignored, and within a decade, the agitation for a separate Telangana gained popular support. Telangana achieved statehood in 2014, and we shall resume the story when we come to the map of 2014!

The commission submitted its report on 30 September 1955. The preface to the report said: 'It is neither possible nor desirable to reorganise States on the basis of the single test of either language or culture, but that a balanced approach to the whole problem is necessary in the interest of our national unity.' As such, in addition to its recommendations about linguistic reorganization, it also offered suggestions to strengthen national unity. These did not have a direct bearing on boundaries but were nevertheless very important in shaping the political and administrative architecture.

The first of these was the abolition of the institution of raj pramukh (and by implication – the sub categories under it – up raj pramukh, and its variants – *jyeshta* and *kanishtha*, senior and junior). With this, the artificial distinction between Part A/B/C/D states also disappeared, and there remained only states and Union Territories. The SRC also recommended the creation of the Indian Forest Service, and advised that at least half the contingent of All India Services officers in a state should not be of that domicile.

The commission suggested that the whole country be divided into sixteen states and three centrally administered areas. The government, while not agreeing with the recommendations entirely, divided the country into fourteen states and six Union Territories. The States Reorganisation Act was passed in November 1956. The states were Andhra Pradesh, Assam, Bihar, Bombay, Jammu and Kashmir, Kerala, Madhya Pradesh, Madras, Mysore, Orissa, Punjab, Rajasthan, Uttar Pradesh and West Bengal. The six Union Territories were Andaman and Nicobar Islands, Delhi, Himachal Pradesh, Laccadive, Minicoy and Amindivi Islands, Manipur and Tripura.

With regard to Mysore, it had all the Kannada-speaking areas from Bombay, Madras and Andhra, besides the Coorg state. In other words, all the recommendations with regard to Karnataka were accepted, except for the name. Thus, Mysore was one of the last princely states to lose its identity. By adding Malabar to Travancore–Cochin, all Malayalam speakers also got their own state of Kerala. The SRC had also suggested that the predominantly Malayalam-speaking areas of Laccadive, Minicoy and Amindivi Islands under the Malabar district of Madras be brought under Kerala. However, while Malabar was made part of Kerala, the islands were organized into a separate Union Territory for administrative purposes. This was on the pattern of the administration for the Andaman and Nicobar Islands, and both island territories came directly under the Union government. The new territory was called Laccadive, Minicoy and Amindivi Islands before the adoption of the name Lakshadweep which in Malayalam and Sanskrit means 'a thousand islands' on 1 November 1973. Incidentally, the Hindi maps, right from 1952 had always referred to these islands as Lakshadweep! A plausible reason for these islands becoming a UT directly under the Union government was the lurking fear of a communist government in Kerala – and the fear of the red flag on these distant lands.

Madras also became a unilingual state – Odiya-speaking districts had been carved out of Madras to make Orissa in 1936; Telugus got their Andhra state in 1953 and Kerala got Malabar. The Travancore Tamil Nadu Congress demanded the merger of Thovalai, Agasteeswaram, Kalkulam, Vilavancode, Neyyatinkara, Senkottai, Deviculam and Peermade with Madras state. However, the commission recommended only the merger of Thovalai, Agasteeswaram, Kalkulam, Vilavancode and Senkottai with Madras state.

The SRC recommended the formation of a separate Vidarbha state by splitting majority Marathi-speaking areas from Madhya Pradesh state. The government did not accept the recommendation and merged these areas in the predominantly Marathi-speaking Bombay state. The States Reorganisation Commission rejected the demand for a Punjabi-majority state saying that it lacked a majority support, and that Punjabi was not grammatically very distinct from Hindi. The Patiala and East Punjab States Union (PEPSU) was merged with Punjab. Although the SRC recommended the merger of the UT of Himachal with Punjab, there was a major uproar against this – and Himachal's status as a UT was retained.

Bombay, like Punjab, continued to be bilingual, though within four years, Bombay was bifurcated into Gujarat and Maharashtra. Punjab was trifurcated into the states of Punjab and Haryana, and the UT of Himachal.

With regard to the state of Assam, the commission held the view that the creation of a hill state was impracticable, and there 'is also no reason, having regard to the peculiar features and circumstances of Assam, why a separate Hill state should be created'. On the contrary, they suggested the merger of Tripura with Assam forthwith, and that of Manipur at a later stage. They also recommended that the arrangements with regard to North-East Frontier Agency[23] should be retained. Likewise, the demand for a separate Gurkha state in Darjeeling was rejected. Thus, technically, West Bengal was, and continues to be, a state in which the official language in the two districts of Darjeeling and Kalimpong is Gorkhali.

With respect to Bihar and Bengal, a portion of the Purnea district east of the river Mahananda, and Puruliya sub district of Manbhum district, were transferred from Bihar to West Bengal. Purnea provided the much-needed link to Jalpaiguri, Darjeeling and Cooch Behar, and Puruliya was predominantly Bengali speaking. The only states and UTs which were left unscathed by the SRC report were UP, Orissa, J&K, Delhi and Andaman and Nicobar Islands. We may note here that the SRC was comfortable with the organization of a linguistic group into two states – Andhra and Hyderabad – as also with a Marathi-speaking state of Vidarbha, and a bilingual (Gujarati–Marathi) state of Bombay.

Dr Ambedkar on Linguistic Provinces

Incidentally, it must be mentioned that one of the first, and more well-thought out, representations to the Linguistic Provinces Commission was submitted by Dr Ambedkar in 1948. In the document, he had argued that 'Bombay as a mixed state consisting of Maharashtra, Gujarat and Bombay should be done away with, and the state of Maharashtra be divided into four states having Bombay city, Western Maharashtra, central Maharashtra and Eastern Maharashtra'. Among all of them, the most disputed subject was the fate of Bombay city. Ambedkar preferred that option, not just to prevent the pressures from both Gujaratis and Maharashtrians, but also as a safe haven for the minorities and the Schedules Castes. 'The minorities need an asylum, a place of refuge, where they can be free from the tyranny of the majority. If there was a united Maharashtra with Bombay included in it, where can they go for safety?'

8

THE LINGUISTIC STATES OF THE SOUTH

Tamil Nadu, Karnataka and Kerala

'The Union of India is far, far away, from the United States of India. But this consolidation of the North and Balkanisation of the South is not the way to reach it.'

~ B.R. Ambedkar

Dravida Politics in Madras

Even though many states – UP, Rajasthan, MP, Andhra, to name a few – gave themselves a new name and identity at the time of commencement of the republic, it took over two decades for Madras to change its name to Tamil Nadu. In 1947, Madras retained its status as a province under the Dominion of India. O.P. Ramaswamy Reddiyar,[1] backed by K. Kamaraj, was the chief minister at the time of Independence. The highlight of this year was the enactment of laws allowing universal access to all temples and the abolition of the Devadasi[1] tradition. When India became a republic in 1950, another Kamaraj protégé, P.S. Kumaraswamy Raja, became the chief minister.

However, as the Dravidian parties decided to boycott the general elections of 1952, the Congress emerged as the single largest party even though the CPI-led coalition was in a better position to form the government. Nevertheless, C. Rajagopalachari was 'nominated' by the then governor to the Legislative Council and took office as the chief minister of the state.

However, Rajaji's regime was very controversial – his first actions after taking charge included removal of controls on food grains and the introduction of a new education policy based on family vocation. The education policy was severely opposed by Dravida Kazhagam and DMK[2] as casteist and dubbed Kula Kalvi Thittam (Hereditary Education Policy).[3] This policy was under attack from within the Congress as well as outside it. In fact, Rajaji had to be replaced by the Congress, and Kamaraj took over as the chief minister in 1954.

One of the first political acts of Kamaraj during his tenure as chief minister was to widen the representation of the non-Brahmins in the Cabinet, but he retained C. Subramanian and M. Bhakthavatsalam, who had contested his leadership. In a move to counter Tamil cultural politics espoused by the DMK, Kamaraj made conscious attempts to partake in the linguistic cultural matters and offered ministerial positions to parties like Tamil Nadu Toilers Party.[4] K. Kamaraj remained the chief minister for three consecutive terms, winning the elections in 1957 and 1962. Had he remained at the helm in Tamil Nadu, the advent of Dravidian parties would have been considerably slower, or perhaps even abated. However, when as per the Kamaraj Plan, he resigned as the chief minister of Madras to take over as the Congress president, he became the kingmaker to the country, but his successor M. Bhakthavatsalam was no match to him. Unlike Kamaraj, his connection with the grass roots was

limited, and being a high-caste Mudaliar was a political liability
in the Dravida politics of those times. The vacuum left in Tamil
politics by Kamaraj was filled by none other than C. Annadurai,
who trounced the Congress party in the 1967 elections. Changing
the name of the state of Madras to Tamil Nadu was an assertion of
Tamil ethnic and linguistic pride.

~

The SRC report also signalled the end of the demand for a
separate Dravidisthan, which had been substantially diluted when
the linguistic reorganization of states took place in 1956. The
movement for Dravida identity was spearheaded by the Justice
Party, which later morphed into the Dravida Kazhagam. The
party had been established in 1916 by Dr C. Natesa Mudaliar,
T.M. Nair and P. Theagaraya Chetty – to protest the domination
of Brahmins not only in government, but also in political, social
and media organizations. Although Brahmins constituted only
3 per cent of the total population, they occupied over 85 per
cent of all senior appointments in government and judiciary,
besides holding sway in the Congress, the Bar associations, the
Home Rule movement and even in the Theosophical Society!
Thanks to the Congress boycotting the elections held under the
Montague–Chelmsford Reforms, Justice Party formed four of the
five ministries in Madras from 1920 to 1937. Their tenures saw
the introduction of reservations in government jobs and reforms
in education – including the establishment of the Annamalai and
Andhra Universities. The Madras University was a stronghold of
the Brahmins.

The most prominent leader of the Justice Party was E.V.
Ramaswamy, who had started his political career with the Congress
in 1919 but resigned after six years when he felt that it was heavily
dominated by the Brahmins. He had participated in the Vaikom

Satyagraha of 1924 but felt that the Congress was prioritizing national causes over social reform, and to him an equal society, based on self-respect and parity amongst caste and gender, was more significant. Under his leadership, the party's anti-Hindi and anti-Brahmin agenda became so prominent that Periyar went to the extent of seeking a separate Dravidisthan: a separate state, loyal to the British Raj and directly under the Secretary of State for India.

However, when it was clear that the British were determined to leave India, he sought a sovereign Dravidian Republic, which would be federal in nature, with four units corresponding to the linguistic divisions (Madras, Kerala, Mysore and Andhra), each having residuary powers and autonomy of internal administration. Earlier, Periyar had also flirted with communism – especially in the early '30s when he visited the Soviet Union and received the hospitality of the foreign department of the Communist Party of Soviet Union (CPSU). After visits to the Lenin Mausoleum, oilfields of Baku in Azerbaijan, hydroelectric power stations in Georgia and the Moscow Automotive Enterprise with its vast assembly lines and dining areas where food was equal and abundant, he was impressed with the great contrast of the Soviet Union with the 'great depression' in the rest of Europe. He saw the May Day celebrations and established contact with Abani Mookerjee, the leader of the Indian communist movement. On his return, Periyar exhorted members of his self-respect movement to desist from using traditional honorifics such as 'Maha-ganam', 'Sri', 'Thiru' and 'Thirumathi', as prefixes and urged them instead to employ 'Thozhar' or 'Comrade'. However, when the CPI was banned in 1934, he changed track by declaring that he was withdrawing his socialist programme in the larger interest of his self-respect movement. The fact that the leadership of the CPI was 'Brahminical' may have contributed to this decision.

~

The Politics of Anna

C. Annadurai joined Justice Party in 1935 and was noticed by Periyar for his oratorical and writing skills. Periyar appointed Anna as the assistant editor of his *Kudiyarasu* magazine. They rallied together for atheism, rationalism and annihilation of caste. By 1944, Anna started his weekly journal, *Dravida Nadu*, to propagate the cause for a separate country. In its Salem conclave in 1944, Anna brought in a resolution to rename the Justice Party as the Dravida Kazhagam. The two leaders, however, fell apart, with Anna going on to form his political party – the Dravida Munnetra Kazhagam (DMK) – in 1949. The trigger for the split was Periyar's stand on Indian independence. Periyar took a stance that Indian independence was merely a transfer from the British to the Brahmin dacoits. However, Anna understood the public mood and acknowledged Independence as the day of deliverance from the British. He used the term 'self-determination', which allowed room for manoeuvre. While highlighting his Dravida identity, he also acknowledged that Dravida was part of India. In his maiden speech in the Rajya Sabha in 1962, he said, 'I claim sir, to come from a country, a part in India now, but which I think is of a different stock … I belong to the Dravidian stock. I am proud to call myself a Dravidian. That does not mean that I am against a Bengali or a Maharashtrian or a Gujarati. I say that I belong to the Dravidian stock and that is only because I consider that the Dravidians have got something concrete, something distinct, something different to offer to the nation at large. Therefore, it is that we want self-determination.'[5] But the Chinese aggression in October 1962 made him give up his separatist notions. Post the Indo-China war, Annadurai said, 'When the country is in danger, for us to advocate separatism would be to give way to the foreigner.'

With this, the DMK shifted its focus to greater autonomy for states, leaving behind its demands for a separate country. However, a dominant faction of the CPI continued to support the Chinese perspective on the border issue, and this, along with the previous record of the DMK, led to the passage of the sixteenth amendment to the Constitution.

The statement of objectives and reasons appended to the 16th Constitutional Amendment Bill read, 'the committee on national integration and Regionalism recommended that Article 19 of the Constitution be amended so that adequate powers became available for the preservation and maintenance of the integrity, and sovereignty of the Union'. It also stipulated that every candidate for the membership of the state legislature or the Union Parliament must pledge himself to uphold the Constitution, and to preserve the integrity and sovereignty of the Union, and that the forms of oath in the Third Schedule should be suitably amended. Incidentally, the committee was headed by C.P. Ramaswami Iyer,[6] who, as the Diwan of Travancore, had moved heaven and earth for the continuance of British rule and had also goaded the Chamber of Princes to declare their independence. Soon after the sixteenth amendment came into effect, the DMK gave up its demand for an independent Dravida Nadu, despite being the only party to have opposed the amendment in the Parliament.

Anna: Master of the Metaphor

Anna was not only shrewd and tactical, he was the master of the metaphor. Thus, he described himself as 'a Hindu sans the sacred ash, a Christian minus the Holy Cross, and a Muslim without the prayer cap'.[7] On 26 January 1965 when the fifteen–year period for retaining English ended, he coined the slogan 'Down with Hindi, Long Live the Republic'. He was thus addressing an audience in his state, as well as the larger polity of India where he sought to make a clear distinction between love for Hindi and love for the country, and the trope which held that both had to go together. In this he received support from several other non-Hindi-speaking states. On the contrary, Bhakthavatsalam could not capture the public mood and rather than make a concession to the growing pro-Tamil sentiment, he attacked Anna's movement as blasphemous at a time when there were hardly any adherents for Hindi. In fact, his critique of Anna tilted the balance in favour of the Dravidian party and, after 1967, the state has been ruled by one of the factions of the Dravidian party.

Here again, it is important to note that DMK could emerge victorious only because of the vehement support of C. Rajagopalachari, who had moved away from the Congress as well as his pro-Hindi stance, and ensured that the anti-Congress vote was not divided.

Immediately on coming to power, Anna legalized 'self-respect marriages'[8] for the first time: these did not mandate the requirement of a Brahmin priest to preside over the nuptials. He encouraged simple, inter-caste marriages. He was also the first to offer subsidized rice as an electoral promise and, in many ways, this was the precursor to the National Food Security Act.[9] Apart from organizing two world conferences on Tamil, he issued an order to remove images of gods and all other religious symbols from government offices. Even though his health had deteriorated on account of his tobacco chewing habit, against medical advice, he continued to address public meetings and breathed his last on 10 September 1968. The Guinness Book of Records acknowledged that this was, till then, the largest number of attendees for a funeral procession!

~

Jayachamarajendra Wadiyar

During this turbulent period of the anti-Hindi agitations in Madras, Jayachamarajendra Wadiyar,[10] the former ruler and later raj pramukh of Mysore, was governor of Madras.

As the ruler of Mysore from 1940, he had ceded his kingdom to the Dominion of India in 1947 but continued as the Maharaja until India became a republic in 1950. He was the raj pramukh of Mysore state from 1950 to 1956. In a rare gesture, even after the reorganization of the state on a linguistic basis, he was appointed governor of the integrated Mysore state in 1956 and held the post until 1964, after which he was nominated as the governor of Madras state (now Tamil Nadu) for two years.

The acceptance of the Wadiyars in the democratic polity of India is best explained by the cardinal principles upheld by their dynasty – political accommodation, enlightened governance and proactive reforms that anticipated and defused any possibility of social unrest. Thus, Mysore had a representative assembly from 1882. Although the franchise was limited and powers were minimal, it marked out this princely state as the most progressive in India.

Mysore was also the first state to allow for reservation based on domicile and caste; the first demand came from the Mysore Brahmins, who were finding it difficult to compete with the Madras Brahmins who had a virtual monopoly over the upper tier of the state's civil service until 1920. This soon led to demands from other groups as well. When Wadiyar IV appointed the Justice Miller Committee[11] to investigate the issue of reservation for Backward Classes (which meant everyone except Brahmins, Anglo-Indians[12] and Europeans), Visvesvaraya,[13] the Diwan of Mysore resigned from his post in protest against reservations for backward classes. However, the Miller Committee recommended 75 per cent reservation in the long run and a time-bound programme to ensure at least 50 per cent posts were kept for the Backward Classes. Thus, seven decades before the implementation of the Mandal Commission recommendations, Maharaja Krishnaraja Wadiyar IV opened the public service to less exalted groups in the caste hierarchy.

Aluru Venkat Rao: Kannada Kula Purohita

Meanwhile, the popular upsurge against Curzon's Partition of Bengal had an all–India impact, and linguistic groups everywhere started their movements. It also galvanized the Kannada-speaking populations living outside Mysore to come together under the leadership of Aluru Venkat Rao.[14] He called for a movement for uniting Karnataka. Popularly known as known the 'Kannada Kula Purohita', or the 'high priest of the Kannada family', he made a case for integrating all Kannada regions of Madras and Bombay presidencies, besides those under the Nizam of Hyderabad, into Mysore. This demand received a fillip when the idea of a separate Karnataka state was ratified by the INC committee led by Motilal Nehru in 1928. According to this, there was a 'strong prima facie case for unification' of all the Kannada-speaking areas, and it was believed that Karnataka could also be a financially strong province.

However, it is interesting to note that unlike language movements elsewhere which looked for an external scapegoat, Aluru Venkat Rao turned the gaze inwards. He wanted the Kannadigas to measure their inadequacies not against the overarching triumphs of the imperial power, but against the modest successes of other linguistic nationalisms within India itself. Aluru Venkat Rao's anguished cry in 1920, 'We don't have a history! We must have a history!'[15] implied that it was only through a recast of history that Kannadiga people could find their identity and their role in Indian history. He deplored the fact that his effort came five decades after Bengali,

Marathi and Hindi counterparts had made their heroes and historic triumphs a part of the Indian nationalist narrative.

Yet it must be placed on record that the impetus for shaping the Kannada identity came not from Mysore, but the Bombay Karnataka region where the Marathi national identity was being reinforced. It was R.H. Deshpande,[16] who strove for the revival of Kannada in a region where Marathi was the language of administration. On the other hand, Mysore was noticed throughout the colonial period for its achievements in statecraft and industrialization.

Divide in the Kannada Movement: Mysore or Karnataka?

With the merger of Mysore into India, there was a clear divide in the Kannada movement. The Mysoreans felt that they were far more advanced in almost all spheres: education and culture, agriculture and industry, health and education. They felt that the merger of the 'backward areas', starting with the six taluks of Bellary, would actually prove to be a drain on the exchequer. They wanted the Kannada-speaking areas outside of Mysore to be constituted into another Kannada-speaking state. This change of attitude is best characterized by D.V. Gundapa (DVG).[17] At the Karnataka Sangha Rajothsava in 1944 at Bangalore's Central College, he called for the consolidation of the Kannada-speaking areas within one, two or more states. However, by the time of the SRC in 1955, DVG had become a staunch opponent of a single Karnataka. Others opposed to the idea of linguistic unification while supporting the idea of two states, namely Karnataka and Mysore, were ex-Diwans Visvesvaraya and M. Mirza Ismail[18], scholars such as M.P.L. Shastry, Congressmen such as A.G. Ramachandra Rao and T. Channaiah (who had also earlier supported unification), and members of caste associations such as Vokkaligara and Kuruba Sangha. This assortment of cultural 'royalists', non-dominant castes and technocrat-administrators wanted to preserve Mysore's formidable reputation as a 'model' state and tried to prevent the linguistic consolidation of the Kannada-speaking people.

However, as per the recommendations of the SRC, a new state of 74,000 square miles and two crore people was formed out of disparate and reluctant entities: the erstwhile Mysore state, the Kannada-speaking areas of Bombay, Madras, Hyderabad and the princely state of Coorg. This was indeed an unprecedented moment, both in Karnataka's history and in the brief history of the independent Indian nation state. Whatever their differences, such was the Congress discipline in those days that the three stalwarts of the Congress, S. Nijalingappa, C. Hanumanthaiah and Devaraj Urs publicly appeared to be on the same page.

Interestingly, Nijalingappa was a Lingayat, Hanumanthaiah a Vokkaliga and Devaraj Urs was an Arusu, a member of the extended clan of the Wadiyars. Although both Lingayats and Vokkaligas (Gowdas) were Kannada-speaking, their differences were quite pronounced. So much so, that even the normally staid SRC commented:

It has been estimated that Lingayats or Veerashaivas constitute about 30% to 40% of the population in the Kannada areas outside Mysore at present. The other important section of the Kannadigas namely the Vokkaligas similarly constitute a little less than 29% of the population of Mysore. In the united Karnataka, it has been estimated that a little more than 20% of the population may be Lingayats between 13% and 14% Vakkaligas and about 17% to 18% Harijans. It is clear therefore that no one community will therefore be dominant, and any one section can be reduced to the status of a minority if other groups combine against it.

The first, and most immediate impact of this demographic change was that Hanumanthaiah moved to the Union Cabinet, making way for Nijalingappa to be elected as the first chief minister by the new Mysore assembly, which consisted of the erstwhile assembly members from Bombay, Madras, Coorg, Hyderabad and old Mysore.

With respect to the retention of the old name, it is interesting to see the difference in perspectives. Nijalingappa wrote in his memoirs: 'The name Karnataka could have been accepted had I pressed for the name change, but I did not want to unnecessarily hurt any feelings. The man who most openly wanted the old name to continue, and did not accept Karnataka, was Devaraj Urs, who subsequently became chief minister and then had the name changed to Karnataka, for his political gain.'[19]

One must mention here that this memoir was written two decades after the incident and, by then, Nijalingappa was a bitter man, and Urs was at the height of his glory. Indeed, one of the first actions of Urs on becoming the chief minister was to change the name of the state from 'Mysore' to 'Karnataka' on 1 November 1973. It is true that the change to 'Karnataka' in 1956 would have made sense: much of the population of the enlarged state lived outside of Mysore, and the INC had described these areas as the 'Karnataka Pradesh Congress Committee'.

However, if at the time of merger, the outsider to 'Mysore' (S. Nijalingappa) retained the name to assuage the feelings of the minority who lived in the former princely state, almost two decades later, the insider (Devaraj Urs) decided on 'Karnataka' to reassure those who were not from Old Mysore that their interests would be uppermost in the polity of the new Karnataka, especially as he pushed the aggressive land reforms policy. The groundwork had been laid in 1961 by Kadidal Manjappa,[20] who had grown up in old Mysore with its marked inequalities in landholdings. His legislation had limited impact, partly because it contained loopholes but mainly because subsequent governments lacked the will to implement it. However, Urs wanted to create a new support constituency – that of the peasant cultivator. All tenanted land passed to the government, which, in turn, transferred it to the tenants. The amended Act also barred the leasing of land, abolished sharecropping and prescribed ceilings for various categories of land.

Kannada Cinema and Identity

However, with the benefit of hindsight, it must be placed on record that while Nijalingappa[21] became the first chief minister and Urs took the credit for renaming the state, it was Hanumanthaiah's[22] dogged persistence that laid the foundations of Karnataka. His articulation of the many 'cusp cultures' of the state on the one hand, and the development discourse on the other, set the tone and the context for integration. Of the two arguments, the state took over the development discourse: 'a 200-mile coastline to landlocked Mysore, three valuable harbours of Bhatkal, Malpe and Karwar; new cities; crops; rivers and waterfalls of north Karnataka as potential hydroelectric dam sites'.[23] The former was ignored, for soon after the merger, much to the chagrin of old Mysoreans like H.R. Ghaffar Khan, the linguistic claims of the eight lakh Urdu speakers were systematically ignored. On this issue, the silence of the state was juxtaposed with the sound of the cinema. In the aftermath of linguistic reorganization of states, cinematic icons in Tamil Nadu, Karnataka and Andhra Pradesh began to supplement the political life of the people in a parallel state form. Thus the role of Kannada cinema, especially the post-1956 productions that also coincided with the emergence of Rajkumar as the larger than life superhero, also contributed in no small way in articulating the popular demand for a Kannada-speaking state.

~

The Union of Travancore–Cochin

When Gopalkrishna Gandhi,[24] the grandson to both Mahatma Gandhi and C. Rajagopalachari, and a former governor of West Bengal, was asked to speak on 'Kerala and Gandhi', his first comment was, 'There is a definitional flaw in the title "Kerala and Gandhi", for Kerala as we know it (now) did not exist in the Mahatma's time. We had the states of Travancore and Cochin, and we had Malabar.'

Malabar[25] was the Malayalam-speaking part of the Madras Presidency, renamed Madras state after Independence. Together these were the three units which the Aikya Kerala[26] movement pressed for as a single entity in the memorandum submitted to the States Reorganization Commission. However, the sentiment was not uncontested, for there was a considerable body of opinion that preferred amalgamation with Madras. In fact, multiple options, including a Dakshin Pradesh with the four linguistic zones of Tamil, Telugu, Kannada and Malayalam prominence were on the table. While Mysore and Andhra had their own linguistic states, given the Malabar connection with Madras, the merger of Travancore–Cochin and Madras was a distinct possibility, and it appears that the Planning Commission and the governor of Madras were in serious correspondence on this subject.

Thus V.T. Krishnamachari,[27] deputy chairman of the Planning Commission[28] wrote to Sri Prakasa, the governor of Madras in November 1955: 'I wonder if it is too late to work for a combined Madras and Kerala. I am not concerned with the political aspects: but from the economic point of view, such a combined state would be of utmost benefit to both the areas.'[29] Krishnamachari also wrote to Home Minister G.B. Pant, 'Proposals for merger or other forms of collaboration between states throw up interesting possibilities of development which are worth exploring. As a case study, some aspects of proposals relating to Madras and Travancore–Cochin have been recently examined in the Planning Commission.' The Home Minister was, of course, more reticent, for he said, 'unless adequate popular support is forthcoming, I doubt if anything will be achieved at this stage'.

In the aftermath of Independence, the states ministry was quite keen to merge the princely states of Travancore and Cochin into one union. While the people of both Travancore and Cochin were of the same stock and spoke the same language and shared the same cultural connect, there were clear differences as well. Cochin had been a 'progressive state', while Travancore was more conservative and 'change-resistant'. Cochin had an effective Legislative Council with an elected majority from 1925 and was the first state to send its representative to the Constituent Assembly, as well as amongst the first to accede to the Indian dominion. Travancore had to be pushed into accession.

~

Vaikom Satyagraha

Travancore was also the site of the famous Vaikom Satyagraha[30] of 1924. The issue was freedom of movement on the roads leading to the entrance of the famous Shiva temple at Vaikom. Not only did the Satyagraha receive support from all sections of society in the state, an Akali delegation from Punjab also joined the protest movement. The Mahatma too lent his fullest support to the movement and stated 'in this age of reason, in this age of universal knowledge, this age of education and comparative theology … untouchability is a blot upon humanity and therefore upon Hinduism. It cannot stand the test of reason'.[31] After an agitation lasting twenty-one months, all public roads and streets were thrown open to all Hindus, irrespective of caste, and the Mahatma called it the 'bedrock of freedom'. However, it was not until the famous Temple Entry Proclamation of 12 November 1936 that all the *kshetrams* (temple spaces) were opened to every Hindu. This action of the last ruling king of Travancore, Chithira Thirunal Balaram Varma, won him accolades from across the country, most notably from the Mahatma.

However, his Prime Minister, Sir C.P. Ramaswami Iyer[32] was quite unpopular, more so with the growing number of communist supporters in the state. Congressmen were also upset with him for, in July 1947, he issued a statement seeking independence for Travancore, and showed extreme reluctance to join the Indian Union. However, he was eased out as the Diwan, and negotiations were opened on the future of the state with the new Prime Minister P.G.N. Unnithan[33] who assisted Maharaja Sree Chithira Thirunal. The Maharaja of Travancore was also appointed the first raj pramukh of the new state, and even though the Maharaja of Cochin was asked to be the up raj pramukh of the new state, he politely declined the offer, but requested that the eldest member of the royal family be designated *Valiya Thampuram*.[34]

V.P. Menon was accorded the honour of inaugurating the new state of Travancore–Cochin on 1 July 1949, with an area of 9155 square miles and population of 75 lakh and an income of 13.5 crore.

The three-dimensional patchwork of Travancore–Cochin (TC), jurisdictions, social groups and political organizations, coupled with an intense struggle between the Congress and the communists, with the socialists playing one against the other to suit their convenience, meant that political stability was a far cry in the short-lived state. As influential, if not more than the political parties, were the Shree Narayana Dharma Prachalan (SNDP),[35] the Nair Service Society (NSS)[36] as well as the Church-affiliated educational and social institutions. The library and reading room movement also played a distinct role for these were 'spaces' where people could read and discuss the newspapers, periodicals and publications with a general affiliation to the ideological dispensation.

In what must be a record, the state had five chief ministers and even a term of President's Rule[37] in its seven years of existence.

The first chief minister, Paravoor T.K. Narayana Pillai,[38] was the secretary of the Travancore Cochin Congress in 1932, and its president in 1938. He took office on 1 July 1949. Part of his organizational strength and reach came from the Aikya Thiruvitahmcore-Cochin Grandhasala Sangham,[39] a voluntary group that promoted public libraries and reading rooms. The state was still reeling under the impact of the Punnapra–Valyar[40] revolutionary upsurge led by the Communist Party of India (CPI). Apart from banning the party, Pillai also took large scale measures to suppress the movement that was organizing demonstrations against the landlords and factory owners. An internecine rift within his own Cabinet saw him tender his resignation within eighteen months.

He was succeeded by C. Kesavan[41] in February 1951 who had strong affiliations with Shree Narayana Dharma Paripalana Yogam, an organization founded by Sri Narayana Guru for the social, economic and educational advancement of Ezhavas,[42] and to impart amongst them a consciousness of their own dignity and strength as an integral part of the wider Hindu consciousness. Although Kesavan was an atheist, his involvement in SNDP arrested the tide of conversions of Ezhavas to Christianity and Islam. He worked for temperance and eradication of untouchability, for he had suffered discrimination as an Ezhava boy on the streets and other public places. Incidentally, the ex–chief minister, T.K. Narayana Pillai, joined his Cabinet. For the record, the historic Land Reforms Bill was piloted by him, but he was not backed by the vested interests within his own party. Of course, in hindsight it can be said that if this Bill had been enacted and implemented, the ideological differences between the communists and the socialists would have been muted. After the declaration of general elections of 1952, he relinquished power.

In the first general elections (1952), the Congress was the single largest party but was eleven seats short of a majority. It, therefore, aligned with the Travancore Tamil Nadu Congress (TTNC) and Kerala Socialist Party to cobble a coalition under the leadership of A.J. John. It was an inherently flawed arrangement as the main plank of the TTNC was the demand for transfer of Kanyakumari district from Travancore–Cochin to Madras. As the ban on the CPI had not been lifted till the announcement of elections, their candidates stood as independents and garnered 33.89 per cent votes as against the Congress share of 35.44 per cent. Thus, the gap was quite narrow, and if the vote share of the other left-leaning parties like the Socialist Party and the Revolutionary Socialist Party (RSP) were also included with those of the independents, the Congress was clearly not in a position of comfort. The government fell within a year when the TTNC withdrew support in September 1953, and fresh elections were called for.

The 1954 elections were a watershed moment in India's Parliamentary history as the socialists and communists together won 60 of the 118 seats in the provincial assembly and was the first major rout of the Congress in a state election, even though with 46 seats, it was still the largest party. A declassified note of US States Department ('Communists may enter Indian state government') notes that this was 'the first opportunity for communists to participate in forming a state government in India'.[43] It also states that socialist leaders at the national level were divided on making a government with support from the Communist Party. Meanwhile, the ex–Prime Minister of Travancore state, Pattom Thanu Pillai,[44] who had made a switch from the Congress to the Praja Socialist Party (PSP), now made an opportunistic alliance with the Congress to lead yet another minority government in Travancore–Cochin, which lasted for only eleven months. He gave way to Panampilly Govinda Menon[45] who was the fifth (and the last) chief minister of the state. He had been the Prime Minister of the state of Cochin at the time of Independence and had served in the Cabinets of T.K. Narayana Pillai, and minister of finance under A.J. John in the Travancore–Cochin state. However, he could only last just little longer than his predecessors: his thirteen-month term gave way to President's Rule till March 1957, by which time the new state of Kerala was formed with the inclusion of Malabar district of Madras, and the transfer of Kanyakumari from Kerala to Madras.

While researching on the history of Kerala, more specifically the rivalry between Cochin and Calicut on the Malabar coast, the role of the Ming dynasty[46] of China comes to the fore. Cochin and its ruler were given a special status and the title of Keyli in 1411 CE by Admiral Zheng. He was instructed by the Ming ruler to confer on them a seal of alliance and special friendship. The Chinese naval armada protected Cochin from its neighbour and rival, the Zamorin of Calicut. Although Calicut was the dominant port city, Cochin had emerged as a rival, and the Chinese Admiral Zheng[47] delivered a stone tablet to its ruler inscribed by the emperor himself. If the Ming treasure voyages had continued, Cochin may have had an upper hand over Calicut. But when these stopped after the decline of the naval power of the Ming dynasty, the Zamorin[48] of Calicut occupied Cochin and installed his representative as the king.

9

THE ROY–SINHA PROPOSALS AND THE BOUNDARIES OF WEST BENGAL

There is an interesting interregnum in the story of linguistic assertions: the Roy–Sinha proposals for the merger of West Bengal and Bihar. This was indeed a novel attempt to settle inter-state border disputes by creating a supra-entity and it had the support of both the chief ministers, Dr B.C. Roy (West Bengal) and Srikrishna Sinha[1] (Bihar), the Union Cabinet, and the Bihar and West Bengal assemblies had resolved in favour of the merger.

What led Dr B.C. Roy – the more influential and better-known leader – to propose a merger that would have made Bengalis a minority in the new state? For Dr Roy, one of main considerations was the rehabilitation of the growing stream of refugees from East Bengal. Roy looked at the reallocation of frontiers of his state 'mainly for solving the linguistic and administrative problems as well as to reallocate the refugees from East Pakistan'.[2] He was most impressed by the manner in which the state of Punjab had been able to rehabilitate Punjabis from across the border on the abundant lands in Kurukshetra, Karnal, Faridabad, Sonipat, Panipat and Gurgaon. On the other hand, refugees from East Bengal were sent to places like Andaman and Nicobar Islands, Orissa, Madhya Pradesh and UP where they did not have a 'political voice', and felt absolutely abandoned. It was also felt that major river basin development projects like Damodar Valley Corporation[3] (for irrigation, flood control and power) covered both the states, and this would make financial and administrative arrangements better. Calcutta had the capital and Bihar had the mineral resources: and this too could have led to rapid industrialization of the new state!

Incidentally, the representations made to the SRC did not include the Roy–Sinha proposal. The four memoranda put up before the SRC were based on different sets of factors, each demanding some area from the neighbouring state. The Pradesh Congress Committee (PCC) memorandum sought an additional area of 21,352 square miles and a population of 8.2 million from the states of Bihar, Orissa and Assam. The state government proposition was far more realistic – it sought the transfer of four districts of Bihar (Purnea, Santhal Parganas, Manbhum and Dalbhum) besides Goalpara from Assam. The third proposal came from the left-dominated Linguistic States Redistribution Committee (LSRC), which claimed all of the territory contiguous to West Bengal in which Bengali-speaking people dominated – a position midway between the state government and the West Bengal PCC. The Jana Sangha came out with yet another formula: the states of Bihar, West Bengal, Orissa, Assam be combined with the centrally administered states of Manipur and Tripura to form one state, to be called Purbanchal[4] Pradesh (Eastern Region).

It must be mentioned that while the editorials and the 'letters to the editor' in the English press (*The Statesman*, *The Times of India*) were supportive of this move of organizing India on administrative convenience, the Hindi and regional language papers were for a reorganization on linguistic lines. The editorial comment in the *Economic Weekly* was more nuanced. It said, 'apart from yielding an ideological dividend in reversing the trend towards linguistic destruction of the nation, the proposal for the merger of Bengal and Bihar hailed so recently as constituting a new dawn of hope does not seem at first sight to have any particularly attractive features and has been so assessed by the general public, at least in Bengal.'

Even though the Roy—Sinha pact on the merger of West Bengal and Bihar was welcomed by the central leadership of the Congress, it was met with vehement opposition from the provincial politicians of both the states. The Bengalis felt that they would be swamped by the Hindi-speaking majority of Bihar. They also felt that as the per capita GDP of West Bengal was double that of Bihar, they would be at a loss should the state be merged. On the other hand, those in Bihar felt that the Bengalis would re-emerge as the 'intermediary ruling class' and dominate the political, commercial and cultural life of the new state. They were also concerned about the possible impact of migration of the nine million refugees from East Bengal, which would certainly alter the demographics of the new state. An excerpt from a report in *The Times of India* on 7 February 1956 read: 'The mounting exodus from East Pakistan has made the authorities in West Bengal aware of the threat of a bulk, if not all, of the nine million members of the minority community in East Bengal ultimately migrating to India as victims of circumstances. The stress on the Islamic nature of the Pakistani constitution, as well as the deteriorating economic conditions in the country has aggravated these fears.'

In any case, the SRC did not comment on or record any suggestion on the Roy—Sinha proposals as they were never formally submitted to the commission. It was opposed tooth and nail by the communists as well as the Praja Socialist Party.[5] Incidentally, the Congress was compelled to review its stand in view of the intense agitation in Kolkata as well as the defeat of the Congress in nine municipalities (including Barrackpore) and in the North West Calcutta Parliamentary Constituency where pro merger Congress candidate Ashok Sen was trounced by the left-supported West Bengal Linguistic States Redistribution Committee nominee Mohit Moitra. Moreover, the local Congress committees failed to convince their workers about the merit of this proposal. As such, Dr Roy reluctantly withdrew his support to the merger plan on 3 May 1956. Therefore, the final territory of Bengal was largely on the basis of territorial readjustments with respect to the districts of Purnea and Purulia. While Purulia came to West Bengal as the majority population was Bengali-speaking, parts of Purnea were added to meet imperative administrative needs and ensure that there was geographical continuity amongst the districts of West Bengal. This allowed West Bengal to become a geographically compact area, with a direct link between the districts of Darjeeling, Jalpaiguri and Cooch Behar with the rest of the state – a link which was snapped by the partition of India.

Consequential changes in the representation of West Bengal and Bihar in the Lok Sabha and the adjustment of the number of seats in the legislatures of the two states followed. Thus West Bengal's representation in the Lok Sabha increased to thirty-six members from the existing thirty-four. In the Rajya Sabha, West Bengal's representation rose from fourteen to sixteen. However there was no reduction in the number of seats to the Lok Sabha and Rajya Sabha from Bihar or in the Bihar assembly. As far as the Kishanganj sub-division was concerned, the SRC recommended that the West Bengal government should give an assurance about its readiness to continue with the teaching of Urdu in schools in that area. An assurance was also given by West Bengal that as the area was already cramped and congested, no refugees would be allowed to settle there.

It is also interesting to note that Jaipal Singh[6] of the Jharkhand Party was rather keen on the merger of the two states as that would have ensured consolidation of the large number of tribals in Midnapore, Bankura and Birbhum districts of West Bengal. In fact, Jaipal Singh wanted to include Orissa in the proposed Purva Pradesh, as all the tribals would have become the dominant numerical force 'under a single state'.

While the inter-state boundary disputes were resolved in 1956, the India–Pakistan (later Bangladesh) dispute over the enclaves proved to be contentious. As mentioned earlier, Cooch Behar was first constituted as a commissioner's province in September 1949 but merged with West Bengal on 1 January 1950. However, this arrangement left 111 enclaves of Cooch Behar in the erstwhile East Pakistan (now Bangladesh) and fifty-one enclaves of Bangladesh in India. An enclave[7] is an area surrounded by another jurisdiction from all sides, which makes access to the citizens of these areas extremely difficult. In fact, the residents of such areas almost become stateless – for they are deprived of access to health, education, development services as well as protection against crime.

The first attempt to resolve this impasse was made in 1958, when India and Pakistan led by their respective Prime Ministers, Jawaharlal Nehru and Feroze Khan Noon, agreed to mutually exchange the enclaves 'without any consideration of territorial loss or gain'. However, this would have involved transfer of territory and the matter came up before the Calcutta High Court. West Bengal legislator Hem Chandra Sengupta argued that as the Legislative Assembly of Bengal had taken the decision of the western districts joining India and eastern districts joining Pakistan, the territorial integrity of the state could not be compromised with. He also described himself as a citizen of West Bengal. Dismissing his appeal the high court held that both the Constitution of India and the Indian Citizenship Act only recognized an Indian citizen, and though states were a constituent part of India, they had no independent or sovereign existence. The high court also held the view that there was no distinction between Part A and Part B states with respect to alteration of boundaries, and that the Union Parliament was competent to do so. While the President could consult the state governments, the views of the state government were not binding on him.

The President of India then requested the Supreme Court of India for its opinion on whether legislative action was necessary for the implementation of the Nehru–Noon Agreement.[8] The Supreme Court opined that this required a Constitutional Amendment (CSTA) because the exchange of enclaves involved cessation of territory to Bangladesh. Article 1, which defined the territory of India, as well as relevant portions of the First Schedule of the Constitution, would have to be amended.

The Supreme Court further clarified that while Article 3 empowered the Parliament to create a new state or alter the boundary or name of an existing state, it was not competent to cede any part of India.

Accordingly, the Ninth Amendment to the Indian Constitution was introduced but it could not be enforced as serious objections were raised by political parties to the transfer of the Berubari enclave to Pakistan. After the liberation of Bangladesh in 1971, yet another attempt was made under the India–Bangladesh Land Boundary Agreement (LBA) as part of the Indira–Mujib Pact of 1972.[9] However, this agreement also required ratification from the Parliaments of both the countries. While Bangladesh ratified the LBA in 1974, India was able to pass the 119th CSTA on the India–Bangladesh LBA only in 2014.

This also shows that while states under military dictatorship (Pakistan under Ayub Khan in 1959) and unitary states (like Bangladesh) find it easier to seek the necessary ratifications and approvals, it became a bone of political contention between the Union government and the Government of West Bengal especially as the ruling dispensations were different.

However, between the Indira-Mujib pact of 1972 and the 119th CSTA, a pragmatic solution to two of the largest enclaves of Bangladesh in India was offered by the leasing of the Teen Bigha Corridor.[10] Technically, there was no bar to India leasing land to Bangladesh, for lease is neither a surrender nor revocation of sovereign authority. But as the Forward Bloc Party (a constituent of the then Ruling Left Front) had raised the pitch, it required the entire might of the state to 'lease out three bighas' in 1992 to Bangladesh to build a bridge to allow access to the inhabitants of Dahagram and Angorpota for upto six hours a day. In 1996, it was opened up from 'sunrise to sunset', and finally in 2011, the corridor was opened for twenty-four hours to the relief of the residents. The lease rent was Rupee 1 per annum, but as a goodwill gesture, the President of India had decided to waive that as well.

10

QUESTIONS OF BILINGUALISM

While the southern states[1] were quite happy with the reorganization and the Hindi-speaking states[2] were not really affected, the report submitted by the States Reorganization Commission received a very hostile reception in the two bilingual states that still remained, viz. Bombay and Punjab.

We shall first discuss the reception of the report in Bombay, which was the commercial hub of India and as important as New Delhi in terms of media influence. The much-awaited report of the SRC was submitted to the government on 30 September 1955 and released to the press on 10 October. However, the key recommendations had been leaked to the print media of Bombay on 28 September itself, using the cover of informed sources in the government. The Bombay government certainly had an inkling of the contents of the report as prohibitory orders[3] on demonstrations and mass meetings for two weeks were imposed in the cities of Bombay and Poona from 28 September itself. However, even though administrative action prevented an immediate aftermath, the simmering tensions found expression in the coming together of almost all shades of political opinion: the CPI, the Praja Socialist Party, the Mazdoor Kisan Party as well as significant sections of the Maharashtra Congress itself under the banner of Samyukta Maharashtra Samiti.[4] In fact, so strong was the popular upsurge that many leaders of the Congress party broke ranks with their national leadership on this issue. The Communist Party of India also found itself walking on a tight rope, for while the Soviet leadership[5] was cozying up to Nehru, the CPI had, till recently, been in complete favour of linguistic self-determination of states. The communist dilemma was indeed quite unique. For while they welcomed the SRC recommendations with regard to the abolition of states under the raj pramukhs, as well as the establishment of linguistic states for Malayalam, Kannada, Tamil and Telegu speakers, they were quite unsure of what to do with the SRC recommendations with regard to Maharashtra.

Meanwhile, the commission did recommend a Marathi-speaking state of Vidarbha,[6] but Bombay was to be retained as a bilingual state, largely because the decision to delink Bombay from Maharashtra could not be taken. As Marshall Windmiller, a visiting political scientist form the University of California at Berkeley, wrote in the September 1956 edition of the *Far Eastern Survey*, 'Bombay, the hub of India's financial and industrial activity, is the product of Gujarati capital and Maharashtra labour.'

However, the resentment among the Marathi-speaking population was at a crescendo, especially because they harboured the impression that the Marathi-speaking unilingual state (Samyukta Maharashtra) was being denied to them on account of the entrenched interest of the Gujarat faction within the Congress. Inside the Bombay state legislature, 111 of 118 Congress Marathi representatives submitted their resignations. The dogmatic statements and stern attitude of Morarji Desai, the then chief minister of Bombay did not help, and the leadership of the Maharashtra PCC itself found it difficult to endorse the decision of the Congress high command.

The Union finance minister, C.D. Deshmukh,[7] resigned from the Cabinet and accused Prime Minster Nehru of 'cavalier and unconstitutional methods'.[8] Passions ran high and violent agitations ensued in Bombay which became quite uncontrollable. There were two distinct phases of violence, first in November 1955 and then in January 1956. In the former, there were at least ten deaths, and in the latter over a hundred by conservative estimates. Meanwhile, the Congress Working Committee (CWC) tried to bring about many a compromise formula, but the main contention was Bombay city, and the dominant view in the Congress high command was that Bombay should be made a Union Territory, which is what the Gujarat MPs wanted. This was, of course, totally opposed by the Samayukta Maharashtra Parishad.

What is interesting to note is that neither the Congress nor the Communist Party could take a clear pan-India position on linguistic states. Even if the national leadership wanted to it could not, because elections had to be fought in the state and voters had to be mobilized on issues that affected them on the ground, rather than on abstract principles.

For the Congress, the biggest challenge lay in the leadership contest amongst their own stalwarts: Morarji Desai from Gujarat, S.K. Patil from Bombay, Shankar Rao Deo and Yashwantrao Chavan from Maharashtra. They were all pulling the party in different directions.

Incidentally, as mentioned earlier, one of the first, and more well-thought-out, representations to the Linguistic Provinces Commission[9] was submitted by Dr Ambedkar[10] in 1948. In the document, 'Maharashtra as a Linguistic Province', he had argued that Bombay as a mixed state consisting of Maharashtra, Gujarat and Bombay should be done away with, and that the state of Maharashtra be divided into four states having Bombay city, western Maharashtra, central Maharashtra and eastern Maharashtra. Among all of them, the most disputed subject was the fate of Bombay city, but Ambedkar preferred this option, not just to prevent the pressures from both Gujaratis and Maharashtrians, but also as a safe haven for the minorities and the schedules castes – the minorities need an asylum, a place of refuge, where they can be free from the tyranny of the majority. If there was a united Maharashtra with Bombay included in it, where can they go for safety?

Meanwhile, lest this impression gain ground that only the Samyukta Maharashtra Movement (SMM) was keen on a unilingual Maharashtra, it should be pointed out that the movement for a linguistic state of Gujarat found its first expression in the 1920s, when Gandhi set up a separate provincial Congress committee for Gujarat, Kathiawar and Kutch. This sentiment was echoed during the inauguration of Saurashtra[11] at Jamnagar on 15 February 1948, by Home Minister Sardar Vallabhbhai Patel, who said 'our dream has been realized, namely, the United States of Kathiawar. The next objective should be to attract the neighbouring states, including Kutch, and pave the way for the ultimate realization of a greater dream – a Mahagujarat – which you can achieve by being strong and self-reliant. You must realize that the freedom which you have won also entails responsibilities.'

After the passing away of Sardar Patel, the Gujarat Congress felt abandoned by the Congress high command. Certainly, no one else could have stepped into his shoes. This sense of neglect became sharper after Independence when the First Five Year Plan did not approve any major river projects for Mahi, Narmada and Tapi. These perceptions coupled with the sense that resources were being channelled to the Maratha-speaking areas culminated in the Mahagujarat movement of 1956. Whatever be the empirical reality of resource allocation, the fact was that both Maharashtrians and Gujaratis felt discriminated against. In a Parliamentary debate in 1956, Shantaram More stated, 'Take the seats in the Cabinet. Take the Congress working committee. Who has the greatest domination? The Gujaratis have the greatest domination, not only in the working committee, but also in the Cabinet.'

Unlike Bombay where the mass mobilization was done by the communists, PSP and the trade unions, the Gujarat movement was led by students and citizens active in the cultural and educational sphere. The turning point came in August 1956 when the students marched to the Congress House, asking for a separate state of Gujarat. Rather than listening to them, the chief minister of Bombay (Morarji Desai, himself a Gujarati) responded with police action, and five students lost their lives. The movement took a decisive turn when Indu Lal Yagnik, the legendary leader of the Kisan Sabha – and the amanuensis to Mahatma Gandhi in Yerawada jail for the first thirty chapters of the latter's autobiography – stepped out of his retirement to lead the agitation. Many leaders of the old guard, including Vidyaben Neelkanth, Shardaben Mehta and Dinkar Mehta not only condemned the Congress, but also supported the movement. The leadership role of the redoubtable women of the Gujarat Congress needs a special mention.

Meanwhile, the Congress realized that its commitment to 'Bilingual Bombay' cost them dearly in the 1957 elections at all levels – municipal, zila panchayat, state and Lok Sabha. It is true that in 1956 Nehru had gone on record to say, 'Let the elections go to hell. I am tired of listening to talks of pleasing this party and that party. To base one's actions and policies on election prospects is the mentality of weak-minded men.'[12] This was a time when the Congress high command was quite convinced of its ability to contain dissension in its ranks.

However, as politics is all about retaining (and expanding) power, there was a volte face in the position of Congress in the aftermath of the 1957 general elections.[13] This was actually the first major electoral debacle faced by the Congress as all those in favour of the unilingual Maharashtra with Bombay came together under the banner of the SMM and swept the Parliamentary, assembly and corporation elections. The Congress did not fare well even amongst the cosmopolitan electorate of Bombay, and was trounced in 'hundreds of panchayats, and scores of municipalities and district boards'.[14] It did retain its influence in the erstwhile Marathwada region of Hyderabad, and partial support in Vidarbha, many of whose legislators would have preferred to go by the SRC recommendation.

Finally, on 1 May 1960, the two states came into existence amidst widespread enthusiasm, bursting of firecrackers and celebratory processions. Prime Minister Nehru took it upon himself to inaugurate the Maharashtra state which saw Yashwantrao Chavan[15] as the chief minister, while for Gujarat the honour of inaugurating the state was extended to Ravishankar Maharaj,[16] and Jivraj Mehta[17] became first chief minister.

For Gujarat, it was a moment of glory, for its identity had been merged 140 ago, first with Bombay Presidency under the British, then the province of Bombay under the dominion and finally the state of Bombay under the republic. For the Maharashtrians, the celebrations commenced quite a few days earlier with illuminations, forts with turrets, gates, watch towers made of bamboo, cloth and paper: it marked, in a way, the return of the reign of Shivaji Maratha! And the iconic Flora Fountain was renamed Hutatma Chowk in memory of the 106 individuals who laid down their lives in the cause of a unilingual Maharashtra with Bombay as the capital.

~

Punjab

Post-World War II, one of the regions in the world that continued to witness bloodshed, violence and political tumult for the next two decades was Punjab. Punjab had been one of the most prosperous provinces of British India, and its boundary extended from Delhi to Dera Ghazi Khan and Rawalpindi (now in Pakistan) to Lahaul Spiti on the borders of Ladakh. However, from 1946 to 1966, the map of Punjab was redrawn several times – and nine politico-administrative units emerged. These included the states of East Punjab, PEPSU, Haryana, the three Union Territories of Chandigarh, Himachal and New Delhi (in India) and West Punjab, Islamabad Capital Territory[18] and One Unit in Pakistan.[19] In fact, the One Unit scheme of Pakistan, which lasted from 1955 to 1970, briefly extinguished the state of Punjab as also Sindh, Baluchistan[20] and NWFP[21] from the geography of Pakistan.

It is interesting to note that just about the time when India was reorganizing its states – acknowledging the linguistic and ethnic aspirations of the people – Pakistan was doing the exact opposite. The 'One Unit' was a brainchild of Mohammed Ali Bogra[22] and Iskander Mirza[23] who argued that having just two geographical units – West and East Pakistan – would end provincial prejudice, reduce administrative expenditure, rationalize resource allocation besides creating parity between the two units. Lahore[24] became the capital of the One Unit of West Pakistan, Dhaka continued to be the capital of the eastern part (which was not really affected), but Sindh felt disenfranchised as the national capital was moved from Karachi[25] to Rawalpindi[26] which became the interim capital till Islamabad could be established as the new capital of Pakistan.

Meanwhile, on the Indian side of Punjab, the agitation for a separate Khalsa Raj[27] (Sikh state) had started even before Independence. 'The Sikhs had been loyal to the British (Master Tara Singh had supported the War effort, even as Congress had given the Quit India call) but they had been abandoned by the British, tolerated by the Congress, taunted by the Muslim League and, above all, frustrated by the failures of their own political leadership. And when East Punjab was constituted, they found that they were again in a minority, and were keen to establish a place where they could exercise unbridled political authority.'[28] Towards this end, a delegation of Sikh leaders comprising Harcharan Singh Bajwa, Bhupinder Singh Mann and Giani Kartar Singh met Dr Ambedkar in January 1948 who advised them to ask for a linguistic rather than a Sikh state. In the aftermath of Partition, the Sikhs were in a majority in the contiguous districts of Amritsar, Gurdaspur, Ferozepur, Kapurthala, Jullundur (as it was then called), Ludhiana, Bhatinda and Patiala, and in substantial parts of Ambala and Sangrur, but the rest of the province was dominated by the Hindus, whose numbers had swelled on account of the incoming refugee population.

Punjab and Bengal were the two Muslim majority provinces where the Hindu minority was as keen on Partition as the Muslims of United Provinces and Bihar. Punjab was a prosperous province; the canal colonies had ushered in unprecedented wealth and the Unionist Party representing the landowners, with explicit patronage of the government, exercised greater salience in public polity than the Congress or the Muslim League in the limited franchise then available. All the princely states – from the Muslim majority Bahawalpur to the Sikh kingdoms of Patiala and the Hindu kingdoms of Punjab Hills states – were pro-British and Punjab continued to be a preferred recruitment base for the British troops in both the Wars, though by the late '30s, Pathans started to get preference over the Sikhs.

However, Punjab also had its share of agrarian unrest – the Ghadar movement amongst expats and the revolutionary stream under the Hindustan Socialist Republican Army (HSRA)[29] of Bhagat Singh, Sukhdev and Rajguru fired public imagination like never before. These movements brought the three major communities together, though not in equal measure. But these were put down with a heavy hand. All the three communities had contributed to the growth of Lahore – the Paris of the East – and like the contested city of Jerusalem, it was much more than a piece of land.

Unlike other parts of the country, there had been no major communal clashes in the Punjab till 1946. However, the simmering tensions between the three communities found an assertion in their preferred language: for the Muslims it was Urdu[30] which, like Arabic, is written from right to left; for the Sikhs, it was the Gurumukhi[31] script, which was given to them by Guru Angad Dev; and for the Hindus, it was Devanagari, the language of the gods.[32]

When it became clear by the end of 1946 that Partition was inevitable, the volcano erupted. While the Muslims of Punjab did not want Pakistan, they were not opposed to it. But, for the Hindus of Lahore and the Sikhs of the canal colonies, the thought of having to uproot themselves from the tracts they had made fertile with their sweat and blood, as well as Nankana Sahib,[33] was absolutely unthinkable.

When the SRC was appointed, the Akali Dal made a strong plea for the Punjabi Suba to the SRC by seeking the merger of PEPSU with contiguous Punjabi-speaking districts and by detaching the Pahadi-speaking areas to Himachal and Hindi-speaking areas to Delhi/Haryana (as it was then called). While PEPSU was merged with Punjab, the Hindi-speaking areas were not detached, and it continued to be a bilingual state for another decade.

When the States Reorganization Committee Report was released on 30 September 1955, Punjab was ravaged by rains and floods of unprecedented intensity. Master Tara Singh of the Akali Dal reacted violently: 'A decree of Sikh annihilation has been passed by the SRC. We are face to face with a calamity greater than that of 1947 ... The report of the SRC wipes us out from the face of the world. With faith in God and our Gurus, we shall fight with our backs to the wall.'

This did not please the protagonists for Haryana Prant either for at least two MPs and over a dozen legislators of the Punjab and Delhi assemblies insisted on the establishment of Haryana with the Hindi-speaking areas of PEPSU, Punjab, Himachal, the Agra and Meerut divisions of UP and Bikaner from Rajasthan. The principal argument was that the Delhi division of the North-Western Provinces[34] was gifted to the Punjab only after 1857 as a reward for their loyalty to the British during the First War of Independence.

Likewise, the majority verdict of the SRC recommending the merger of the hill districts of Himachal with Punjab was received with grief and frustration, especially because as a chief commissioner's province from 1952, it had its own Legislative Assembly and council of ministers. However, it is important to point out that the chairman of the SRC gave his dissenting note against the merger of Himachal with Punjab and wanted it to be retained under the Centre.

The main criticism of the SRC report was that the recommendations on Punjab were just a minor modification of the Maha Punjab demand by the Hindu organizations, notably the Jana Sangh, the RSS and the Arya Samaj. The Punjab Congress committee gave freedom to their members to give their own individual representations to the SRC, but the official position of Punjab government was more in alignment with the views of the Hindu Congress members and Jana Sangh which favoured something akin to Maha Punjab.

Though they had received initial support from the Hindi-speaking Hindus of Haryana, they were now more inclined towards a separate Haryana, for they felt that they were being dominated by the Punjabis. Speaking in the Parliament in December 1955, Thakur

Das Bhargava[35] showed that the representation from Haryana region was less than 6 per cent in the higher echelons of the state's political, judicial and administrative set-up.

The sense of discrimination was quite deep-rooted and predates the Independence movement. As early as 1923, the idea of a separate Haryana Prant comprising Delhi, Ambala division of Punjab, besides the Agra and Meerut divisions of UP, was mooted by Swami Satya Nand, Chaudhari Shadi Ram and Suraj Mal who persuaded the then Unionist leader and agriculture minister of Punjab, Sir Chhotu Ram,[36] to preside over the All India Jat conference. The conference demanded a separate province of Delhi comprising the districts of Ambala, Agra, Meerut besides the districts of Moradabad, Saharanpur, Bijnor, Pilibhit and Badayun in United Provinces, and Alwar, Dholpur and Bharatpur in Rajasthan. This was reiterated in 1928 by an all-parties conference in Delhi and submitted as a memorial to Sir J.P. Thompson, the chief commissioner of Delhi. Lala Desh Bandhu, the erudite editor of *Tej* said, 'The Hindi speaking region has never really been a part of Punjab. Ever since its inclusion in Punjab, this region has been suffering economically, politically, and culturally. It was essential for the development of this region to separate it from Punjab proper and form a new state by uniting with it certain adjoining parts of Delhi, Rajasthan and UP.'[37]

In fact, the proposal for formation of Haryana on these lines was put up before the Indian Statutory Commission (Simon Commission) – but the separation of Ambala and Delhi from Punjab would have upset the fragile denominational balance among Muslims, Hindus and Sikhs. Moreover, it was felt that 'Delhi as the capital of India, should remain as at present, a unity by itself unaffected by leanings and prejudices of other provincial units' (Simon Commission). Mahatma Gandhi was presented with the demand for a separate province of Haryana in 1931 when his train stopped at Badli railway station. It was mentioned that

'Ambala division is not irrigated from the five rivers of Punjab but from the Jamuna system, on which the adjoining districts of UP are also dependent'.[38] The separation of Haryana from Punjab was vociferously opposed by Pandit Madan Mohan Malviya[39] and Master Tara Singh as well. While Malviya did not like the idea of detachment of any part of UP, Master Tara Singh felt that it would make Punjab 'overwhelmingly Muslim' if the Ambala division was taken out of Punjab.

After 1947, Master Tara Singh sought an autonomous region for the Sikhs – but the question of linguistic reorganization of states was put on the backburner by the Linguistic Provinces Commission, as also by the JVP Committee. To a large extent, the conflict between the Hindi- and Punjabi-speaking regions of Punjab was resolved by the Sachar[40] Formula which stipulated that Hindi in the Devanagari script and Punjabi in the Gurumukhi script would both be recognized as the regional languages of the province, and the state itself was divided into Hindi- and Punjabi-speaking zones. The Hindi zone comprised Rohtak, Gurgaon, Karnal and Kangra districts, as well as a portion of Hissar lying in the south of Ghaggar river, besides the Jagadhari and Naraingarh tehsils of Ambala. The Punjabi-speaking zone had Amritsar, Jullundur, Gurdaspur, Ferozepur, Ludhiana and Hoshiarpur districts, all portions of Hissar district lying to the east of Ferozepur and the Patiala side of Ghaggar river, besides Ropar and Kharar tehsils of Ambala district. Simla and Ambala tehsils were declared to be bilingual.

The Sachar Formula was acceptable to the Akali Dal – but faced severe criticism from the Hindu organizations like the Arya Samaj, Hindu Mahasabha and the Jana Sangh. Nehru supported the Sachar Formula for he was opposed to the immediate reorganization of states – he felt that this was important, but not urgent. At a public rally at Patiala in 1952, he said, 'I will not allow India to be divided again. I will not allow any further trouble. If there's trouble in any part of India, I would put it down with all my strength.'[41] However, Nehru had to backtrack from this statement after Potti Sriramulu's fast unto death for the separate Telugu-speaking state of Andhra later that year.

As a matter of fact, the Sachar Formula had 'seeded' the possibility of the Hindi-speaking state of Haryana, and it received a fillip when the SRC was appointed. So, while on the one hand the Akali Dal presented the demand seeking a separate Punjabi-speaking area, and by implication a Hindi-speaking Haryana and a Pahari-speaking Himachal (which was already a UT) the Communist Party and Praja Socialist Party also sought the reorganization of the state on linguistic lines.

Master Tara Singh and the Akalis were not alone in condemning the SRC recommendations with respect to the Hindi- and Pahari-speaking regions of Punjab. Prof. Sher Singh, Sriram Sharma and Dr N.M. Jessore rallied together in favour of Haryana and said that 'ninety percent of the people of Haryana were of the opinion that they should have no connection whatsoever with Punjab'.[42] Perhaps, the best comment came from Bahadur Singh who stated on the floor of the Lok Sabha, 'as far as Northern India is concerned, the recommendations of the Commission are totally incorrect, contradictory and unconvincing. The people demanded Punjabi speaking state, Haryana, and Himachal Pradesh, but the Commission has recommended the formation of a Maha Punjab, with the integration of Punjab, PEPSU and Himachal Pradesh.'

Just as it appeared that Punjab was on the brink of an administrative collapse and breakdown of the law and order machinery, Pratap Singh Kairon, the prosperous and enterprising Jat Sikh, educated at Colonel Brown's school at Dehradun, Khalsa College Amritsar[43] and at Michigan and Berkeley in the US, took over as the chief minister of Punjab, and for the next eight years, ruled it with an iron fist. Under his leadership, the Regional

Formula was put into practice in both the linguistic units (Hindi- and Punjabi-speaking) and regional committees, consisting of MLAs belonging to each region, constituted to deal with specific matters.

The Akali Dal accepted this proposition – for this was in many ways the implicit acceptance of the Punjabi Suba. Kairon also played the Jat Sikh card, opened the membership of the Congress to the Akalis and sidelined Master Tara Singh by propping up Sant Fateh Singh. While both sat on 'fasts-unto-death', their withdrawal on 'general assurances of goodwill' did not enhance their reputations. The Master had led the movement for over three decades but found that on account of his Khatri birth and urban background, the rural Jat Sikhs who now held sway in the Akali and SGPC referred to him derisively as a Bhapa Sikh (one who has migrated from Pakistan) – a rather sad commentary on the state of politics across party lines in the country. The Regional Formula did not work, but Kairon's firm grip on the state ensured that all protest movements – from the Akali Morchas to the Save Hindi protests – were put down with an iron hand. That was not all: Kairon also laid the foundation of the Green Revolution[44] in rural areas as well as industrial estates[45] in the urban areas, thereby building successful alliances with the vocal and dominant sections of both the communities.

While Sant Fateh Singh had started out as the Master's protégé, he soon understood that politics is about building bridges and speaking the right thing at the right time to the right audience. He always spoke of Punjabi, rather than a Sikh Suba, and during the 1962 and 1965 wars, he offered his unconditional support, leveraging the fact that Punjabis and Sikhs were very well represented in the army – both as soldiers and officers. After the war, a Cabinet committee headed by Lok Sabha Speaker Hukam Singh, which included Y.B. Chavan and Indira Gandhi, was appointed to make a recommendation on Punjabi Suba. Given the popular mood and support from most sections, including the

Hindu legislators from Haryana and Himachal, the Hukam Singh committee recommended that the Punjabi-speaking region be reconstituted into a unilingual Punjabi state, Hindi-speaking areas into the Haryana state, and the hill areas of erstwhile Punjab be merged into Himachal.

This was the triumph of Punjabi Suba over Maha Punjab. And of course, the state of Haryana and the Union Territory of Himachal Pradesh.

~

The difference between the *truth* and the *whole truth* is best illustrated by the oft-repeated comment that Himachal Pradesh is the fallout of the Punjabi Suba agitation. This is true, but it does not consider the aspirations and the struggles of the people of the princely states for participatory democracy and the merger of the states with the Union of India. In fact, even though the Congress had been supporting the activities of the All India State's Peoples Congress (AISPC) (Praja Mandal) it was only in the Haripura session[46] of the Congress in 1938 under the leadership of Subhas Bose that 'states were declared as an integral part of India, whose Purna Swaraj was as much its object, as for the rest of India'. In 1939, the idea of forming Praja Mandals was conceived in the session of All India State Peoples' Conference at Ludhiana, and the Himalayan Riasti Praja Mandal was made responsible for directing the activities of the political workers in Chamba, Sirmaur, Mandi, Bushahr, Sundernagar and other princely states. It was a daunting task, as the rulers were dependent for their *gaddi*, their seat of power, not on the goodwill of the people but the patronage of the Raj.

In the aftermath of Independence, the rulers of the hill states met in Delhi in January 1948 and proposed a union of states for the Himalayan region, but when the Raja of Mandi called on the Mahatma the latter advised them to call a joint meeting of the Praja

Mandals and the rulers to deliberate on this. A meeting was indeed held at Solan later that month, but it was confined to the Shimla Hill states only. The name Himachal Pradesh was coined there. Because of the opposition of the dominant faction of Praja Mandal led by Dr Y.S. Parmar,[47] the ministry of states (under Patel and Menon) refused to acknowledge its formation, and the Praja Mandal supporters started an agitation for the merger of the states with the Union of India (rather than amalgamation on the lines of PEPSU). The Raja of Suket, Lakshman Sen, was the first to capitulate, and all others, with the exception of Bilaspur, viz. Chamba, Mandi, Bushahr and its tributaries Kaneti and Delath; Keonthal and its tributaries Koti, Theog, Madhan, Ghund and Ratesh; Baghat, Jubbal with its tributaries Rawin and Dhadi; Kumarsain, Bhajji, Mahlog, Balsan, Hami, Kuthar, Kunihar, Mangal, Beja, Darkoti, Tharoch, Sangri and Sirmaur followed suit. This led to the formation of the chief commissioner's province of Himachal Pradesh, but this was not to the liking of Dr Parmar who felt that unlike other parts of the country, those in the forefront of the freedom movement were being denied the role of political leadership. Three years later, a partial democratic set-up was introduced with a Legislative Assembly with limited powers under a lieutenant governor, but controlled by the President of India. The first lieutenant governor of Himachal was Major General Himmat Sinhji, a royal from Nawanagar who was a distinguished sportsman and cricketer.

Another important milestone in the consolidation of Himachal was the merger of Bilaspur in 1954. Its ruler, Aman Chand, had insisted on being the first chief commissioner, and the Government of India conceded this point as the Bhakra Nangal site was in Bilaspur.

However, it was still a truncated Himachal, as Shimla, the summer capital of India from 1864 to 1947, as well as of East Punjab from 1947 to 1960, besides the hill areas of Kangra, Kullu, Lahaul and Spiti were still under Punjab. Most of the Dogra Paltan[48] of the British Army was recruited from that region.

Meanwhile, in the aftermath of Independence, *begar* (compulsory labour without any payment) was abolished, *bethu* (free service to the landlord in lieu of homestead land) was regulated and the pernicious practice of *reet* (state sanctions and tax for purchase of women for purposes of matrimony) was banned. The introduction of commercial crops like apple and potato brought about a major change in the agricultural economy of the state.

As mentioned earlier, the SRC report of 1955 caused substantial consternation in the hills as the majority verdict sought its merger with Punjab. However, the chairman of the commission, Fazal Ali, in his dissenting note[49] said that given the communal situation and the law-and-order problem in Punjab, it made better sense for this region to retain its identity. The fear of a potential merger with Punjab continued to haunt the people of Himachal till the Punjab Boundary Commission[50] headed by Justice Shah recommended that the districts of Kangra, Shimla, Lahaul, Spiti besides the Una tehsil of Hoshiarpur in Punjab, should be transferred to Himachal on account of geographical continuity and lingual affinity.

The territorial consolidation of the state was complete by 1966, but it took another five years for the ultimate dream of the hill people to have their own state. Finally, a unanimous resolution of the Himachal Assembly House for the transition from a UT to a state was adopted by the Union Parliament, and Himachal became a state one day before the twenty-first anniversary of the Indian Republic.

11

THE END OF FOREIGN JURISDICTIONS

Three strips of black tape were pasted on the 1961 edition of the Map of India, published by the Survey of India, as it had been printed before 18 December, the day operation Vijay[1] saw the liberation of Goan territories from the Portuguese, and their final merger with India.

Operation Vijay had been a very smooth operation led by Gen. J.N. Chaudhary[2] of Operation Polo (Hyderabad fame) and lasted just about twenty-eight hours – the operation started at 0930 hours on the 17 December; the Portuguese began their retreat by 1230 hours on 18th; and the first batch of troops surrendered at 1530 hours. The Instrument of Surrender was signed at 2 p.m. on 19 December by Portuguese governor general Manuel Antonio Vassalo e Silva[3] at Vasco da Gama[4], the then capital of Goa.

However, the moot point about the liberation of Goa is not about what happened in December 1961, but why it took India so long to settle the Goan question, especially because the freedom movement in Goa had taken roots as early as 1928 when T.B.

Cunha[5] founded the Goa Congress Committee.[6] Just as the rest of India was protesting against the visit of Simon Commission, the Goans were agitating against the 1930 Colonial Act of Portugal[7] which made a clear distinction between Portugal and the overseas territories. Meanwhile, the Congress played an important role in getting back the Kunbi[8] workers of Goa from the British plantations in Assam, where they were working in 'miserable, and slave like conditions'. During his presidency in 1938, Subhas Bose established the Provisional Goa Congress Committee[9] in Bombay to work with the parent body in Goa for restoration of civil liberties and to agitate for responsible government in Goa. In March 1946, the resolution of the Goa Congress read, 'The Goa Congress committee adheres to the national call of Quit India demand of the INC and calls upon the Portuguese to leave the shores of Goa, Daman and Diu, so that we can achieve our destiny in common with the rest of India.'

In 1946, the first civil disobedience movement against the Portuguese rule was launched in Goa under the leadership of Dr Lohia,[10] and for the first time the Goan nationalists and Indian freedom fighters held hands to break the artificial divide between Goans and Indians. Mahatma Gandhi wrote in the *Harijan*,[11] 'He (Lohia) has thereby rendered a service to the cause of civil liberty and specially to the Goans. The small Portuguese settlement, which merely exists on the sufferance of the British government, can ill afford to ape its bad manners.' However, according to Durga Das,[12] a contemporary chronicler of history, there was some difference of opinion among the Indian leaders about the timing for liberating the foreign possessions of India. Patel wanted immediate action, but Nehru and Gandhi were willing to enter into diplomatic parleys with the French and the Portuguese.

However, much to the consternation of the Goan nationalists, the Foreign Office of India was taking a 'legalistic view'. It was obvious that while the nationalists looked at Goa as an internal issue, Prime Minister Nehru and the foreign ministry were quite fine with seeking international mediation on this. Much was made of our opposition to Portugal's membership of the UN, but finally Portugal did secure a place in the UN, and promptly filed a case against India with the International Court of Justice (ICJ)[13] in 1955 about its right of passage to Dadra and Nagar Haveli. Both India and Portugal claimed victory, for while the ICJ upheld the Portuguese claim, it denied them the right of passage to their positions in Dadra and Nagar Haveli.

The case is interesting, for it also shows that while the MEA was engaged in diplomatic niceties, Goanese activists under the banner of Azad Gomantak Dal[14] from Bombay marched to Dadra in the midnight of 21 July 1954, took over the police station and hoisted the tricolour. Later, they were joined by the volunteers of the RSS and Goa Peoples Party[15] and the Indian flag was unfurled at Silvassa on 2 August 1954. From 1954 to 1961, the 'Varishta Panchayat of Free Dadra and Nagar Haveli'[16] held sway. The Varishta Panchayat, having already voted to join India that June, appointed the administrator K.G. Badlani,[17] a member of the IAS, as the Prime Minister, putting him on par with Nehru, and a legal signatory to the Document of Accession to India on 11 August 1961.

Earlier, Portugal had tried its best to play the victim card in the context of Dadra and Nagar Haveli, shedding off the colonial yoke by popular will in July–August 1954. The Salazar regime tried to mobilize opinion amongst their NATO allies,[18] especially the UK, which found itself on a rather sticky wicket: for while the sovereigns of England and Portugal had signed several treaties of eternal support and co-operation, the Queen was also the head of the Commonwealth,[19] and India was the 'jewel'! Even as it treaded cautiously, trying to balance both sides, India took umbrage and the British press reported 'Nehru's Snub to Britain',[20] while Portugal protested that the BBC[21] coverage had been pro-India.

This dispatch from UK's Lisbon Mission (2 August 1954) says it all: 'The Portuguese are not foolish as to imagine that the UK would go to war with India. All they ask us to do is to bring home to the Indian government that their present behaviour is such as to benefit no one in the long run but the Russians.'

In a bid to de-escalate the tension, India did accept the Portuguese proposal (8 August 1954) of a joint team of observers with three to be nominated by each side, but this never got off the ground because of procedural issues. Portugal had in fact approached Denmark, Belgium, Canada, Brazil, Argentina, Chile, Switzerland, Luxembourg, the US, the UK, Italy and Vatican.[22] But the UK developed cold feet for it realized that if this principle were to be accepted, there would be many more Joint Observers in its existing colonies. Once this became a global issue, opinions were divided on predicted lines, with Belgium, Italy, Chile, South Africa, Brazil, Spain, Argentine and the 'Holy See' making oral representations to the Government of India and the USSR, China, Nepal, Iraq and Burma coming out to defend the Indian position. Egypt was guarded in its response. Canada agreed to take up the matter privately with Nehru, but recused itself from the Joint Observers' team.

A perusal of the now unclassified confidential documents also shows that Salazar did consider a 'frontier modification'[23] : surrender of Dadra and Nagar Haveli in lieu of a formal Indian recognition over Goa, Daman and Diu. Fortunately, this was not seriously followed up by the UK or any other government, and there was no formal proposal made in this regard. The public opinion of India would have been aghast, for the entire opposition (PSP, CPI, Jana Sangh, Swatantra Party) and the Goan nationalists led by T.B. Cunha and P.D. Gaitonde,[24] among others, were anguished by the 'legalistic' interpretations of Nehru and his team. They pointed out that less than 50,000 of the 6,38,000 eligible voters of Goa, Daman and Diu chose to exercise their ballot in the elections called by the Portuguese state in 1955.

Writing in *Free Goa* of 25 May 1957, T.B. Cunha said, 'The Prime Minister's statement about the Portuguese possessions in India betrays a perplexed state of mind and shows a lack of determination on the part of the government.' Efforts at economic blockade of Goa were not successful as the Karachi port became active to extend logistics support for import of oil and export of minerals.

Meanwhile, the Afro-Asian bloc under the NAM[25] and the UN Trusteeship Council were putting tremendous pressure on Portugal, and it was finding itself increasingly isolated. On 15 December 1960, the UN General Assembly voted overwhelmingly (sixty-eight to six with seventeen abstentions) that Portugal was obliged under the UN charter to furnish a report on its colonial territories (including Goa). This gave India the confidence to pass the legislation to incorporate Dadra and Nagar Haveli into India on 11 August 1961. Meanwhile, the construction of the Berlin Wall[26] began on 13 August and the attention of US and NATO shifted to the European theatre. The US made it clear to Portugal that its military assistance was only in the context of NATO. This was quite a relief for India, and on 17 August Nehru informed the Parliament that 'the steps for the liberation of Goa could include the use of Indian Army at the appropriate time'.[27] Soon thereafter at the Belgrade NAM conference in September, he came under fire from the African delegates for not doing enough to liberate Goa, which would signal the end of Portuguese colonies in Africa. Thus, by the time he returned to India, the die had been cast and instructions were given to the Indian Army to take steps for Operation Vijay, which lasted around twenty-eight hours.

The French Settlement in India

Unlike the difficult and contested transfer of Portuguese enclaves (Goa, Daman, Diu and Dadra and Nagar Haveli), the settlement with the French was smooth, though not without its share of problems. As early as 28 August 1947, India and France issued a joint declaration to resolve the question of settlements, taking into account the 'aspirations and interests of the people'. For India, it meant that they would eventually negotiate the peaceful transfer of the five settlements (*comptoirs*): Pondicherry, Chandernagore, Karikal, Mahe and Yaman, covering a little over 200 square miles of territory with a population of less than three lakh. In popular Indian imagination, the French settlements had provided asylum to Indian revolutionaries and freedom fighters – from Aurobindo Ghosh[28] to Subramania Bharathi.[29]

Scattered along the Eastern coast, linguistically these settlements had much more in common with their British Indian neighbours than with each other; there was free movement of people from Chandernagore to Calcutta and Pondicherry, Karikal, Mahe and Yaman to Madras for work and education. In fact, 'the geographical marginality of these enclaves made them invisible in Indian historiography'[30] but from the point of France, their future was linked to their colonial possessions elsewhere, especially IndoChina.[31]

With the advent of freedom for India on 15 August 1947, the popular mood in the French territories was overwhelmingly in favour of a merger. The ferment was strongest in Chandernagore[32] (August 1947/March 1948) and Mahe (October 48) where popular demonstrations gave way to full-fledged rebellions. As the situation in Chandernagore was getting out of hand, the French government held a plebiscite in Chandernagore in June 1948 in which 97 per cent of the electors opted to join India. However, Mahatma Gandhi, the Constituent Assembly and the Government of India were all convinced that the process of transfer should be a negotiated settlement under the auspices of the Government of India – for there was a genuine fear that such movements could be driven by the communists or other fissiparous parties.

The suspicions of the Government of India with regard to the communists and a section of the socialists were not unfounded because a part of the politically conscious electors in the enclaves saw in the Fourth French Republic,[33] established in 1946 after WWII, the possibility of achieving greater autonomy besides higher representation in the French Senate and Assembly. This brought all the local political parties, the communists, nationalists and socialists together under the banner of the National Democratic Front (NDF),[34] which won all the thirty-four seats. These included the communist leader Subbiah[35] and socialist leader Sarvanae.[36] However, after Independence, the NDF faced a fierce ideological contest, with the communists coming out in favour of an immediate merger with India, but Sarvanae and Goubert,[37] a French Indian lawyer, sought autonomy within the French Union. The communist support for the merger was also not unconditional – for while they were all for liquidation of the French Imperialism, they were also struggling against the collaborationist Indian Union government, and working for the establishment of a people. Meanwhile, the Muslim League of French India sought a separate electorate for Muslims in the referendum on the future of these settlements, claiming that their population was at least one third, and that Muslims had fled Chandernagore for Pondicherry after its merger with India. The Indian consul general in Pondicherry mentioned in his reports that most Muslims in French India harboured pro-Pakistani sympathies, which were being exploited by the French for anti-merger purposes. Last, but not the least, there was the very strong Dravidian movement in south India, and two newspapers,

Velli[38] in Tamil and *Republique Francaise* in French, strongly advocated French India as an integral part of the proposed Dravidistan.

As Akhila Yechury[39] put it: 'In a period when the integration of princely states was not yet complete, and the problem of Kashmir loomed large, India's uncertain future found a reflection in French India.'[40]

However, all of this convinced Indian officials that going in for a plebiscite would be akin to opening Pandora's Box, because the possibility of an autonomous region within the French Union was also becoming distinct. However, with the rout of the French at Dien Bien Phu[41] in May 1954 – the first time a major colonial power was defeated in open warfare – the French lost their nerve, and the most vocal supporters of autonomy within France realized that the future was with India. In a clearly opportunistic move, the Socialist Party's vocal leader Goubert decided to cast his lot with India. Therefore, on 18 October 1954, of the 178 delegates of French India, 170 voted in favour of the merger. On 1 November, Pondicherry, Yanam, Mahe and Karikal were de facto transferred to the Indian Union, and became the Union Territory of Pondicherry to be administered under the Foreign Jurisdiction Act of 1947. The *de jure* union of French India with India took place in 1962 after the ratification of the French Parliament.

Incidentally, the Foreign Jurisdiction Act[42] was repealed only five years ago, on 13 May 2015, when the Indian Parliament was officially informed that from 1962, no territory of India was under the control of any colonial power.

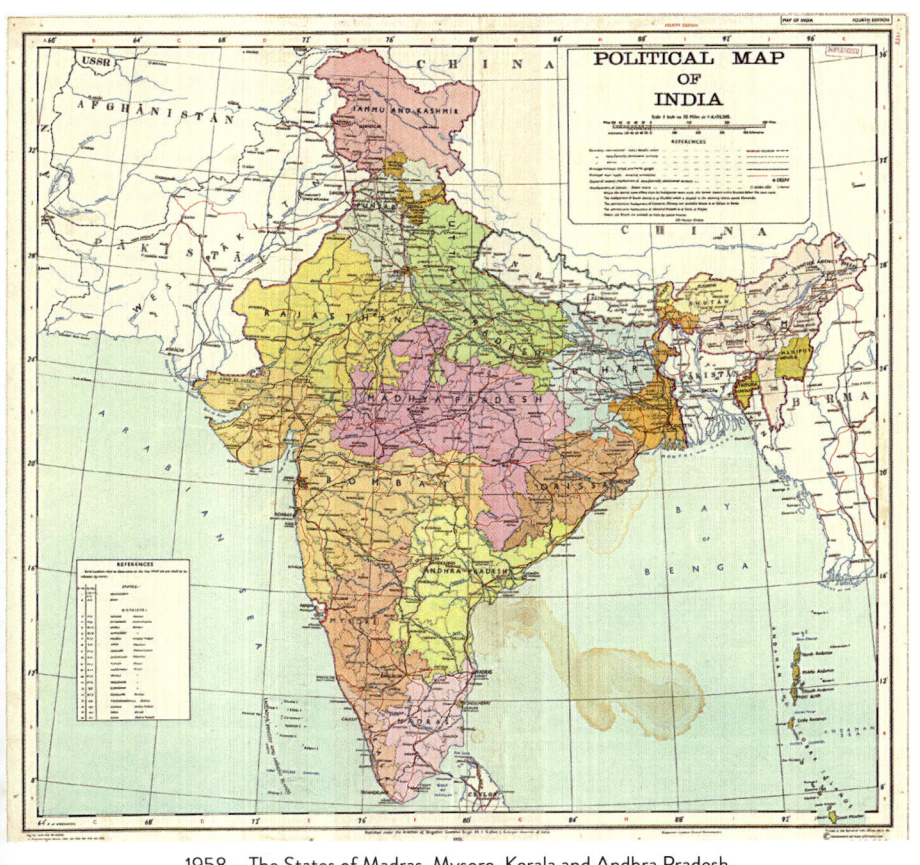

1958 – The States of Madras, Mysore, Kerala and Andhra Pradesh

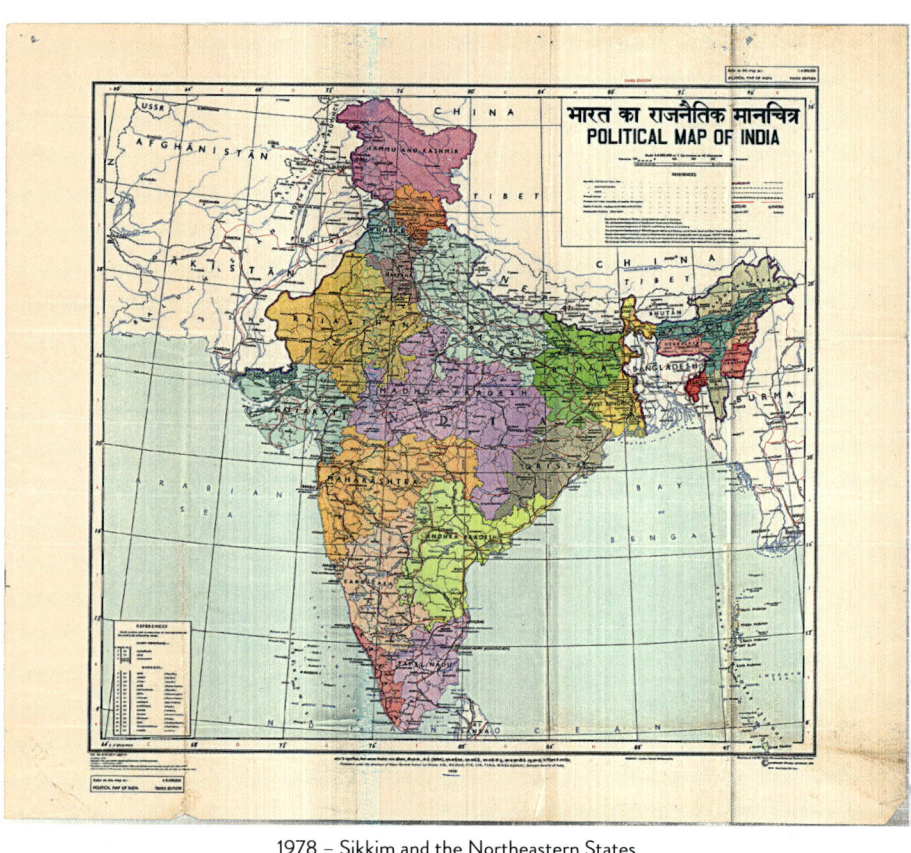

1978 – Sikkim and the Northeastern States

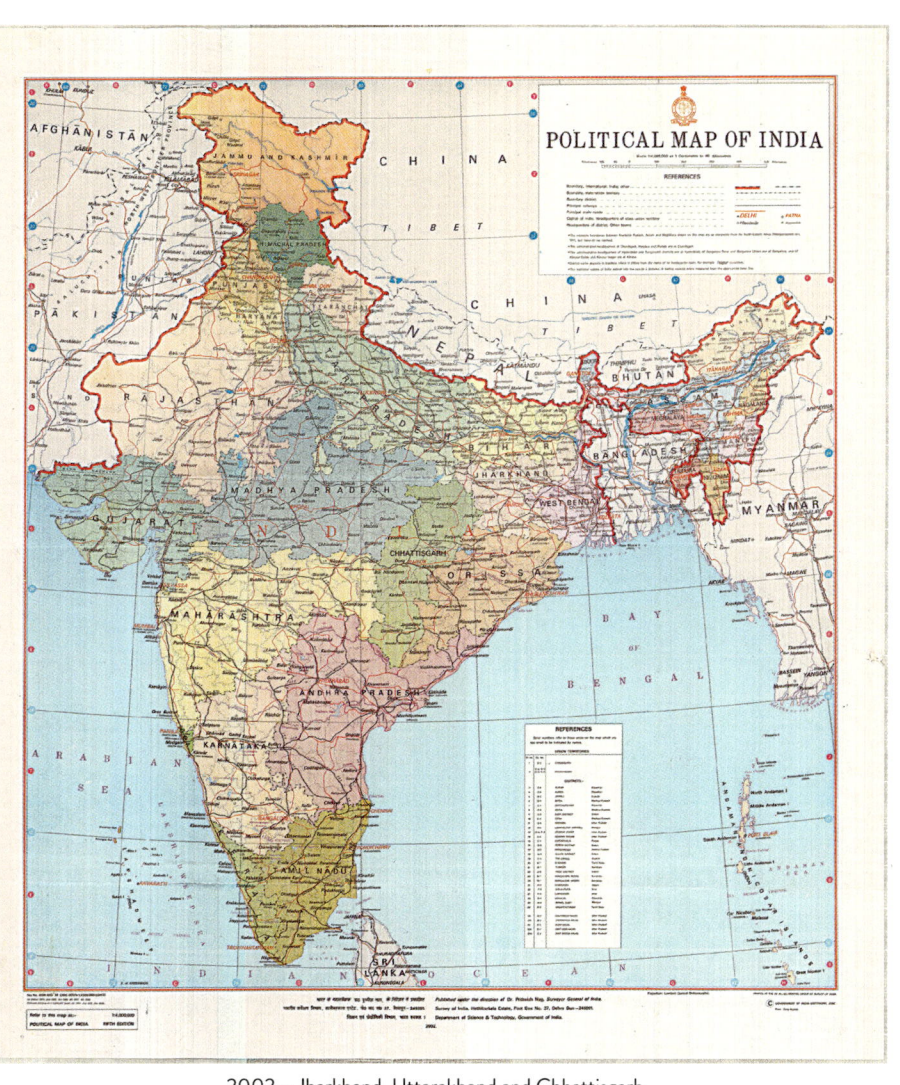

2002 – Jharkhand, Uttarakhand and Chhattisgarh

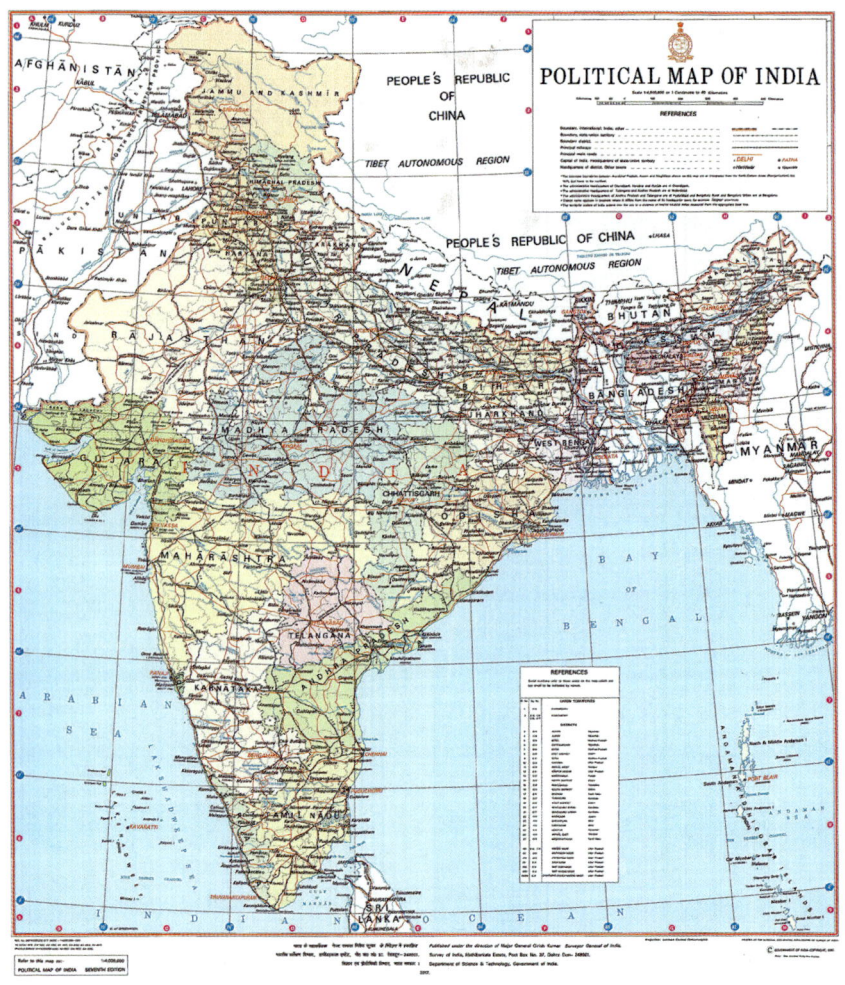

2017 – Telangana – the Second State for Telugu Speakers

12

THE FRONTIERS OF THE NORTH-EAST

The 'making' and 'unmaking' of Assam goes on to show how frontier boundaries[1] have played a seminal role in the political history of this region. Not only was Assam a frontier state in British India, but it has also been so from the times of the Mahabharata. Even for the Mughals and the subedars of Bengal, it was the last outpost. The many changes in the frontiers of this state, therefore, make for a very interesting story!

In most writings on Assam, it is assumed that the story starts when Assam became a chief commissioner's province in 1874. However, that 'Assam' was different from the Ahom[2] kingdom on the Brahmaputra Valley which comprised the districts of Goalpara, Kamrup, Darrang, Nagaon, Sibsagar and Lakhimpur. All of these, with the exception of Goalpara, were taking a distinct shape in the nineteenth century, with Guwahati[3] as the headquarters of the provincial administration. In 1874, four new districts – Cachar, Garo Hills, Khasi and Jaintia Hills and Naga Hills – were appended to Assam. Sylhet too was brought under Assam in September of the same year. As Rajen Saikia has noted, 'This was the beginning of the separation of the political geography of the region from its social and historical roots.'[4] Two decades later, the Lushai Hills district was also added.

However, it must be pointed out that the annexation of the Garo Hills, the Naga Hills and the Lushai Hills by the British was a violation of the Queen's proclamation of 1858[5] which promised an end to the era of territorial expansion of the Empire in India.

The first chief commissioner of Assam, Col. Richard Harte Keatinge, assumed office in February 1874 at Guwahati but shifted the capital to Shillong. The move was opposed by the *Bangabandhu* of Calcutta which said: 'Guwahati was the centre of the province, had a good climate and a better claim as a capital than Shillong which was not connected by good roads.' The annexation of the districts of Cachar and Sylhet also came in for intense criticism. Historian J.B. Bhattacharjee[6] called this the first partition of Bengal. 'Surma valley being a natural continuation from Bengal plains and peopled by the Bengalees, it was logical that Cachar and Sylhet should continue as parts of Bengal.'[7]

But the real change in the profile of the state came from the intertwined factors of Christianity and the Inner Line Regulation (ILR)[8] issued under the Bengal Frontier Regulations. These regulations published in 1873 transformed the cultural, social, educational, denominational and political landscape of the hill districts. The torch bearers of Christian proselytization were the American Baptists in the Naga and Garo Hills, and the Welsh Missionaries in the Mizo, Khasi and Jaintia Hills. Although criticized as an indirect instrument of colonial control, there were positive aspects as well: the Church brought about a total change in the outlook of the head-hunting tribes by ensuring the development of local languages, publication of dictionaries and grammar, popularization of English, expansion of secular education, measures of healthcare and cultural change, etc. However, the 'nationalist' opinion was rather sceptical of the missionary role, especially with regard to proselytization. One reason for the success of the missionaries was the disdain with which the Assamese elite looked upon the hill tribes. 'They did not have any curiosity about the hillman – his food, dress, hearth and home. Localised border trade helped them realise the benefit of friendly relations. But there was no promise of long-term friendship from either side.'[9]

Let it also be added that while the ILR was designed to be a protective measure for the security of the British subjects, it did not recognize any 'pretension to sovereignty of the hill tribes living beyond that imaginary line'. However the ease with which the missionaries were allowed to cross the ILR for evangelical work and conversion did raise questions about the real intent of the colonial administration, all of whom were Christians, and even after Indians started joining the ICS, there was a deliberate attempt at keeping them away from the Assam hill districts.

The demographic transformation of Assam had started with tea plantations – it was easier to manage 'coolies' from outside, than insiders. The planters[10] preferred tribals from Central India as workforce and Bengalis in supervisory roles.

Just as the planters needed Bengali clerks, the administrators who were making a transition from Persian to English and Bengali as the administrative language began to depend more and more on Bengalis in this endeavour, and they became the intermediary ruling class.

The third group that stepped into Assam was the Marwari[11] business class, which monetized the economy for the native Assamese who were just not inclined to change their set mores. The Marwaris reached the farthest interior with finished goods and extracted the disposable surpluses. Then there were the Nepali workers who were engaged in road construction, coal mining and other sectors which required hard physical work. Last but not least, were the Muslim agriculturists who brought new land as well as 'char lands',[12] under the plough, and transformed the landscape with their distinct sartorial identity as well as places of worship. Their integration with the Assamese society was a major challenge as unlike the Santhals, the Marwaris, the Bengalis and the Nepalis, they were not part of the larger Hindu pantheon.

The Partition of Bengal[13] in 1905 saw the creation of a new province with Eastern Bengal and Assam. Dhaka, Chittagong and Rajshahi divisions were cut off from Bengal and lumped with the province of Assam to carve out a new province. Rajen Saikia called this the 'the second vandalization of the political geography of the region'. This 'short lived artificial province' came to an end with the annulment of the Partition of Bengal in 1911.[14] However, the political geography of the fleeting province had devastating results in the long run for the state of Assam. This was the period of 'open sesame' for migration of peasants from eastern Bengal to the lower Assam districts. The Chittagong port and Lumding railway line in central Assam became the highway of migration, changing for all times the demography of the state.

Although the Congress party under the leadership of Gopinath Bordoloi[15] won the highest number of seats in the provincial elections, the Congress decided to sit in Opposition, which gave an opportunity to Sir Saadullah Khan from the Muslim League to become the premier of the province. Sir Saadullah not only wanted the abolition of the ILR system, he also encouraged settlement of Muslim immigrants to make Assam a permanent base of the Muslim League. His 'Grow More Food' or 'Land Development Scheme' was turned down by Viceroy Lord Wavell[16] as a ploy 'to grow more Muslims'. Saadullah's sixteen-month regime was not exactly popular, and given the contradictions in his ragtag coalition, he had to resign in August 1938. Gopinath Bordoloi then formed the Congress ministry in Assam and amongst his first steps was the reversal of the Saadullah policy of encouraging Muslim immigration to Assam. Bordoloi felt that the 'unrestricted occupation might drive away the indigenous inhabitants and the (Congress) government prohibited the settlement to persons who came after 1 January 1938'.[17] But Bordoloi had to resign again when British India joined the Second World War, and Saadullah again became the premier till 1946, when he was replaced by Bordoloi once more. Saadullah's premiership brought about the demographic transition in Assam that led Jinnah to remark to his Private Secretary Moin-ul-Haque Chaudhury, 'Wait, I shall present you Assam on a silver plate'.[18]

The establishment of the dominions of India and Pakistan was no deterrent to the ingress of the Bengali Muslims into Assam. In spite of the Pakistani passport system, Pakistan (Control) Act and Migrants Act 1950, the inflow of migrants continued unabated. As the earlier migrants had settled down in districts of Assam bordering East Pakistan, the newcomers found no difficulty in crossing the porous borders[19] and settled down through the *matbars* or petty zamindars.

In the immediate aftermath of Independence, the entire province was in turmoil. The Sixth Schedule[20] was applied, *mutatis mutandis* to the Excluded and Partially Excluded areas under the GoI Act of 1935 under which an autonomous district council of not more than twenty-four members was invested with legislative powers to make laws for administration of land, management of non-reserve forests regulation of jhum cultivation, appointment and succession of chiefs and matters having a bearing on personal and social life of the tribals. The council was empowered to set up various types of courts, including appellate ones, construct and manage primary schools, dispensaries, roads and prescribe language and manner in which primary education would be imparted. It had the power to assess and collect land revenue on the same principle as followed in the states and to levy and collect certain taxes. Thus, while the tribals in other states were governed by the Fifth Schedule, the tribes of Assam hill tracts were accorded autonomous status under the Sixth Schedule. More significantly, unlike panchayats in other parts of India, the district council had parallel legislative powers with the state government in respect of certain subjects. The council also had a 'separate budget head' in the general budget of the state. They enjoyed exemption from payment of income tax, reservation in services and special facilities for students and in matters of admission into educational institutions, besides scholarships and stipends.

However, even with the best intention of the framers of the Constitution, the councils could not achieve their intended objectives. While the Nagas rejected it outright, the remaining five councils – Garo Hills, United Khasi and Jaintia Hills, Lushai Hills, the United Mikhir (Karbi) and North Cachar Hills – also started on a rather inauspicious note as Assam was most reluctant to give up any powers. The chauvinistic elite of Assam wanted to hasten extension of Assamese influence into the interior of the hills. Unfortunately for them, as well as for the diverse ethnic groups in the state, they could make no distinction between 'integration' and 'assimilation', and herein lay the genesis of the fragmentation of Assam. Constant harping on assimilation with 'Greater Assam' alarmed the highlanders with regard to their land, language and cultural identity.

As such, within the first decade of Independence, the ethnically and linguistically diverse groups sought the reorganization of the state. The representatives of all the hill tribes of Assam met in Tura in 1954 to prepare a memorandum for the States Reorganization Commission demanding a hill state as 'the autonomy granted by the Sixth Schedule was not real and substantial'. The structure of the proposed hill state included a Legislative Assembly, a council of ministers and a governor who would also be responsible for the administration of NEFA,[21] which ultimately should be a part of the hill state. It was agreed that the hill state and the residual state of Assam should have a common high court, public service commission, accountant general and, in the interim, Shillong as the common capital. However, the counter proposal from Assam was a state for the entire eastern Himalayas, including Darjeeling, Jalpaiguri, Cooch Behar and NEFA!

Proposals were also made for the formation of a Kamatapur state[22] consisting of Goalpara, Garo Hills, Cooch Behar, Darjeeling and Jalpaiguri, besides a Purbanchal state consisting of areas in and around Cachar.[23] However, the commission was guided by the principle that a border state should be a well-administered, stable and resourceful unit capable of meeting emergent problems arising out of military exigencies. The commission felt that it should be safer to have on our border relatively larger and resourceful states rather than small and less-resilient units. Even while recognizing the multi-racial and multi-linguistic character of the state, it recommended that the new state of Assam should include all the existing areas, besides incorporation of Tripura and Manipur. The SRC thought that this would bring the entire border between India and Pakistan under one single control, namely the Government of Assam. The commission was of the view that 'separation will add to the cost of administration and render difficult the coordination of policies and programmes between the State of Assam and hill areas, on the one hand, and the hill districts themselves, on the other'.

Even though the SRC was not in favour of any division of Assam, the Government of India, especially Prime Minister Nehru, was keen to enter into a political settlement with that section of Naga leadership that agreed to eschew violence and enter into negotiations. The central government realized that the main antipathy of the Nagas was with the conduct of overzealous officials of Assam rather than with the Government of India.

When the Indian Statutory Commission (Simon Commission) visited India in 1929, the Naga Club,[24] a representative body of the Nagas, in their petition prayed for exclusion of the Naga Hills from the reform scheme and wanted to be placed directly under the British Government.

The formation of Nagaland is also closely aligned to the question of the construction of Naga identity, the British quest for having frontiers as buffers,[25] their ideas about retaining Nagaland as a Crown colony, the implicit support for the missionary activities and the distrust amongst the highlanders and the plainsmen (as in many other regions across the world), besides the easy availability of ammunition dumps left by the armies of the Allied and Axis powers at the end of the Second World War.

From a chronological point of view, the story of 'the district becoming a state' starts with the establishment of the Naga Hills district in 1866 with its headquarters at Samaguiting, and from 1878 at Kohima with a subdivision each at Wokha and Mokokchung. By the Bengal Eastern Frontier Regulation of 1873, the Inner Line Permit (ILP) was introduced, thereby legally restricting the contact with the rest of the country. The GoI Act of 1935 created the Excluded and Partially Excluded Areas and outlined the relationship of the viceroy/governor general towards these territories.

The iron curtain, created by the ILP, was breached by the two World Wars. Nearly four thousand Nagas were recruited during WWI for a Labour Corps[26] in France, and during the WWII, the entire region became a theatre of war. The Axis (Japanese) troops were at the steps of Kohima before they were finally routed, and Field Marshall Sir William Slim acknowledged the role of the brave Nagas in his monumental book, *Defeat into Victory*. 'There was the gallant Nagas whose loyalty even in the most depressing times of the invasion had never faltered. Despite floggings, torture, execution, and the burning of their villages, they refused to aid the Japanese in any way, or to betray our troops. Their active help to us was beyond the value of praise. Under the leadership of devoted British political officers, they guided our columns, collected information, ambushed enemy patrols, carried our supplies, and brought in our wounded under the heaviest fire – and then being the gentlemen they were, often refused all payment. Many a British and Indian soldiers owe his life to them.'

No wonder then that the administrator–anthropologist J.H. Hutton, who had been a deputy commissioner in Assam, and Governor Sir Robert Reid were keen to place these frontier areas on the Burmese border as a Crown territory directly under Whitehall, but as V.P. Menon in the newly constituted states ministry got wind of it, he had it stalled at the level of the secretary of state.

Meanwhile, a delegation of Naga leadership including A.Z. Phizo[27] and T. Sakhrie[28] met Mahatma Gandhi in May 1947 at New Delhi, who conveyed to them that although he felt that the Nagas were an integral part of India, it was for them to decide the modalities of their participation in the Indian Union, and that the use of force was out of question. The governor of Assam, Sir Akbar Hydari,[29] signed a Nine Point Agreement[30] with the Naga leaders at Kohima in June 1947 wherein the Nagas were given full autonomy in judicial, legislative and executive matters, and guaranteed non-alienation of their lands. The ninth point read: 'The Governor of Assam, as the agent of the Government of the Indian Union, will have a special responsibility for a period of ten years to ensure due observance of this agreement: at the end of the period, the Naga Council will be asked whether they require the above agreement to be extended for a further period, or a new agreement regarding the future of the Naga people would be arrived at.' While Phizo interpreted this to mean the option of Independence after ten years, for the Government of India, it meant a choice between remaining a part of Assam, or having a separate status within the Union of India.

The Naga Autonomous Hills district within Assam was given representation in the Lok Sabha and the Assam Legislature under Part XVI of the Constitution (Articles 330 and 332). However, the Nagas under Phizo's leadership did not participate in the first general elections of 1952 and took up armed insurrection with active connivance from China and (East) Pakistan. Fed up with the continual violence perpetrated by Phizo and his unwillingness to negotiate with the government, the moderate faction of the Naga National Council (NNC) led by T. Sakhrie decided to hold talks on the issue of autonomy within the Indian Union. Even after he was kidnapped and killed by the extremist faction, the momentum built by him found expression in the Naga Peoples Convention held in August 1957, which authorized Imkongliba Ao to start the negotiations. After discussions with Prime Minister Nehru in September 1957, it was agreed that 'the Naga Hills district (of Assam) and the Tuensang frontier division (of NEFA) would be constituted into one unit, to be administered by the Governor of Assam on behalf of the President of India'.

Subsequently, two more conventions were held at Mokokchung in 1958 and 1959 when Major Bob Khathing[31] was the deputy commissioner, and a decision was taken to press for a state of Nagaland within the Indian Union, as well as the formation of a Naga regiment[32] within the Indian Army, besides the continuation of the Inner Line Permit. In July 1960, Prime Minister Nehru overruled both the recommendations of the SRC and Home Minister G.B. Pant to announce the establishment an interim body of forty-two elected members for the regulation of Nagaland, and matters connected therewith until the creation of Nagaland as a state under the Indian Union. Unfortunately, Imkongliba Ao was also assassinated, but after the initial setback, Shilu Ao, who later became the first chief minister, ran the council for the next two years.

And finally, on 1 December 1963, Nagaland, the sixteenth state of India with a territory of 6300 square miles and a population of approximately 3,70,000 people, was inaugurated by President S. Radhakrishnan at a colourful ceremony in Kohima, with Shilu Ao as the first chief minister.

The statehood for Nagaland established the principle of the supremacy of political settlement with regard to ethnic issues. The SRC's argument of financial and administrative viability was no longer the only determinant. Right from its very inception, it was clear that the state would be heavily dependent on the Union government for funds as well as functionaries. It also meant that the SRC recommendations with respect to NEFA, Manipur, Tripura, Garo and Jaintia Hills as well as Lushai hill tracts would sooner rather than later be set aside in favour of smaller states and UTs.

As mentioned earlier, much against the wishes of Manipur and Tripura – which had been chief commissioner's provinces after their merger with India – the SRC wanted these two to be part of Assam. Even though Manipur and Tripura were quite apart geographically, ethnically, culturally and linguistically, the fates of the two states have been intertwined from 1947 – both the rulers had sent C.S. Guha as their common representative to the Constituent Assembly. Both signed the Instrument of Accession in 1947 and merged their states to the Indian Union in 1949. Both were initially placed under chief commissioners and narrowly missed integration with Assam in 1956 and became Union Territories in 1963. Both received statehood in 1972, but that did not mark an end to ethnic insurgencies, extremist ideologies and clashes. Both states also shared a common cadre for the All-India Services from 1972–2014, and there have been no territorial alterations to these states post 1947.

Let us, however, step back two centuries. Tripura accepted the protection of the British in 1809, while Manipur accepted the subsidiary alliance in 1824. Both were salute states, with Tripura's status being a notch higher – it had a thirteen-gun salute as compared to eleven guns for Manipur. It may also be mentioned that during the Raj, the superintendence of Manipur was with the governor of Assam, while for Tripura it was with the governor of Bengal. The ruling family and the elite in both the states were heavily influenced by Bengali language, art, culture and religious mores, but to a substantial tribal population, that was a sign of cultural imposition.

In fact, when the rulers of Tripura were encouraging Bengalis – both Hindu and Muslim – to settle in their state, as well as their estate of Chakla Roshananbad (granted to them by Nawab of Bengal in 1720), they could have never imagined that their indigenous Kokborok[33] language and ethos would be on the verge of extinction. When the Tripura royalty was hosting Gurudev Rabindranath Thakur[34] and promoting Bengali art and culture, no one could have imagined the partition of the country and its consequences especially for Tripura; for its extensive zamindari,[35] which was also the main source of revenue, was assigned to East Pakistan on account of its Muslim majority.

The last king, Bir Bikram, who was on the throne immediately before India's independence, died just eleven weeks before independence (17 May 1947), and he was succeeded by his minor son Kirri Bikram Mannikya, with his widow queen Kanchan Prabha taking over the regency of Tripura. She was instrumental in the merger of the Tripura kingdom to the Indian Union in November 1949.

However, post Independence, large parts of Tripura territory, especially its zamindari, went to East Pakistan, and it lost most of its income. But the real tragedy of Tripura stemmed from the demographic transformation which rendered the Tripuri tribe with an unbroken line of 183 successions into a minority even before India's independence. Just to place some facts in perspective: the tribal population was 64 per cent in 1875, 52 per cent in 1931, but by 1951 it was only 37 per cent. It had dipped to 27 per cent in 2001. There has been an increase of the tribal population to 31.8 per cent in the 2011 census, which is indeed an encouraging sign – certainly there is no further in-flow of population into the state.

The movement of Hindu Bengalis started well before Partition as Tripura was considered to be a safe haven. After the unprecedented Rajpura (Dhaka) riots of 1941, Tripura offered free and planned rehabilitation at Arundhutinagar, near Agartala. Hindus also sought shelter in the state after the Noakhali[36] riots in 1946. Another exodus from East Pakistan followed the Partition riots in 1950, 1952 and 1956 when seventy, eighty and fifty thousand refugees respectively stepped into the state. Although the formal registration of refugees stopped in 1958, there were waves of migration before the wars of 1965 and 1971 as well. Till the grant of statehood, and the deployment of BSF in the mid '70s, 'it was India's most porous border of a thousand kilometers'.[37] But 1971 was not the end of the story. Fleeing persecution on account of race and religion, there was an exodus of Chakmas from the Chittagong hill tracts (CHT).[38]

Needless to say, the Bengalis who moved into Tripura were politically conscious, keen to assert their citizenship and, compared to the tribes people, involved in the mainstream political parties. Both the Congress and the communists tried to woo them by offering concessions/raising demands in their favour, including the use of *khas* land (state-owned wasteland) in tribal areas, which was the last straw on the camel's back. Bir Bikram Tripur Sangha (1947), Paharia Union (1951) and the Tribal Union (1955) resisted rehabilitation efforts, but to the credit of the Congress and the communists, it must be said that they did not give an ethnic colour to the issue. But the mode of agriculture, as well as the world view of settled agriculturists and shifting cultivators (*jhumias*) was so different that over time the tribal found that land was no longer in abundance for their way of life and livelihood. The Land Revenue and Land Reforms Act, 1960, did prevent further alienation, but a lot of damage had already been done.

In 1967, the Tripura Upjati Juba Samiti (TUJS) was formed, for by this time tribal youth had also been educated and Christianized by the missionaries, and they demanded Kokborok in the Roman script as the language for education and affairs of the state. TUJS also received help from the Mizo National Front (MNF), and both organizations set up training camps in CHT with cross border support.

In a bid to finding a long-term solution to the tribal issue, the Tripura Assembly unanimously passed the Tripura Tribal Areas Autonomous District Council Bill in 1979, which was incorporated into the Sixth Schedule in 1984 through the 49th Constitutional Amendment. This was a sign of great maturity and sagacity as there were only seventeen tribal members in the sixty-member Assembly that transferred over 68 per cent of the area of the state to the council, which now has its own administrative headquarters at Khumulwng, about 26 km from Agartala.

At the time of writing this chapter (August 2021) the end to Tripura's travails is in sight, for the isolation that began with the disruption of road and rail links from Agartala to Kolkata, increasing the distance from 550 km to 1645 km, ended with the restoration of the 12.3-km-long Akhaura rail line. This along with the bridge over the Feni river near Sabroom has connected the port city of Chittagong directly to Agartala. This is a good augury, not just for Tripura, but the entire North-east, West Bengal and Bangladesh which share a common ecosphere but diverse political arrangements.

Although Manipur did not see an ingress of refugees from East Pakistan, its problems lay in the interpretation of the Indian Independence Act by the Maharaja and the Manipur Durbar. A few

days before Independence, Maharaja Bodhchandra Singh[39] signed
the Instrument of Accession in the same format as was done with
the other princely states. This was followed up by the Manipur
State Constitution Act, 1947,[40] and elections based on universal
adult franchise were held in Manipur in June 1948. However, the
Manipur State Constitution Act, 1947, was not recognized by the
Government of India, and as such the elections were 'void' from
the perspective of the ministry of states. The Centre's view was that
the Instrument of Accession should be followed by an Agreement
of Merger so that all Indian citizens – irrespective of whether they
were living in British India or in the princely states – had the same
rights and privileges. Whether or not the Maharaja was authorized
to sign the Merger Agreement after the passage of the above Act
is a contested issue. The allegations that the treaty was signed by
him under duress dominated the political discourse till Manipur
made the final transition from a Part C state (chief commissioner's
province) to a UT and finally to a state in 1972.

However, this was not the most contentious issue for Manipur.
The real challenge lay in the internecine conflict among the three
major ethnic groups: the Meiteis,[41] the Kukis[42] and the Nagas. While
the Meiteis, who were also the ruling clan, dominated the Imphal
Valley, the hills were controlled by the Kukis and the Nagas – both
in longstanding and violent conflict with each other as well as with
the Meiteis. The Kukis and Nagas had their distinct systems of land
management and governance. While Naga lands were held by the
community, Kukis were oriented towards a hereditary chiefship.
As if this was not enough, the ethno-religious group of Meitei
Muslims, called Pangals or Pangams,[43] was also engaged in violent
assertions of identity.

Manipur was one state where every ethnic group had its own
militia, and at some point in time had also engaged in guerrilla
warfare with each other as well as with security forces. The groups

splintered and proliferated, both on ideological and personality factors, but in general, the Meitei insurgents sought independence from India, the Kukis wanted a separate state and the Nagas wished to merge with Greater Nagaland or Nagalim, which was in sharp conflict with Meitei insistence on the territorial integrity of their state. One must acknowledge that Manipur was also home to Rani Gaidinliu who led the resistance movement of the Heraka[44] cult in the 1930s among the Zeliangrong tribes: Kabui, Puimeis, Zemi and Liangmeis against the British, as well as against the missionaries, whom she felt were destroying their traditional belief systems. Arrested at the tender age of seventeen, she was released after 1947 and was opposed to Phizo's struggle for Naga independence. She received the Tamra Patra for freedom fighters in 1972, and the Padma Bhushan in 1982, but is now a forgotten figure as many of her own kinsmen are now Christians, and the movement for the revival of Heraka is now liminal.

Another hero from Manipur, whose contribution to the determination of India's borders is unparalleled is Major Ralengnao (Bob) Khathing, who, with the blessings of Jairamdas Daulatram,[45] the then governor of Assam, led the contingent of Assam Rifles[46] to Tawang in 1952 and directed the Lamas to refrain from sending their ritual tribute to Lhasa. Thus, it was Tawang where the Dalai Lama made his first halt in 1959 during his escape to India. Khathing was also the deputy commissioner of Mokokchung when the Naga conventions were held in 1956 and 1959 to renounce violence and accept statehood within the Indian Union. He rose to be the chief secretary of Nagaland, and later became our ambassador to Burma, as Myanmar was then known. He was also accorded the honour of the Padma Shri in 1957.

Manipur and Tripura became Union Territories (along with Himachal) as per the Government of Union Territories Act, 1963. The first chief minister of the Union Territory of Tripura was Sachindra Lal Singh[47] and of Manipur was Mairembam Koireng Singh.[48]

The next major change in the North-east came about with the enactment of the Northeastern Areas (Reorganization) Act, 1971, which provided for the establishment of the states of Manipur and Tripura besides the formation of the state of Meghalaya and of the Union Territories of Mizoram and Arunachal Pradesh by reorganization of the existing state of Assam.

Thus, Meghalaya became a state along with Manipur and Tripura in 1972. However, the major difference lay in the fact that both Manipur and Tripura made the transition from being princely states to chief commissioner's provinces in 1949; to Union Territories in 1963; and full-fledged states in 1972. For Meghalaya, statehood was the fulfilment of a longstanding demand – first of a really effective Autonomous District Council within Assam, with an insistence on statehood after attempts were made to impose Assamese throughout the state. The story of Meghalaya is also intertwined with the lost glory of Shillong, as well as the shrinking territorial contours of Assam.

The creation of Meghalaya is best expressed by Swarna Rajagopalan in her 'Report on Peace Accords in Northeast India', 'The formation of Meghalaya began as a demand for a stable hill state in the Northeast but was replaced by demands from several groups for their own states, and the All-Party Hill Leaders Conference [APHLC] focused its attention on the Khasi–Jaintia and Garo Hills, which already had autonomous councils provided by the sixth schedule. A proposal to create a Hill Areas committee in the Assam state Assembly quickly yielded to the demand by the residents of Khasi–Jaintia and Garo Hills for statehood for Meghalaya when the Assamese language was adopted state-wide as a medium of instruction.' It must be mentioned that in the early '50s most legislators from the hill districts were pressing for greater autonomy for the councils within the Sixth Schedule and elected chairmen for all the district councils besides representation from the councils in the Cabinet. They also wanted a limitation on the 'veto powers' of the governor. And last, but not the least, the control of Shillong Municipality by the Khasi Hills Council. In fact, the wish to control Shillong was also at the root of the contest between the state of Assam and the protagonists of Khasi assertion.

By 1962, the APHLC had become a political party, contested elections and achieved outstanding success in all the autonomous districts except Mikir and North Cachar districts. However, discussions with PM Nehru were inconclusive and his successor Lal Bahadur Shastri[49] appointed the Pataskar Commission, whose recommendations stopped short of a separate state, and were hence rejected by the APHLC. In 1967, the Centre proposed a reorganization of Assam on the basis of a federal structure, with a sub-state for the hills. The sub-state would comprise the two districts of Khasi and Jaintia and Garo Hills, with the option to the 280,000 people of the United Mikir and North Cachar (UMNC) district to join the council if they decided to do so by a two-thirds vote. The sub-state was to have the same administrative set-up, with a chief minister and chief secretary as any other state, but the powers transferred to it would not include such subjects as law and order, highways, major industries, major irrigation, drainage, power and navigation projects, and control over the municipality and cantonment of Shillong, the state capital, located in the Khasi and Jaintia district. Moreover, a standing committee consisting of the sixteen hill representatives in the Assam Assembly had a 'pre-emptive right' to pass laws on subjects of interest to the hill districts.

The Creation of North Eastern Council (NEC)[50]

The most interesting part of the sub-state scheme was the proposal for a North Eastern Council (NEC) to be presided over by the governor of Assam. The chief ministers of Assam, Nagaland and the new autonomous state would be members, along with one other minister from each. The Union Territories of Manipur and Tripura were to be represented by their chief commissioners and the chief ministers of the territorial councils. The NEC was to undertake integrated development planning for the whole region, and its Security Sub-Committee had the mandate to look at policies in the context of external and internal threats. This was also an answer to the criticism that reorganization may expose Assam to security risks. Only the Jana Sangh, the precursor to the BJP, had reservations about what this 'fragmentation' would do to the unity and security of India. However, the leadership of the armed forces was strongly in favour of a negotiated settlement with the hill people, lest the situation deteriorate into yet another insurgency.

Mizoram: First as UT, then as State

Although Mizoram became a state only in 1987, it got the status of a Union Territory (UT) in 1972 along with the statehood for Manipur, Tripura and Meghalaya. Interestingly, while the APHLC was up in arms against the Pataskar Commission for not recommending statehood for Meghalaya, one of the key recommendations of the commission was the creation of a UT in the area covered by the Lushai Hills. It may be mentioned that both the Mizo Union and the MNF had boycotted the commission because they said that they had already submitted their memorandum to Prime Minister Lal Bahadur Shastri, which inter alia read:

A step motherly treatment meted out to the Mizo Hills (by Assam government) is responsible for the unfortunate feeling of discontent that we are being treated as second rate citizens ...unless the political aspirations of Mizos are fulfilled through the creation of Mizoram, as there is no desire to remain part of Assam, there is still that sincere desire in the hearts of majority of Mizos to feel themselves as Indians.

Having said this, it must be pointed out that while there was absolute unanimity about separating from Assam, the Mizo Union wanted a state within India, whereas the MNF, which had its origins in the Mizo National Famine Front[51] established in 1960, wanted a sovereign Mizo state. Since 1959, the entire region had been ravaged by a debilitating famine, but the attitude and response of the Assam government had been absolutely callous and indifferent. This alienated all sections of the Mizo society, and the attempt to impose Assamese as the administrative language for the entire state aggravated the feeling of discontent and frustration.

In fact, right from 1952, when the district council in the Lushai Hills was established under the Sixth Schedule, there was a clear feeling that the government of Assam was hell-bent on making it a moribund entity. While the old chieftain system had collapsed, the new council was quite weak to step into its shoes. Even though the Mizo Union had won the elections both to the Advisory Council in 1948 and the Territorial Council in 1952, the traditional chiefs, who held hereditary power under the old dispensation, were clearly opposed to them.

In their memorandum to the SRC, the Mizo Union which was dominating the District Council sought the inclusion of Mizo-dominated areas of Manipur and Tripura in the Lushai Hills. This reconstituted district was to be part of the Eastern Hills State comprising Manipur, Tripura along with the autonomous districts of

Assam and NEFA. However, given the linguistic and ethnic diversity in the proposed hill state, the Mizos reneged from their position, and pressed for a separate Mizoram state within the Indian Union.

After 1961, there was a clear split between the Mizo Union and the MNF, which declared its aim of a sovereign Mizoram. By 1963, the party gained currency, especially among the youth, and though it captured 145 village councils, the Mizo Union was still the dominant political force – it had 220 village councils with them. But the Laldenga[52] led MNF, egged on by its supporters in East Pakistan, launched Operation Jericho, an armed struggle for a sovereign Mizoram, by launching simultaneous attacks on the Assam Rifles (AR) garrisons at Aizawl, Lunglei and Champhai, BSF outposts and the Aizawl Treasury on 1 March 1966. Even the deputy commissioner of Aizawl, T.S. Gill, had to take shelter in the Assam Rifles camp. But the AR garrison held on, and the proposed victory parade scheduled for 2 March could not be held for the insurgents had underestimated the strength of the Indian Army and overestimated the support of the Inter-services Intelligence (ISI)[53] and East Pakistan.[54] But even though the insurgents could not hoist the flag, they released the prisoners from the Aizawl jail and looted the shops of the non-Mizos (*Vais*).

On 2 March 1966, the Armed Forces Special Powers Act (AFSPA)[55] was invoked, curfew imposed in Aizawl and reinforcements sent for Assam Rifles by helicopters. After the attack on the chopper of Eastern Army commander Lt Gen. Sam Manekshaw, Indian Air Force (IAF) jets strafed the MNF insurgent posts using machine guns on 4–5 March, the one and only instance of combat action by IAF within the country.

In all this, the Mizo Union was steadfast in its support for India. Their biggest grouse was that the chief minister of Assam, B.P. Chaliha,[56] was supporting the MNF – a secessionist organization – because, for him, 'the disintegration of the state of Assam is more serious than the amputation of Mizo Hills from India'.[57] It may not be true, but this was certainly the popular perception. Meanwhile, in October 1966, the governor of Assam, Vishnu Sahay, suggested that 'Mizo hills should be plucked from Assam and formed into a Union Territory'.[58] The GoI was also cognizant of the fact that the Autonomous Council under the Sixth Schedule had failed to meet the political aspirations. The Mizo Union presented a memorandum to Prime Minister Indira Gandhi in December 1970 for a full-fledged state, but a compromise was struck with the enactment of the Northeastern (Areas) Reorganization Act, 1971, under which Mizoram was formed into a UT with thirty-three legislators and one seat each in the Lok Sabha and the Rajya Sabha. The veteran Mizo Union leader Ch. Chhunga took the oath of office as chief minister in 1972.

The Loveliest and the Loneliest Frontier: Arunachal

The establishment of Arunachal, first as a UT and then as a state, runs counter to the general format: the aspiration, if at all, for a separate entity was rather muted, and there was no assertion either. While Arunachal does have a boundary dispute with Assam, and there are issues with regard to the Tibetan settlements, the Chakmas[59] and the Hajongs,[60] this does not take away from the description of the state as 'the loveliest, loneliest and the least known outpost of the Northeast, a vast variegated swathe of territory that encompasses much of Brahmaputra Valley in a giant horseshoe'.[61] The state is marked with extraordinary diversity: with one hundred and ten tribes, of whom twenty-six are considered to be major tribes. Many of these tribes migrated centuries ago from Tibet and Burma, stayed on in isolated hamlets as movements across the mighty rivers were not easy to negotiate – thereby explaining the diversity of culture and the babel of tongues.

While the earliest history is now being reconstructed on the basis of archaeological finds, Dr Suniti Kumar Chatterjee[62] opines that this region was part of the sacred geography of the Mahabharata and Jambudweep. As per popular legend, this is where sage Parashuram atoned for his sins, king Bhismaka founded his kingdom and Lord Krishna married Rukmini. During the medieval period, Mahayana Buddhism held sway over Tawang, Dirang, Kalaktang and Mechuka. We also get some idea about these tracts from the writings on Mir Jumla's[63] campaign against the Ahom kingdom in 1662, which apart from describing the rugged terrain, also talk of the mesmerizing beauty of the Mishmi women. Détente ensued between the Ahoms and the Mughal governors of Bengal, but as the East India Company, with its capital in Calcutta became the dominant political power, in 1818 the Ahom king sought the assistance of the British against the armed incursions from Burma. The Treaty of Yandaboo[64] saw the Ahom kingdom cede part of its territory to the Company. From 1875 to 1904, the areas inhabited by sub-Himalayan tribes on the borders of Darrang and Lakhimpur between the Bar Nadi on the Darrang Kamrup boundary on the north of Brahmaputra and the Disang river on the extreme southeast of Lakhimpur district on the south bank of Brahmaputra, touching the Sibsagar district, were brought under British control. In 1914, the Foreign and Political Departments extended the Assam Frontier Tracts Regulation, 1880, to the hills inhabited or frequented by Adis, Miris, Mishmis, Singphos, Nagas, Khamtis, Bhutias, Akas, Nyishis, and designated it as the North-East Frontier Tract.

With the Constitution of India coming into force, a change was visible in the administrative set-up of the Frontier Tracts. The Government of Assam was relieved of its responsibility for the administration of North-East Frontier Tract and the discretionary powers were re-vested in the governor of Assam, as the agent of the President of India. Although the region was still a part of Assam, the legislative jurisdiction was not extended to the Frontier.

Prime Minister Nehru's policy was based on the views of the defrocked missionary, Verrier Elwin,[65] who as the adviser on tribal affairs had considerable clout in the policymaking for the region. In 1954, a full-scale administration of the area was inaugurated, with the promulgation of North-East Frontier Agency (Administration) Regulation of 1954 and the acronym of NEFA became the new descriptor. The establishment of the Indian Frontier Administrative Service (IFAS)[66] was not without strong resistance from the home ministry, the Government of Assam and the members of the Opposition, and it was perhaps because of this that NEFA was placed under the MEA, of which Nehru was also the minister. Writing to Foreign Secretary Subimal Dutt, Nehru said, 'The real question is of building up a cadre, specially selected, and specially trained … I think that Mr Verrier Elwin could be of great help to us because of his wide knowledge and experience and human sympathy for these (tribal) folk.'[67]

However, after the 1962 debacle, when the Chinese forces occupied substantial parts of NEFA, and certainly after Nehru's death, NEFA was moved from the external affairs to the home ministry, the IFAS officers were seconded (and finally merged) with the IAS and the IPS, and the isolationist policy was reversed. It was rightly felt that political participation of the people at all levels would be the best way to integrate the region with the country. In fact, based on the recommendations of the Daying Ering[68] Committee, the President promulgated the North-East Frontier Agency Panchayati Raj Regulation, 1967. It can be said that this was the precursor to the seventy-third Constitutional Amendment for the implementation of Panchayati Raj structure in the rest of the country in 1992.

The North-East Areas (Reorganization) Act, 1971, provided a new political status to the region as Arunachal Pradesh, and in 1972 it became a Union Territory. The credit for the new name goes to Bibhabasu Das Shastri, the then director of research, and K.A.A. Raja, the then chief commissioner of NEFA.

By creating these new states and UTs, Assam was 'freed from the burden of geography'. However, even as several issues relating to ethnic and linguistic assertions have been resolved, many others, especially those relating to citizenship, economic aspirations and contested inter-state borders, will continue to impact the political economy of the states in the North-east.

13

ISLAND TERRITORIES

Andaman and Nicobar (A&N) Islands are two archipelagos of 572 islands/islets located in the Bay of Bengal, of which only twenty-five in Andamans and twelve in Nicobar group are inhabited. Together, they provide India a great strategic advantage over the Straits of Malacca,[1] one of the most important 'Sea Lane of Communication' (SLOC) critical to trade and movement of oil from Gulf to the South China Sea, East China Sea and the Pacific. They also provide India with tremendous economic potential for tourism, fisheries and deep-sea exploration for oil and gas. Nearly one-third of our Exclusive Economic Zone (EEZ)[2] is derived from these islands. Besides boosting our Look East Policy[3] and our soft power on the Indo–Pacific region, the islands have given the Indian Navy a salient role to play in containing China's intransigence in the blue waters. It must be mentioned that of the 7,500 km coastline of India, nearly 2,000 km comes from this archipelagic chain.

Although the Andaman and Nicobar Islands have been under a common system of administration from 1869, and both are home to pre-modern, indigenous societies, and both started as penal settlements, the two sets of islands had different encounters with the colonial powers.

The official website of the Andaman and Nicobar Islands administration traces the history of this archipelago to the times of the Ramayana, when the place was called Handuman, a name closely linked to Hanuman. Sanat Kaul[4] says that the name was given by the Malays who called Hanuman by this name.[5] Since prehistoric times, some of the islands have been inhabited by the primitive tribes: Onges, Jarawas, Sentinelese, Andamanese, Nicobarese and Shompens – the last two being of Mongoloid stock, and the former four trace their origin to Africa.

The famous Greek geographer Ptolemy called it Agadaeman in his work published in the first quarter of second century CE. The seventh-century Chinese Buddhist monk I–Ching and the Arab travellers of the ninth century also talked of the sweet waters of these islands. Marco Polo visited the islands in the thirteenth century and referred to the islands as Angamanian. There are documents which record the visit of Friar Odoric[6] in the fourteenth and Caesar Fredricke[7] in the sixteenth centuries. In 1789, Archibald Blair[8] tried to establish a base on the Chatham islands,[9] which was later shifted to Port Cornwallis. To clear the forest and establish the colony, the first set of three hundred convicts were transported from Bengal, but the idea was abandoned when many of them died of disease, and in 1796, the colony was closed, and the survivors were sent to another penal settlement in Penang.[10]

However, given the strategic location of the islands, the British retained their interest in Port Cornwallis. It lay on the trading route of the East India Company. They also wanted a haven for shipwrecked vessels, sailors and prospectors, and by the 1840s, the interest was rekindled when they made plans for the recolonization. This received a fillip after the Great Indian Revolt of 1857, when the rebels destroyed the jails and released the prisoners. In fact, such was the impact of the insurrection that the British penal settlements in Burma and Straits refused to accept the rebel convicts. The first 'challan' of 200 freedom fighters were shipped to Andamans in 1858, where they were put to work in the most inhuman conditions.

However, even during their transportation, the rebel convicts displayed a remarkable degree of agency as well as self-respect. Fazal Haq Khairabadi, a renowned poet of the Mughal court, a friend of Mirza Ghalib, and a mentor to David Ochterlony, refused to plead 'not guilty' or seek amnesty even when it was offered. Using charcoal sticks and cloth rags, he penned a contemporary narrative of the First War of Independence as well as the experiences of Kala Pani in Arabic as *Al-Surat-ul Hindia* and *Al Fitnat-ul Hindia*. Four days after the first landing, another rebel, Narain Singh, tried to escape, but was caught and shot dead. His colleague, Naringun Singh, committed suicide by hanging. Many went slow at work, feigned illnesses, attacked their overseers and escaped into the jungles. Two of them were picked up in the sea as 'shipwrecked sailors' and got all the way to London where they were lodged in the Strangers Home for Asiatic Seamen and were taken to visit the Crystal Palace as well.

Within two months of their arrival, a daring escape attempt was made by eighty-one of them, but facing acute hostility from the indigenous tribes, they returned to the prison camp and surrendered, but they were put to 'death by hanging' on a single day by Dr James Pattison Walker.[11] Even when J.P. Grant, the president in council in Calcutta complained to the governor general about the severity of the punishment, Walker was not reprimanded. However, he was removed in 1859 when he clamped an 'iron collar' on the convicts, and suggested branding their forearms.

The next set of twenty-two inmates were transported in 1864 – they were the leaders of the Wahabi[12] movement and the loyal supporters of the royal family of Manipur. Of the Wahabi leaders sent to the settlement, Sher Ali fatally assaulted Viceroy Lord Mayo when he was returning after a pleasant trip to Mount Harriet on the evening of 8 February 1872. In what could only be described as ironical, just before the attack, Lord Mayo[13] was heard saying that the place was ideal to hold at least two million people. Sher Ali was in Mount Harriet on sick leave, and the evening before he had thrown a dinner for his comrades and friends on the island. Later investigations revealed that he was keeping abreast of the movement in the mainland.

After the first set of politicals – those involved in the 1857 revolution – prisoners of the Wahabi movement and the Manipur rebels, the penal settlement was opened to general convicts between the ages of eighteen to forty – for the islands had the space, and the British needed free labour to develop the settlement and maintain places like Ross Island and Mount Harriet, which boasted of large spacious bungalows, club houses, dance halls and swimming pools. All this was built with the sweat, blood and toil of the Hindustani prisoners.

However, even amongst the politicals, not all those who were sent to the islands retained the fervour of revolution. Some made 'intelligent compromises' and became part of the intermediary class which helped the superintendent of prisons in the task of the day-to-day administration. We have, for example, the interesting case of Maulana Muhammad Jaffar Thanesari, a Wahabi arrested in 1863 for conspiring to smuggle funds to anti-British mujahideen in Afghanistan. He was initially sentenced to death, but his punishment was commuted to life in penal transportation, which meant exile in the Andaman Islands. Beginning 1866, he spent nearly eighteen years in the penal colony, and then returned to Punjab with a new wife, new children and considerable wealth and social status. His status and utility in the penal colony was derived from his literacy in multiple languages: Urdu, Farsi, Hindi and English. The work that

Thanesari did in the penal colony demonstrates that punishment in the Andamans operated on a market principle of sorts. Because the British needed loyal intermediaries at every level of the prison administration, they were obliged to bargain with convicts who agreed to serve in such positions, and to reduce the punitive content of punishment.

In addition to men like Thanesari who were 'sent' to Andamans, the prison administration also sought 'volunteers' from amongst the Eurasian (Anglo-Indian convicts) to assist them. In fact, soon after the establishment of the penal settlement, the British transferred Eurasian convicts in India and Burmese jails to the islands to work as convict-overseers. Eurasian prisoners from the mainland were offered remission after a three-year stay in the islands, as well as a stipend of fifty rupees per month. Prisoner skills included fluency in Hindustani, rope-, mat-, shoe-making and baking, as well as carpentry and weaving. By 1867, there were thirty-four Europeans, Eurasians and Americans employed as clerks, painters, fishermen and carpenters for the seven thousand odd Hindustani prisoners. They were all clubbed together in the 'Christian barrack' where they lived a life of relative luxury. Their barracks were stone built, and some even had cubicles with beddings like the European soldiers. The Indian prisoners on the other hand were housed in wooden barracks – each holding hundred to hundred fifty men, divided into groups of twenty-five each.

The living and working conditions for Indians were deplorable and sub-human, and in the 1870s, intense rain, malaria, pneumonia and dysentery caused many deaths. The prisoners were also used as 'guinea pigs' as the doctors embarked on testing of pharmaceutical drugs like quinine (cinchona alkaloid) by forcibly feeding it to the ten thousand prisoners who were now in the islands. Cinchona was a tree imported to Asia from Peru whose bark would later be distilled to make quinine an effective and natural anti-malarial drug.

But the rough preparation and dosage experimentations by the prison doctors caused acute side-effects like nausea and diarrhoea on the convicts. It was also a depressant. In monthly reports for the period of the test, the chief commissioner, Lieutenant Colonel T. Cadell, observed[14] 'a remarkable increase in suicides'. Convicts 'weary of life' would literally hack each other to pieces, hoping to secure the death penalty. But Cadell had a solution: 'Flogging and a reduced diet.' Everyone under the age of twenty-two was now required to sleep in 'a sort of trellis-work cage'.

Another fallout of the European presence was the decimation of the indigenous population on account of sexual assault by soldiers and naval ratings. Later, measles, flu, tobacco, opium and whisky played their part in wiping out more than half of the indigenous population from the main island of Andamans in the 1870s.

After the Anglo Manipur War of 1891,[15] Manipur war hero Yuvraj Tikendrajit and General Thangal were publicly hanged in Fida, Imphal. But Maharaja Kulachandra Dhwaja Singh and twenty-two freedom fighters were sent to Kala Pani and kept on Mount Harriet. In October 2021, the island was renamed as Mount Manipur. A memorial plaque for the Manipur heroes is now being put up by the Manipur government and the island administration.

~

Lest an impression is created that the penal settlement housed only political prisoners, it must be placed on record that as per the study of Clare Andersen, between 1858 and 1937 there were over eighty thousand convicts, but the political prisoners did not exceed a thousand. In order to make the islands 'revenue neutral', convict labour was used for all kinds of productive purposes. 'Nationalist prisoners', on the other hand, were subject to a very different penal regime. They were isolated from the mass of convicts and after the cellular jail was operational from 1910, they were confined there for the whole term of their sentence and put to non-productive (penal) forms of labour like oakum picking and grinding thirty pounds of oil every day, yoked like oxen to the oil press.

Of the 16,000 odd residents counted in the census of 1901, there were 12,000 convicts, 2000 free residents (ex-convicts and their descendants), about 300 Europeans and over a thousand Eurasians (Anglo-Indians). While the Europeans lived on the Ross Island 'with its grand colonial residences, swimming baths, tennis courts, clubs and bazaars', the Anglo-Indians lived in Port Blair and socialized in the Temple Club. The relatively large number of Eurasians living in Andamans at the start of the twentieth century reflected the extent to which the British relied on them to run the penal settlement. They occupied almost all the senior positions in the management and operation of jails, telegraph, forest and wireless services. The Eurasians, though not at the helm, lived a 'resplendent life' with their weekly dances, piano lessons and convict-servants.

However, even though the administrative apparatus to manage the islands was in place, what the island needed was 'settlers' – people who would ensure self-sufficiency, at least in terms of cereals, milk, poultry, fish, betel, coconut plantations and basic services. Prisoners from across the mainland were offered remissions and incentives to settle in the islands with their families. It was different for the political detenus – for the purpose was to 'humiliate them, and break their spirit forever, or make them subservient – as in the case of "approvers" like Thanesari'.[16]

The mindset that guided the authorities in the penal settlement is best illustrated by the talk given by Richard Carnac Temple, the chief commissioner of the Andamans, at a lecture at London's Imperial Institute on 24 February 1899. 'Political prisoners would no longer live in barracks scattered across the malarial islands. Instead, a 698-cell panopticon was being established on mangrove swamps on a promontory called Atlanta Point, overlooking the main town of Port Blair. From its Central Tower radiated seven 150-yard wings that rose to three levels, each level fitted with 52 cells, 13.5 ft by 7.5 ft, each supplied with a 6 ft by 3 ft wooden slat bed and ventilated by a barred 3 ft by 1 ft grate.' Here was a 'huge, practical reformatory' that would carry the work of the Andaman Islands' authorities into a new age. Every arrival would be forced 'to bend his rebellious nature to the yoke'. Carnac Temple promised them a fate 'even more dreadful than the hangman's noose'. This was the place where the political prisoners were to be held, and they were the ones for whom the most humiliating forms of punishment were proposed.[17]

Manmath Nath Gupta, a revolutionary himself, writes about the place, 'The cells were of the worst type prevalent, there was no provision for lavatories; an earthen pot smeared with coal tar in a corner of the cell served the purpose. There was no cover of any sort, so in time, a prisoner slept in a sort of open lavatory.'[18]

It was to this 'facility' that 149 revolutionaries were sent from prisons across the country in 1909. In 1910, the convicts of the Khulna, Alipore and Nasik conspiracy cases were also sent to the Cellular Jail. Among them was Damodar Vinayak Sarvarkar who wrote about his lived experience in *The Story of My Transportation for Life*. As news about the treatment meted out in the prison came to be published, there was universal opprobrium, and by 1919–20, the Indian Jails Committee[19] recommended the general abolition of transportation to the islands. The announcement was made by Sir William Vincent, ICS, vice president of the Indian Legislative Council on 21 March 1921. The process of phased repatriation to jails in the mainland was initiated as there were twelve to fifteen thousand prisoners at that time. However, as provincial governments were unable to cope with the resultant prison overcrowding, the practice of transportation for male, non-political convicts was renewed in 1922. Normal convicts perhaps had a 'tolerable time' for they were encouraged to take to agriculture and other productive works, marry with the female inmates if both parties agreed and get their families from the mainland after their prison term was over. They were also given regular remissions from time to time.

After the mass convictions of the Malabar Rebellion in 1922,[20] the convicts were offered the status of 'self-supporters' and encouraged to move to the islands with their families. Another two thousand Moplah rebels were also transferred to the islands, and the government even paid the passage money for their families. The government then invited applications for land grants, and some Anglo-Indian families took the plunge. However, as they had not worked on the land earlier, and were men with professions – station masters, police sergeants and wireless operators – the experiment was a failure. Another attempt was undertaken by the Salvation Army to rehabilitate three hundred families of Bhantus (classified by the British as a criminal tribe).[21] Thus in 1926, Salvation Army[22] captain, Edwin Sheard (known in India as Fauj Singh), settled them in Ferrargunj, Cadlegunj and Anikhet. While the community became self-supporting in a few years' time, the conversion project was not quite successful, as only sixty-six of the 295 Bhantu adults had become Christians. In 1929, another two hundred families of another so-called criminal tribe – the Karwals – were packed off to the Andamans.

By 1932, as the revolutionary fervour gripped the nation and Bengal and Punjab became the hotbed of revolution, the government decided to remove the 'nationalists' as far away from their support base, and the Cellular Jail was back in the reckoning. However, as the 'transportation of prisoners' was against the declared policy of the government, it was essential to justify reneging from a commitment made in the Legislative Assembly. The legal adviser to secretary of state, Sir Charles Tegart, rationalized that under Section 29 of the Prisoners Act, convicts were liable to be 'removed to any

Indian prison, and Andamans was a part of British India'. Thereafter, based on reports received from governments of Bengal, Bihar, Orissa and Punjab, nationalist prisoners from these states were sent to Andamans. This is how the last set of 386 'politicals'[23] were sent to the Cellular Jail, which had by this time become a synonym for notoriety for those who took cudgels against the Raj. And politicals continued to assert their rights even in the Cellular Jail. At least six of them were below eighteen – Anand Prasad Gupta, Sahairam Das, Fakir Mohan Sen, Haripada Bhattacharya, Sudhendu Bikash Dastidar and Hira Mohan Chatterjee. The inmates gave a one month notice to the authorities to redress their grievances which included their rights to entitlement as B class prisoners, provision of reading material, mosquito nets, tooth powder, sandals and improvement in the quality of food. After the stipulated period, they started a hunger strike in the Cellular Jail, to which the authorities responded with force feeding – which led to a struggle between the prisoners and the warders. The entire process was dehumanizing, to say the least, and at least three prisoners died in the process, forcing the authorities to relent especially as the matter was raised in the Legislative Assembly, as well as by the newspapers. The concessions included the establishment of a library, the right to play football, management of a common kitchen, political classes and circulation of a handwritten newspaper. After this, life was bad, but it was 'not like hell'.

The passage of the GoI Act of 1935 gave a fair amount of autonomy to the provinces. The Congress was able to make ministries in most of the states, and one of their first actions was the release of political prisoners in 1937. However, for the political inmates of A&N Islands, the wait was longer with the last batch leaving the penal settlement in January 1938. After that, only volunteer prisoners were sent to the islands, mainly for labour work, and they were given incentives like remissions on their period of sentence as well as a 'working wage'.

The Nicobar Group of Islands

We will take a detour to the Nicobar group of islands, which were of great interest to the mercantile nations on account of their strategic location in the Bay of Bengal, and at the mouth of the Straits of Malacca. By the eighteenth century, the European powers were keen to look for safe havens on their sea-faring routes and had already established settlements at St Helena and Mauritius. They were willing to look beyond. But before we talk about the interest shown in the islands by the Danes, the Norwegians, the Austrians, the Italians and of course, the British, we may look at the connect of these islands to Sri Lanka and Thanjavur. The islands were first mentioned in the Sri Lankan Pali Buddhist chronicles, the *Dipavamsa*, (third or fourth century CE) and the *Mahavamsa* (c. fourth or fifth century) as Naggadipa – or the island of children – perhaps because of the short stature and primitive nature of existence of the inhabitants. The modern name is likely derived from the Chola dynasty name for the islands, *Nakkavaram* (meaning 'open/naked land' or naked man's land in Tamil) and inscribed on the Thanjavur inscription of 1050 CE.

During his extensive travels and diplomatic missions to India and Burma, Marco Polo (twelfth and thirteenth century) also recorded these islands as 'Necuverann'. Probably because of the references gathered from his journeys, the fifteenth century Chinese admiral, Zheng He, anchored on these islands and recorded them as Cui Lan Island in the Mao Kun map of the *Wu Bei Zhi*.

The first colonial power to take interest in these islands were the Danes. It is recorded that in November 1754, an assembly of high-ranking Danish officials, including the directors of the Danish Asiatic Company and Governor Krog of the Tranquebar colony, deliberated on the report of the Moravian Missionary Husfield, who had spent considerable time on these islands. His report suggested that the Nicobars were an excellent place for the cultivation of pepper, cinnamon, sugarcane, coffee and cotton, in addition to the existing (natural) crop of coconut and arecanut. The Danes also looked at the abundant timber resources which could be used for the shipbuilding industry.

However, all their attempts at settling in the Nicobar Islands failed – most likely due to malarial climate and inadequate support from the government. That the Danes were not really invested in the islands was clear from the fact that between 1778 to 1783, the islands were taken over by the Austro Hungarians, and later by the British from 1807 to 1814. Italy made an attempt at buying the Nicobar Islands from Denmark between 1864 and 1865. Denmark's presence in the islands ended formally on 16 October 1868 when it sold the rights of the Nicobar Islands to Britain, which, in 1869, made them part of British India.

The British began with a penal colony at Nancowry which was developed as a settlement with the help of convict labour, and production of yams, pineapples, mangoes, vegetables was taken up. However, after nineteen years, the penal settlement was closed and all the convicts shifted to Andamans, and the focus was on missionary activity, with the Anglicans taking the lead in establishing a school. By 1897, Rev. Solomon had been appointed as the government agent and in 1918, an assistant commissioner was stationed in Car Nicobar and a tehsildar at Nancowry. Nancowry had emerged as an important trading post for it was customary for vessels sailing to Rangoon (Yangon) from the Straits of Malacca to visit Nicobar to barter rum and salt for coconuts. It was at Nancowry that the technique of copra-making was developed, and it soon became a game changer for the Nicobars. It was more profitable to export dried copra as it saved transport cost. When copra godowns were set up, semi-permanent establishments followed, and traders started staying there for longer durations.

The profile of the traders kept changing. In the initial years, the traders from Myanmar were dominant, followed by those from Sri Lanka, Maldives and Minicoy Islands and Madras. However, the most successful firm was R. Akoojee Jadwet & Company which ran a flourishing trade between Gujarat and Myanmar. Their vessels regularly frequented the Nicobar Islands to obtain copra and betel nuts to be traded in Myanmar. In the early '30s, they obtained a long-term lease from the British government over the produce of Great and Little Coco Islands even as they maintained very cordial relations with Edward Kutchat, the chief captain of the Nicobars, and the tribal leaders.

Tricolour over the Islands

The next major milestone in the history of the islands was the abdication by the British during the Second World War, and the smooth takeover by the Japanese, who were initially welcomed by the inhabitants of both the islands. The garrison at Port Blair consisted of a 300-men Sikh militia with twenty-three British officers, augmented in January 1942 by a Gurkha detachment of the 16th Indian Infantry Brigade. Following the fall of Rangoon, the British recognized that Port Blair had become impossible to defend, and the Gurkhas were withdrawn to the Arakan peninsula. In March 1942, the garrison offered no resistance to the Nippon landings. The troops were disarmed but most members of the Sikh militia enlisted in the Indian National Army (INA). The army was first formed in 1942 by the Indian soldiers of the British–Indian Army in Malaysia and Singapore. It got a fillip when Subhas Chandra Bose took over as the supreme commander of the INA after his arrival in South East Asia in 1943. The army was affiliated to the *Arzi Hukumat-e-Azad Hind* (the Provisional Government of Free India).

In the early days of the occupation local intellectuals (mostly officials and doctors) were encouraged to join Rash Behari Bose's Indian Independence League (IIL), and a 'Peace Committee' was formed from its members, headed by Dr Diwan Singh.

Meanwhile, on 29 December 1943, Netaji accompanied by Anand Mohan Sahay, Captain Rawat, ADC, and Col D.S. Raju, the personal physician of Netaji, landed at the Port Blair aerodrome in the Andamans. He was received by the Japanese admiral at Port Blair. The enthusiastic Indians and Burmese also accorded a warm reception to him. The Indian tricolour was hoisted by him on the 30 December 1943.

Bose named Andaman Island as Shaheed and Nicobar Island as Swaraj and appointed INA general, A.D. Loganathan, as the governor of the islands. Azad Hind Government was not merely a Government in Exile anymore but had its own land, currency, civil code and stamps.

However, even though the islands were formally handed over to the INA, the Japanese troops behaved like an army of occupation. Amongst the first victims was a young man, Zulfiqar Ali, who took umbrage at the unauthorized entry of troops into his house. Although no one was hurt in the air gun firing, Zulfiqar Ali was captured and marched to the maidan. Here his arms were twisted until they broke, and he was eventually shot dead. The memorial to him is now called Sunny's Mazar. Later, Dr Diwan Singh, and most other members of the IIL were also arrested, tortured and killed.

Although the Japanese burnt all the records before they surrendered, the reconstruction of the period of Japanese occupation is documented in Jayant Dasgupta's *Japanese in Andaman & Nicobar Islands: Red Sun over Black Waters*. Dasgupta refers to the hitherto unpublished accounts of a local resident Rama Krishna, *The Andaman Islands under Japanese Occupation: 1942–5*, and of a

British officer, D. McCarthy, *The Andaman Interlude*. From these records, it appears that as food became scarce, the Japanese forced the residents of Port Blair to move to uninhabited islands, and many were drowned, or bayoneted, or shot when they tried to escape. T.R. Sareen, however, gives a more nuanced picture of the role of the Azad Hind Fauj and the role of Subhas Bose.[24] He holds the blockade of the islands by the British as the principal reason for the acute shortage of food and argues that the Japanese authorities were trying to send people from Port Blair to uninhabited islands to bring new land under the plough.

In December 2018, the seventy-fifth anniversary of Netaji Subhas Chandra Bose's hoisting the national flag at Port Blair was commemorated with the renaming of three of the most-frequented islands in the archipelago. Ross Island was renamed Netaji Subhas Chandra Bose Dweep, Neil Island as Shaheed Dweep and Havelock Island as Swaraj Dweep. It was the fulfilment of a long-standing demand that the islands should not be named after the colonial masters, two of whom – Havelock and Neil – as commanders of the British Indian army had the blood of thousands of Indians on their hands. Ross was an exception – he was a marine biologist who spent his time documenting the underwater beauties in the surrounding seas. Ross Island served as the capital of the islands till a major earthquake destroyed the facilities, and subsequently the administration shifted to Port Blair.

In his seminal work *Andaman & Nicobar Islands: India's Untapped Strategic Assets*, Sanat Kaul mentions that at the time of Independence, the British weighed four possible options regarding the islands. One proposal was to keep the islands as a Crown colony – like many others in the Caribbean and Pacific Islands. There are unconfirmed reports that as there were many Christian converts in Nicobar, Bishop Richardson sent a wire to London asking for the islands to be retained directly under Whitehall. Pakistan too laid a claim on the islands on account of their proximity to the Chittagong and Dhaka ports. The possibility of transferring the islands to Burma was also under consideration. Finally, it was decided that the islands would remain under the Union government as a Union Territory, and Imam-ul-Majid was appointed as the first chief commissioner.

Immediately after Independence, the first wave of migration into the islands was for rehabilitation of refugees from East and West Pakistan. From the first to the fifth Five-Year Plans, nearly six hundred families were allotted over 4100 acres of cleared forest land in Middle Andaman, Neil Island and Little Andaman. However, in addition to the officially settled refugees, post 1971 several Bangladeshis also intermingled with the Bengali settlers. The Burmese and Karens who had decided to stay back after their prison terms were also allotted lands, especially for the purpose of rubber cultivation.

An attempt was also made to resettle ex-servicemen in Great Nicobar. Over three hundred of them were given land with a view that they would ensure that nothing untoward happened in these marine frontiers of the country. As Kaul says, 'the main aspect of this rehabilitation was strategic. By putting ex-servicemen in Great Nicobar, it was felt that India would create a small group of well-trained Indians who would be able to provide the initial intelligence to any untoward activity in the area'.

Thus, the population mix of Andaman Islands is quite eclectic – a veritable mini-India. There are Punjabis, Tamils, Bhantus, Karens, Bengalis, Moplahs, Ranchis and, of course, a category called Local Born – the sons and daughters of the erstwhile prisoners who chose to settle there. Hindi has emerged as the new lingua franca, though the regional languages continue to flourish in the cultural communities to which most residents are now affiliated.

The island territories today are a significant strategic asset for India, especially on account of the proximity to Malacca Straits, an important SLOC, critical to trade and movement of oil from Gulf to the South China Sea, East China Sea and the Pacific. In fact, India's salient position in the QUAD is largely on account of its proximity to the Straits of Malacca. These islands also provide India tremendous economic potential for tourism, fisheries, forests besides enabling India to add 30 per cent of its additional EEZ. They also boost our Look East Policy and showcase India's maritime and air power in the India Pacific region. These considerations also led to the establishment of the first integrated command in India in which the Army, Air Force and Navy work together as a unified force. In 2001, Vice Admiral Arun Prakash took over as the first commander-in-chief of this unified command. The command moves to each of the three forces – Army, Navy and Air Force – every two years.

The big question today is whether the islands should be opened for high-end tourism, mineral reserves in the deep ocean as well as for deep-sea fishing, or left 'preserved' as they are. Both views have their pros and cons and the NITI Aayog proposal for a Rs 75,000-crore plan for the development of a new 'greenfield city' with a diverse and robust economy based on maritime services and tourism, amongst other drivers, has received intense criticism. The proposal includes an international container transshipment terminal, a greenfield international airport, a power plant and a township complex at the 166-acre Great Nicobars Island. Over half a million people are expected to stay there by 2050, if the development pans out as per the growth projections.

Even though the National Board for Wildlife, India's apex body for wildlife conservation, has denotified the Galathea Bay Wildlife Sanctuary in its entirety, critics have pointed out that this is the most iconic nesting site for giant leatherback turtles. Experts have also raised concerns over the impact all these activities will have on the rich forests and coastal and marine ecosystems of Great Nicobar. The island hosts a UNESCO World Heritage Site, multiple forest types and one of the best-preserved tropical rainforests in the world. It is also home to 648 species of flora and 330 species of fauna, including rare and endemic ones like the Nicobar wild pig, Nicobar tree shrew, the Great Nicobar crested serpent eagle, Nicobar paradise flycatcher and the Nicobar megapode. The proponents say that the of the 921 sq. km area, 640 sq. km is under reserve forest, and another 450 acres is protected under the Onge Tribal Conservation Area. They argue that making such a hue and cry over 166 acres is not justified, for other islands in the Pacific and Caribbean are doing very much the same and creating employment options for the residents.

Lakshadweep – A Hundred Thousand Islands

The literal meaning of Lakshadweep is 'one hundred thousand islands' in Sanskrit, Malayalam and Marathi. However, in that historical context, where Bharat Varsha was a part of Jambudweep,[25] Lakshadweep included the archipelagos of Maldives[26] and the Chagos,[27] a British Overseas Territory which includes the US naval base, Diego Garcia. The islands have long been known to sailors, as indicated in an anonymous reference from the AD first century in *Periplus*.[28] These were also mentioned in the Buddhist Jataka stories of the sixth century BCE. Islam was established in the region when Muslims arrived around the seventh century. During the medieval period, the region was ruled by the Chola dynasty[29] and later by the Kingdom of Cannanore. The Catholic Portuguese arrived around 1498 but were expelled by 1545. The region was then ruled by the Muslim house of Arakkal, which had to cede some areas to Tipu Sultan. By the early part of the nineteenth century, most of the region passed on to the British, though for all practical purposes, the islanders were left to fend for themselves. Amini, Kalpeni, Andrott, Kavaratti and Agatti were the oldest of the inhabited islands.

In 1956, the SRC had suggested that the predominantly Malayalam-speaking populations of Laccadive and Minicoy Islands under Malabar district, and Amindivi Islands of the South Canara district (both in the erstwhile Madras state) be integrated with the new linguistic state of Kerala. However, the islands were detached from their respective districts and established as a new Union Territory with a population of just 21,000 (census 1951) for administrative purposes. The district of Malabar was made part of Kerala, and South Canara (Dakshin Kannada) was attached to Karnataka. Meanwhile, a referendum was held in Minicoy in 1956 as this island was directly under the Crown, and only notionally attached to Malabar district for purposes of administration. That is how the islands of Laccadive, Minicoy and Amindivi became a Union Territory in 1956.

In 1973, the islands were renamed Lakshadweep, although the first Hindi map of India in 1952 had also referred to the islands by this name. It must be mentioned here that while the Amindivi group of islands had been under the control of Tipu Sultan,[30] the Laccadive group (Kavaratti, Agatti and Andrott) were under the Arakkals.[31] Minicoy island – the farthest island outpost of India – is situated mid-way between India and Maldives, and the language of this island is Dhivehi[32] although the rest of the islands speak Jeseri.[33] Dhivehi is the official language of Maldives. There were two possible reasons for placing these islands directly under the Union government. The stated reason was, of course, the long-term naval interest in the region, about which K.M. Panikkar started articulating his concerns from the time of India's independence. However, another plausible and more direct reason was the lurking fear of a possible communist regime in Kerala, and the Union government was paranoid about the implications of a red flag on any of the islands.

Before November 1956, the administration in the islands was only nominal and the trade to the mainland was done in boats called 'odams'. The islanders traded fish, copra and coir in exchange for rice, salt and other essentials. Lakshadweep's first representation to the Indian Parliament was based on nomination. From 1956 to 1967, the MP was K. Nalla Koya Thangal who served two terms. Although the overwhelming majority (99 per cent) of the population is Muslim, for reasons of geographical isolation, the entire population of the islands has been designated as Scheduled Tribe. It is also the smallest Lok Sabha constituency.

The first elections were held in 1967 and P.M. Sayeed went on to win the next ten elections consecutively. He was first elected to Lok Sabha in 1967 at the age of twenty-six. He served as Union minister of state for steel, coal and mines (1979–80), home affairs (1993–95) and information and broadcasting (1995–96). He was the Deputy Speaker of the Lok Sabha from 1998–2004. The credit for initiating most of the development interventions in the islands, including the establishment of the Island Development Authority, the introduction of air services, linkages with National Agricultural Cooperative Marketing Federation of India (NAFED) for the procurement of copra and modernization of ports and fishing, goes to him. Another milestone in the history of Lakshadweep was the shifting of the headquarters from Cochin to Kavaratti on 26 March 1964. Once the 'Administrator' started staying in the islands, the progress was substantial, and gradually government infrastructure, especially schools and hospitals, came up in all the inhabited islands. Interventions in the health sector are especially commendable and noteworthy, as leprosy was a major issue in the islands. Administrators like Omesh Saigal[34] helped in ensuring regularity in transport and communication services. His book,

Lakshadweep, published by the National Book Trust, helped bridge the information gap about the islands. Today, Lakshadweep has the second-highest literacy rate in the country, and women are not far behind men in this accomplishment. In terms of HDI, Lakshadweep is fourth in the country, just behind Kerala, Chandigarh and Goa, and above the NCT of Delhi! NITI Aayog has recently drawn up a strategy paper, 'Transforming the Islands through Creativity and Innovation', for the development of Lakshadweep Islands with a focus on sustainable eco-tourism and fishing as the key economic drivers in the islands, and over the next decade, these islands will actually be exemplars of how development interventions ought to be made.

14

FROM SUBJECTS TO CITIZENS – SIKKIM JOINS INDIA

The transition of Sikkim from one of the 562 princely states to a Protectorate,[1] then to an Associate State[2] and finally to an integral part of India is a fascinating story. The Maharaja of Sikkim was the vice president of the Chamber of Princes (*Narendra Mandal*)[3] established in 1920 by King-Emperor George V[4] for rulers of the princely states to voice their concerns and aspirations. As such, Sikkim was clearly more like Patiala and Baroda, rather than Nepal and Bhutan with whom the British arrangements were different. The relations between Britain and Bhutan were defined by the Treaty of Sinchula signed in 1910. In fact, in 1924, the British government confirmed that Bhutan, though under British suzerainity, was outside India, and not a native state. Another difference between Sikkim and Bhutan lay in the fact that the majority population of Sikkim was Nepali and had no intrinsic affiliation to the ruling Bhutia clan, which ran the kingdom in an absolutely autocratic manner through their own clansmen, the Kazis, who were the hereditary feudal lords with revenue and magisterial ownership over their disenfranchised Nepali serfs and the dispossessed Lepchas. The condition of the region in 1947 is best described in the words of Tashi Tshering:[5]

> Sikkim is a small Indian state tucked away in a corner of the Himalayas. Its ruler Sir Tashi Namgyal, KCSI, KCIE is of Tibetan descent and so are his personal adherents called Kazis who form the majority of the landlords of Sikkim. His Highness has a state council consisting entirely of the landlords and a Secretariat which is largely controlled by the landlords, the subject people or Eyoys (peasants) have no voice in administration, and they have long groaned under the pernicious yoke of landlordism.[6]

This was also the time when the redoubtable Sardar Patel and the constitutional expert B.N. Rau[7] pressed for the integration of Sikkim to India, but they were overruled by Prime Minster Nehru who, under the influence of Verrier Elwin, believed that *not only should the tribal way of life be preserved, it should be insulated from the impact of modern civilization*. He thus prevented integration with India, and also indulged the Maharaja of Sikkim by anointing him the Chogyal and the Maharani as the Gyalmo, thereby giving the ruler ideas about being 'sovereign' and independent. The second blunder was to place Sikkim as well as NEFA under the specially constituted IFAS, and placing these territories under the MEA, thereby setting them apart from the administration elsewhere in the country.

As such, for nearly two decades, the democratic movement in Sikkim was placed on the back-burner and India preferred to run Sikkim as an estate of the external affairs ministry. While Nehru had his own ideas about these frontier areas, and Shastri did not have the time to look into these issues, Prime Minister Indira Gandhi was different. She not only got India its first decisive military victory, but was also determined to defend the borders, and show the world that India had emerged as the dominant regional power of South Asia. The UN recognition for Bhutan had taken her by surprise and she was upset with the MEA for its mishandling of the situation. More of a realpolitik than a dreamer, she put the Chogyal in his place; and when he assumed 'sovereign and royal airs', he was hoisting his own petard.

Even under the highly distorted electoral system, the Sikkim National Congress led by Kazi Lhendup Dorjee had always scored the highest percentage of votes, but in the rigged elections of 1973, the Darbar Party[8] scored a landslide victory, which was suspect in the eyes of all concerned, and violent crowds moved to Gangtok and besieged the palace. Demands for the Chogyal's abdication became the dominant slogan. He was compelled to sign the India–Sikkim Treaty, which called for the establishment of a fully responsible government in Sikkim, with a democratic Constitution, fundamental rights, rule of law, independent judiciary and voting on the basis of one-man-one-vote. The Chogyal was to be the Constitutional head of the state. In the elections that followed, the Sikkim National Congress[9] led by the Kazi won 29 of the 32 seats, and the assembly passed a resolution asking for greater participation in the economic and political institutions of India. This was followed by the 36th Constitutional Amendment Act of 1974, which made Sikkim an Associate State.

This was a compromise between the various factions in the political ecosystem of Sikkim, which had as the key players: the Chogyal, Chief Minister Kazi Lhendup Dorjee, the radical faction of the Nepali peasantry led by the erstwhile protégé of Kazi Dorjee, Narbahadur Khatiwada,[10] and the civil servants under the darbar. This arrangement, though unstable, would allow the Chogyal to continue as the titular and hereditary head of Sikkim.

However, the personal ambitions of the Chogyal (which were more temporal than spiritual) coupled with the imprudent advice from his American Gyalmo[11] and his complete misreading of the person, persona and determination of Prime Minister Indira Gandhi were not in sync with the times. The impertinent remarks made by him to the foreign press during his visit to Nepal on the occasion of the coronation of the king, as well as his parleys with the Chinese delegation, were the last straw on the camel's back. Over the next few months the stage would be set for Sikkim's merger with India.

Was there an *ab initio* default in the 35th Constitutional amendment making Sikkim an Associate State of India? Or did it collapse because of the failure of the Chogyal to read the changing circumstances? It is true that Kazi Dorjee would have preferred 'merger', but even the Sikkim Assembly Resolution of 20 June 1974 asked for 'fuller participation of Sikkim in the economic and social institutions of India'. Had the Chogyal gone along with the popular mandate, could he have maintained his 'kingdom' where the overwhelming majority was ethnically apart?

After the status of Sikkim changed from a Protectorate to an Associate State, the subjects of Sikkim were almost equal in status to the citizens of India. They could be elected to the Lok Sabha and Rajya Sabha, and take the civil services exam at par with Indian students. Had the Chogyal reconciled with this situation, he could have continued to exercise the moral, cultural and spiritual leadership not just in Sikkim, but perhaps on the larger canvas of India. However, in a complete misreading of the situation, he preferred to internationalize the issue, which was an unwise move, considering the attitude of the then PM as well as the popular sentiment of the majority population of Sikkim. His statements casting aspersions against the newly elected government saw a massive anti-Chogyal upsurge in the streets of Gangtok, and when the Palace Radio called for a referendum on the status of Sikkim as an Associate State, the Chogyal unwittingly gave the Kazi a golden opportunity to organize a referendum. However, the agenda was now in the hands of the Kazi. Sikkim did have a referendum on 14 April 1975, but on a different issue: that of abolition of the office of Chogyal and complete merger with India. The results were on expected lines: an overwhelming support for joining India and ending the monarchy. Within two weeks, the Parliament approved the 36th Amendment, facilitating the incorporation of Sikkim as an integral part of India.

One must mention that there are four eminently readable texts on Sikkim – and each one lends an in-depth understanding of the issues surrounding Sikkim. Of these, *Smash and Grab*[12] by Sunanda K. Datta-Ray and *The Sikkim Saga*[13] by B.S. Das were published by Vikas Publication in 1984. Both, incidentally, had similar cover pages – shades of blue – and none carried the map of Sikkim on the cover or the back page. The third and the fourth books: *Sikkim: Requiem for a Himalayan Kingdom*[14] by Andrew Duff and *Sikkim: Dawn of Democracy*[15] by G.B.S. Sidhu were published by Penguin in 2015 and 2018 respectively. While they all agree on the events, incidents and issues, the treatment meted out is quite different, and reading these books side by side also confirms that history is but an interpretation and perspective of facts, and that no one, especially the contemporary observer, can claim to be 'objective'.

In *Smash and Grab*, Sunanda K. Datta-Ray's dedication of the book to Jungkhyang – the term used for the Chogyal in reverence – makes it clear that this is the perspective of the Chogyal. *The Sikkim Saga*, on the other hand, is the narrative from the point of view of B.S. Das, who served Sikkim as the chief executive officer, maintaining a fine balance between the Chogyal, in whose name he carried on the administration, and the Foreign Office in Delhi which, under Kewal Singh,[16] was quite adept at back-seat driving. Then we have the Scotsman Andrew Duff, tracing his grandfather's travels to the Sikkim Himalayas undertaken a century ago. He was given Datta-Ray's book as the first source but supplemented it with the reports from the FCO, in-depth interviews with key stakeholders, but most of all, from the weekly letters of the Scottish Headmistress(es) of the Paljor Namgyal Girls school in Gangtok: Martha Hamilton and Isabel Ritchie. Both had access to the Palace and were indeed beholden to their royal patrons. Their letters gave a first-hand, contemporaneous account for the years from 1959 to 1975, albeit from the Chogyal perspective. One must add that his book is quite nuanced, for he gives adequate coverage to the views of the other dramatis personae as well.

The fourth book is by G.B.S. Sidhu, an officer of the R&AW posted as an officer on special duty (OSD) in Sikkim to bolster the pro-democracy forces, led at that time by Kazi Lhendup Dorjee,[17] who he feels was short-charged by the Congress in the Emergency years and later. He mentions quite candidly that his purpose of writing the book was to salvage his reputation. He makes the point that 'kingdoms are created by force, military might, brotherhood, treaties or deceit. They crumble when people realize that the unpopular king has become powerless, as the very power (in this case India's protective cover) which had propped up the king or even sustained his unpopular rule, had disappeared, or withdrawn its protection, and was now willing to make amends for its past acts of omission or commission. Thondup Namgyal's dynasty lasted for 333 years. It could have survived longer had there been an enlightened ruler willing to adjust to changing environment by trying to accommodate the democratic aspirations of his people. But Thondup was not a person made out of that mould.'

15

DELHI, NEW DELHI, NCT AND NCR

The story of the capital city of India is so intertwined with the history of Bharat, Hindustan and India[1] that it is indeed difficult to talk of one without the other. The formidable challenge is not dearth of sources or reference material: on the contrary, it is about sifting the 'salient' from the plethora of information about a city with a living tradition from the second millennium BCE and projected to be the world's most populous city by 2030. The first known version of city of Delhi, Indraprastha, was established by the Pandavas in the Mahabharata period: it was one of the five settlements sought by Krishna from the Kuru kingdom[2] of Hastinapur (present-day Meerut) to avert the war, the other four being Swarnprastha (Sonipat), Panprastha (Panipat), Vyaghrprastha (Baghpat) and Tilprastha (Tilpat). Incidentally, even though these are not part of the National Capital Territory (NCT) of Delhi, they are all part of the National Capital Region (NCR).

The discovery of an Ashokan[3] edict in Brahmi script[4] (circa third century BCE) on a rock exposure at Bahapur in Srinivaspuri, near

Kalkaji temple, suggests that it marked an important trans-regional trade route of north India connecting the Gangetic Delta with the northwestern part of the Indian subcontinent. Another view is that this was the location of one of the five temples built by the Pandavas. The city found a mention as 'Indapatta' or 'Indapattana' in Buddhist texts, where it is described as the capital of the Kuru kingdom, situated on the Yamuna river.

Indraprastha was known to the Greco-Roman world as well: Ptolemy's *Geography* (second century CE) described the city as 'Indabara'. Although during the Maurya, Kushan, Gupta, Vardhan and Gurjara Pratihara dynasties, it continued to be a garrison outpost, as well as an important centre for trade and pilgrimage, political power had moved to Pataliputra in the Maurya and Gupta periods, Paurashpura (Peshawar) in the times of Kushans, Kannauj in the times of Vardhans and Ujjain in the times of the Pratiharas. The Tomar dynasty resurrected the political fortunes of Delhi by establishing Surajkund[5] and Lalkot in the ninth century. Quila Rai Pithora[6] was built by Prithvi Raj Chauhan in 1180 CE, but in 1192, he lost the city to Mohammad Ghori,[7] and, in a manner of speaking, this also marked the erasure of Bharat, and the advent of Islam to the subcontinent – first under the Mamluks, Khiljis, Tughlaqs, Sayyids and Lodhis (from the thirteenth to the fifteenth centuries) and then the Mughals who made it the world's most resplendent city. The Mamluks first camped in Mehrauli and established the Qutub Minar[8] complex in the thirteenth century. However, the iconic three tonne Iron Pillar (23 feet and 8 inches in height and a width of 16 inches) was originally erected during the time of Emperor Chandragupta II (375–413/14 CE) and moved to its present location by Anangpal Tomar[9] in the eleventh century. The Siri Fort established by Alauddin Khilji in 1300 CE was followed by Tughlaqabad, Jahanpanah and Firozabad by the

Tughluqs from 1320 to 1354. Between 1538 and 1545, Humayun developed Dinapanah,[10] and Feroze Shah Suri built Shergarh, both in the vicinity of the site of Indraprastha (Purana Quila area). When the Mughal Empire was at its zenith (1638–49) Shah Jahan built Shahjahanabad with Chandni Chowk, the Jama Masjid and the Lal Quila, where the Mughal dynasty lived till the fall of the empire in 1857. However, the Mughals had lost effective power to the Marathas in 1759 and, in 1783, the Khalsa armies under the combined leadership of Baghel Singh of the Karorsinghia, Jassa Singh of Ahluwalia and Jassa Singh of Ramgharia Misls[11] occupied the Red Fort, and took possession of the Mughal throne on which Aurangzeb had sentenced Guru Teg Bahadur to death and built gurudwaras across Delhi, including the historic Sis Ganj, Rakab Ganj and Bangla Sahab. But the Khalsa army left Delhi after making its presence felt and the Marathas held on till 1803, when the British took effective control after the Anglo–Maratha War[12] in which the Marathas were trounced. In 1857, disaffection on account of the annexation of Oudh (Awadh) and the introduction of 'greased cartridges' which both Hindu and Muslim soldiers felt was an act of sacrilege, the soldiers rallied behind Bahadur Shah Zafar[13] who was cast into the leadership role 'most reluctantly'. But he was a convenient scapegoat who spent his last years in exile in Rangoon. However, even when the capital of British India was Calcutta, Delhi continued to be the venue for the most significant political events and announcements, till it became the first city of India again. Three extracts from a book *Delhi: The Capital of India* by John Capper, FRAS,[14] are given below to describe the salience of Delhi to the governance of India:

(i) It is therefore no wonder that from time immemorial, Delhi has been the chief city of Bharat. All roads from the four points of the compass converged towards Delhi, and from Delhi marched forth in all directions hosts of army and caravans of merchants to conquer territories and capture markets. The Musalmaans in their onward march of conquests cast covetous eyes on Delhi … It was around Delhi that the Hindu kings made their last stand against the Muslim invasion. It was the capture of Delhi that brought India under the Muslim rule.

(ii) The Mahrattas had captured the city in 1759, but were defeated by Ahmad Shah Durrani in 1761. However, from 1788 to 1803 – they were the supreme power of North India, but and because of the failure to include Delhi in it, the Mahratta rule dwindled into a number of principalities, instead of becoming an empire of India that it bid fair to become at one time. After the Anglo Maratha War of 1803, Delhi came under the EIC and was placed under General David Ochterlony who was responsible for advising the 'dejure' sovereign the Mughal Badshah on issues related to governance, succession and protection from external aggression. It became part of the Northwest Province with Agra as the capital.

(iii) It was Delhi that the sepoy rebels in 1857 betook themselves to and sought the tottering shadow of the nominal ruler of Delhi to give their revolt a higher significance. It was on the recapture of Delhi that the British rule was firmly established. And it continued to be the site for the performance of the principal and most important functions of the capital town of the Indian empire even when the actual seat of government (Calcutta) was a thousand miles away from it.

As Simarpal Singh writes in his book *The Siege of Delhi*, 'In 1803, the Company considered it expedient to retain the emperor as a puppet – for a time at least – rather than abruptly terminating the dynasty. The holding of the Great Moghul as a pensioner under its protection gave the Company a significance, prestige and most importantly legitimacy to their status as the new paramount power in India.'

Be that as it may, after the reconquest of Delhi, it was detached from the North-Western Provinces and Oudh, and made part of the newly constituted state of British Punjab which had been annexed by the East India Company in 1849. In 1858, the Punjab, along with the rest of British India, came under the direct rule of the British crown. It had an area of 358,354.5 sq. km and five administrative divisions – Delhi, Jullundur, Lahore, Multan and Rawalpindi – and a number of princely states. From 1858 to 1911, Delhi was only one of the divisions of Punjab.[15] Even though Lahore was now the capital of Punjab, Delhi's significance lay in the fact that it was the venue for the Imperial Delhi Durbar of 1877[16] in which the Queen of Great Britain and Ireland was declared as the Empress of India.' The viceroy, Lord Lytton, held an Imperial Assemblage at Delhi to which all governors, lieutenant governors, heads of administrations, ruling chiefs, princes and nobles were invited. On the occasion of the second Coronation Durbar in 1911, King George V announced Delhi as the new capital of India. In 1912, Delhi became a chief commissioner's province with William Malcolm Hailey (on whom the Hailey Road is named) as the first incumbent. The Government of India Acts of 1919[17] and 1935[18] classified Delhi as a chief commissioner's province, which meant that Delhi was to be directly ruled by the governor general through his representative – the chief commissioner – a senior civil servant appointee who reported directly to the governor general.

The name 'New Delhi' was given in 1927, and the formal inauguration took place on 13 February 1931. Also called 'Lutyens' Delhi' after the architect who designed the Raisina Hill and the surrounding buildings, it continued to be a chief commissioner's province and its status (along with that of Ajmer-Merwara and

Coorg) came up for discussion in the Constituent Assembly debates where Deshbandhu Gupta and B.K. Sidhwa raised the issue of popular government in Delhi. In July 1947, the Pattabhi Sitaramayya Committee[19] set up to study the territorial and administrative structures of the chief commissioner's provinces singled out Delhi as a special case to formulate a road map for its autonomy and governance as a National Capital Territory. Given its complicated and overlapping jurisdictions, the committee paid considerable attention to study the administrative systems of various federal capitals such as Canberra in Australia, Washington, D.C. in the United States and London in the United Kingdom. Considering the circumstances that led to the formation of the Delhi Province in 1912, the committee concluded that the 'province which contains the metropolis of India should not be deprived of the right of self-government enjoyed by the rest of their countrymen living in the smallest of villages'.

The recommendations of the Sitaramayya Committee included the following: 'province' should function under a lieutenant governor (to be appointed by the President); a council of ministers headed by a chief minister to aid and advise the lieutenant governor; concurrent powers of legislation to Union Parliament even in matters included in the 'Provincial List'. The central government was also vested with special responsibilities for the 'good governance' and financial solvency of the province.

However, both Nehru and Ambedkar had serious reservations with the recommendations of the Sitaramayya Committee. They felt that being the national capital of India, it could not be placed under the administration of a local government. Opposing the recommendations of the committee, Jawaharlal Nehru observed, 'Ever since the committee was appointed the world has changed; India has changed, and Delhi has changed vitally.'[20] Delhi had indeed changed in the aftermath of the Partition.[21] The infrastructure and resources required for the rehabilitation of refugees from Punjab and Sindh, as well for the new institutions of governance required 'the resources of the entire nation'.

As Veronique Dupont[22] wrote, 'the demographic evolution of the city of Delhi during the twentieth century is closely linked to the history of the country. Following the announcement of Delhi as the capital of the British Empire in 1911, the population grew from 2,38,000 to 6,96,000 in 1941. Just after Partition, Delhi's demography changed forever – over 4,70,00 refugees moved in from West Punjab and Sindh, while over 3 lakh Muslims left for Pakistan.'[23]

As such, Delhi became a Part C State (Union Territory) and the national capital would be administered by the President through a lieutenant governor (LG) to be appointed by him and it forfeited the right to have a Legislative Assembly or a council of ministers. Subsequently, Articles 239 and 240[24] were added to provide more layers to the governing space of Delhi.

Following this, the Government of Part C States Act (1951) was passed, under which provision was made for a council of ministers in Delhi, albeit with limited mandate. Key subjects such as public order; police (including railway police); municipal corporation and lands were left with the central authorities. As a result, Delhi, for the first time, had a Legislative Assembly, a council of ministers and a chief minister. The first Delhi Legislative Assembly was constituted in March 1952, and Chaudhary Brahm Prakash[25] took over as the first chief minister, albeit with limited powers, and an advisory role to the then chief commissioner.[26] This was a short-lived experiment – for as per the recommendations of the States Reorganization Commission which came into effect from November 1956, Delhi became a Union Territory under the direct

administration of the Government of India (MHA). The majority
view in the commission (Chairman Fazal Ali and H.N. Kunzru)
was that the commission observed that the dual control over the
national capital had led to 'marked deterioration of administrative
standards'. Citing the examples of Paris and London, the
commission observed, '... capital cities possess or come to possess,
some degree of political and social predominance' and went further
to claim, '... any constitutional division of powers, it is applicable
to units functioning in the seats of national governments, is bound
to give rise to embarrassing situations.' The commission, however,
noted the need for an autonomous Municipal Corporation to
provide 'greater local autonomy than is the case in some of the
important federal capitals ... in fact, the only solution to the
problem of Delhi State'.

However, it must be placed on record that in 1956, a resolution of
the Delhi Legislative Assembly 'recommended to the Government
of India that boundaries of Delhi state be enlarged to include the
neighbouring districts of Punjab and UP so that an administratively
and economically sound state is created'. A memorandum submitted
to the SRC on behalf of the Delhi state government stated, 'the
people of this area (Delhi and the surrounding districts) have
historic, cultural and economic ties. They have common language,
dress, marriage rites, laws of succession, system of land tenure and
customs.' The representation went on to add that the province of
Delhi had been broken up artificially 'both as a punishment for
taking part in the so-called Mutiny of 1857, as well as a device to
break down their morale and to crush their spirit'. The territories
proposed to be included were the Agra, Meerut and Rohilkhand
divisions of UP, the Ambala division of Haryana, and the Alwar
and Bharatpur districts of Rajasthan. This proposal did not find a
positive response, either from the Union government, or the states

of UP, Punjab and Rajasthan. Meanwhile, a similar memorandum was submitted by ninety-seven MLAs from the western and hill districts of UP wanting to merge their areas with Delhi. The five points made in favour of their demand were: a) the sheer size of the (UP) state, which often led to the neglect of the western districts and the hill areas; b) lesser development expenditure; c) need for rapid industrialization; d) geographical proximity to Delhi rather than Lucknow and e) the new state would not need a new capital for Delhi could serve the purpose.

The news that a hundred legislators could get together and submit a memorandum to the SRC caught the state and the central leadership of the Congress unawares, and they stepped in immediately to stall the move. P.D. Tandon[27] and G.B. Pant[28] closed ranks and nipped the idea in the bud, and gave a counter memorandum to the SRC on why the territorial boundaries of UP should remain unchanged. They averred that the large size of UP was good for large-scale development projects and for mobilization of resources. While the chairman of the SRC, Justice Fazal Ali, and H.N. Kunzru were convinced with this argument, the third member K.M. Panikkar gave a strong note of dissent. He made the point that UP was too large to be administered. It may be noted that earlier Dr Ambedkar had expressed the view that a state of the size and population of UP was creating political asymmetry. Had the views of Dr Ambedkar, as well as the legislators of UP and Delhi, prevailed the political geography of India would have been quite different from what it is.

Unsurprisingly, SRC's recommendation of abolishing Legislative Assembly and reducing the national capital's autonomy to the level of Municipal Corporation invited the strongest criticisms from key figures from Delhi. Reacting to the commission's report tabled in Parliament, member of Parliament Sucheta Kriplani[29] raised her concerns against the change of Delhi's status thus: 'Delhi is going to lose its democratic setup. We are going to lose the status of State. Our people will be disenfranchised. In place of legislature, we are going to be given Corporation with limited powers. Therefore, I feel Delhi is not being dealt fairly.' Another lawmaker, C.K. Nair, observed: 'But what we expected is a fair deal for Delhi just as every Part C State was added to Part A State, which means greater advantage and greater freedom for people of those areas. It is not so with regard to Delhi.'

To give Delhi some elected leadership, the Municipal Corporation of Delhi Act, 1957 was passed by the Parliament, establishing the now-trifurcated Municipal Corporation of Delhi. Delhi, however, did not come under the Government of Union Territories Act, 1961, which allowed for Legislative Assemblies and councils of ministers in some large Union Territories. There were widespread demands for Delhi to get statehood and more elected representatives in its general governance.

As a compromise, the Delhi Metropolitan Council was formed in 1966 with the passing of the Delhi Administration Act, 1966, by the Parliament of India; the council had fifty-six directly elected members (called councillors) and five members nominated by the newly created position of lieutenant governor(LG). The council had only advisory powers with regards to legislative proposals, budget proposals and other matters referred to it by the lieutenant governor. The lieutenant governor succeeded the chief commissioner as the administrator of Delhi. The Delhi Metropolitan Council's chairman and deputy chairman acted as speaker and deputy speaker for the council, which elected a chief executive councillor (CEC) and three executive councillors, much like a state chief minister and council of ministers elected by – and responsible to – the council. During this twenty-four-year period, the chief executive councillors emerged as the 'de facto' political leaders of Delhi with V.K. Malhotra[30] and

Kedar Nath Sahni[31] of the BJP and Jag Parvesh Chandra[32] of the INC holding the position for significant periods of time.

After two decades of haphazard governance through multiple agencies, the Centre finally agreed to set up the Justice R.S. Sarkaria[33] Committee (later renamed Balakrishnan[34] Committee when Justice Sarkaria resigned) to look at the 'Reorganisation of Delhi Set-up' in 1987. The committee was tasked to study the administrative processes, issues plaguing the administration process of the national capital and offer solutions. While the BJP and the Janata Dal made a strong plea for full statehood before the committee the (then) ruling Congress party at the centre took a more restrained view. It expressed support for maximum autonomy but was opposed to statehood. In its report submitted in 1989, the committee admitted that most of the difficulties faced by the citizens of Delhi were due to the structural inadequacies and flaws of the existing system. However, it was reiterated that, 'Delhi as the national capital belongs to the nation as a whole.'

It further held that while the federal government should have substantial control over the governance of the national capital, the people in the city also needed a representative body to look into those aspects of administration that impact their daily lives. Even as it maintained Union Territory status for Delhi, the report made a strong recommendation for the restoration of legislative assembly with appropriate powers to deal with matters concerning the citizenry. The report had envisaged that Delhi cannot have a situation where the national capital has 'two governments run by different political parties. Such conflicts may, at times, prejudice the national interest'.

The report foresaw that if Delhi became a full-fledged state, there would be a constitutional division of sovereign, legislative and executive powers between the Union and the state of Delhi. The Parliament would have limited legislative access and that too only in special and emergency situations. The Union would be unable to discharge its 'special responsibilities in relation to the national capital as well as to the nation itself'.

In accordance with the recommendations of the Balakrishnan Committee, the Parliament passed the Constitution (69th Amendment) Act, 1991, which inserted the new Articles 239 AA and 239 AB[35] in the Constitution providing, inter alia, for a Legislative Assembly for Delhi. Another comprehensive legislation passed by Parliament, the Government of National Capital Territory of Delhi (GNCTD) Act, 1991 supplemented the Constitutional provisions relating to the Legislative Assembly and the council of ministers and matters related thereto. Section 33 of the Government of National Capital Territory of Delhi Act provided for the framing of the Rules of Procedure and Conduct of Business of the Legislative Assembly. The assembly was invested with the power to make laws with respect to all the matters in the State List or in the Concurrent List of the Constitution of India except Entries 1 (Public Order), 2 (Police) and 18 (Land). In short, the 69th Amendment Act roughly restored the kind of governance system that was offered to Delhi in 1952: a Union Territory with a Legislative Assembly, council of ministers and an elected chief minister with a limited mandate. However, the LG continued to exercise overriding powers, especially in matters concerning land, law and order and appointment of senior officials.

In 2016, the Government of NCT of Delhi[36] approached the Delhi High Court seeking a clarification on the powers of the LG. The court held that the lieutenant governor of Delhi exercised 'complete control of all matters regarding National Capital Territory (NCT) of Delhi'. An appeal was filed in the Constitution Bench of the Supreme Court which opined that 'the status of NCT of Delhi is *sui generis*, a class apart, and the status of the Lieutenant Governor of Delhi is not that of a Governor of a State, rather he remains an Administrator, in a limited sense, working with the designation of Lieutenant Governor'. It said the lieutenant governor of Delhi had no independent decision-making powers and was bound to follow the 'aid and advice' of the Delhi 'chief-minister-headed council of ministers' on all matters except those pertaining to police, public order and land. However, as experts have pointed out, while the court's interpretation of Article 239 AA of the Constitution was sound and correct, all it did was to restore 'an unhappy status quo as regards the government of the National Capital Territory of Delhi'. The flaw was in Article 239 AA itself. While giving Delhi a legislature that drew its powers from the Constitution (like a state), it also left it with an administrator in the form of an LG (like a Union Territory) with more powers than the governor of a state.

The situation has not been eased by the enactment of the GNCTD (Amendment) Act, 2021, which allows the LG of Delhi to refer to the President any Bill passed by the Delhi legislature that may even incidentally fall outside the purview of the Delhi legislature (Section 3), curtails the powers of the Legislative Assembly and its committees to look into matters of 'day-to-day administration' or 'administrative decisions' (Section 4) and mandates that all executive actions can only be taken by the Delhi government after seeking the opinion of the LG (Section 5). Needless to say, the Act has been challenged in the Supreme Court by the GNCTD.

Is there a way out of this impasse? One must reckon with the fact that Delhi is one of the fastest growing regions of the country, is already ahead of many states (Uttarakhand, Himachal, Tripura, Meghalaya, Manipur, Nagaland, Goa, Arunachal and Sikkim) and the highest among the eight UTs in terms of population. By 2028, it will equal or exceed the population of Haryana and Chhattisgarh. Also, if one went by the population criterion, Delhi would have a substantial raise in the number of its MPs (from seven to twelve) after the next round of delimitation.

The best option is to reconstitute Delhi as two UTs – NCTD and NCR. The NCTD should be confined to NDMC, Delhi Cantonment and the Aerocity – these are geographically contiguous and compact – and placed under a chief commissioner or LG reporting to the MHA. The most important buildings and establishments of the Government of India, including the Rashtrapati Bhavan, the new Parliament complex, all the ministries, departments, state bhawans, diplomatic missions as well the defence establishments and the airport will come within this area. Except for Red Fort where the PM unfurls the flag on the Independence Day, every other venue, including the National War Memorial and Rajghat are in New Delhi. If required, the jurisdiction of the NCTD may be extended to cover Red Fort as well – and it is just a few kilometres from the Bahadur Shah Zafar Marg, which is in New Delhi.

The rest of Delhi with the addition of districts and tehsils of UP, Haryana and Rajasthan which are part of the NCR, should be constituted as the UT of NCR but with a higher degree of devolution of political authority. This region too should belong to the entire nation, and every Indian should have a right to study, work and settle in the region. This NCR will be the magnet of entrepreneurial growth as well as the hub for education, media, commerce, green manufacturing, ministry of micro, small and medium enterprises (MSME) and the services sector. This UT should have a Legislative Assembly and an effective chief minister with 'almost' the same powers as a regular state. The NCR was defined by NCR Act in 1985, and at the time of its inception, it included the whole of Delhi – the districts of Gurgaon, Faridabad and Sonipat, Rohtak (including Jhajjar tehsil) and the Rewari tehsil then in Mahendragarh district in Haryana, Bulandshahr,

Muzaffarnagar, Meerut (then including Baghpat tehsil), and Ghaziabad (including Hapur tehsil) of UP and some parts of Alwar in Rajasthan. This NCR covered an area of 34,144 sq. km. Gautam Budh Nagar district was created in 1997 out of the existing NCR districts of Ghaziabad and Bulandshahr. The city of Noida was the location of the new district's headquarters. Also, in 1997, Baghpat district was created from Baghpat tehsil of Meerut district.

In July 2013, the NCR was expanded to include three more districts, Bhiwani and Mahendragarh in the state of Haryana, as well as Bharatpur in the state of Rajasthan. This brought the number of districts, outside of Delhi NCT, to nineteen, and with the total NCR area was now 45,887 sq. km. In 2015, the Government of India approved the inclusion of three more districts in NCR – Jind, Panipat, Karnal in the state of Haryana and Muzaffarnagar in Uttar Pradesh, thereby extending the total area to 50,566 km. Shamli district of UP was added to the NCR in December 2017. In 2018, the Government of Uttar Pradesh formally proposed the extension of the NCR to cover the districts Aligarh, Bijnor, Hathras and Mathura and Agra. Punjab pitched for the inclusion of Patiala and Mohali in the NCR. It was as if inclusion in NCR was a panacea for all the infrastructure and development issues.

While UP, Rajasthan and Punjab were keen on expanding the circle of NCR, it caused a major concern in Haryana, for almost the entire state was coming under its ambit. It was felt that after a few decades, the very existence of the state may come under a cloud. Moreover, the NCR itself was becoming quite unwieldy, and the criterion for inclusion rather 'subjective'. A course correction was done in 2021, restricting NCR to a 100-km radius from the Rajghat, as against the earlier criterion of including areas up to 175 km. This would also reduce the size of the NCR to a manageable 37,115 sq. km.

This is certainly not an easy task, and there will be tremendous opposition from the constituent states from which districts will be cut off for the NCR. As such this must be part of the larger exercise of reorganization of states that ought to be done before the next round of delimitation which must address the issue of the great asymmetry among the states. However, whenever this exercise is undertaken, there will be a strong case for a new UT of NCR besides, of course, a compact UT for NCTD.

16

REGIONAL ASPIRATIONS

Chhattisgarh, Uttarakhand and Jharkhand

At the turn of the millennium, three new states were formed out of the three of the largest states[1] in the country: Madhya Pradesh, Uttar Pradesh and Bihar. All three were in the Hindi belt, but there was a rare bipartisan consensus on the creation of the new states, based not just on ethnicity or language but on 'regional aspirations'. The three states also marked a new phase in the construction of a modern regional identity. Chhattisgarh was formed on 1 November, Uttarakhand on 9 November and Jharkhand on 15 November 2000.

Chhattisgarh

Chhattisgarh, or the region with thirty-six forts as mentioned in inscriptions, literary works and foreigners' travelogues, covered an area of 135,000 sq. km, had a population of about twenty million and was the largest of the three new states. One-third of the territory and population of Chhattisgarh was formed by the sixteen eastern districts of MP.

The state's ancestry can be traced to the legendary Dakshin Kosala, the kingdom of Rama's mother Kausalya, as well as Dandakaranya[2], where he, along with Lakshman and Sita, had to spend fourteen years in exile from Ayodhya. The capital city Shripur (etymologically the city of wealth) on the banks of Mahanadi became an important centre of Buddhism, at par with Nalanda, for its hundreds of monasteries and thousands of monks from the fifth century BCE to the twelfth century CE. From the tenth century, the Chedis[3] and the Chalukyas[4] ruled the region directly, and then it was under the suzerainty of the Mughals from the sixteenth century. By the late eighteenth and early nineteenth century, the British extended the colonial enterprise to this region. As Nandini Sundar,[5] an insightful scholar and chronicler of contemporary Chhattisgarh, puts it, 'the colonial situation meant that the primary impulse for extension of administration did not come from the changing exigencies of local society, but from the colonial authorities' perception of the necessity to govern'.[6] The superabundant forest wealth drew the colonial gaze, and thus began the reservation of forest, organized timber felling, infrastructure for the 'hunt', and the systematic curtailment of rights of forest dwellers over the forest produce, thereby upsetting the ecological balance and livelihood opportunities of the forest dwellers. These conflicts over traditional rights to forest produce versus the 'legal grime of the colonial state' often led to revolts and rebellions, which were intense and violent, but spatially confined to the region. However, the central narrative remained common and unchanged: the inalienable right of tribals over local land resources and forests. The Bastar tribals, therefore, sought a separate state of Gondwana,[7] but the movement petered out as they could not mobilize political support from the Congress or Acharya Kirplani's Kisan Mazdoor Praja[8] (later Praja Socialist Party) which was the lead Opposition in the region. Also, the Bastar tribals could not make common cause with the people from pre-dominantly rice-growing plains areas around Raipur, where political mobilization for Chhattisgarh had started from the '20s and the former's conception of Chhattisgarh included the forest and hill regions. It may also be mentioned that while Raipur and the adjoining plains were part of the erstwhile Central Provinces and Berar, the tribal areas came under a variety of princely and feudatory states, and were also linguistically and geographically separated.

The first stirrings of the national movement in the region were felt when Mahatma Gandhi toured Raipur on 20 December 1920 to mobilize support for the Khilafat and Non-Cooperation movements, and to raise resources for the Tilak and Swaraj funds. He was accompanied by the Ali brothers,[9] and the arrangements for a conference were made by the political stalwart of the region, Ravi Shankar Shukla,[10] who later became the premier of Central Provinces and Berar, and the first chief minister of Madhya Bharat. A flavour of the times is captured in the repartee of Ravi Shankar Shukla to Asgar Ali who thanked the Hindu brethren of Raipur for supporting the Moslem cause of the Khilafat. Shukla responded: 'We do not consider ourselves Hindus or Moslems: we are all Hindustanis.'[11]

This led to the formation of the Raipur District Congress Committee, which raised the demand for a separate province of Chhattisgarh in 1924. This was also raised in the Tripuri session[12] of the Congress, but there it did not gain much traction on account for the domination of Shuklas in the larger arena of state and national politics.

Nevertheless, a memorandum was submitted to the SRC in 1954, and the demand for a separate state came up in the Nagpur Assembly of the then state of Madhya Bharat, which was in many ways the reiteration of a demand that had been raised in the Central Provinces and Berar Assembly prior to Independence as well. But even though the demand was not accepted by the SRC, the 'seed had been sown'.

Although the demand for Chhattisgarh was rejected by the SRC on the grounds that Madhya Pradesh would not be economically viable without the forest and mineral wealth of Chhattisgarh, it was revived again in the 1960s, especially as the leadership of the Shuklas came to be contested by Khubchand Baghel.[13] Baghel was a popular leader of the Mahanadi Valley, and had established the Chhattisgarh Bhratru Sangh (CBS) not only to give a distinct flavour to Chhattisgarhi dialect and culture, but also to articulate the demand for statehood. In many ways, it was the revival of the Prathak (separate) Chhattisgarh movement of the '20s. The objective of CBS was to ensure that the drain of wealth from this region to the larger entity of MP was curtailed, and there was preference in jobs and contracts for the locals. The CBS argued that in terms of education and entrepreneurship, the region was a laggard. The CBS emerged as a major force in the Mahanadi Valley. One must also make a reference to the Chhattisgarh Samaj, an organization formed under the umbrella of the Proutist Sarva Samaj, it was devoted to the development of a political, social and cultural consciousness of Chhattisgarh. Since the late '60s, the Samaj had been publishing a weekly newspaper in Chhattisgarhi. Like the Chhattisgarh Mukti Morcha (CMM), it had been fielding candidates in the Chhattisgarh elections, but could not make a significant impact in electoral politics.

Meanwhile, one needs to discuss another mass movement led by the intrepid Shankar Guha Niyogi.[14] It started as a trade union movement in Bhilai, where in addition to the Bhilai Steel Plant, there were over a dozen big industries and a hundred steel-based industrial units. The conventional trade unions had left out the contract workers, and their affiliation to the political parties

(INTUC[15] with Congress), (AITUC[16] with CPI) and (CITU[17] with CPM) always made it possible for the managements to engage with the highest echelons of those parties, thereby reducing the negotiating ability of the local units. Niyogi was an organic intellectual on the lines of Gramsci, but he was serially thrown out of the CPI, CPM, CPI (ML) as his grassroots style of politics which included prohibition, primary schools, women's issues and working in collaboration with civil society and support to constructive work was an anathema to the conventional communist politics. His concept of a Chhattisgarhi was 'one who lives in the geographical region of Chhattisgarh, earns his livelihood through honest work, and is dedicated to the cause of emancipation of Chhattisgarh'.[18] He also sought to unite the peasants with the workers – hence, the red-green flag – of the CMM and the organization of Chhattisgarh Mahila Mukti Morcha (CMMM), for women's emancipation and equal participation was another of his priorities. He also started the tradition of observing the day of Shahid Vir Narain Singh's execution by the British as Martyr's Day. The idea was to evoke a sense of pride and conviction in one's own ability to affect change. While he did not make non-violence the credo of his movement, he was veering towards Gandhian ideology with respect to empowerment of the self and the community. 'CMMs notion of New Chhattisgarh for a New India resembles Gandhian notion of the Indian state as the outermost circle of several concentric circles with the individual at the centre and the village as the innermost circle.'[19] CMM did enter electoral politics but could not make a dent in the salience of the INC and the BJP in the state.

In the late '80s and early '90s, Chandulal Chandrakar[20] of the Indian National Congress formed a bipartisan political forum known as Chhattisgarh Rajya Nirman Manch. This forum successfully organized region-wide bandhs and rallies, which were supported by major political parties including the Congress and the BJP. By this time, the BJP had let go of its reservations with regard to small states. It felt that the grassroots work done by the Vanvasi Kalyan Ashram[21] would ensure electoral success in a new state in which tribes made up one-third of the overall population. In fact, there was one-upmanship between the BJP and the Congress regarding whose support for the new state was stronger

The Congress Government of Madhya Pradesh under Digvijay Singh took the first institutional and legislative initiative for the creation of Chhattisgarh in March 1994. Four years later, the NDA-led Union government drafted a Bill for the creation of a separate state of Chhattisgarh from sixteen districts of Madhya Pradesh. This draft Bill was sent to the Madhya Pradesh Assembly which approved it unanimously, albeit with minor modifications, and after the approval of both the Lok Sabha and the Rajya Sabha, the President of India gave his consent to the Madhya Pradesh Reorganization Act, 2000, on 25 August 2000, and the first day of November was designated as the 'appointed date' for the establishment of the new state of Chhattisgarh.

While both the BJP and the Congress had supported the formation of the state, the contest for the position of the first chief minister was bitter. Though the Congress had 48 seats as against the BJP's 36 in a 90-member house, the Congress was a house divided with V.C. Shukla,[22] a lead contender, staying away from the swearing-in ceremony after his last-minute attempts to cobble an alliance with the BJP failed. Ajit Jogi was made the first chief minister though his tenure was not very smooth, both on account of the controversy regarding his status as a tribal and his involvement in a political murder.

Uttarakhand

Before the Gurkhas[23] established their rule in 1790, the Garhwal and Kumaon regions were ruled by the Parmar/Panwar[24] and Chand[25] dynasties respectively. After the Anglo Gurkha War of 1815, the Treaty of Sugauli allowed Sudarshan Shah to rule over Tehri Garhwal, while the Pauri Garhwal and Kumaon was brought under the governor general, who administered it as a Non-Regulation Area, with the commissioner of Kumaon being more powerful than any other commissioner in the United Provinces. The commissioner had both executive and judicial powers and also acted until 1937 as the British agent to the Tehri principality. It was then placed under the Punjab Hill States Agency. Between 1815 and 1947, Kumaon had some legendary commissioners, and the tenures of G. W. Trail (1816–36), Henry Ramsay (1856–84) and Percy Wyndham (1913–24) are remembered in local folklore as well.

However, by 1864, the operational 'power' in the hills started shifting to the forest department. In 1868, the management of the forests of Kumaon was handed over to this department. The Indian Forest Act of 1878 outlined a process whereby the state could take over forest areas for its exclusive use. This has to be seen in the context of the great railway expansion project by the Empire, especially after the Crown took over the direct administration. The objective was to ensure the movement of men and materials across the length and breadth of the subcontinent. Even in the administrative headquarters of Kumaon, the forest around the town of Nainital was demarcated and declared 'protected'.

The kingdom of Tehri Garhwal followed the British example even more brazenly, for there was money to be made from 'wooden sleepers' and the income from forests was the mainstay of the revenue of the Tehri Raj. Tehri was also home to Frederick Wilson,[26] who began collecting the pelts of animals and stuffing the skins of monal pheasant, rare white tigers, black and brown bears, and the musk deer for commercial profit. Later, he used his extensive knowledge to provide a major chunk of the two million sleepers requisitioned by the railways.

However, all this meant that the peasants, artisans and craftsmen who lived in the vicinity of the forest lost their traditional sources of livelihood. The boundaries of the reserved forest now extended right up to their fields and houses. Forest exploitation was proceeding apace even as villagers were no longer allowed to practice shifting cultivation. The consequence of all this was sporadic *dhandaks*[27] under the leadership of Badri Singh Aswal and Lachhman Singh Kathait. The prominent nationalist leader G.B. Pant drew up a detailed chart to show the reality of this 'resource kidnap' between 1897 and 1916. The First World War intensified the demand for timber and 4,00,000 sleepers were sent out of Kumaon, but by this time, the peasants rose in revolt against the restriction on their traditional and customary rights. The other irksome issue was the institutionalized system of begar, working for the visiting officials of the forest and revenue departments without remuneration.

In 1916, with the formation of the Kumaon Parishad[28] and a clear position taken by the local press, protests began to take the shape of an organized movement. Forest issues had merged with the strife against begar. The merger had lent depth to the struggle. In various gatherings the abolition of begar and the restoration of forest rights were permanent demands presented repeatedly. On 11 May 1919, a gathering chaired by Hargovind Pant in the Nandadevi Prangan (temple compound) of Almora demanded the abolition of begar and the restoration of full rights over forests.

In 1921, a Kumaon Forest Grievances Committee (KFGC) was constituted to understand problems relating to forest land. To a large extent, this committee restored the forest rights of local farmers. While valuable forest areas remained with the state, villagers were encouraged to manage the areas close to their settlements – those designated as 'Van Panchayats'. By the time of Independence, there were close to 500 Van Panchayats in the Kumaon Division.

Meanwhile, in 1938, the Congress party held a conference at Srinagar in Garhwal and raised the issues pertaining to both Kumaon and Tehri. Jawaharlal Nehru participated in this conference held under the presidency of Pratap Singh Negi. Nehru agreed that the people in these hills had a right to take their own decisions and enrich their culture in view of their peculiar circumstances. Later, in 1939, the Congress in its political meet at Pauri witnessed the emergence of Garhwal Jagrit Sanstha (GJS) that comprised Congressmen (like Pratap Singh Negi), who were not satisfied with the progress in regard to the demands of the hill people. At a meeting held at Haldwani in 1946, the Kumaon leaders like Badri Dutt Pande, popularly known as Kumaon Kesari, and Puran Chand Tiwari demanded a separate administrative unit for the hills in a meet held in 1946 at Haldwani. Later Badri Dutt Pande sent this demand for the consideration of the States Reorganization Commission.

Meanwhile, the popular protest movements in Tehri were also gaining strength, and even though the Maharaja had banned all political activities in his state, the Rawain dhandak over forest restrictions, cess on potatoes, and the resistance to Pontoti Tax (customs duty) were the precursors to the freedom movement in princely Garhwal. Meanwhile, a Praja Parishad came up in Dehradun and leaders like Sridev Suman, Paripoornananda Penyuili and Virendra Datt Saklani fought for the fundamental political and economic rights of the people of Tehri. Immediately after Independence, the Saklana dhandak was organized in which Kirti Nagar was 'liberated' from the Tehri Raj. Vir Chandra Singh Garhwali[29] took on a leadership role, which ultimately led to the full and final merger of the Tehri Raj with India on 1 August 1949.

Given the limited scope of farming, cattle rearing and forest-based entrepreneurship, the youth of Kumaon (and Garhwal) found in the British Indian Army an unparalleled opportunity to show their strength and valour, travel across the country, even the world, and win laurels. Together with the Gurkhas from Nepal, Pathans from the NWFP and the Jat Sikhs of Punjab, the highlanders of the Kuman hills were amongst the 'prominent martial races'[30] of British India. The headquarters of the Kumaon and Garhwal Regiment were established in Ranikhet and Lansdowne respectively, and the Garhwalis also took pride in the Victoria Cross winners, Darwan Singh Negi (from Chamoli) and Gabbar Singh Negi (of Chamba in Tehri Garhwal), in the First World War. However, the counter fact was equally strong. As mentioned earlier, Rifleman Chandra Singh Garhwali refused to open fire on an unarmed procession of Congressmen in Peshawar in 1930, and over 2500 soldiers of this regiment opted to join the Azad Hind Fauj under Subhas Bose in 1945 when the occasion arose. Captain Chandra Singh Negi rose to be a lieutenant colonel in the Azad Hind Fauj, and Captain R.N. Awasthi and Buddhi Singh also held responsible positions.

In the aftermath of Independence, the entire region, as well as the princely Tehri Garhwal, was brought under the administration of Uttar Pradesh (the new name of the erstwhile United Provinces). It may be mentioned that as Tehri was under the Punjab States Agency[31] from 1936, and then under Punjab States (in the ministry of states), the possibility of a larger Himalayan state – Ladakh, Lahaul–Spiti, Garhwal and Kumaon – was under active consideration for a brief period. Be that as it may, by 1950, the first map of the Republic of India had both Kumaon and Garhwal under the state of UP.

In the post-Independence period, the first political party to take up the issue of a separate Uttarakhand was the Communist Party of India. The undivided CPI took it up in 1952 when its former general secretary P.C. Joshi[32] sent a memorandum in this regard to the Government of India. This was forwarded to the States Reorganization Commission which did not accede to the demand even though K.M. Panikkar's note of dissent mentioned that the sheer size of UP made it administratively unmanageable. The ex-Maharaja of Tehri, Manabendra Shah, revived the issue of a separate state in 1957, and later in 1966, after the creation of Himachal as a UT, he sent a memorandum in this regard. Perhaps the prominent positions held by leaders from Uttarakhand in the national polity – G.B. Pant,[33] H.N. Bahuguna,[34] N.D. Tiwari[35] and K.C. Pant[36] – in the first three decades of Independence never let the feeling of regionalism come to the fore. In many ways, the rise of the 'Uttarakhand sentiment' coincided with the marginalization of these leaders, both in the politics of UP and the Centre.

Earlier the National Forest Policy of 1952 had laid down that properly managed forests must not only supply raw materials for industry, export and defence, but also secure a balanced ecosystem, while ensuring local people's demands for firewood, grazing land and minor forest produce for livelihoods and entrepreneurship. However, the forest department was set in its old ways, and discouraged all forms of small-scale commodity extraction. More importantly, under the extant rules, it was difficult for small-scale local entrepreneurs to compete at the forest department auctions with merchants and traders from outside the region who had the capacity to mobilize finance through their links in the capital and credit markets. They also brought with them skilled and semi-skilled labourers, mostly Nepalis, who were more 'biddable' and willing to work for lower wages.

Another factor that led to the 'economic marginality' of the region was the closure of the Indo-Tibetan border[37] in the late '50s when relations with China began to sour. The immediate impact of this was again borne by the communities that were dependent on trade for their income and livelihood and in the absence of any economic alternative, the situation became even worse. The Five-Year Plans did not have anything specific for agriculture and livelihoods of the hill people, and the forest department was not forthcoming in supporting the locals over the established contractors.

By the '70s, these practices of commercial exploitation, as well as the severe restrictions faced by the villagers, resulted in open discontent. In central and eastern Garhwal and in Kumaon, Gandhian workers and political activists from the CPI succeeded in mobilizing local villagers (of all status groups, men and women) to save the surrounding forests from large-scale commercial felling. The tree-saving activities – well-known as the Chipko Movement – had a clear economic and political target: to stop exploitation by 'outsiders' and to grant local people the autonomy to manage and use the forests and forest produce, and to generate local employment. This was best exemplified by the Dasholi Gram Swaraj Sangh[38] (DGSS), a small agro industrial cooperative with strong Gandhian overtones based in Gopeshwar. Under the leadership of Chandi Prasad Bhatt it ran a small turpentine unit, manufactured agricultural implements and organized demonstrations against liquor sales, untouchability and the forest contractor system. In 1973, it clashed with the forest department over the provision of allocation of hundreds of trees to Symonds, a sporting company, after they had been refused just a few trees from the same forest. They intervened by literally hugging the trees, and with women like Gaura Devi[39] in the forefront, they were able to save the trees from the axe. The protests spread to other areas and by traversing beyond their immediate local needs to a wider spatial and temporal perceptive, Chipko became a meaningful social movement with regional implications. Although Chipko did not start out as a movement for statehood, it did create a grassroots movement with a high degree of political consciousness.

The spark that lit the embers for statehood was the introduction of a Uttar Pradesh Government Order dated 29 March 1994,[40] providing 27 per cent reservation of seats for the Other Backward Classes(OBCs), both in the institutions of learning and in employment. However, the vast majority of the highlanders were Brahmins and Rajputs (about 83 per cent), the latter often claiming descent from famous clans of Rajasthan and Gujarat. Scheduled Castes (SC) constituted another 10 per cent. This led to spontaneous bursts of protests in the hills as the order would have excluded a considerable percentage of the hill population from the two most important routes to economic and social mobility – education and government posts.

The government of Uttar Pradesh took no account of this, and the legislation was widely seen as the final straw in what was perceived to be decades of neglect and exploitation. Moreover, the people felt voiceless and marginalized as the region has only 19 MLAs in an assembly of 431 (including one nominated Anglo-Indian MLA).[41]

In the opening weeks of the mass agitation two critical themes emerged which created the shift from an 'anti-reservation' struggle to the demand for a separate state. These centred on the closely related issues of development and politics. While there was a feeling that the region was subjected to 'internal colonialism' by Uttar Pradesh (voiced in newspapers, at meetings and in discussions), it was generally conceded that the region had started to receive more 'development' funds from both the state and central governments over the past decade. The main grievance now was that the economic and developmental marginalization of the hill areas were due to the fact that plains-based planners in the distant state capital of Lucknow were unable (as well as unwilling) to understand the development needs of the *hill* population, environment and economy.

The insensitivity of the state government to the concerns and issues of the highlanders, especially the firing at Rampur Tiraha in Muzaffarnagar on 2 October 1994, which led to confirmed death of six activists and allegations of molestation and rape of women by UP police, was the final nail in the coffin. Although the then chief minister Mulayam Singh Yadav ordered a judicial enquiry, the hills were aflame with anger and indignation, and government employees and students organized protest marches. The anger was directed against the state government, and relief was sought from the Union government, as the protestors were proud Indians opposed to the politics of the SP–BSP[42]. Incidentally, in the initial phase, both the Congress and the BJP were 'quiet' for they were also looking at the larger picture of UP and India. For the record, the BJP MP from Tehri, Manabendra Shah (the ex-Maharaja of Tehri) did file a petition against the OBC reservation order. The high court gave relief only with respect to admissions in educational institutions.

By 1996, the Union government under H.C. Deve Gowda[43] had conceded the demand for the formation of a new state, and the BJP then took it up officially. In the new round of state reorganization in 1998, the party preferred the name Uttaranchal for its 'allegedly fewer separatist connotations'. However, the vast majority of those who actively participated in the movement for statehood preferred Uttarakhand as the name of the new state.

With the BJP firmly supporting the reorganization of the state, and the changed political complexion, both in the state and the Centre, the UP Legislative Assembly and council passed the Uttar Pradesh Reorganization Bill, and after seeking Presidential approval, the then Deputy Prime Minister and Home Minister

L.K. Advani[44] introduced the same in the Union Parliament on 22 December 1998. The reasons for the delay were twofold: the reluctance of the prosperous Punjabi landowners who felt that they would lose their 'clout' in the new state, and the resistance on the inclusion of Haridwar district, the majority population of which was ethnically more aligned with the state of UP. As most MLAs from these two sections were also aligned to the BJP, the resistance was overcome, and the new state of Uttaranchal came into existence on 9 November 2000, amidst much fanfare in the interim capital of Dehradun. Nityanand Swami, a BJP legislator from Dehradun, was sworn in as the first chief minister by Surjeet Singh Barnala, the first governor of the state. But the first chief minister was not from the hills and the capital was Dehradun, not Gairsain.[45] This led to a pithy comment by Shekhar Pathak,[46] a well-respected activist and the chronicler of the Chipko movement: 'We are happy (*khushi*) to have our own state, we feel sadness (*udasi*), because our hopes did not come true, we are full of resentment (*akrosh*) because our demands were not respected.'[47]

However, the controversy over the name continued to simmer, and the activists who led the agitation for statehood were keen on Uttarakhand as the name of the state. This was also the name of the only regional party, the Uttarakhand Kranti Dal (UKD), formed for the sole purpose of creation of the state. Ironically, after the state was formed, the UKD lost the rationale for its existence, and the state has been alternately voting the BJP and the Congress to power. In 2006, just as the movement for the change of name was gaining ground, the then Chief Minister N.D. Tiwari took the 'wind out of the sails' of this agitation by getting the State Assembly to pass a unanimous resolution for changing the name to Uttarakhand[48] from 1 January 2007.[49]

Jharkhand

'*As long as the Jharkhand region remains divided into four states and the centres of political power remain at Patna, Calcutta, Bhopal and Bhubaneswar, the people of Jharkhand region will continue to be victims of cultural suppression and economic exploitation ... therefore the districts of Palamu, Hazaribagh, Giridih, Dhanbad, Deoghar, Godda, Sahibganj, Ranchi, Lohardaga, Gumla and Singhbhum from Bihar, Sarguja and Raigarh from MP, Sundargarh, Sambalpur, Kendu, Jhargarh and Mayurbhanj from Orissa and three districts – Midnapore, Bankura and Purulia – from West Bengal should be merged to make the new entity of Jharkhand ...*'[50]

– Jaipal Singh Munda, founder–president of the
Jharkhand Party (JHP).

Given the multitude of languages spoken by the thirty-two tribes in the proposed region, and the growing numbers of 'outsiders/settlers/dikus' who became the majority by the time the demand for statehood took firm ground, it is clear that Jharkhand was not a demand from a specific ethnic or linguistic group, but emerged as a 'regional construct' in which the dominant discourse was that of 'inequity, inequality and a sense of alienation'. There was a feeling that if these districts constituted a separate political entity, the interests of the tribals and local inhabitants would occupy the centre stage of economic development. Therefore, it is important to make a distinction between the movement for the linguistic states of Gujarat, Orissa, Andhra and Punjab, and the demand for Jharkhand. The latter was driven by the feeling of belonging to a region, which was being deprived of its natural resources by the state on account of comparative demographic disadvantage. There was also a move to call the new state Vananchal[51] rather than Jharkhand, but even though the tribal population was less than one-third, they were firm that the new state should have an association with the historical struggle for a separate state.

The assertion for a separate and unique identity of the region was manifest in a series of agrarian uprisings, the most significant of which was the insurrection led by Birsa Munda[52] from 1895 to 1900 and the Tana Bhagat[53] movement in the second decade of the last century. While these were very powerful movements, the British were able to suppress them with superior firepower and the coordinated effort of the civil and military administration. From time to time, the tribals received concessions with regard to collection of minor forest produce (MFP) as well as permission to brew *hadiya*, the local rice beer, for non-commercial use. Missionary activity was given implicit support by the colonial administration, but did not cut as much ice as it did in the hill tracts of the North-east. However, by the first decade of the twentieth century, the Church-led, ethno-centric movements, the Christian Students' Union, for example, were established under the leadership of J. Bartholomew[54] which drew up detailed memoranda on the tribal situation and the problems of tribals.

The missionary angle cannot be discounted, for the government had received a major setback during the Santhal Revolt of 1917,[55] the immediate cause of which was the recruitment campaign to mobilize two thousand local tribals to serve in Egypt, Iraq and Mesopotamia during the First World War. Prior to this, during March and April, a war loan propaganda had been mounted and 'the combination of these novel proceedings not unnaturally exited uneasiness and alarm in the aboriginal mind'.[56] The idea of serving across the seas in a foreign country in a semi-military capacity was a strange and alien idea.

Perhaps the British recruiters did not reckon with the fact that unlike the Christianized tribals in Nagaland and Mizoram, less than 4 per cent of the tribes in Jharkhand were baptized, and it was the

Hindu pantheon that provided the umbrella to their belief systems. Moreover, the Santhals resented the fact that they were recruited as non-combatants and porters, whereas in the Naga and the Lushai Hills, the missionaries had been able to portray the recruitment as an opportunity to go to war for Christ and the king.

By 1920, the first ever systematic effort to get all the tribals on an interdenominational platform was made by the Chota Nagpur Unnati Samaj.[57] The leadership was provided by tribal teachers, and 'it sought to secure employment for educated tribals, reservation in the services and the legislative bodies, and the formation of a sub-state, joined to Bengal or Orissa'.[58] This was also the main thrust of the memorandum submitted to the Simon Commission and the Cripps Mission. Later a Kisan Sabha and an Adivasi Mahasabha were also organized. After Independence, all these were brought together as the Jharkhand Party by the Oxford-educated Jaipal Singh Munda, a recent convert to Christianity who was equally passionate and committed to his tribal ethnicity. During the Second World War he had made efforts to mobilize recruitment for the British Indian Army which met with partial success, mostly amongst the converts and the Mundas. But he certainly became a well-known leader during this period. Under his mentorship, the Jharkhand Party became the main elected opposition to the Congress in Bihar in the 1950s. He was quite distraught when the Roy–Sinha proposal for the merger of West Bengal and Bihar was dropped, for he was keen on a united Purva Pradesh (Bihar, Bengal and Orissa), for the tribal population in Purva Pradesh would have been quite substantial.

The first general elections of 1952 firmly established the political dominance of the Jharkhand Party in the region, and soon thereafter the demand for the creation of a separate province gained ground. The culmination of this campaign was a well-attended demonstration by the tribals in 1955 at Ranchi to show the numerical support for a separate state before the States

Reorganization Commission. However, the SRC also had to face counter demonstrations that favoured the territorial integrity of Bihar. The anti-Jharkhand camp accused the 'Jharkhandis' of playing into the hands of foreign missionaries. There were quite a few contradictions at play: tribal and non-tribal, and within the tribals, there was conflict based on Christian and non-Christian tribals, and within the Christian tribals, there were issues between the Catholics and Protestants.

Be that as it may, the Jharkhand Party (JHP) submitted a memorandum to the SRC stressing the economic, socio-political and cultural grounds for demanding the creation of a new state. It emphasized that linguistically, culturally and ethnically, the tribal population was separate from the non-tribal people, and, hence, geographical contiguity and a separate administrative unit was required. Here again, the dilemma was apparent: while on the one hand, the JHP was trying to mobilize people on the issue of Jharkhand, it was eager to secure the support of both tribal as well as non-tribal populations. The SRC did not pay any heed to the cultural distinctness of the region and built its case on purely lingual basis of reorganization. Hence, the claim of the Jharkhandis for a separate state was rejected on grounds that the multiplicity of tribal languages did not permit the creation of a new state in the Jharkhand region.

The failure of JHP in convincing the SRC affected its popularity. Gradually, even its key supporters began to doubt the intentions of the JHP and its leaders, and a mood of disillusionment set in. The final nail in the coffin was the merger of JHP with INC in 1963 as a quid pro quo for a ministerial berth in the Vinodanand Jha[59] Bihar Cabinet for Jaipal Singh.

Although the JHP was merged into the INC, many splinter groups appeared on the firmament, and representations were made to Prime Minister Indira Gandhi in 1969, and again in 1973 by

Jharkhand Party leader N.E. Horo. This was followed by a third representation by the Jharkhand Coordination Committee leader B.P. Keshari in 1989 to the President of India.

Meanwhile, the '70s saw the second phase of the movement. Here the issues of farmers and workers were in the forefront, and the political demand for Jharkhand took a back seat. The ever-increasing resource extraction from Jharkhand, massive displacement of the indigenous and other rural population, and the unprecedented exploitation of the miners and unorganized industrial workers was the immediate cause of the emergence of the Jharkhand Mukti Morcha (JMM) – literally, Jharkhand Liberation Front – under the mentorship of the Marxist A.K. Roy,[60] Kurmi leader Binod Bihari Mahto[61] and the tribal supremo Shibu Soren.[62] While Mahto successfully brought the Kurmis into the fold of the Morcha, Shibu Soren, a charismatic Santhal leader, became instrumental in forging a Santhal–Kurmi unity. However, the epicentre of the movement shifted from the tribal-dominated Ranchi and Dumka to the mining and industrial belt around Dhanbad, Bokaro and Jamshedpur.

The JMM also demanded statehood, but this was not a primary tool of mobilization. Instead, the JMM sought to provide leadership to existing protest movements. They also appealed to a common identity of Jharkhandis as 'workers' in both rural and urban areas. The main ideologue, A.K. Roy, argued that the Jharkhand 'nation' was suffering from a situation of 'internal colonialism', exploited by outside interests.

However, this consolidation did not last long because of serious ideological differences and personality clashes between the three very strong leaders, all of whom wanted the movement to have different orientations: thus A.K. Roy was opposed to capitalism itself, Shibu Soren wanted to dispense 'instant justice' and the ouster of 'dikus' from tribal lands, and Mahto was keen on electoral politics. As such, the movement petered out.

The '80s saw the emergence of the Jharkhand Coordination Committee (JCC) and the All-Jharkhand Students' Union (AJSU). These were movements for assertions of the 'Jharkhandi identity', and they consciously eschewed politics.

More than this, it was the mainstreaming of the statehood demand by the leading opposition party, the BJP, which till recently had been opposing the formation of new states in the country, that gave a boost to the formation of Jharkhand. In the first three decades after Independence, the Jana Sangha and RSS had been opposed to the linguistic reorganization of states: they regarded it as a fissiparous tendency. However, in both Jharkhand and Chhattisgarh, the BJP found it easier to mobilize support in the newly established industrial townships, as well as in mining and irrigation project areas, for these were the places to which the new migrants – professionals as well as workers – were attracted. Another reason why the BJP and the RSS became active in these regions was to prevent any further attempts at proselytization by Christian missionaries.

Thus the bifurcation of the state had the bipartisan support of both the Congress and the BJP, and though the RJD had its initial reservations, there was a rare political consensus in the country at the turn of the century with regard to the formation of the three new states, of which Jharkhand was the largest. Thus, as per the Bihar Reorganization Act, 2000, on the 'appointed day, viz the 15th of November 2000' which coincided with the birth anniversary of Birsa Munda, the great Adivasi leader, the state of Jharkhand was carved out of Bihar. Jharkhand had a population of about 2.2 crore and an area of about 80,000 sq. km, which was half of the territory of Bihar. However, since the districts in MP, West Bengal and Orissa were not touched, it can be said that the demand for Jharkhand was fulfilled substantially, but not fully!

17

BANDE UTKALA JANANI

One hundred and eight years after this song by Laxmikanta Mahapatra[1] was rendered at the meeting of Utkal Sammelani[2] in 1912, the Odisha Cabinet accorded it the status of the 'state anthem'[3] on 7 June 2020. Now it has to be officially sung in all academic institutions and at state functions. Earlier, on 9 November 2010, the enactment of Orissa Bill gave the state the new name of Odisha, besides changing the name of the language from Oriya to Odiya. Thus, Odiya nationalism is in the 'present continuous', but its protagonists contend that the cultural construction of Odisha blends with and strengthens the nationhood of India. They go on to ask: if each state had its anthem and flag, and if regional icons (leaders, monuments, texts) were to be placed on the Indian currency, will it not strengthen people's identification with India?

There are many 'firsts' to the Odisha story. Orissa, along with Sindh[4] and Bihar, was the first of the 'linguistic states' conceded by the British on 1 April 1936, after a long and persistent demand of the Oriya-speaking population. Orissa's case is quite different from that of Sindh, for the Oriya-speaking population was spread across four administrative entities: as a division in the Bengal Presidency,[5] in Central Provinces,[6] in the Madras Presidency[7] and as small kingdoms under princely states. This also gave rise to the concept of Natural Orissa to which we shall refer to in the later part of this chapter.

Second, the assertion of the Oriya identity was primarily against the control of Bengalis, who dominated the administration, judiciary and the educational institutions, and these were the only employment avenues open at that time. Commissioner T.E. Ravenshaw's[8] contribution to the Oriya language have to be placed on record.

Third, the Oriya elite had a clear two-pronged strategy in place for a linguistic province. While on the one hand, they were making an appeal to the colonial state through memorials, petitions, signature campaigns and references in the state and central legislatures, on the other they were educating their own brethren about the salience of Oriya as a language, and Utkal as a territory, and invocation of Lord Jagannath as the unifying force for all those who lived in the region. Fourth, we see the transition in leadership – from the constitutionalism of Madhusudan Das[9] to the 'mass movement' of Gopabandhu Das.[10] Fifth, we see the tension between the central and the provincial leadership of the Congress, as also the multiple factions within the party, as well as their attempts at one-upmanship. Sixth, we note that linguistic and cultural nationalism – whether of the Oriyas or Telugus or Kannadigas – was in tandem with political nationalism for independence from the colonial regime.

Seventh, mobilizing people on the basis of popular demands was different from the task of governance, and this became apparent when there was a clear clash of class interests, especially between the landlords and the sharecroppers. Eighth, the dominant discourse on development was so strong that considerations of ecology, livelihoods and cultural mores were often brushed aside. The concerns of the tribal population (or aboriginals, as they were referred to, even by V.P. Menon[11]) were not part of the political discourse, for while they constituted over 40 per cent of the population, as a group they were a disenfranchised community, and could be used as cannon fodder by different interest groups – by the rulers of feudatory states, by the communist insurgents, as well as by the Congress and the Praja Mandal,[12] as and when the need arose. Last, but not the least, the acceptance of the Gandhian ideals of swaraj[13] as the end, and satyagraha[14] as the means for its political realization came to the fore as the most potent political forces in the region.

Let's start with the first stirrings. Nivedita Mohanty in her work *Oriya Nationalism* points out that as early as 1866, the Utkal Bhasha Unnati Bidhayani Sabha was founded at Balasore, and Commissioner T.E. Ravenshaw attended the meeting of the association in 1868. Then came the Cuttack Debating Club in 1869 and a host of other societies and clubs, all of which were affiliated to the Utkal Sabha or the Utkal Union Conference founded in 1882 with Gouri Shankar Ray as the secretary and Madhusudan Das, the Calcutta-returned lawyer, as its vice president. Ray was also nominated by the Sabha to attend the first session of the INC in 1885. In 1886, it confronted the government for meddling in the affairs of the temple of Lord Jagannath in Puri, and in 1895, it urged the government to reconsider its decision regarding imposition of Hindi (in place of Oriya) in the schools and courts of Sambalpur. With the introduction of Oriya as a subject under Calcutta University in 1902, the differences between S.N. Banerjea (the Congress leadership under him had been opposed to linguistic provinces) and Madhusudan Das came to the fore, and the latter founded the Utkal Sammelani. Earlier, in 1898, Madhusudan Das was also elected to the Bengal Legislative Assembly and became the minister for local self-government in the short-lived state of Bihar and Orissa in 1911.

However, the constitutional methods and overt loyalty to the Crown were no longer acceptable to the next generation Oriya leaders like Gopabandhu Das, who had established the Satyabadi Bana Bidyalaya in 1909 to encourage youth to engage actively with the social, educational and economic upliftment of the Oriyas. Gopabandhu Das had to decide between 'loyalty to the Crown' and commitment to the nationalist causes – swaraj and satyagraha: he chose the latter. Gandhi's first visit to Orissa was in 1921, and he supported the cause of a 'linguistic state for Orissa'. By this time, the difficulties in the rather unnatural state of Bihar and Orissa were coming to the fore, and there was a very strong demand for the establishment of Natural Orissa, which would include all the Oriya-speaking areas in the different administrative jurisdictions.

In her essay, 'Vernacular in the Making of Modern Orissa', Pritipuspa Mishra says that by the third decade of the last century, Oriya groups lobbying for the formation of a separate province of Orissa had named the proposed province Natural Orissa. The term 'natural' was deployed strategically: it lent both historical and political legitimacy to the demand for a separate province. In 1903, it found support in H.H. Risley,[15] the colonial administrator, ethnographer and linguist, who argued that the 'Oriya-speaking plainsmen' and 'hill men' (read Adivasi) should be united under a single administration despite the racial difference, because the connection between a spoken language and its dialect or patios is a more potent ground of union. The same year, the Utkal Sammelani or the Utkal Union brought the Oriya-speaking elite of Bengal, Central Provinces and Madras as well as of the princely states to press the demand for a Natural Orissa, in contrast to the Colonial Orissa where the Oriyas were subject to the domination of the intermediary ruling class.

The Intermediary Ruling Class

This term was first used by Madhusudan Das to refer to the Bengalis and Biharis in the context of their sway in the district and subdistrict level administration – as revenue, judicial and police officers, besides, of course, teachers, postmen and railway employees. The day-to-day contact of the layperson in the mofussil was not with the ICS officer, but with the functionaries mentioned above: this refrain was seen even in Assam where the anti-Bengali sentiment also became strong, reinforced by the superior and patronizing attitude of the *bhadralok*.[16] This term became part of the memorandum submitted to the Orissa Boundary Commission.[17]

Sometimes one wonders that if the Bengal intelligentsia – starting from Rajender Lal Mitter and S.N. Banerjea – had accepted the fact that Oriya was an independent language, and not opposed its teaching tooth and nail, Bengal could have continued as a bilingual state in which two languages could have existed side by side. Recent scholarship also shows that perhaps the 'commercial interests' of the Calcutta publishers of textbooks in Bengali led Headmaster K. Bhattacharya to write the polemical *Odiya Is Not an Independent Language*.

Strategies for the Linguistic Province

A threefold strategy was put in place. The first was an appeal based on facts and figures to the provincial and imperial (viceroy's council) governments, the second was an impassioned plea to the Congress leadership, and the third was a passionate campaign amongst the masses through the Oriya press. Madhusudan Das was the lead exponent of the first and Gopabandhu Das of the second. Works of popular authors like Fakir Mahapatra,[18] especially his translations of the Mahabharata and the Ramayana, played a stellar role in making

Oriyas feel proud of their language. Mahatma Gandhi's support for linguistic provinces was important for Oriyas – because prior to this, the Congress leadership under S.N. Banerjea had been opposed to this assertion. However, the credit for the standardization and printing fonts in Oriya should be given to the missionaries: in fact, it can also be postulated that but for the spread of printing, the Oriya language movement could not have gained the form it took.

It must also be noted that both Madhusudan Das and Gopabandhu Das did not posit Oriya nationalism against Indian nationalism. Rather, it was part of the Indian nation or Bharat Varsha. 'Orissa's river is called Mahanadi, or the great river, Orissa's sea is the Mahodadhi, or the great sea, Orissa's hill is Mahendra or the great mountain. Orissa's tree is Kalpabatta (Kalpataru) or the tree of wish fulfilment, Orissa's Lord is Jagannath, or the Lord of the Universe and Orissa's cremation ground is the Swargadwara or the gateway to heaven.'[19]

The Cult of Jagannath

This brings us to the cult of Jagannath, the most potent symbol of Oriya nationalism and pride. It served as a site that did not practise caste and religious exclusion by allowing lower castes and Adivasi communities to have access to the deity during the Annual Rath Yatra. In fact, this single annual event came to serve as an example of enduring inclusion of religious and caste differences in Orissa as a region. It included within its frame multiple identities: the regionally important folk deities and the diverse motifs of tribal religions. Lord Jagannath, the Supreme Lord, also incorporates a distinct Sabara Adivasi origin. Telugu fishermen look up to him as their Lord Father and women from all strata, including the outcaste chandala women like Shreya Chandaluni[20] were believed to be his ardent worshippers, while all the little kingdoms were happy to be part of the great tradition of Jagannath in some form or the other. Also, Lord Jagannath had adherents from all groups, including Christians and Muslims. In fact, one of the first acts of the first Prime Minister of the newly carved province of Orissa, K.C. Gajapati Narayan Deo, the raja of Paralakhemundi,[21] was to pay a ceremonial visit to Lord Jagannath. Even the roots of Mahatma Gandhi's decision to start his *padyatra*, a journey on foot, from Puri may be traced to the nationalistic feelings of Oriyas for Lord Jagannath.

Mobilizing popular opinion for the establishment of a linguistic state for the entire Oriya-speaking population spread over different provinces and princely states was relatively easy; managing contradictions, especially those relating to land reforms, was indeed a challenge, especially as the Congress was committed to abolition of intermediaries in land and recognition of the rights of the cultivators. Meanwhile, the Praja Mandals in the princely states were determined to replace the rule of the Rajas with that of elected representatives. While there was power struggle within the Congress even when it was still a 'movement for independence', it intensified after the 1935 GoI Act when the party participated in elections, and was invited to form ministries, albeit with limited powers.

In the case of Orissa, the Congress did emerge as the largest party, but the first premier of Orissa was K.C. Gajapati Narayan Deo of the Paralakhemundi royal family who held office for a few months before handing over to Biswanath Das[22] from the Congress party. The first budget speech of Orissa was delivered by Biswanath Das on 29 August 1937, in which the ambivalence of the Congress towards the new arrangement is spelt out quite clearly: 'The new Government of India Act of 1935 has been thrust upon us against our will, and in spite of our stringent opposition. When this measure became an Act of (British) Parliament and was set to be enforced, the INC changed its tactics and took a dual parliamentary

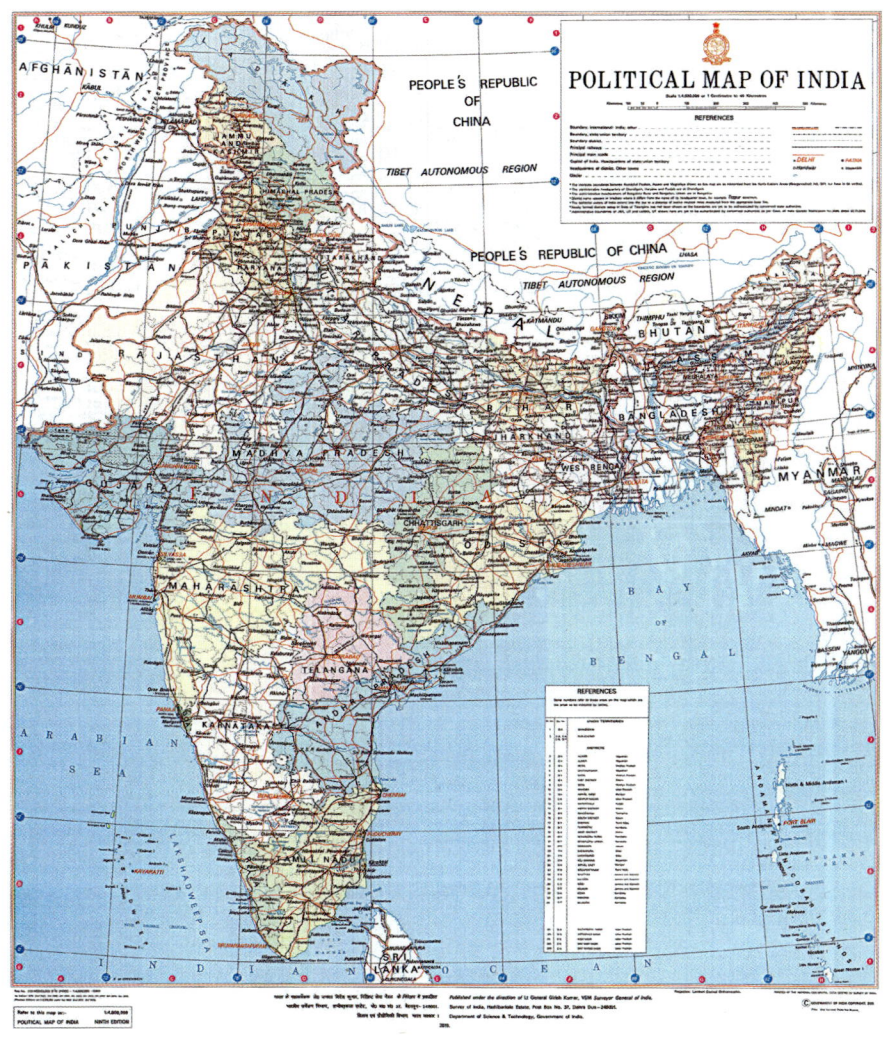

2019 – The Union Territories of Ladakh and J&K

2017 – Telangana – the Second State for Telugu Speakers

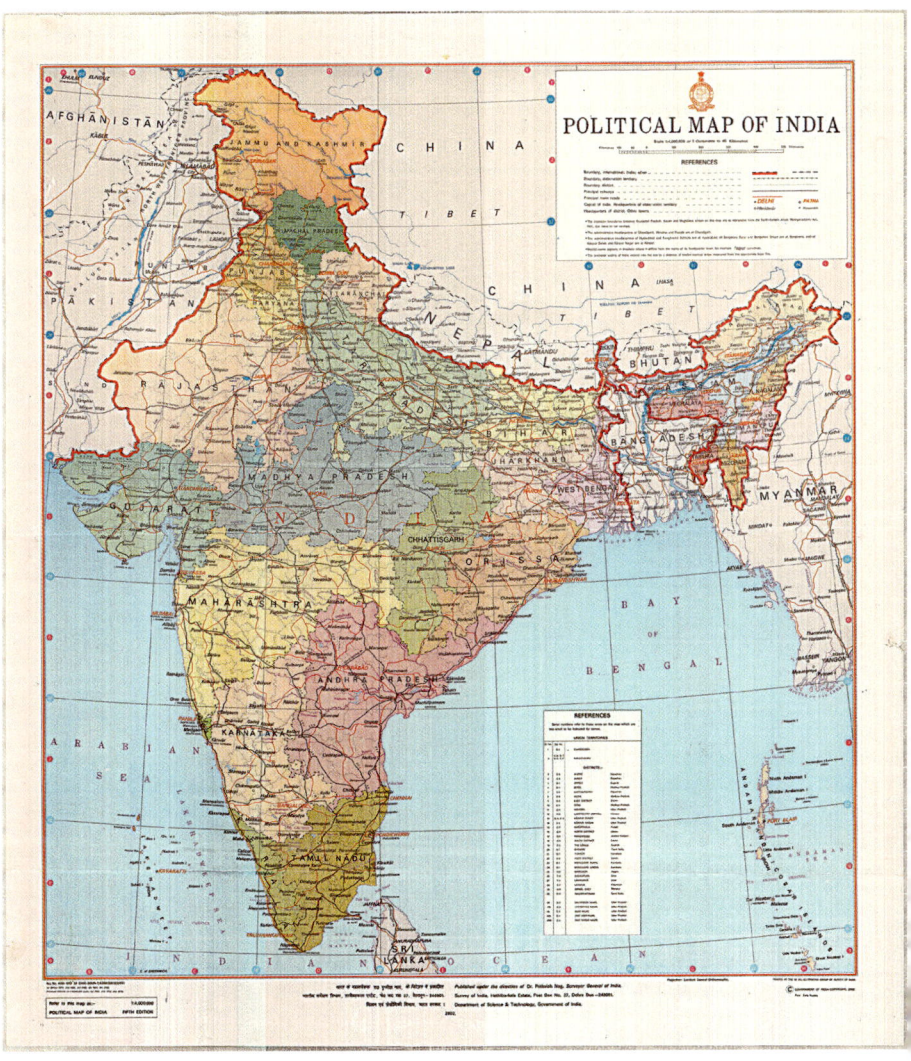

2002 – Jharkhand, Uttarakhand and Chhattisgarh

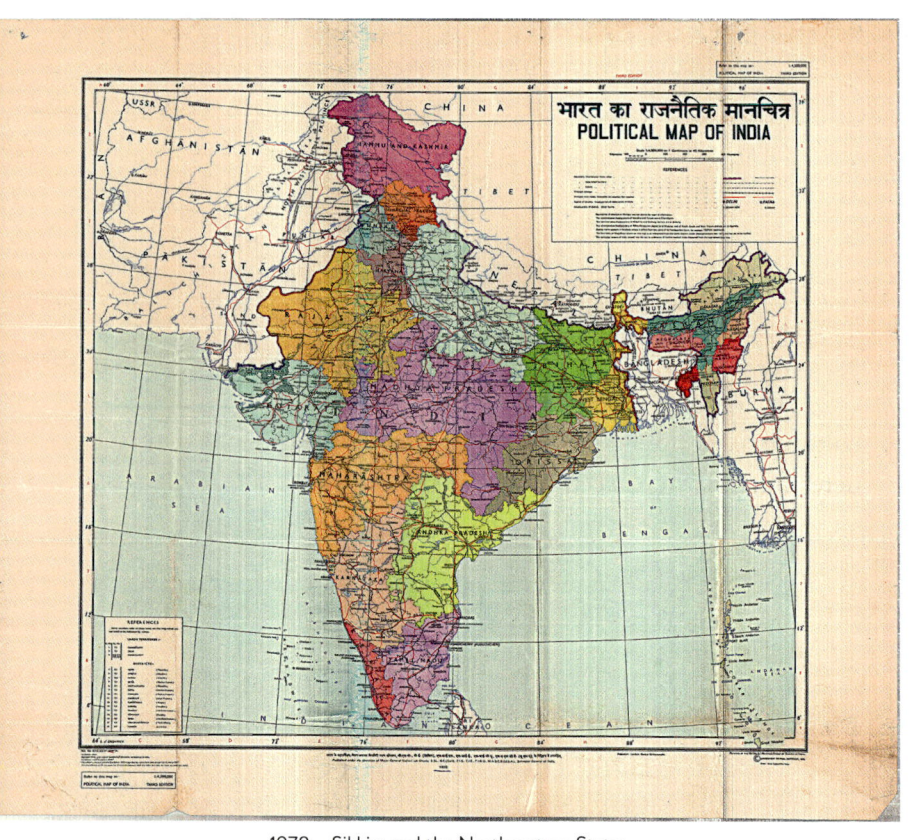

1978 – Sikkim and the Northeastern States

programme of combat and construction in order that this imported Constitution may go, and we have the Constitution of our own through a Constituent Assembly to be formed by ourselves. Then only we will have real Swaraj and our real growth.'[23]

The first budget was difficult. It involved settling administrative and financial issues with the predecessor governments of Madras and Bihar. Das also made the point about 'unfairness in the distribution of assets' and requested the GoI for immediate release of Rs 50 lakh for the Orissa Flood Relief Committee. Irrigation, flood control and agriculture – all interrelated – were on the top of the agenda of the first government, as also the spread of agriculture, cooperatives, cottage and khadi industries. Three important tenancy legislations – Madras Estates Land (Orissa Amendment Act), Orissa Tenancy (Amendment Act) Bill and the Money Lenders (Regulation) Bill were introduced during his tenure.

The budget speech highlighted that more than half the area of the state (over 20,000 sq. miles and a population of 2.67 lakh) was under the Partially Excluded Areas, in which the writ of the governor ran supreme. Another takeaway was that the main income in excise came, not from liquor, but from opium, and the budget pointed out to the difficulties in imposing prohibition especially the neighbouring princely states. However, before the Das ministry could actually come to grips with the situation, the Congress directed its legislators to quit the government in 1939.

After brief spells of Governor's Rule and the second tenure of K.C. Gajapati Narayan Deo, the Congress resumed power in 1946 with Hare Krishna Mahtab[24] as the chief minister. Such was the strength of big zamindars that Mahtab actually claimed that the big landlords 'will remain at least neutral', and that he would prevent any organized party from contesting the 1946 elections. Thus, at freedom's doorstep, one observes a strengthening of alliance between the landlords and the Congress. In 37 out of the

60 constituencies, the Congress was elected unopposed, and with another 11 seats in the contested constituencies, the Congress tally was 47 in a 60-member house.

The positive steps taken by his ministry included the abolition of the salt tax, provisions for temple entry, and abolition of untouchability. But with regard to agrarian reforms, a committee was set up to 'make land revenue uniform, remove intermediaries, prevent fragmentation of holdings, provision of common lands, amendment of laws relating to tenure, simplify sale laws, rent ceiling, agricultural income tax, as well as laws to make it easier for government to acquire land for private companies in the interest of planned economic development'.[25] It was clear that the proactive land legislation, which was so central to the polity in the previous decade, had been sidetracked.

However, it is also important to look at the context from the point of view of Mahtab. He wanted to unite the princely states with Orissa, on the one hand, and integrate the Adivasis in the agrarian economy of the state – and he had to choose the middle path between these spectrums.

Meanwhile, the CPI-led Kisan Sangha[26] started direct action against the zamindars and mobilized the peasants for a Bhagchashi movement (sharecropper) to claim three-fifth of the gross produce as the farmers' share as well as written lease agreements. In November 1947, the Sharecroppers Act officially accepted this proposition, but the government of the day was rather indifferent to this responsibility.

As far as the princely states were concerned, they made a last ditch effort at trying to assert their sovereignty and independence, which led Biswanath Das, then a member of the Constituent Assembly, to forcefully argue that with the lapse of paramountcy, sovereignty vested with the people of India. The Praja Mandals were clear that these principalities had to be merged with Orissa.

Although Mahtab also broached the idea of an 'administrative merger' over complete merger, the states ministry under Sardar Patel and V.P. Menon were clear: no exceptions were to be allowed. And though some Rajas tried to mobilize Adivasis against the farmers in the plains, they were up against a wall. It must be placed on record that the Praja Mandal and the communists worked together and in unison to get the princes to sign the Instrument of Accession for the merger of twenty-four princely states into Orissa.

18

TELANGANA

The Second State for Telugu Speakers

Telangana Redux[1]

Political events make history: but history is also 'always in the making',[2] as the present is contextualized in the 'present continuous'. This becomes so apparent when one looks at the imagination of Telangana's history. While most observers would trace the history of the twenty-ninth state of India to 1955 when a section of intellectuals and the political leadership of erstwhile Hyderabad were wary of the attempts to merge it with the Andhra state, some have traced this to 1799,[3] when the Nizam had to give up his territories in coastal Andhra and the Rayalaseema region to the British in lieu of the tribute he had promised them for their support in his war against Tipu Sultan. In 1852, a decision was taken to build an anicut across the Krishna and Godavari rivers. This too was an important milestone — for while this ushered unprecedented prosperity in the undivided districts of Krishna, Guntur and Godavari, the areas that remained directly under the Nizam lost out on account of lack of access to water for their fields

However, when the Telangana movement was at its height, its adherents asserted that Telangana refers to Trilinga Desha[4] to celebrate the presence of ancient Shiva temples at Kaleshwaram, Srisailam and Draksharamam. Even more credible is the argument that during the reign of the Nizam, the region was known as Telugu Angana, to differentiate it from the areas where Marathi and Kannada were spoken – for polyglotism was a hallmark of the Hyderabad state in which people spoke Urdu, Telugu, Kannada and Marathi.

As the formation of Andhra state in 1953 and Andhra Pradesh in 1956 has already been discussed, the genesis of Telangana can be traced to the failure of the Gentleman's Agreement.[5] The agreement was violated in both letter and spirit and was one of the persistent tensions underlying the discourse of the '60s: was it possible for the political elite of a resource-poor region to ensure an agreement of this kind when the interests of the dominant elite were at stake? Linguistic determination was important, but development aspirations could not be overlooked.

Another factor that is often overlooked in the debate is the critical role of the then CPI in supporting the merger of the two regions. The party was guided by the Marxist notion of a 'linguistic nationality'.[6] There was widespread belief that in the second general elections of 1957, there was a fair chance of the party being voted to power in the integrated state. What the comrades overlooked was the ability of the Congress to adopt the socialistic rhetoric and befriend the leadership of the Communist Part of the Soviet Union (CPSU)[7] whose global interest were now aligned with those of Nehru, much to the chagrin of a section of the CPI[8] leadership (which later became the CPI[M]). As Hargopal[9] puts it 'in the process, the dream of the Communist party for the formation of Vishalandhra became true, their hopes of coming to power were totally belied'.[10]

Meanwhile, given the success of the Green Revolution technologies in the Andhra districts which had assured irrigation as well as access to seeds, fertilizers and markets, the region saw abundance, whereas the Telangana districts continued to lag behind. While Andhra moved from the peasant mode to a market mode of production[11] with enough surpluses to invest in agro industries, manufacturing and real estate, including investments in Hyderabad, the other regions – Telangana, Rayalaseema and North Andhra – were still dependent on rain-fed agriculture and the peasant mode of production. The extant Hyderabad elite – Punjabis, Marwaris and Gujaratis – also joined hands with the Separate Telangana agitation which reached a crescendo in 1969. Led primarily by students and government employees citing violations of this agreement and discrimination in education and employment, the agitation claimed over 350 lives. Marri Chenna Reddy[12] broke ranks with the ruling Congress party to establish the Telangana Praja Samithi (TPS) to spearhead the movement. Indira Gandhi, who was then at the helm of both the government and the party, though opposed to the division of the state, accommodated the Telangana leadership both in the party and government. In a bid to assuage the Telangana sentiment, Narasimha Rao, a Telangana politician, was brought in as chief minister of Andhra in the place of Brahamananda Reddy. This also marked the beginning of the complete domination of the Congress high command,[13] and the end of the regional satraps in the Congress, which in the long run led to the rise of regional parties in both Andhra and Telangana.

Narasimha Rao decided to go ahead with land reforms and redistribution, which till then had never been strictly enforced. Enraged by this shift in leadership, and the threat of land reforms, the Andhra elite started their own parallel Jai Andhra[14] agitation in 1971–72, also seeking a bifurcation of the state. As they could not directly challenge the question of land reforms, they took the validity of Mulki[15] rules in the city of Hyderabad. To start with, the employees' federations of Andhra filed cases in the high court challenging the legal validity of the Mulki rules. While the high court declared these rules as ultra vires, the Supreme Court upheld their validity, but so strong was the Andhra lobby that they were able to prevail upon the Parliament to amend the law and declare that they would not be valid anymore.

Post the Emergency period, Andhra and Karnataka were the two states that did not face the anti-Indira Gandhi wave, and when the Janata coalition collapsed in three years, the Congress returned to power. However, the new campaign was not 'Garibi Hatao (abolish poverty)', but the unity and integrity of India. This period also marked the transition from politics of ideology to politics of identity.

The public upbraiding of T. Anjaiah[16] by the then Prime Minister Rajiv Gandhi did not go well at all, especially as Anjaiah broke down at his humiliation. That, coupled with the frequent changes of the chief minister of the state at the insistence of the Congress high command, created the ground for the rise of Nandamuri Taraka Rama Rao, popularly known as NTR, and his brand of politics. Renowned in both Andhra and Telangana on account of the mythological and social roles played by him in Telugu films, his popularity soared on the rhetoric of the welfare state, which the Congress was abandoning. His Telugu Desam Party (TDP) was an assertion of Telugu pride and identity. As Hargopal put it succinctly in his lecture on the evolution of the Telangana state, 'the pan Telugu identity resulted in the eventual subjugation of other regional identities within Andhra Pradesh'.[17] It had always been a case that such subsuming forms of identity politics – instead of negotiating with sub-identities – left the space and scope for aggressive reemergence of sub-identity politics. The rise of Telangana identity at the turn of the millennium was thus part of the social and political dynamic of change which received a further fillip when Chhattisgarh, Jharkhand and Uttarakhand were carved out of MP, Bihar and UP respectively. Moreover, the clash amongst Kapus, the Kamas, the Dalits, tribal communities and women as a group broke the 'TDP consensus' and paved the way for the assertion of the Telangana sub-identity.

NTR was ousted by his son-in-law, Chandrababu Naidu,[18] who projected himself as the CEO rather than the CM of the state. A large section of the national (English) media projected him as a twenty-first century CEO who would transform the landscape through IT, e-governance and foreign investments. Hyderabad became the 'poster city' of India's liberalization, but the contrast with the districts in the immediate vicinity of Hyderabad – Mahbubnagar, Ranga Reddy, Medak and Nalgonda – only aggravated the feelings of neglect. The withdrawal of government from health and education and the increasing visibility of 'private providers' for these services further alienated the people of Telangana districts.

The Telangana Rashtriya Samithi (TRS) emerged from this deep-rooted feeling of discontent and deprivation: as people rallied to the call for a separate state, both the pan-India parties, the Congress and the BJP, were compelled to support the statehood demand, especially as the parties had supported the formation of new states in the Hindi heartland. Thus, the BJP extended its support to Telangana as early as 1997. The real momentum was built in 2001, when K. Chandrashekhar Rao[19] (KCR) resigned from the TDP and floated the TRS. In the 2004 elections, TRS, in alliance with the Congress, won twenty-six assembly and five Lok Sabha seats, thereby making its mark.

TRS became part of the United Progressive Alliance (UPA) 1,[20] and the demand for a separate state was included in the Common Minimum Programme with riders on 'consultations and consensuses'. In 2006, the Committee for Consultations on

Situation in Andhra Pradesh (CCSAP) was constituted. Popularly called the Srikrishna Committee after its head, the former Chief Justice B.N. Srikrishna, it did not give any conclusive report except to state that the development of all the regions of the state, including Telangana and Rayalaseema, should be 'balanced'. It submitted its (inconclusive) report in 2010.

Meanwhile, fed up with procrastination on the part of the Congress leadership, TRS quit the alliance and, wonder of wonders, entered into an alliance with the TDP and the left. The alliance got a major drubbing as Y.S. Rajasekhar Reddy[21] of the Congress had been able to contain the movement (much like Pratap Singh Kairon in Punjab) by applying both patronage and coercion against his opponents. His sudden death in a helicopter crash in 2009 left a leadership vacuum in the state Congress, and KCR began his fast unto death in December of that year.

Perhaps the MHA based its strategy on the experience of violence in the aftermath of earlier hunger strikes especially that of Potti Sriramulu and hastily announced that it would start the process. To step up pressure on the Union government a Telangana Joint Action Committee comprising political and non–political groups was formed under the leadership of the Osmania University[22] professor M. Kodandaram Reddy as its convenor. A similar Joint Action Committee also came up in Andhra under the leadership of Prof. N. Samuel of the Nagarjuna University.[23] Although these committees were headed by academics, it was clear that they were not really autonomous – both were actually advocacy groups for their respective causes. It was also quite clear that the genie was out of the bottle, and that even if the political parties wanted, the chasm had widened, and there was no going back. Internally, the TDP, the Congress and the BJP were a house divided because their leaders and workers had no option but to support the 'majoritarian' view in whichever region they were.

The demand for Telangana was also articulated by folk artistes – especially those who engaged with song and dance – in village-level programmes called 'Dhoom Dham' where songs relating to the demand for a separate state and injustices to the region were received with a hearty applause. Elected representatives, especially from parties like TDP and the Congress, which were perceived to be anti-Telangana, were heckled and humiliated. The electronic media also took upon itself the task of organizing live debates and opinion polls called 'Dasha Disha' (direction and destination). This was also a forum in which people from all walks of life, especially those not directly engaged with politics, were invited to participate.

Finally, in 2013, the UPA announced the formation of Telangana, and even though there were loud protests by the Seemandhra MPs and the Andhra Assembly rejected the resolution by a voice vote, President Pranab Mukherjee gave his assent to the Telangana Bill in 2014, with Hyderabad[24] as the joint capital of both the states for a period of ten years. However, such was the animosity between the two newly formed states over distribution of assets as well as cadre allocations that Chandrababu Naidu, the Andhra chief minister, decided to carve out a new capital of Amravati.

TRS won the first elections to the Telangana state in 2014, and KCR was elected as the first chief minister of the state. He won the second term in 2019 with an even higher majority. He along with his son and likely successor KTR are now trying to project Telangana as the most investment-friendly state in the country with equal priority to irrigation, agriculture, livelihoods and poverty alleviation. This model of regional development poses a major challenge to another dominant narrative which argues that if there is a convergence of ruling parties in the Centre and the state, the growth trajectory is faster.

EPILOGUE

The book is about the making and remaking of the states of Bharat, but before we close, we have to discuss the J&K Reorganization Act which led to the creation of two UTs: J&K and Ladakh from the territory of the state of J&K. The identity which Ladakh had lost when Ladakh and Tibet were dropped from the official name of the Riyasat e Jammu wa Kashmir wa Ladakh wa Tibet ha is now resurrected. It is currently India's biggest UT in terms of size, and at 59,000 square kilometres, it exceeds the territory of J&K by nearly 17,000 square kilometres. From a visual and a cartographic perspective, it is now the crest of India.

It is also interesting to note that when Ladakh became a UT, the formation of Telangana found a reference. The noted scholar and former diplomat, and a proud Ladakhi, P. Stobdan, wrote in an August 2019 article for *The Week*: 'Ladakh feels liberated after 185 years of slavery and coercion. The demand for a separate state of Ladakh has been pending since 1947 – older than the demand for Telangana.' It was seen as the fulfilment of a long-standing demand of the Ladakh Buddhist Association (LBA) which had been wanting to dissociate Ladakh from Kashmir from the time of the organization's inception in 1933 by Jigmet Dadul Namgyal, Kalon Tsewang Rigzin, Kalon Bankapa Morup Gyaltsan and Munshi Sonam Tsewang. A probable reason for its formation was to select the two members from Ladakh for the Praja Parishad which was created by Maharaja Hari Singh in the same year. As mentioned earlier in the book, this was more symbolic than effective, for the majority was made up of officials and nominees of the Durbar.

Be that as it may, with the signing of the Instrument of Accession on 26 October 1947 by Maharaja Hari Singh and its acceptance by Governor General Mountbatten a day later on 27 October, the erstwhile wazarat of Ladakh in the princely state of J&K became an administrative district under the Kashmir division of the state of J&K. Moreover, Kashmir continued to dominate the political discourse both nationally and globally, followed by Jammu, which was the winter capital of the state, and also the commercial centre and logistics hub on account of the railhead for all supplies to and from the state. Ladakh, with its relatively small population and just four seats in the State Assembly – Nubra, Leh, Kargil and Zanskar – and one in the Union Parliament, was politically marginalized.

As such, as early as 1949, Cheewang Rigzin of the LBA gave a memorandum to Prime Minister Jawaharlal Nehru which read as follows:

> In case the result of the plebiscite is favourable to India, we simply go a step further than other people of the state in seeking a closer union with that great country and in case it is otherwise, our verdict stands clear and unchallengeable ... we have decided to cut ourselves asunder from the state itself ... We have indeed made up our mind to join India ... We certainly make the offer for our own advantage; we see in our merger with India the only hope of our salvation ...

The head lama of Ladakh, Kushak Bakula, believed to be a reincarnation of Arahant Bakula, a contemporary of the Buddha, went a step further. He wanted an autonomous Ladakh linked directly to the Union, or in association with Lahaul–Spiti and the Punjab hill states. Bakula said that they would prefer to join Tibet, rather than be a part of Kashmir. However, Nehru prevailed upon Kushak Bakula, who was a member of the INC, to join the J&K Cabinet, and seek development within the framework of J&K because of the difficulties posed by Article 370. But as confirmed by the Justice P.B. Gajendragadkar Commission appointed in 1968 to investigate the charge of regional imbalances in the state, Ladakh was certainly receiving only a marginal share in the development expenditure of the state.

As the state government did not take any follow-up action on this report, movements for UT status were started by Ladakhis such as Thupstan Chhewang in 1974 and again in 1982.

Meanwhile, in 1979, Kargil was carved out as a new district. The LBA felt that this was a cynical move on the part of Sheikh Abdullah to drive a wedge between the Ladakhis on the basis of religion, although they had all descended from the same ethnic stick and spoke the same language.

After the establishment of the Darjeeling Gorkha Hill Council in Darjeeling in 1987, there was little ground to deny a similar body for Ladakh. As protests continued through 1991 and 1992, the state government took the view that the proposal would call for an amendment in the State Constitution as well as threaten the existence of Article 370 of the Indian Constitution. However, finally, the MHA saw merit in the argument of LBA and, in 1995, a democratically elected Leh Autonomous Hill Development Council (LAHDC) came into existence, followed by the Kargil Autonomous Hill Development Council in 2003.

And when Article 370 was removed altogether, the two districts of Leh and Kargil were constituted as the UT of Ladakh. However, even as the LBA, and other Leh-based organizations, including the Gyalrung Drukpa and Anjuman Moin-ul-Islam, welcomed the move, there were murmurs of protest in Kargil as many of its residents felt that in popular perception, Leh – with its monasteries, stupas, landscapes and the serene lakes – has become synonymous with Ladakh. Historically, Kargil suffered neglect as the trade routes would get disrupted and it also bore the brunt of all the attacks from the Pakistani intruders in 1948, 1965, 1971 and 1999. However, the recruitment to the SSB, ITBP and Ladakh Scouts mostly came from Leh. It was only after 1999 that the first induction of Kargil youth in the armed forces began. Kargil residents complained of a double jeopardy: under the erstwhile state government, they were neglected because they were Shias – now they are being discriminated because they are not Buddhists. They point out that Kargil district with 1.40 lakh residents has a marginally higher population than Leh which is 1.33 lakh – although in terms of area, Leh at 45,000 square kilometres is three times the size of Kargil. However, there is a consensus that in the last decade there has been a major thrust on infrastructure projects, including the Zojila Tunnel and the Kargil Zanskar Highway to ensure connectivity of the region with the rest of the country. This is expected to receive even greater impetus with the declaration of Ladakh as a UT.

As such, the abrogation of Article 370 and the creation of the UT has had both external and internal implications. As long as it was a part of J&K, it had little political voice, for even after the creation of the councils, the key officials continued to report to the state government. Now the Union government can monitor development interventions – from highways to telecom to power grids directly. Both Leh and Kargil have been brought under the ambit of the Smart Cities programme, and officers from across the country are being assigned to the region. The key demand of reservation of jobs for the residents of Ladakh and control over land has also been accepted. A significant challenge would be to ensure that both Leh and Kargil feel equally empowered and involved in the institutions of governance and get a fair chance of employment in all sectors, including defence.

With regard to the external front, the possibilities are best expressed by Stobdan: 'It also opens doors for a fresh look at territorial disputes with China. Granting Ladakh UT status was a masterstroke. It is a strategic move. Now that Jammu and Kashmir is gone, there is no longer a need to remain hung-up on its territorial integrity – the Aksai Chin issue should be flexible.' This is indeed a very bold statement, but coming as it does from a seasoned diplomat and a resident of Ladakh, it should merit dispassionate consideration. The one thing that history teaches us is that there are no permanent enemies or friends, only permanent interests, which keep evolving!

~

Every new book on contemporary history offers a new insight. India, that is Bharat, is such a vast country that many generalizations inevitably enter the popular discourse: it is the task of the historian and the chronicler to amend/supplement the anecdotal with the empirical. Take, for example, the role of Hindi and Punjabi newspapers in Punjab. Growing up in Jullundur (as it was then called) one saw the vitriol spewed by the *Veer Pratap* and *Punjab Kesari* on the one hand, and *Akali Patrika* and *Ajeet* on the other. I had assumed that these papers must have played their role in the Punjabi Suba agitation. However, after reading Ramesh Inder Singh's book *Turmoil in Punjab* I realized that the battle for Hindi and Punjabi was actually being fought by the *Ajeet* and *Hind Samachar* group in Urdu! *Ajeet* became a Punjabi newspaper later on and then the Hindi edition of *Punjab Kesari* came up. Although

Operation Blue Star did not have an impact on the boundary of Punjab, and was therefore outside the ken of this study, yet the observations of B.D. Pande in his book *In the Service of Free India* would have shaped the writing of this chapter. Likewise, the *Long Game* by Vijay Gokhale, published in 2022, gives us very fine insights into the reasons for and the circumstances under which Tibet got excluded from India's cartographic imagination. Then, there is Manu Pillai's book *False Allies* which looks at the relationship of the princes with the Raj – but by the time I saw it, the chapters on integration of states had already been 'locked'.

I have in the course of the book mentioned the contribution of the Nagas as well as the reluctance of the Santhals to be part of the Indian Labour Corps. Now there is an academic work by Radhika Singh from JNU called *The Coolie's Great War*. This list could go on, but my editors at HarperCollins have warned me that unless the camera-ready version of the final manuscript is received by them before Independence Day, there is no way this book will be published in the seventy-fifth year of our independence.

~

What next? Well, the demand for new states, autonomous councils and changes in nomenclature will never cease. Many states – Punjab and Haryana, Assam and Mizoram, West Bengal and Orissa, Maharashtra and Karnataka, to highlight a few – are still contesting their borders and claim to each other's territory. Then there are disputes over the sharing of waters, which get aggravated before each election. The councils established under the Fifth and Sixth Schedules are crying for attention, even as there continues to be greater devolution of funds, functions and functionaries. They have not quite met the expectations with which they had been created. Are there any lessons to be learnt? State governments have refused to let go of their control over revenue and police functions, and the question may well be asked of those in politics – does power mean anything if those at the helm have neither a patronage nor a nuisance value?

The acceptance of Telangana has certainly rekindled the hopes for a second state for Marathi and Bengali speakers. Although the decennial census scheduled for 2021 was postponed on account of Covid, it cannot be delayed forever; when the results are out, one can certainly expect intense political contestation on the principle to be adopted for determining seats for the Lok Sabha and the Rajya Sabha – for if population is the only criterion, then the share of the Hindi-speaking states, especially UP, will certainly go up. It is clear that the new Parliament building can accommodate 888 MPs in the Lok Sabha and 384 in the Rajya Sabha. It also has a provision for a joint sitting of all 1272 together. But the regional and state-wise distribution will be both a challenge and an opportunity to reshape political discourse for the years to come.

ACKNOWLEDGEMENTS

My gratitude, first and foremost, to my alma mater as well as my *karmabhoomi* – the Lal Bahadur Shastri National Academy of Administration (LBSNAA), Mussoorie, which I had the privilege to helm from 2019 to 2021. I started this project a few weeks before almost everything came to a halt on account of Covid in March 2020. However, the rich collection of material available at the Gandhi Smriti Library in LBSNAA ensured that I had everything needed for this research. The Library was fortunate to have the services of Sivaprasad Senapati, a fine and enthusiastic librarian on deputation from the National Library, Kolkata. In addition to sourcing all relevant books, journals, e-resources and state papers, he helped me access declassified records of the Foreign and Commonwealth Office of the UK. His efforts were supplemented by Ramesh Goel and Bhupinder Kaur.

The maps were provided thanks to Lt Gen. Girish Kumar, the DG of the Survey of India in Dehradun, and the very competent deputy DG, Pankaj Mishra. The Survey of India is indeed one of the finest 'knowledge institutions' in the country, and its contribution to nation-making – both literally and metaphorically – has to be placed on record.

A very special thanks is due to the team at the director's office. Led by the able Vijender Singh Rana, it included Preeti R. Bhandari, Y.S. Preeti, Y.S. Meena, Akshay Pandey and Narayan Bunker who typed out passages from archival material, as well as Shaayeque Sohail who helped convert PDFs into text files and incorporated various maps into my presentations. In retrospect, it all looks quite easy, but I was not very tech-savvy to begin with and their assistance was invaluable. Ankit Kumar and Mayank Yadav ensured that I was comfortable at my perch in the library by taking care of my addiction to Darjeeling tea and Arakku Valley coffee. The pleasant disposition of my driver Vikas Bhairav kept all of us in good cheer.

Srishtee Sethi joined the Academy as a Research Fellow in February 2021. Her scholarship and interest in the area of migration and borders was in broad alignment with my research, and she rendered indispensable assistance in getting my references and links sorted out. Her contribution to the research work is nothing short of sterling. Around this time, the Academy was also hosting Prof S.V. Subramanian (Subbu) from the Harvard Centre for Population Health and Geography. The three of us would often have lunch together and review the chapters. Subbu's insights into cartography, demography and geographic determinants are reflected in many passages of this work.

My colleagues in the LBSNAA Academic Council: Manoj and Arti Ahuja, P. Amudha, Raghuraj Rajendran, N.K. Sudhanshu, C. Sridhar, Nandini Paliwal, M.H. Khan, Monika Dhami, Vizay B. Vasanta, Vidya Bhushan, Alankrita Singh, Gauri P. Joshi, Anandhi, Abhiram G., Disha Pannu, Sunita Rani, Nitesh Jha, Hari Prakash, Milind Ramteke and Vinod Taneja were supportive of this endeavour, and I am grateful to each one of them. Being at the Academy also gave me an opportunity to share my research-in-progress with the JCM, MCTP, Induction, Professional and Foundation batches.

Lok Ranjan, who succeeded me as director, encouraged the continuation of my work at the Library and invited me to share my findings as part of the Azadi ka Amrit Mahotsav celebrations at the Academy. Thanks also to the DGs of the two premier forest institutions of Dehradun: Arun Rawat and Bharat Jyoti from the Indian Council for Forestry Research and Education (ICFRE) and the Indira Gandhi National Forest Academy, respectively. I was invited to these institutions to make presentations of this work to officers of the Indian and State Forest Services.

My dear friend Hridyesh Mohan from the West Bengal cadre has been supporting all my research efforts – from intra-SAARC border trade to understanding Indo-Bangladesh enclaves. Through his efforts, along with those of Satyabrata Mookerjee who talks with authority on politics, philosophy and practical matters in the same breath, a session on my project was organized at the BCCI in Kolkata. Sanjay Singh, then-head of the India Harvard office, arranged a Lakshmi Mittal and Family South Asia Institute seminar at India International Centre, New Delhi; in fact, the title of this book is drawn from that talk. Harshit Gupta and Dhruv Seth from Young Indians of the Confederation of Indian Industry gave me the opportunity to talk to bright young entrepreneurs. Two seminars – one at the Centre for Policy Research in Delhi and the other at Bangalore International Centre – could not be held because of Covid, but I would like to thank Deepak Sanan and Manish Sabharwal for arranging them. I have gained from my interactions with both on this subject. The intrepid Debashis Mitra, who moves between Siliguri, Bhubaneshwar, Bangalore and all frontiers of his father's Dogra paltan, has been the sounding board for many propositions in this book.

I would like to thank Durbar Ganguly at Millennium Post for carrying out the series called 'Mapping the Indian States'. However committed one may be to a research project, a firm weekly deadline helps – special thanks to Arif Mohammed for reminding me every week to submit the 1000-word column by Thursday evening. Now it has become such an ingrained habit that he does not need to remind me for the ongoing column on Geographical Indicators. I also thank Jagdish Chandra and Anita Hada of First India, Satish Sharma of *Garhwal Post* and Atul Singh of Fair Observer for carrying out articles which drew heavily upon research for this book.

I must acknowledge that feedback on my column from two former directors of the Academy, B.S. Baswan and Wajahat Habibullah, was of tremendous help. Likewise, for comments and suggestions from my former colleagues in the Krishi Bhawan, New Delhi, from 2010 to 2015: P.K. Basu, Anup K. Thakur, Sanjay Bhoosereddy, S.G. Rahate and Mukesh Khullar. Two former chairmen of the UPSC, Deepak Gupta and Arvind Saxena, a former member, Air Marshall Ajit Shankarrao Bhonsale, as well as ex-CVC Sanjay Kothari have been following this work and giving me encouragement. A word of thanks to Wing Commander Kuldip Shiva, Sanjay Abhigyan, Subhasis and Suyasha Chattopadhyay, Manu Dev Gautam, Rajneesh Chaudhary, Geeta Gopalakrishnan, Pravir Krishna, V. Srinivas and Sanjay Bhatia who share my work and give it wider currency.

My colleagues on the board of the Valley of Words Festival have always been very supportive of this endeavour: Robin Gupta, Lt Gen. P.J.S. Pannu, Dr Rajendra Dobhal, Dr Amna Mirza, Jyoti Dhawan, Brigadier Ashwini Kumar and Kishore Menon. Although we could not ultimately use Kishore's design options for the front cover of the book, I have made a collage of all those images which now occupies pride of place near my workstation. Rohan Talwar helped me download all the Supreme Court judgments on the contentious transfer of enclaves to

Bangladesh. Much gratitude to Dr Tania Saili Bakshi and Bikram Singh for their constant support.

I would also like to acknowledge the contribution of late D.P. Tripathi, a former member of the Rajya Sabha. I had several rounds of discussion with him on issues of delimitation and reorganization of states. Thanks also to Mukesh Tyagi and Brijesh Tripathi who were present in most of these debates.

In January 2022, Ashish Srivastava who was then heading the Information Technology Development Agency (ITDA) of Uttarakhand assigned Vaibhav Bahuguna to help me with the task of putting everything together in the form of a manuscript which I could share with my publisher. My journey with HarperCollins started through Krishan Chopra and Siddhesh Inamdar, who helped conceptualize the book. Paloma Dutta, who has a very fine eye for detail, brought my long sentences down to manageable lengths in her excellent editing. Suchismita Ukil ensured that deadlines were met, and if this book is released in the seventy-fifth year of our Independence, a fair share of credit must go to her.

There would still be names that I have missed out, and I request indulgence from those who may feel that they have not been acknowledged. A senior citizen is entitled to unintentional lapses of this nature!

My daughter Yauvanika has made me revise my work by insisting on a shift from compulsory to compulsive reading. Although still not up to her exacting standards, my writing is perhaps better now despite thirty-six years of writing officialese. Thank you for holding a mirror to me. My wife Rashmi has always been a pillar of support for all my *sensible* endeavours – and if she had not endorsed this project, it would not have seen the light of day. There were times when I nearly gave up because research is a painstaking and lonely track, but she put me back with her disarming smile. Thank you. This book is dedicated to both of you.

NOTES

1. Maps and Milestones: The Marking of Internal Boundaries in India

1. 'The Preamble', as drafted by Dr B.R. Ambedkar, had the words 'Sovereign, Democratic, Republic' describing India. The 42nd Constitutional Amendment added the words 'Socialist' and 'Secular' in 1976.

2. Article 1 : India, that is Bharat, shall be a Union of States.

   Article 2 : Admission or establishment of new States: Parliament may by law admit into the Union, or establish, new States on such terms and conditions, as it thinks fit.

   Article 3: Formation of new States and alteration of areas, boundaries or names of existing States: Parliament may by law

   (a) form a new State by separation of territory from any State or by uniting two or more States or parts of States or by uniting any territory to a part of any State;

   (b) increase the area of any State;

   (c) diminish the area of any State;

   (d) alter the boundaries of any State;

   (e) alter the name of any State;

3. See, Catherine Clémentin-Ojha, "'India, That is Bharat …'": One Country, Two Names', *South Asia Multidisciplinary Academic Journal* (2014).

4. Survey of India, the national survey and mapping organization of the country. It was set up in 1767 in Calcutta. The history of the Survey of India dates back to the eighteenth century. 'Chapter XI: Geographical Maps', *Handbook of Topography*, Survey of India, Government of India (2009). During the last two decades there has been a major change in concept and technique of map-making. Conventional mapping technique has already been superseded by digital technology. There have been major changes in specifications too.

5. Nine provinces: East Punjab, West Bengal, Unite Provinces, Bihar, Bombay, Madras, Assam, Orissa and Central Provinces.
    Five provinces that became part of Pakistan included West Punjab, East Bengal, Sindh, Balochistan, North West Frontier Province.

6. Sanjeev Chopra, 'Prestige for Loyalty', http://www.millenniumpost.in/amp/mapping-the-states-of-india/prestige-for-loyalty-436820
    Also see, Sanjeev Chopra, 'Pakistan and the Princely Order', *First India*, 17 May 2020.
    William S. Niederkorn, 'A Scholar Recants on His "Shakespeare" Discovery', *The New York Times*, 20 June 2002.

7. See, Valentine Chirol, *Indian Unrest*, Createspace, 2018.

8. One of the reasons for Uttarakhand's sense of alienation was that in the first three plans there was no mega project for the state.

9. Gandhi's *Hind Swaraj* lays down the concept of minimal state which privileged rural over the urban.

10. Ambedkar's thoughts on social justice included that all benefits and privileges in the society should be shared by all its members. If there is any structural inequality towards any particular section, the government should take affirmative action in eliminating such inequalities.

11. See, Bipan Chandra, Mridula Mukherjee, Aditya Mukherjee, K.N. Panikkar, Sucheta Mahajan, *India's Struggle for Independence* (2016). The linguistic principle of provincial organization was among the fundamental ideas that inspired the Indian freedom struggle.

12. As detailed in Narayani Basu's book *V.P. Menon: The Unsung Architect of Modern India*, Simon & Schuster India, 2020.

13. The Union of India, also called the Dominion of India, was an independent dominion in the British Commonwealth of Nations between 15 August 1947 and 26 January 1950.

14. See, Manan Ahmed Asif, 'Introduction: The End of Hindustan'. In *The Loss of Hindustan: The Invention of India*, Harvard University Press, 2020.

15. Chamber of Princes or Narendra Mandal was a representative body of 'India Princes' which was established in 1920. The key members were Maharaja of Bikaner, Maharaja of Patiala, Maharaja of Nawanagar, Nawab of Bhopal. Sikkim's Maharaja was the vice-president of the Narendra Mandal at the time of India's independence. Many photographs of the annual conference of the Narendra Mandal can be seen in the lobby of Imperial Hotel, New Delhi.

16. K. Adeney, *Federalism and Ethnic Conflict Regulation in India and Pakistan* (2016). Katharine Adeney demonstrates that institutional design is the most important explanatory variable in understanding the different intensity and types of conflict in the two countries rather than the role of religion. Adeney examines the extent to which previous constitutional choices explain current day conflicts.

17. The Haripura Session of Indian National Congress is where Subash Chandra Bose became its president.

18. The 1935 Act gave new dimensions to the affairs of the country by the development of an All-India Federation, provisional autonomy and the removal of the diarchy. It was also the last Constitution of British India, before the country was divided, in 1947, into two parts – India and Pakistan.

19. Sanjeev Chopra, 'Prestige for Loyalty', http://www.millenniumpost.in/amp/mapping-the-states-of-india/prestige-for-loyalty-436820
Also see, Sanjeev Chopra, 'The Great Game and the Frontier States of Pakistan', *First India*, 24 May 2020, and 'Kalat, Balochistan and Pakistan', *First India*, 8 June 2020.

20. Col. Gambhir Singh, MIS (Officiating Surveyor General of India) 'Bharat ke Rajnaitik Vibhag or India's Political Map' (1952). The first Hindi map of independent India was published in 1952; the map classifies states under raj pramukhs, Union Territories under lieutenant governors and chief commissioners under the Union government. It also carries the usual disclaimers regarding the India–Pakistan boundary still being indicative, and not an international boundary.

21. Accordingly, section 3(2) of the Official Languages Act, 1963 (amended in 1967) provides for continuing the use of English in official work even after 25 January 1965.

22. Until 1949, Tibet was an independent Buddhist nation in the Himalayas, which had little contact with the rest of the world. Tibet's political and spiritual leader, the Dalai Lama, fled to India in 1959.

23. 'Ralengnao Khathing MC', MBE (1912–1990), popularly known as Bob Khathing, was an Indian soldier, civil servant and diplomat and the first person of tribal origin to serve as an ambassador for India to Burma now Myanmar.

24. C. Rajagopalachari was the governor general of India (1948–50) and first governor general of Bengal (1947–48).

25. 'Report of the States Reorganization Commission' (1955). The notification read, 'The Commission will investigate the conditions of the problem, the historical background, the existing situation and the bearing of all important and relevant factors thereon. They will be free to consider any proposal relating to such reorganization.'

26. James Tod, *Annals and Antiquities of Rajasthan: Or, 'The Central and Western Rajpoot States of India Asian Educational Services'*, H. Milford, Oxford University Press, 2001.

27. Roy–Sinha Declaration, *Hem Chandra Sen Gupta and Ors. vs The Speaker of Legislative* in the assembly of West Bengal (17 April 1956).

28. Ajit Singh Sarhadi, *Punjabi Suba* (1970); Punjabi Suba Movement, a long-drawn political agitation launched by the Sikhs demanding the creation of Punjabi Suba or Punjabi-speaking state in the Punjab. At the time of Independence, it was commonly recognized that the Indian states then comprising the country did not have any rationale or scientific basis. They were more the result of the exigencies of the British conquest.

29. Under Pratap Singh Kairon, the Akalis were allowed dual membership in the Akali Dal and in the Indian National Congress.

30. Pluricentralism was a concept propagated by António de Oliveira Salazar who was the finance minister and then Prime Minister of Portugal to legitimize overseas territories (colonies) by giving them a representation in the Senate and Parliament of Portugal.

31. 'Gorkha' is a term that refers to Gurkha soldiers from Nepal who have served or are serving in the British Army. Gurkhas have been part of the British Army since 1815 and Bodos are the original inhabitants of Assam.

They ruled Assam till around 1854. They belong to the Indo-Mongoloid stock and their language is derived from the Assam-Burmese branch of Tibeto-Burman sub-family.

32. Om Marathe, 'Explained: Sikkim, from Chogyal Rule to Indian State', *The Indian Express*, August 2019.
    For 333 years before 1975, Sikkim was ruled by the Chogyals (or kings) of the Namgyal dynasty of Tibetan descent. According to one account, the first ruler, Penchu Namgyal, was sworn in as king by Tibetan lamas in 1642.

33. Kazi Lhendup Dorjee was the first chief minister of Sikkim from 1975 to 1979 after its union with India.

34. Bhutia-Lepcha is an ethnic grouping consisting of people of the Bhutia and Lepcha communities in Sikkim state of India. Both these groups are listed as Scheduled Tribes by the Government of India.

35. See, Francine Du Plessix Gray, 'The Fairy Tale That Turned Nightmare?', *The New York Times*, March 1981.

36. As per the J&K Reorganization Act, 2019, Ladakh's total area is 59,146 sq. km and Jammu and Kashmir's total area is 222,236 sq. km.

37. M. Saleem Pandit and Sanjay Khajuria, '50 Per Cent Voter Turnout in 4th Phase of DDC Polls in Jammu and Kashmir', *The Times of India*, December 2020.

38. See, Stephen Cohen, *The Idea of Pakistan*, Brookings Institution Press, 2004.

39. See, Dr B.R. Ambedkar, *Thoughts on Linguistic States, 1955*, Samyak Prakashan, 1955.

40. 'How 1976 Seat Freeze Has Altered Lok Sabha Representation', *The Times* of India, March 2019.

2. 1947: The First Map of Independent India

1. Article 3: Formation of new states and alteration of areas, boundaries or names of existing states. Parliament may by law (a) form a new state by separation of territory from any state or by uniting two or more states or parts of states or by uniting any territory to a part of any state; (b) increase the area of any state; (c) diminish the area of any state; (d) alter the boundaries of any state; (e) alter the name of any state.

2. Ship of Theseus: Theseus owned a ship and the ship was entirely made of wood. Every time a piece of the ship needed replacing it was substituted with a metal part. This went on for a few years until eventually it was entirely made of metal. It is on expanding the metaphysics of identity, a thought experiment that raises the question of whether an object that has had all of its components replaced remains the same object.

3. This was published under the direction of Brigadier G.F. Heaney, Commander of the British Empire (CBE) and surveyor general of India at the Survey of India office at Dehradun. Incidentally, Survey of India Press has the distinction of also printing the first stamp of India, as early as 1854, and later the first Constitution of India.

4. Cyril John Radcliffe, 1st Viscount Radcliffe, GBE, PC, QC, FBA was a British lawyer and Law Lord. He was born on 30 March 1899 and died in 1 April 1977. He was tasked in June 1947 to assign territories between the Dominions of India and Pakistan. In order to determine exactly which territories to assign to each country during the Indian independence and creation of Pakistan, on June 1947, Britain appointed Sir Cyril Radcliffe to chair two boundary commissions – one for Bengal and one for Punjab.

5. 'Partition', W.H. Auden, https://www.poeticous.com/w-h-auden/partition, 1966. Accessed on 5 February 2021.

6. This was published under the direction of Brigadier G.F. Heaney, Commander of the British Empire (CBE) and surveyor general of India at the Survey of India office at Dehradun. Incidentally, Survey of India Press has the distinction of also printing the first stamp of India, as early as 1854, and later the first Constitution of India.

7. Justice M.C. Mahajan, *Looking Back*, Har-Anand Publication (revised edition), 2018.

8. Admiral of the Fleet Louis Francis Albert Victor Nicholas Mountbatten, 1st Earl Mountbatten of Burma was born Prince Louis of Battenberg and lived between 25 June 1900 and 27 August 1979. He was a British Royal Navy officer and statesman. He was the last viceroy of India and the first governor-general of independent India.

    In March 1947, Lord Mountbatten arrived in India as the last viceroy, with an explicit mandate to achieve the transfer of power before June 1948. Mountbatten had accepted the post as viceroy on the condition of an early deadline.

9. Richard M. Langworth, *Churchill by Himself: The Definitive Collection of Quotations*, PublicAffairs, 2008, 163.

10. The Indian Independence Act, 17 July 1947 once the whole partition scheme was agreed by major political parties, stage was set for introducing Independence Bill in the House of Commons, which was introduced on 4 July 1947. This was the culmination of India's struggle against colonialism and imperialism.

11. See, Sanjeev Chopra, 'Prestige for Loyalty', http://www.millenniumpost.in/amp/mapping-the-states-of-india/prestige-for-loyalty-436820

12. Kashmir as a princely state appears on the map in 1846 and is located differently in the subsequent map in 1948.

13. The Instrument of Accession was a legal document first introduced by the Government of India Act, 1935, and used in 1947 to enable each of the rulers of the princely states under British paramountcy to join one of the new dominions of India or Pakistan created by the partition of British India.

14. *Jinnah: His Successes, Failures and Role in History*, Ishtiaq Ahmed, Penguin Random House India, 2020.

15. Ibid.

16. Bihar and Orissa province: the province of Bihar and Orissa was created in 1912. However, there were inherent flaws in this formation as there was neither a common language nor a cultural tradition.

17. Bibek Debroy, 'An Area of Light', *The Indian Express*, 20 September 2010.

18. The Temple Entry Authorization and Indemnity Act was passed by the government in 1939 by which restrictions prohibiting Dalits from entering Hindu temples was removed.

19. *The Story of the Integration of the Indian States*, V.P. Menon, Longmans, Green & Co., 1955.

20. The state of being paramount – the highest rank or authority, dominion, rule; dominance or power through legal authority.

21. *The Story of the Integration of the Indian States*, V.P. Menon, Longmans, Green & Co., 1955.

22. Foreign Jurisdiction Act, 1947: An Act to provide for the exercise of certain foreign jurisdiction of the central government. Whereas by treaty, agreement, grant, usage, sufferance and other lawful means, the central government has, and may hereafter acquire, jurisdiction in and in relation

to areas outside India. The Act was on the statute till its repeal in 2014 when the ministry of external affairs spokesperson informed the Standing Committee in the Parliament that as India was not in possession of any foreign territory, there was no justification for the Act. See annexure for the full Act.

3. Riyasat e Jammu wa Kashmir wa Ladakh wa Tibet ha

1. The First Anglo-Sikh War (1945–1946) was fought between the Sikh Empire and the British East India Company.
2. It was the part of territory ruled by Maharaja Ranjeet Singh.
3. Ladakh is a region of India which has been administered as a Union Territory since 5 August 2019.
4. Chitral, previously the largest district of Khyber-Pakhtunkhwa, is a region which shares its eastern border of Gilgit–Baltistan.
5. Gilgit is the capital city of Gilgit–Baltistan, under the occupation of Pakistan. The Gilgit region is part of Greater Kashmir.
6. Baltistan is a mountainous region under the occupation of Pakistan. It is also part of Gilgit–Baltistan. To note, Gilgit–Baltistan, formerly known as the Northern Areas, is a region administered by Pakistan as an administrative territory, and constitutes the northern portion of the larger Kashmir region, which has been the subject of a dispute between India and Pakistan since 1947.
7. Historically, Tibet was an independent state and a buffer between India and China. Several perspectives exist on the region. It is important to note that on 29 April 1959, His Holiness the Dalai Lama established the Tibetan administration in exile in Mussoorie (Uttarakhand). Named the Central Tibetan Administration (CTA) of His Holiness the Dalai Lama, this is the continuation of the government of independent Tibet. In May 1960, the CTA was moved to Dharamshala. The Tibetan people, both in and outside Tibet, look to the CTA as their sole and legitimate representative.
8. *Rajatarangini* is a historical record of Kashmir composed by Kalhana in 1148 CE. It claims to have the recorded the history of Kashmir of over four millennia.

9. Kalhana, known for his work *Rajatarangini*, was a Sanskrit scholar who was born and lived in twelfth-century Kashmir.

10. Rishi Kashyap is one of the Saptarishis, i.e., one of the seven great sages of Vedic times. It is generally believed that Kashmir is named after Rishi Kashyap.

11. Ptolemy was an Egyptian astronomer, mathematician and geographer who lived in second century BC.

12. Herodotus was an ancient Greek writer, geographer and historian who lived in fifth century BC.

13. Kaspapapyros was mentioned by Hecataeus in his book *Periēgēsis* (Tour around the World), which is thought to be a reference to Kashyapa-pura.

14. Hecataeus of Miletus was an ancient Greek historian. His work *Periēgēsis* (Tour around the World) is considered to be a major historical and geographical work.

15. Stephanus of Byzantium was a Greek who was the author of *Ethnicia*, a historically important geographical dictionary.

16. Jambupura was the capital of Raja Jambulochan and named after him too. It was built on the right bank of Tawi.

17. Raja Jambulochan was a powerful local chieftain who ruled during the ninth century.

18. Jambudwip is the ancient name of Greater India geographical area.

19. Nund Rishi, who is also known as Alamdar-e-Kashmir, (1377–1440) was a Kashmiri.

20. Durrani Afghans refer to the Afghans of one of the two major Pashtun tribes, Durrani. The Durrani Empire was established by Ahmad Shah Durrani in mid eighteenth century. The Durrani Empire is considered to be the foundation of modern-day Afghanistan.

21. Zorawar Singh was a military general under King Gulab Singh of Jammu. He is known for conquering Ladakh and parts of Tibet. He is also known as the 'Conqueror of Ladakh' and the 'Napoleon of India'.

22. Khalsa Raj was also known as Sikh Empire. It was established by Maharaja Ranjit Singh and based majorly in Punjab.

23. Raja Gulab Singh (1792–1857) was the founder of the Dogra dynasty.

24. Nanak Shahi was the ruling currency of the Sikh Empire also known as the Khalsa Raj.

25. Robert Thorpe was an officer of British Indian Army and is remembered for his chronicles on the life of Kashmiris under Maharaja Ranbir Singh.

26. Cashmere is an alternative spelling of Kashmir used by the British.

27. *Cashmere Mismanagement*, Robert Thorpe, Wyman Bros, 1968.

28. Aligarh Muslim University was established by Sir Syed Ahmad Khan in 1875. It is now a Central University.

29. Sir Bertrand James Glancy (1882–1953) was the governor of Punjab between 1941 to 1946.

30. *The Blazing Chinar: Autobiography*, Sheikh Abdullah, Pragun Publications, 2013.

31. RSS or Rashtriya Swayamsevak Sangh is a Hindu nationalist organization founded by Kehsav Baliram Hedgewar in 1925.

32. All Jammu and Kashmir Muslim Conference is a political party based in Pak-occupied Kashmir. It was founded by Sheikh Muhammad Abdullah in October 1932.

33. Budh Singh was a Kashmiri politician who was also the president of the All Jammu and Kashmir National Conference.

34. Pandit Prem Bazaz was a Kashmiri politician and an advocate of 'Kashmir for Kashmiris'.

35. Tripuri Session of Congress was held in a small town called Tripuri near Jabalpur, Madhya Pradesh, in 1939. In this session, Subhas Chandra Bose was re-elected as Congress president.

36. All India States Peoples Conference was organized in 1927. It was formed as a result of political movements in the erstwhile princely states of British India.

37. Sir Muhammad Iqbal (1877–1938) was an author and an advocate for creation of Pakistan. He is the national poet of Pakistan. However, prior to his advocacy for Pakistan he wrote the famous work 'Sara Jahan se Accha'.

38. Ghulam Mohammad Abbas (1904–1967) was a Kashmiri politician and president of the Muslim Conference party. He later became the head of Azad Kashmir government.

39. Quit Kashmir Agitation was a movement started by Sheikh Abdullah against both the British and Maharaja Hari Singh in 1936.

40. Swami Sant Dev was an occultist who became close to Maharaja Hari Singh of Kashmir and became a member of his court.

41. Grigori Rasputin (1869–1916) was a mystic who became a close confidant of both Emperor Nicolas II and his wife Empress Alexandra.

42. Janak Singh (1872–1972) was an army minister under Maharaja Hari Singh and later became the Prime Minister of Jammu and Kashmir from 11 August 1947 to 14 October 1947.

43. Liaquat Ali Khan (1895–1951) was one of the founding fathers of Pakistan and the first Prime Minister of Pakistan. He remained the Prime Minister of Pakistan till his assassination in 1951.

44. Akbar Khan (1912–93) was a member of British Indian Army and then Pakistan Army. He retired as Major General of Pakistan Army in 1951.

45. Shaukat Hayat Khan was an officer of the British Indian Army and a prominent member of Muslim League. He was part of the Constituent Assembly of Pakistan.

46. Ram Chandra Kak (1893–1983) was the Prime Minister of Jammu and Kashmir under Maharaja Hari Singh from 1945 till 1947.

47. Mehr Chand Mahajan (1889–1967) was the third chief justice of India. He was also the Prime Minister of Jammu and Kashmir under Maharaja Hari Singh from 15 October 1947 to 5 March 1948.

48. *1947 Kashmir Invasion: Why Stalemate? (Who Failed India)*, P.C. Dogra, Manas Publications, 2020. P.C. Dogra is a former Punjab director-general of police. He is a 1968 batch Punjab cadre IPS officer.

49. *My Life and Times*, Syed Mir Qasim, South Asia Books, 1993. Mir Qasim (1921–2004) was the second chief minister of the erstwhile Indian state of Jammu and Kashmir. He was awarded Padma Bhusan posthumously in 2005.

50. *Mission with Mountbatten*, Alan Campbell-Johnson, Atheneum, 1985.

51. Thomas Christopher is the author of *Faultline Kashmir*, Brunel Academic Publishers, 2000.

52. Asian Relations Conference was a conference hosted by the Provisional Government of India in April–May of 1947.

53. Cold War refers to the period of high tension between USA and USSR, which ended with the dissolution of USSR in 1991.

54. Commonwealth is a voluntary organization of fifty-six independent countries all of which were former British colonies.

55. Sir Zafarullah Khan (1893–1985) was the first foreign minister of Pakistan, who also served as president of the UN General Assembly (1961–62) and president of the International Court of Justice (1970–73).

56. http://www.jammu-kashmir.com/documents/abdulun48.html

57. United Nations Commission for India and Pakistan was formed to investigate and mediate the India–Pakistan dispute over the future of the state of Jammu and Kashmir. It existed from June 1948 until March 1950.

58. Shimla Agreement of 1972 was a peace treaty signed by the prime ministers of India and Pakistan (Indira Gandhi and Z.A. Bhutto, respectively) on 2 July 1972 in Shimla.

59. United Nations Military Observer Group in India and Pakistan was established in January 1949 to supervise the ceasefire between India and Pakistan in the state of Jammu and Kashmir.

60. Sir Owen Dixon (1886–1972) was an internationally prominent jurist who served as the sixth chief justice of Australia.

61. https://www.jammukashmirnow.com/Encyc/2020/9/16/16-September-1842-Treaty-of-Chushul-History-of-Dogra-Tibetan-War.html

62. *India after Gandhi*, Ramachandra Guha, HarperCollins, 2007.

63. *1962 and the McMahon Line Saga*, Claude Apri, Lancer, 2013.

4. The Nizam and His Firmans

1. A unique and hybrid version of 'Highness' conferred to only the Nizams of Hyderabad by the British Government.

2. A royal decree issued by a royal sovereign.

3. Emperor of the Ottoman Empire, the most influential Islamic Empire for most part of its existence.

4. A Khalifa or a Caliph is a Muslim ruler of an Islamic State who is looked at as one of the successor to Prophet Muhammad.

5. Maulana Shaukat Ali (1873-1938) was a prominent leader of the Khilafat Movement.

6. Osmania University is a public University in Hyderabad. It was founded by Nawab Osman Ali Khan, the seventh Nizam of Hyderabad.

7. Aligarh is a city in the state of Uttar Pradesh. Aligarh Muslim University is located there.

8. Deoband is a town in the Saharanpur district in the State of Uttar Pradesh. It is known for Darul Uloom Deoband, one of the most prominent Islamic Seminary of India.

9. 'Federating the Raj: Hyderabad, Sovereign Kingship, and Partition', Sunil Purushotham, *Modern Asian Journal*, Vol. 54, Issue 1, 4 July 2019.

10. 'Council of Indian Muslim Theologians' is an organization of Islamic scholars belonging to the Deobandi school of thought in India.

11. 'The Princely States, the Muslim League and the Partition of India', Ian Coplan, *International History Review*, 1991.

12. Lord Charles Hardinge (1858–1944) was the viceroy and the governor general of India from 1910 to 1916.

13. Rufus Issac (1860–1935), the first Marquess of Reading, was the Viceroy and the governor general of India from 1921 to 1926.

14. *The Story of the Integration of the Indian States*, V.P. Menon, Longmans, Green & Co., 1955.

15. Champaran Satyagraha was the first satyagraha led and launched by Mahatma Gandhi in 1917. It was launched for the rights of Indian Indigo Planters.

16. Khilafat or Caliphate is an Islamic state ruled by an Islamic ruler with the title of Khalif/Caliph.

17. Andhra Jana Sangham was a people's movement in the state of Hyderabad which was launched to fight for the interests of Telugu-speaking population in the state of Hyderabad.

18. Konda Venkata Ranga Reddy (1890-1970) was a politician who was active in Telangana Rebellion and then went on to become the deputy chief minister of Andhra Pradesh.

19. Madapati Hanumantha Rao (1885–1970) was the first mayor of Hyderabad and also the founding member of Andhra Jana Sangham. He is known as Andhra Pitamah.

20. Andhra Mahasabha was formed after Andhra Jana Sangham grew exponentially. Andhra Mahasabha played a very important role in the Telangana Rebellion.

21. Arya Samaj is a reformist Hindu movement started by Dayanand Saraswati with the aim to establish the Vedas as the truth.

22. Dayanand Saraswati (1824–83) was a social reformer who advocated Vedas as the truth. He also founded Arya Samaj.

23. 'Shudhi' as a concept and process was promoted by Arya Samaj. Shudhi refers to purification and included removing untouchability and converts outcasts from other religions to Hinduism.

24. Hindu Mahasabha is a Hindu political party founded by Vinayak Sarvarkar, Lala Lajpat Rai and Madan Mohan Malaviya in 1915.

25. Sanatana Dharma is an alternative term used for Hinduism and covers much more than Hinduism under it.

26. Keshav Rao Koratkar (1867–1932) was a social reformer and educationist. He was elected president of Hyderabad Arya Samaj in 1904.

27. Government of India Act, 1935, was a legislation passed by the British Parliament dealing with the system of government and governance in India. This also acted as a major influence for the Indian Constitution.

28. Haripura Resolution was passed during the Haripura Session of Congress in 1938. The resolution identified princely states as an integral part of India.

29. 'Last Phase of Freedom Struggle in the Hyderabad State', G. Meeneshwar Rao, Indian History Congress, 1991.

30. Asaf Jahi Dynasty was a ruling dynasty of the Kingdom of Hyderabad. It was founded by Asaf Jah I in 1734.

31. Public Safety Act, 1938, was passed by the Nizam of Hyderabad to counter the rising popularity of Hyderabad State Congress and the act deemed the Hyderabad State Congress as unlawful.

32. Padmaja Naidu (1900–1975) was an Indian freedom fighter who served as the fifth governor of West Bengal. She was the daughter of the prominent Indian freedom fighter Sarojini Naidu.

33. Born in Lucknow in 1902 and educated at Aligarh Muslim University, Kasim Rizvi entered the service of the Nizam, established the Majilis-e-Ittehadul Musilmeen and later the Razakar militia in the state of Hyderabad. He fled to Pakistan in 1948.

34. Ittehad refers to a member of Majlis-e-Ittehadul Muslimeen.

35. Razakars was a private militia maintained by Kasim Rizvi. The militia on principle opposed the integration of Hyderabad into India, and tried to convince the Nizam to accede to Pakistan.

36. Operation Polo was the operation carried out by the Indian Armed Forces to integrate the state of Hyderabad into the Union of India.

37. Standstill Agreements were agreements signed between the newly independent dominions of India and Pakistan and the princely states of the British Indian Empire. It agreed to continue the administrative process as they were under British Raj until the integration with either dominion happened successfully.

38. Sir Walter Monckton (1891–1965) was a British politician who was the Constitution advisor to the Nizam of Hyderabad.

39. Muhammad Ahmad Said Khan Chhatar (1888–1982) was the 39th and 41st Prime Minister of Hyderabad.

40. *Mission with Mountbatten*, Alan Cambell-Johnson, Atheneum, 1985.

41. Sidney Cotton (1894–1969) was an Australian inventor and aviator. He supplied guns and ammunition to the state of Hyderabad to help them resist integration to India.

42. *The Story of the Integration of the Indian States*, V.P. Menon, Longmans, Green & Co., 1955.

43. Mullath Kadingi Vellodi (1896–1987) was an Indian diplomat who was appointed as the chief minister of Hyderabad by the Indian government after fall of Nizam of Hyderabad.

5. India as a Republic!

1. PEPSU: The Patiala and East Punjab States Union (PEPSU) was a state of India, uniting eight princely states between 1948 and 1956.

2. Raj pramukh was an administrative title held by the governors of India's princely states from 1947 to 1956. The raj pramukhs were mostly former rulers of the states themselves.

3. The Indian National Congress held its 51st session during last month at Haripura in the district of Bardoli. Under the leadership of Jawaharlal Nehru, who held office as president for more than eighteen months, the Congress had grown by leaps and bounds. This growth of support to the Congress was reflected at the Haripura session. Mammoth crowds, estimated at more than half a million people, witnessed the procession and paid homage to the President-Elect, Subhas Chandra Bose.

4. *The Indian Princes and Their States*, Barbara Ramusack, Cambridge University Press, 2004.

5. The payments of 'privy purse' were made to the former rulers under constitutional provisions of Article 291 and Article 362. Privy purse conferred 'special status' to the ruling class, which continued the British practice of ruler and ruled..

6. A short-lived union of the eastern princely states. It was formed right after the British left and India became independent.

7. Second chief minister of West Bengal and remained in office between 23 January 1948–1 July 1962. Bidhan Roy, often considered the 'Maker of Modern West Bengal', was a physician, educationist and freedom fighter.

8. The twelve sovereign states of the Punjab confederacy during the eighteenth century.

9. The initial Peshwas were all ministers who served as the chief executives to the king. The later Peshwas held the highest administrative office and also controlled the Maratha confederacy. Under the Chitpavan Brahmin Bhat family, the Peshwas became the de facto hereditary administrators of the confederacy.

10. *The Story of the Integration of the Indian States*, V.P. Menon, Longmans, Green & Co., 1955.

11. The term Mahagujarat included all Gujarati-speaking areas including mainland Gujarat and peninsulas of Saurashtra and Kutch. Writer-politician Kanaiyalal Munshi had coined the term Mahagujarat at the Karachi meet of Gujarati Sahitya Parishad in 1937.

12. Sisodia is an Indian Rajput clan who claim Suryavanshi lineage. A dynasty belonging to this clan ruled over the kingdom of Mewar in Rajasthan.

13. Cutch or Kutch comprises mostly of salt marshes, share a conflicted international borderline with Pakistan.

14. *The Story of the Integration of the Indian States*, V.P. Menon, Longmans, Green & Co., 1955.

15. Ibid.

6. The First Hindi Map of India

1. Col Gambhir Singh, MIS (Officiating Surveyor General of India), 'Bharat ke Rajnaitik Vibhag or India's Political map' (1952). The first Hindi map of independent India was published in 1952; the map classifies states under raj pramukhs, Union Territories under lieutenant governors and chief commissioners under the Union government. It also carries the usual disclaimers regarding the India–Pakistan boundary still being indicative, and not an international boundary.

2. North-east Frontier Agency or NEFA, originally known as the North-East Frontier Tracts, was one of the political divisions in British India and later the Republic of India until 20 January 1972, when it became the Union Territory of Arunachal Pradesh and some parts of Assam. Its administrative headquarters was Shillong (until 1974, when it was transferred to Itanagar). It received the status of state on 20 February 1987.

3. *Region, Nation, 'Heartland': Uttar Pradesh in India's Body Politic,* Gyanesh Kudasiya, Sage Publication, 2006.

4. Ibid.

5. The Maharaja of Darbhanga maintained good relations with both the Raj and the Congress. Lakshmeshwar Singh was one of the founders of the Indian National Congress (INC) in 1885. Darbhanga was one of the major donors to the party despite the family maintaining its proximity to the British Raj. During British rule, the INC wanted to hold their annual convention in Allahabad but they were denied permission by the government to use any public place for this purpose. The Maharaja of Darbhanga bought an area and allowed Congress to hold their annual convention there. The annual convention of Congress of 1892 was held on 28 December on the grounds of Lowther Castle, purchased by the then Maharaja.

6. *The Story of the Integration of the Indian States,* V.P. Menon, Longmans, Green & Co., 1955.

7. Ibid.

8. Ibid.

9. *1962 and the McMahon Line Saga,* Claude Apri, Lancer, 2013.

10. *The Long Game: How the Chinese Negotiate with India,* Vijay Gokhale, Penguin Random House India, 2021.

11. *The Man Who Saved India,* Hindol Sengupta, Penguin Random House India, 2018.

7. The Andhra State and the SRC

1. The Hindi heartland supports about a third of India's population and occupies about a quarter of its geographical area. The population is concentrated along the fertile Ganga plain in the states of Uttar Pradesh, Madhya Pradesh, Chhattisgarh, Jharkhand and Bihar. It is a linguistic region encompassing parts of northern, central, eastern and western India where various Central Indo-Aryan languages subsumed under the term 'Hindi'.

2. The Government of India formed the Linguistic Provinces Commission in 1948 under the chairmanship of S.K. Dhar, to recommend whether the states should be reorganized on linguistic basis or not.

3. JVP committee was set up to study the recommendations of the Dhar Commission. The committee, comprised Jawaharlal Nehru and Vallabhbhai Patel, in addition to the Congress president Pattabhi Sitaramayya.

4. S.K. Dhar was a retired judge of the Allahabad High Court and the Government of India formed the Linguistic Provinces Commission, 1948, under his chairmanship.

5. Professor of linguistics, Rapoport Professor of liberal arts at the College of Liberal Arts.

6. *Nehru and the Language Politics of India*, Robert D. King, OUP, 1997.

7. Tanguturi Prakasam was an Indian politician and freedom fighter, chief minister of the Madras Presidency, and subsequently became the first chief minister of the new Andhra state, created by the partition of Madras state along linguistic lines.

8. Hyderabad State Praja Party was a political party in the Hyderabad state. It was formed in 1951 when Tanguturi Prakasam and Acharya N.G. Ranga broke away from the Indian National Congress.

9. Vishalandhra was a movement in post-independence India for a united state for all Telugu-speaking regions.

10. Omandur P. Ramaswamy Reddiyar (1895–1970) was a freedom fighter and the first chief minister of the Madras Province after Independence.

11. Indian freedom fighter, a Gandhian, undertook a fast unto death, which created an explosive situation in Andhra.

12. P.S. Kumaraswamy Raja an Indian politician who served as the chief minister of Madras Presidency from 6 April 1949 to 10 April 1952 and Governor of Orissa between 1954 till 1956. He was born in Rajapalayam in Tamil Nadu.

13. Sri Prakasa was born in Varanasi in 1890. He was an Indian politician, freedom fighter and administrator. He served as India's first high commissioner to Pakistan from 1947 to 1949, governor of Assam from 1949 to 1950, governor of Madras from 1952 to 1956, and governor of Bombay from 1956 to 1962. In his early days, he participated in the Indian independence movement and was jailed. After India's independence, he served as an administrator and Cabinet minister.

14. A.N. Khosla was an Indian engineer and politician. He was the chairman of the Central Waterways Irrigation and Navigation Commission of India. He was the governor of Orissa from September 1962 to August 1966 and again from September 1966 to January 1968.

15. Potti Sriramulu was an Indian freedom fighter and revolutionary. Sriramulu is revered as 'Amarajeevi' (Immortal Being) in the Andhra region for his self-sacrifice for the Andhra cause. He became famous for undertaking a hunger strike for fifty-six days in support of having a separate state for Andhra Pradesh; he died in the process.

16. Dr Burgulla Ramakrishna Rao was the first elected chief minister of the erstwhile Hyderabad state. Prior to the independence of India and the political integration of the princely states into the Union, he was among the Telugu-speaking leaders to resist the Nizam in the princely state of Hyderabad.

17. *Nehru and the Language Politics of India*, Robert D. King, OUP, 1997.

18. Mulki agitation in 1952 was a political movement for the safeguarding of jobs in Hyderabad state government for native residents, or Mulkis. It was the first event in Telangana movement.

19. Dr Fazal Ali was an Indian judge, the governor of two Indian states (Assam and Orissa), and the head of the States Reorganisation Commission which determined the boundaries of several Indian states in the December 1953. Their commission submitted the report in September 1953, broadly accepting the language as the basis of reorganization of states.

20. H.M. Kunzru was an Indian freedom fighter and public figure. He was a long-time Parliamentarian, serving in various legislative bodies at the provincial and central level for nearly four decades. He was a member of the Constituent Assembly of India (1946–50) that drew up the Constitution of India.

21. K.M. Panikkar popularly known as Sardar K.M. Panikkar, was an Indian statesman and diplomat. He was also a professor, newspaper editor, historian and novelist. He was appointed a member of the States Reorganisation Commission set up in 1953. He was also India's ambassador to France and a member of Rajya Sabha, the upper house of the Indian Parliament. He also served as vice chancellor of the University of Kashmir and the University of Mysore.

22. Bharat Ratna is the highest civilian award of the Republic of India. Instituted on 2 January 1954, the award is conferred in recognition of exceptional service/performance of the highest order, without distinction of race, occupation, position, or sex.

23. North-east Frontier Agency or NEFA, originally known as the North-East Frontier Tracts, was one of the political divisions in British India

and later the Republic of India until 20 January 1972, when it became
the Union Territory of Arunachal Pradesh and some parts of Assam.
Its administrative headquarters was Shillong (until 1974, when it was
transferred to Itanagar). It received the status of state on 20 February 1987.

8. The Linguistic States of the South: Tamil Nadu, Karnataka and Kerala

1. Devadasi in Sanskrit means the female servant or maid of gods and
   goddesses. Under Devadasi tradition, a pre-puberty girl would be married
   to the presiding deity of a temple. This girl would then remain a devadasi
   for life and would spend her life doing her duties around the temple.
   They were also required to sing devotional songs and dance in devotion
   to their deity.

2. Dravida Munnetra Kazhagam is an Indian political party and one of the
   two major Dravidian parties in Tamil Nadu. DMK was founded by C.N.
   Annadurai as a breakaway party from Periyar's Dravida Kazhagam.

3. Kula Kalvi Thittam (Hereditary Education Policy) was the name given
   to Rajaji's Madras Scheme of Elementary Education. Under this scheme,
   schools were to conduct two sessions. In the first session, regular teaching
   would be done. In the second session, the students would go back home
   and learn their parents' trade. It was scrapped after coming under criticism
   for promoting and upholding casteism.

4. Tamil Nadu Toilers Party was formed by the members of the Vanniyar
   caste to represent their interests in the first general elections and state
   elections of 1952. The party won 17 out of 309 constituencies in the
   state elections and 4 seats in the general elections. By 1957, the party
   had disbanded with most of its leaders having joined the Congress party.

5. *Carry on, but Remember! Selected Speeches of C.N. Annadurai in the Indian
   Parliament*, C.N. Annadurai, Thannatchi Pathippagam.

6. Sir Chetput Pattabhiraman Ramaswami Iyer (1879–1966) was the Diwan
   of the erstwhile princely state of Travancore at the time of independence
   of India from 1936 to its accession to India. As the Diwan of Travancore,
   he oversaw the setting up of University of Travancore and Travancore
   Bank, issuance of Temple Entry Proclamation, etc. At the time of
   Independence, he was an advocate for an independent Travancore and
   supported Maharaja Sri Chithira Thirunal's issuance of declaration of

independence. Later, after much negotiation and an assassination attempt on him, Travancore's accession to India was completed.

7. *Carry on, but Remember! Selected Speeches of C.N. Annadurai in the Indian Parliament*, C.N. Annadurai, Thannatchi Pathippagam.

8. Self-respect marriages are those which are conducted without being officiated by a Brahmin priest. Self-respect marriages were promoted and advocated by the leaders, like Periyar, of the Self-Respect Movement. The leaders alleged that conventional marriages were a way of strengthening Brahmin influence on Tamil culture. Self-respect marriages also promoted inter-caste and love marriages.

9. National Food Security Act, 2013, is an Act passed by the Indian Parliament 'to provide for food and nutritional security in human life cycle approach, by ensuring access to adequate quantity of quality food at affordable prices to people …' This Act provides for maternity benefits, food security allowance and implements Targeted Public Distribution System.

10. Jayachamarajendra Wadiyar (1919–74) was the twenty-fifth and the last Maharaja of Mysore. He ascended to the throne in 1940 and ruled Mysore till 1947. He was one of the first kings to agree to accede and merge his kingdom with the newly formed Union of India. He signed the instrument of accession in 1947. He was known for his love of music and philosophy.

11. Justice Miller Committee was appointed by the then Maharaja of Mysore Krishnaraja Wadiyar IV in 1919. It was headed by Sir Leslie Creery Miller. The objective of the committee was to 'consider steps necessary for the adequate representation of communities in the public service'.

12. 'Anglo-Indian' generally referred to persons of mixed British and Indian ancestry or is of British ancestry but is an Indian native. The Government of India Act, 1935, defined an Anglo-Indian as 'a person whose father or any of whose other male progenitors in the male line is or was of European descent but who is a native of India'.

13. Sir Mokshagundam Visvesvaraya (1861–1962) was an Indian civil engineer and the Diwan of Mysore from 1912 to 1919. He was the chief engineer of Krishna Raja Sagara dam and also served as one of the chief engineers of the flood protection system for the city of Hyderabad. His birthday, 15 September, is celebrated as Engineers' Day in India, Sri Lanka and Tanzania in his memory.

14. Aluru Venkat Rao (1880–1964) is known for his role in the unification of Kannada-speaking areas and formation of Karnataka under the Karnataka Ekikaran Movement. He is generally considered as the main leader of the movement.

15. *Outlines of South India History*, M.N.Venkata Ramanappa, Vikas Publishing House, 1975.

16. Ramachandra Hanamanta Deshpande (1861–1931) established Karnatak Vidyavardhak Sangha in 1890. He promoted the Kannada language, the local language, in the North Karnataka which was back then under the hegemony of Marathi as this part was under Maratha rule. He apparently also coined the slogan '*Sirigannadam gelge*' (Long live, Kannada!).

17. Devanahalli Venkataramanaiah Gundappa (1887–1975) was a renowned Kannada philosopher and author. He started a number of Kannada newspapers and magazines, most prominently, *The Karnataka*. His most famous literary work is *Mankuthimmana Kagga*.

18. Sir Mirza Muhammad Ismail (1883–1959) was born in a Persian family settled in Bangalore in the year 1883. He was successively the Diwan of three princely states, Mysore (1926–41), Hyderabad (1942–46) and Jaipur (1946–47). He is mainly remembered for the beautification of Bangalore and Mysore.

19. *My Life and Politics*, S. Nijalingappa, Vision Books, 2007.

20. Kadidal Manjappa (1908–1992) was the third chief Minister of Karnataka. He was the chief minister from 19 August 1956 to 31 October 1956. He was a Gandhian and is remembered for the various land reforms he brought in, like the Tenancy Act and the Inam Abolition Act.

21. Siddavanahalli Nijalingappa (1902–2000) was the fourth chief minister of Karnataka and the first after the state reorganisation in 1956. He was a strong supporter of Karnataka unification. He also strongly advocated the formation of linguistic states. He also offered refuge to Tibetans in Karnataka.

22. Kengal Hanumanthaiah (1908–1980) was the second chief minister of Karnataka. He was also a freedom fighter and a member of the Constituent Assembly of India. He was the main force behind the construction of Vidhan Soudha of Karnataka.

23. *Outlines of South India History*, M.N.Venkata Ramanappa, Vikas Publishing House, 1975.

24. Gopalkrishna Devdas Gandhi, born in April 1945, is an Indian politician and a former diplomat who served as the 23rd governor of West Bengal from 2004 to 2009. He is the grandson of Mahatma Gandhi. As a former IAS officer, he served as secretary to the President of India and as high commissioner to South Africa and Sri Lanka, among other administrative and diplomatic posts.

25. The term Malabar (often referred as the Malabar coast), in historical contexts, refers to India's southwestern coast, which lies on the narrow coastal plain of Karnataka and Kerala states between the Western Ghats range and the Arabian Sea. The coast runs from south of Goa to Kanyakumari on India's southern tip.

26. Aikya Kerala, the movement for a united (Aikya) Kerala gathered momentum with the attainment of independence. The first concrete step in this direction was taken on 1 July 1949. Following the national policy of integration, the state of Kochi and Travancore were merged into Travancore-Kochi State under a raj pramukh. The next step came with the reorganization of states on a linguistic basis in the light of the report of the States Reorganisation Commission. It was decided to add Malabar district and the Kasaragod taluk of south Canara district to Travancore–Kochi and to separate the Tamil-speaking southern region of old Travancore from Travancore–Kochi for inclusion in Madras state. On 1 November 1956, the new state of Kerala was formally inaugurated.

27. V.T. Krishnamachari was an Indian civil servant and administrator. He served as the Diwan of Baroda from 1927 to 1944, Prime Minister of Jaipur State from 1946 to 1949 and as a member of the Rajya Sabha from 1961 to 1964.

28. Planning Commission was an institution in the Government of India, which formulated India's Five-Year Plans, among other functions. It was formed in March 1950.

29. *The Story of the Integration of the Indian States*, V.P. Menon, Longmans, Green & Co., 1955.

30. Vaikom Satyagraha was a satyagraha (social protest) in erstwhile Travancore (now part of Kerala) against untouchability and caste discrimination in Hindu society of Kerala. The movement was centred around the Sri Mahadeva Temple at Vaikom, in the present-day Kottayam district.

31. https://www.mkgandhi.org/epigrams/u.htm

32. C.P. Ramaswami Iyer, popularly known as Sir C.P., was an Indian lawyer, administrator and politician who served as the Advocate-General of Madras Presidency from 1920 to 1923 and the Diwan of Travancore from 1936 to 1947. He was also a member of the 1926 and 1927 delegations to the League of Nations.

33. P.G.N. Unnithan was the last Diwan (Prime Minister) of independent Travancore (Thiruvithamkoor).

34. Darsanakalanidhi Parikshit Thamparan, the last official ruler of the princely state of Cochin. The state of Cochin was merged with that of Travancore and in 1949 his rule ended, but he continued as the Valliya Thampuram of Cochin.

35. Shree Narayana Dharma Prachalan (SNDP) was founded in 1903 by Dr Padmanabhan Palpu with the guidance of Sree Narayana Guru. SNDP was the first organization to envisage Kerala as a whole.

36. Nair Service Society (NSS) is an organization created for the social advancement and welfare of the Nair community that is found primarily in the state of Kerala. It was established under the leadership of Mannathu Padmanabha Pillai. The NSS is a three-tier organization with Karayogams at the base level, taluk unions at the intermediate level and a central headquarters operating from Perunna, Changanassery, in Kerala.

37. President's Rule refers to the suspension of a state government and the imposition of direct rule of the Centre. The central government takes direct control of the state in question and the governor becomes its constitutional head.

38. T.K. Narayan Pillai was an Indian freedom fighter during the colonial rule in India and was a member of the Indian National Congress (INC) which fought against the British. He was the last Prime Minister of Travancore and the first chief minister of Travancore–Cochin at the time of its formation in 1949.

39. Aikya Thiruvitahmcore-Cochin Grandhasala Sangham (Public Library Movement) in Kerala is older than of any other state in India and is unique in many respects. In the erstwhile Travancore, Cochin and Malabar which formed the constituent areas of the present Kerala state, public library development occurred at different periods. In 1949, with the merger of the two princely states of Travancore and Cochin the Travancore Grandhasala Sangham became the Thiru-Cochi Grandhasala Sangham. With the formation of the linguistic state of Kerala in 1956, the three

former political units were united. A common apex body covering the entire state became an imperative. In 1958, Kerala Grandhasala Sangham came into existence with a governing body elected from among the library workers of the state.

40. Punnapra–Valyar was a communist movement in the princely state of Travancore, British India, against the Prime Minister, C.P. Ramaswami Iyer and the state.

41. C. Kesavan was a politician, social reformer, statesman and the chief minister of Travancore-Cochin during 1950–52.

42. Ezhavas are a community with origins in the region of Kerala, India. They are also known as Ilhava, Irava, Izhava and Erava in the south of the region; as Chovas, Chokons and Chogons in central Travancore; and as Thiyyar, Tiyyas and Theeyas in the Malabar region. They used to work as agricultural labourers, small cultivators, toddy tappers and liquor businessmen. Some Ezhavas were also involved in weaving and some practised Ayurveda. In the present day, the Ezhavas are classified as an Other Backward Class by the Government of India under its system of positive discrimination.

43. *India: The Most Dangerous Decades*, Selig S. Harrison, Princeton University Press, 2016.

44. Pattom Thanu Pillai was a participant in the Indian independence movement who later served as the chief minister of Kerala from 22 February 1960 to 25 September 1962.

45. Panampilly Govinda Menon was an Indian politician, freedom fighter and lawyer. He served briefly as the Prime Minister of Cochin state in 1947. After the union of Travancore and Cochin, he served as minister for education under T.K. Narayana Pillai and minister for finance under A.J. John, Anaparambil. He was the chief minister of Travancore–Cochin in 1955–1956. He became Union minister for law and railways (1969–70) and minister of state for food and agriculture.

46. The Ming dynasty ruled China from 1368 to 1644 AD, during which China's population would double. Known for its trade expansion to the outside world that established cultural ties with the West, the Ming dynasty is also remembered for its drama, literature and world-renowned porcelain.

47. Admiral Zheng was a Chinese mariner, explorer, diplomat, fleet admiral and court eunuch during China's early Ming dynasty.

48. The Samoothiri (anglicised as Zamorin) was the hereditary monarch of the kingdom of Kozhikode (Calicut) on the south Malabar region of India. Calicut was one of the important trading ports on the south-western coast of India

9. The Roy–Sinha proposals and the Boundaries of West Bengal

1. Shri Krishna Sinha, also known as Shri Babu, was the first chief minister of the Indian state of Bihar.
2. 'Bengal–Bihar Merger Movement of 1956', Arun Ghosh, Karatoya, vol. 10, March 2017.
3. Damodar Valley Corporation is an Indian governmental organization, which operates in the Damodar river area of West Bengal and Jharkhand states of India. The corporation operates both thermal power stations and hydel power stations under the ministry of power, Government of India.
4. Purvanchal is a geographic sub-region of Uttar Pradesh that is within the larger Bhojpuri region. It comprises the eastern end of Uttar Pradesh.
5. The Praja Socialist Party, an Indian political party, was founded when the Socialist Party, led by Jayaprakash Narayan, Acharya Narendra Deva and Basawon Singh, merged with the Kisan Mazdoor Praja Party.
6. Jaipal Singh Munda was an Indian politician, writer and sportsman. He was the member of the Constituent Assembly, which debated on the new Constitution of the Indian Union. He captained the Indian field hockey team to clinch gold in the 1928 Summer Olympics in Amsterdam.
7. As per the 1971 census, an estimated 34,000 people lived in the Indian enclaves and 17,000 people in the Bangladesh enclaves. Bangladesh enclaves in India measured 17,000 acres and the figure for Indian enclaves in Bangladesh was 7100 acres (approximate figures).
8. The desire to 'de-enclave' most of the enclaves was manifested in a 1958 agreement between Jawaharlal Nehru and Feroz Khan Noon, the respective Prime Ministers, for an exchange between India and Pakistan without considering loss or gain of territory.
9. The India–Bangladesh Treaty of Friendship, Cooperation and Peace was a twenty-five-year treaty that was signed on 19 March 1972, forging close bilateral relations between India and the newly established state of Bangladesh.

10. Teen Bigha is a strip of land lying in the south-east of Mekhliganj Block of Cooch Behar District of West Bengal State in India. The Teen Bigha strip of land situated 10 km south-east of Mekhliganj measures 178 metres x 85 metres, comprises parts of 146 Upanchowki Mouja of Kuchlibari and 139 Fulkadabri of Kashiabari Mouja in Mekhliganj Block. It is located strategically between the Bangladesh enclaves of Dahagram and Angorpota on the west and Panbari Mouza of Bangladesh on the east.

10. Questions of Bi-lingualism

1. Andhra Pradesh, Kerala, Madras (Tamil Nadu) and Mysore (Karnataka).
2. UP, MP, Bihar and Rajasthan.
3. Orders issued by a district magistrate or police commissioner under Section 144 of Criminal Procedure Code restricting the number of people in a gathering or an assembly.
4. Founded on 6 February 1956 in Pune, it was an all-party forum to demand the creation of a new Marathi-speaking state with its headquarters at Bombay. Communist leader S.A. Dange was the President of the Samiti.
5. After the death of Stalin, the Soviet leadership was in the hands of Georgi Malenkov, Lavrenti Beria, Vyacheslav Molotov and Nikita Khrushchev.
6. Comprising the predominantly Marathi-speaking divisions of Amravati and Nagpur. It was also called Berar and had been attached to the Central Provinces for purposes of administration.
7. Member of the ICS, the first Indian governor of RBI and finance minister in the Union Cabinet from 1950–56.
8. *Nehru and the Language Politics of India*, Robert D. King, OUP, 1997.
9. Established by Dr Rajendra Prasad, president of the Constituent Assembly in June 1948, to recommend whether states should be reorganized on linguistic lines. The members were Justice S.K. Dhar, Jagat Narain Lal, lawyer and member of the Constituent Assembly and Panna Lal, a retired ICS officer.
10. Submitted a memorandum to the LRC supporting the formation of linguistic states, specifically the formation of a Marathi-speaking state with Bombay as the capital. He also suggested that the official languages of each state should be the same as that of the Central government.
11. Also called Sorath or Kathiawar is a peninsular region of Gujarat. It became a union of Gujarati speaking princely states from 1948 to 1956

and was a part of Bombay till May 1960, when it joined the newly carved state of Gujarat.

12. This is how Prime Minister Nehru was quoted by *The Times of India*, Bombay on 3 June 1956.

13. Although the Congress party fared well in the rest of the country, they suffered reverses in the Bombay region.

14. *India: The Most Dangerous Decades*, Selig S. Harrison, Princeton University Press, 2016.

15. First chief minister of Maharashtra, he is also called the architect of modern Maharashtra. In 1962, he was inducted as the defence minister, and he continued to occupy the position during the premiership of Lal Bahadur Shastri as well. Also served as the home, external affairs and finance minister. He also became the Deputy Prime Minster for a brief period under the Charan Singh ministry.

16. Freedom fighter and Gandhian social activist who accompanied Vinobha Bhave on a 6000-kilometre yatra to convince zamindars to give up their surplus land voluntarily to the landless (*bhoodan*: gift of land).

17. Joined the Congress movement after receiving his FRCS from London, where he also became the President of the Indian Students Association. He was also the personal physician to Mahatma Gandhi.

18. The Islamabad Capital Territory is the only territory of Pakistan which is administered directly by the Federal Government, just like a Union Territory in India.

19. One Unit refers to the Pakistani Government Plan, announced on 22 November 1954, under which the four provinces of Pakistan were clubbed into one unit.

20. Baluchistan is one of the four provinces of Pakistan and is the western part of Pakistan. The Balochis resent being 'coerced' into joining Pakistan against their will. There is an active insurgency in the region.

21. North-West Frontier Province was a province of British India and later of Pakistan. It is now known as the province of Khyber Pakhtunkhwa. The former Pakistan PM Imran Khan is from this state.

22. A career diplomat from East Bengal in East Pakistan, he became the third Prime Minister of Pakistan, but within two years, he was relieved of his position and made Pakistan's ambassador to USA.

23. Born in Murshidabad, he was educated at the University of Bombay and Sandhurst Military College. After a brief stint in the British Indian

Army, he joined the Indian Political Service, and made the first defence secretary of Pakistan after 1947. He was appointed the governor of his home state (East Bengal) to quell the situation after the language riots of 1952. He became the acting governor general, and then the first President of Pakistan.

24. Lahore was the capital of British Punjab from 1858 to 1947. It was a major centre for arts, culture and kingdoms for undivided India. It was made the capital of Punjab by Maharaja Ranjit Singh in 1799. It is now the second largest city in Pakistan.

25. Karachi is the largest city of Pakistan and the capital of province of Sindh. It was also the first capital of Pakistan till 1958.

26. Rawalpindi is the fourth largest city of Pakistan which acted as the interim capital of the country till the capital was shifted to Islamabad.

27. Khalsa Raj refers to an area in which the Sikhs as a community exercise political hegemony. Maharaja Ranjit Singh's empire is also called the Khalsa Raj, and it extended from the Punjab region to Khyber Pass in the west, to Kashmir in the north, Sindh in the south and Tibet in the east.

28. *Language, Religion and Politics in North India*, Paul R. Brass, iUniverse, 2005.

29. Hindustan Socialist Republican Army (HSRA) was founded in 1928 at Feroze Shah Kotla, New Delhi. Under the leadership of Bhagat Singh, it took a turn towards Marxist ideology. HSRA's manifesto 'Philosophy of the Bomb' was written by Bhagwati Charan Vohra.

30. One of the twenty-three official languages of India and the state language of Pakistan. Derived from the Turkish word Ordu, meaning the army, it was the language developed in the Mughal cantonments which saw so many languages and people come together. Amir Khosrow (1253–1325) is credited with the development of the language, which is also called Rekhta, Hindvi, Zaban-e-Hind.

31. The script of the Holy Guru Granth Saheb. It was formalized by the second guru of the Sikhs, Guru Angad Dev. Its roots can be traced to the Brahmi script, and the colloquial Lande.

32. Also called the Nagari, it is a left to right abugida based on Brahmi script. Evolved between the first and fourth centuries, it has been in regular use from the 7th CE. In addition to Hindi and Sanskrit, the script is also used (with one or more additional consonants) by Nepali, Gorkhali, Bodo, Marathi, Pali, Prakrit, Haryanvi, Garhwali, Kumaoni, Maithili, Dogri, Kashmiri, Nagauri and Rajasthani languages.

33. Nankana Saheb is the birthplace of the founder of Sikhism, Guru Nanak Dev ji. It is now a district in Pakistan.

34. This British Indian province was created in 1836 by merging the administrative divisions under Agra Presidency. Later Awadh (Oudh) was added, and it included the Delhi territory from 1836 to 1858. Allahabad was the capital of the province, as well as for the entire British India for one day.

35. Member of the Constituent Assembly and later an MP from Hissar. His brother Gopi Chand Bhargava was the first chief minister of East Punjab.

36. Prominent leader of the Unionist Party in undivided Punjab. Very articulate in defending the rights of farmers and cultivators. Did not hold the Congress party in high esteem, for it was, in his view representing the interests of the urban elite.

37. 'Sub-Nationalism in Indian Politics: Formation of a Haryanavi Identity', Pradeep Kumar, *The Indian Journal of Political Science*, vol. 52, no. 1, 1991.

38. *Haryana: Studies in History and Culture*, Kripal Chandra Yadav, Kurukshetra University, 1968.

39. President of the Indian National Congress from 1909–10, he was a scholar, administrator, educationists and freedom fighter. Founder of the Benares Hindu University as well as the All India Hindu Mahasabha.

40. Recognized both Punjabi and Hindi as the official languages of the state and carved out zones for the teaching of both languages in the schools falling in the jurisdiction. This was a compromise formula suggested by Bhim Sen Sachar, who was the chief minister of Punjab twice – first in 1949 for a period of seven months, and then from 1952 to 1956.

41. *Nehru and the Language Politics of India*, Robert D. King, OUP, 1997.

42. *Haryana: Studies in History and Culture*, Kripal Chandra Yadav, Kurukshetra University, 1968.

43. Leading college of Punjab. Both Kairon, and his principal protagonist, Master Tara Singh, were products of this institution. Another chief minister of Punjab, Darbara Singh, is also an alumni of this institution.

44. Green Revolution refers to the package of institutional credit, hybrid seeds, fertilizers, water supply and MSP for the final produce. Green Revolution bought about a major transformation in the agriculture of Punjab, and made it one of India's most prosperous states.

45. Established to provide the required infrastructure for industry: roads, power, water, service centres, tool rooms, waste management and retrieval, besides effluent treatment.

46. Prior to this, the Congress policy towards the Indian states was ambivalent. Many princely states 'funded' the Congress party, and many more had prominent Congressmen as their legal advisors. In the Haripura session it was clarified that the people living in the states would have the same rights and freedoms as their brethren elsewhere.

47. Was at the helm in Himachal Pradesh from 1952 to 1956, and again from 1963 to 1977. He had been a member of the Constituent Assembly and played a lead role in the integration of all the erstwhile Punjab Hill states into Himachal.

48. Traces its lineage to 1858 when it was established as an infantry with Dogra soldiers from Jammu and the Punjab Hill states. The Paltan saw action in both the World Wars, the Indo-Pak War of 1947–8, India–China War of 1962, the Indo-Pak War of 1965, the liberation of Bangladesh in 1971, Kargil War of 1999, besides UN Peace Keeping Forces.

49. In retrospect, it seems that Justice Fazal Ali was correct – Himachal retained its identity and became a state in 1971.

50. The Punjab Boundary Commission was established by the MHA under the chairmanship of Justice J.C. Shah with S. Dutt and M.M. Philip as members to demarcate and adjust the boundaries between the three states of Punjab, Haryana and Himachal.

11. The End of Foreign Jurisdictions

1. Operation Vijay was the code name for the military operation carried out by Indian Armed Forces to integrate Goa, Daman and Diu.

2. General Jayanto Nath Chaudhari (1908–1983) was the sixth chief of Indian Army Staff.

3. Manuel Antonio Vassalo e Silva (1899–1985) was the last governor general of Portuguese India.

4. Vasco Da Gama is a city in the Indian State of Goa, which is named after the Portuguese explorer Vasco Da Gama.

5. Tristao de Bragança Cunha (1891–1958) was an Indian freedom fighter from Goa. He is known as the Father of Goan nationalism.

NOTES

6. Goa Congress Committee was formed by T.N. Cunha in 1928. He later merged it with Indian National Congress.
7. Portuguese Colonial Act, 1930, was an act adopted by the Portuguese Government. The Act had provisions differentiating between Portuguese of colonies and Metropolitan Portuguese.
8. Kunbi are believed to be one of the original inhabitants of Goa and are now generally low-income farmers or farm labour.
9. A provisional Goa Congress Committee was formed in Bombay (now Mumbai) to mobilize the Goans in Mumbai for the Goa Liberation Movement.
10. Ram Manohar Lohia (1910–1967) was a prominent Indian freedom fighter and socialist leader.
11. *Harijan* was a weekly English newspaper published by Mahatma Gandhi. He began publishing it in 1933 and continued till his death.
12. Durga Das is a prominent Indian historian and is the author of *India: From Curzon to Nehru and After.*
13. International Court of Justice is the judicial organ of the United Nations. It was established in 1945 and is located at The Hague, Netherlands.
14. Azad Gomantak Dal was a group formed to fight for Goa's liberation by using direct action.
15. Goa People's Party was a regional political party based in Goa.
16. Varishta Panchayat of Free Dadra and Nagar Haveli was a body formed to administer the area of Dadra and Nagar Haveli after pro-Indian forces took control of the area in 1954.
17. K.G. Badlani was an IAS officer of Gujarat Cadre who was made the Prime Minister of Dadra and Nagar Haveli by the Indian government in 1961.
18. North Atlantic Treaty Organization is a military alliance of twenty-eight European countries and two North American countries.
19. Commonwealth is a voluntary organization of nations, mostly comprising of nation states, which were formerly British colonies.
20. Papers of the Foreign and Commonwealth Office. Drawn from the declassified records.
21. British Broadcasting Company (now Corporation) is the national broadcaster of United Kingdom.

22. Vatican City is a city state located in Italy and is the world's smallest country by area and population. It also serves as the seat of the Catholic Church.

23. Refers to Salazar's willingness to change his demand and concede the loss of Dadar and Nagar Haveli.

24. Pundalik Dattatreya Gaitonde (1913–96) was an Indian freedom fighter and an active participant in the Goa liberation movement.

25. Non-Aligned Movement is a movement and group of countries who don't align themselves with any major power bloc. This was started in response to the Cold War between the United States and the Soviet Union.

26. Berlin Wall was built up in 1961 to mark the line between the East Germany and West Germany. It was torn down in 1981.

27. *Jawaharlal Nehru: A Biography*, vol. 3: 1956–1964, Sarvepalli Gopal, Harvard University Press, 1984.

28. Aurobindo Ghosh (1872–1950), now known as Sri Aurobindo, was an Indian nationalist who later became a spiritual guru.

29. Subramania Bharathi (1882–1921) was a Tamil author, social reformer and a freedom fighter. He is known as Mahakavi Bharathi.

30. 'Imagining India, Decolonizing "L'inde Française", C. 1947 – 1954', Akhila Yechury, *The Historical Journal*, vol. 58, no. 4, 2015.

31. The French had their overseas territories : Vietnam, Laos and Kampuchea (Cambodia). Collectively, they were called IndoChina.

32. Chandernagore (now Chandannagore) is a city in the Hooghly district of West Bengal.

33. French Fourth Republic was for the government of France from 1946 to 1958.

34. National Democratic Front was a political coalition in French India, mainly consisting of socialists and communists.

35. Varadarajulu Kailasa Subbiah (1911–93) was the general secretary of the Communist Party of French India and later became a member of CPI.

36. Édouard Goubert (1894–1964) was the first chief minister of Pondicherry (now Puducherry).

37. Akhila Yechury is a lecturer based in Edinburg, Scotland.

38. 'Imagining India, Decolonizing "L'inde Française", C. 1947–1954', Akhila Yechury, *The Historical Journal*, vol. 58, no. 4, 2015.

39. Dien Bien Phu is a city located in north-western region of Vietnam.

40. An Act to provide for the exercise of certain foreign jurisdiction of the central government.

12. The Frontiers of the North-east

1. Refers to the region of the last geographical outposts of a country. While the frontier is a vast zone without any clear lines of demarcation, a boundary is a fixed land line between two political entities or even administrative units.

2. The Ahom kingdom was a late medieval kingdom (1228–1826) in the Brahmaputra Valley which successfully resisted Mughal expansion in the North-east. It was established by the Ahom king Sukaphaa. He entered Brahmaputra by crossing the rugged Patkai mountain range with an entourage of nine thousand (including his queens, concubines, nobles and soldiers). Ahoms brought with them the technology of wet rice cultivation, and over the next century, the process of Ahomization struck a deep chord in the region, though by the fourteenth century, the Ahoms had ceased to be a numerical majority in the territory over which they ruled.

3. Also called the 'gateway to Northeast of India', it is situated on the south bank of the Brahmaputra; this was also the site of the capitals (Prayagjyotishpur and Durjaya) of the ancient state of Kamrup.

4. *Social and Economic History of Assam*, Rajen Saikia, Manohar Publishers, 2002.

5. The Proclamation was made in Allahabad, and specifically stated 'we desire no extension to our present territorial possessions'.

6. Bhattacharjee has worked on state formation in the North-east, roots of insurgency as well as on historiography of the region.

7. 'The Political Geography of Colonial and Post-Colonial Assam: Construction and Contestations', Rajen Saikia, Proceedings of the Indian History Congress, vol. 70, 2009–10.

8. Introduced by the British in 1873 as part of their 'isolationist' policy. The declared objective was 'protection of culture and identity of indigenous tribes in the region and autonomy in the management of their affairs'.

9. 'Colonial Encounter and Christian Missions in Northeast India', David R. Syiemlieh, Proceedings of the Indian History Congress, vol. 73, 2012,

10. Refers to tea planters. The planters organized their social and cultural life around their estate bungalows, as well as the Planters' Clubs in which they could socialize and play games like golf, tennis, squash, billiards. Women organized their own flower shows, hat shows and balls on different occasions.

11. An ethnic group from Rajasthan, well-versed in business and trade. Members of this clan moved to Bombay, Bengal, Assam (and wherever else opportunity arose) from the nineteenth century. Marwaris have been bankers to the Mughals, nawabs as well as the East India Company. Marwaris would issue 'Hundis' which would be valid across their extensive network that covered most of South Asia.

12. A non-permanent tract of land surrounded by waters of a stream, river, lake or sea. These are usually accretions in a river course or estuary. Makes it difficult to demarcate river boundaries.

13. Officially described as 'territorial reorganization of the Bengal Presidency', the decision of Lord Curzon was seen as an attempt to divide Bengal on communal lines – with the Muslim majority districts being constituted into East Bengal with Dhaka as the capital

14. The annulment was announced by Lord Hardinge on the occasion of the visit of King George V. This was accompanied by an announcement that the capital of British India would be shifted from Calcutta to New Delhi.

15. Indian independence activist, Gandhian, Congress leader and the first chief minister of Assam. He was the first person to understand the long-term implications of the demographic changes in Assam.

16. Succeeded Lord Linlithgow and as the governor general and VC of India from 1943 to 1947. Known for his plain speaking, he tried to ensure that India should remain a single dominion with maximum autonomy to the provinces.

17. *Lokopriya Gopinath Bordoloi: An Architect of Modern India*, Lily Mazindor Baruah (ed.), Gyan Publishing House, 1993.

18. *Jinnah: His Successes, Failures and Role in History*, Ishtiaq Ahmed, Penguin Random House India, 2020.

19. When natural and/or physical barriers are ineffective in stopping the movement of people across countries.

20. The sixth schedule deals with the administration and management of tribal areas in the states of Assam, Meghalaya, Tripura and Mizoram. The

schedule has been prepared as per the provisions of Articles 244 (2) and 275 (1) of the Constitution.

21. The NEFA agency was placed under the ministry of external affairs (MEA) – mainly because Nehru was also the external affairs minister, and he wanted to manage the affairs of the Frontier directly.

22. Demand raised by the Rajbanshi population of North Bengal, especially Cooch Behar and the contiguous districts in Assam.

23. The pre-Independence Cachar is now four districts: North Cachar Hills, now called Dima Hasao, Cachar, Hailakandi and Karimganj. Dima Hasao district is now administered by the North Cachar Hills Autonomous Council (NCHAC) as per the Sixth Schedule.

24. The Naga Club was established by the members of the Indian Labour Corps who were recruited from this region. They developed a close affinity with their British officers on account of their affiliation to the Church. They made a representation to the Simon Commission wanting to have a direct relationship with the Crown.

25. The concept of 'Buffer regions and Buffer states' was expounded by Lord Curzon at the annual Romanes Lecture at Oxford in 1906, one year after his return from India.

26. The Indian Labour Corps was tasked with digging trenches, building roads, bridges and clearing up of mines. Although recruitment was voluntary, village heads were often 'nudged' to fulfil their quotas.

27. Naga Nationalist leader who received British citizenship and was in the forefront of leading an armed struggle against the Indian republic with support from China and East Pakistan.

28. Sahkire broke rank with Phizo as he felt that the solution to the Naga issue did not lie in armed confrontation with the Indian state. He was the one who initiated the talks with the Union government.

29. A member of the ICS from 1919, he served in the Madras Presidency and as secretary to Government of India before being appointed as the governor of Assam.

30. See Annexure for the Text of the Agreement.

31. A Tangkhul Naga from Manipur, he started his career as a teacher, joined the army during WWII and the Indian Fronter Administration service thereafter and rose to become the chief secretary of Nagaland, and India's ambassador to Myanmar (then Burma).

32. Raised as an infantry regiment in the Indian Army, at least 50 per cent of the jawans are Nagas, with the remaining half coming from Garhwal, Kumaon and the Gurkha recruitment zone.

33. Also called Tripuri, this has been notified as a state language from 1979, and all government notifications are issued in Kokborok as well as in Bangla. The languages wing of the Tripura Autonomous District Council has been publishing translations from classics like Rabindranath Tagore's *Gora*, Shakespeare's *Merchant of Venice* and *Candide* of Voltaire in the Kokborok language.

34. A Nobel laureate and polymath, he reshaped Bengali literature, art, music and was responsible for the extreme popularity of Bengali literature throughout the subcontinent.

35. Introduced by Lord Cornwallis, it made the zamindars responsible, not just for the collection of land revenue, but also for the internal administration of the vast estates. Many Rajas and Maharajas were 'kings' in their own territory, but also held zamindaris in British India, where their status was similar to that of other rent-paying landlords. However, as the zamindaris were quite lucrative, the Rajas and Maharajas continued to hold on to them.

36. Mahatma Gandhi camped here for four months after the gruesome violence that left over five thousand Hindus dead in the organized reign of terror unleashed by the Muslim League in October–November of 1946. However, even though the peace mission stemmed the violence, the survivors refused to return to their villagers for fear of reprisal and, more importantly, to ensure the safety of their women.

37. 'Reorganization of Northeast India', V. Venkata Rao, *The Indian Journal of Political Science*, vol. 33, no. 2, 1972.

38. Now divided into three districts of Khagrachari, Rangamati and Bandarban, the CHT is the only hilly area of Bangladesh. Although Muslims constituted only 3 per cent population of the CHT, it was assigned to East Bengal on the principle of geographical continuity.

39. The last ruler of the Manipur state was at the helm from 1941 to 1949. Although he had signed the Instrument of Accession on 11 August ceding defence, foreign affairs and communications, he was most reluctant to sign the Instrument of Merger, which would have meant effective transfer of power to an elected legislature.

40. Although the Act was approved by the Maharaja on 26 July, before he signed the Instrument of Succession, the ministry of states did not recognize the Act, because it had not been approved by the governor general and viceroy, and the Maharaja of Manipur was only a quasi-sovereign.

41. Meiteis represent 53 per cent of the ethnic population of Manipur; they also inhabit the neighbouring states of Assam, Tripura, Nagaland, Meghalaya and Mizoram, besides Bangladesh and Myanmar. The Meitei language is also called Manipuri, and now included as an official language in the Eighth Schedule of the Constitution.

42. They inhabit the hills, but have major differences with Nagas, and want a separate homeland/territory. There have been very violent clashes between the underground faction of the Nagas. Kukis mark 13 September as Remembrance Day as over a hundred Kukis were massacred on this day by the NSCN (IM) as they claimed the territory for Nagalim (greater Nagaland).

43. Also called Mei-Mughals, they trace their origin to the expedition of Mubariz Khan, a Mughal commander, who annexed this territory to the Bengal Subah.

44. Based on the ancestral Naga religion, the leading proponent was Haipou Jadonang, who was in the forefront of violent opposition to the Christian missionaries and the officials of the British Raj.

45. A prominent Congress leader of Sindh, he was appointed as the governor of Assam from 1950–56. It was per his advice that Major Bob Khathing (then with the Assam Rifles) took possession of the Tawang monastery where His Holiness the Dalai Lama took refuge in 1959.

46. Oldest paramilitary force in the country with the motto 'sentinels of the northeast'. They are now tasked with guarding the border with Myanmar.

47. Was a member of the Indian National Congress and was the chief minister of the state from 1963 to 1971. Prior to Independence, he had started the Gana Parishad to seek greater participation of the people in the administration of the state.

48. Was the chief minister of the state for three terms (first, second and fourth terms). Had extended support to the Azad Hind Fauj (INA) and was awarded the Tamra Patra as a mark of his contribution as a freedom fighter. Immediately after Independence, he led an agitation against the erstwhile ruler (Bodhchandra Singh) for the control of Thangjing

Temple. Prior to this agitation, the ruler used to appropriate all the temple offerings to himself.

49. The second Prime Minister of India on whom the apex training institution in the country is named. He was the home minister in 1963, and as such had a fair idea of the developments in the region.

50. Now functioning under the ministry of the Development of North Eastern Region (DONER), it takes care of economic, social, administrative and infrastructure needs of the eight states (Arunachal, Assam, Manipur, Meghalaya, Mizoram, Nagaland, Tripura and Sikkim). It is also supposed to provide mediation in inter-state disputes.

51. The predecessor to the MNF, the organization was formed to protest against the apathy of the Government of Assam to the famine situation in and around Aizawl in 1959.

52. Founder of the Mizo National Famine Front, which morphed into a political, and later an underground movement. Renounced violence and became the first chief minister of the newly carved state of Mizoram.

53. The Inter-services Intelligence is the premier intelligence agency of Pakistan. Also referred to as the 'deep state', it has funded secessionist groups seeking to dismember India.

54. East Pakistan was the province of Pakistan that later became Bangladesh after the 1971 War of Liberation. Prior to this, the territory of East Bengal was used by rebel groups from across the North-east.

55. Armed Forces Special Powers Act allows the personnel of the Indian defence forces to maintain law and order and fire in self-defence in 'disturbed areas'. After the mistaken killing of seventeen Naga miners in Mon district on 4 December 2021, the demand for repeal of AFPSA has become very vocal.

56. During his tenure as the chief minister of Assam, he ended the Assam Official Language Act, 1960, which led to the alienation of Mizos, Nagas, highlanders of Jaintia and Khasi hills and Bodos. During his second term as the chief minister, he raised the issue of illegal cross-border movement.

57. *The Mizo Uprising: Assam Assembly Debates on the Mizo Movement 1966– 1971*, J.V. Hluna and Tochhawng, Cambridge Scholars Publishing, 2012.

58. 'Assam Reorganization', Dilip Mukherjee, *Asian Survey*, vol. 9 (4), April 1969.

59. Belong to the Chittagong Hill tracts but facing religious persecution, as well as natural and environmental dislocation. Large numbers (over

fifty thousand) have settled in Arunachal thereby causing demographic imbalance in a sparsely populated landscape.

60. Part of the Bodo-Kachari tribe with recorded settlements in the Garo Hills and Mymensingh districts. Now settled across the North-east and the Chittagong division in Bangladesh.

61. *India's Northeast Resurgent: Ethnicity, Insurgency, Governance, Development*, B.G.Verghese, Konark Publishers, 1996.

62. Indian linguist, educationist and litterateur, and the recipient of India's second highest civilian award, the Padma Vibhushan.

63. Born in Iran to a family of oil merchants, he became a diamond trader and merchant in Golconda, joined the service of the Sultan, rose to be a Vizier (Prime Minister), organized his merchant ships and coastal trade, fell out with the Sultan, joined the service of the Mughal Emperor Shah Jahan, and supported Aurangzeb in the war of succession, for which he was made the governor of Bengal Subah. Mir Jumla captured Kamrup, Cooch Behar and all the frontier tracts.

64. Signed at the end of the first Anglo-Burmese War, which marked the end of Burmese influence in Assam, Manipur, Rakhine (Arakan), Cachar and Jaintia, besides a war indemnity of one-million-pound sterling in four instalments. However, the British spent at least five to ten times more money and lost fifteen thousand lives in the campaign.

65. British-born Indian anthropologist, ethnologist and tribal activist who started life as a Christian missionary but became a Gandhian after his extended stay in India. Became a close adviser to Nehru, received the Padma Bhushan in 1961 and the Sahitya Akademi Award for his autobiography, *The Tribal World of Verrier Elwin*.

66. The Indian Frontier Administration Service was created to serve the North-East Frontier Agency. Members were drawn from the defence services, administrative and diplomatic corps to give a 'direct administration' to the people.

67. 'Reorganization of Northeast India', V. Venkata Rao, *The Indian Journal of Political Science*, vol. 33, no. 2, 1972.

68. Member of the IFAS, nominated to the Lok Sabha from NEFA. He became deputy minister in the food and agriculture ministry, but better known for his report on local government, which formed the basis of the Panchayati Raj system.

13. Island Territories

1. The Straits of Malacca is a narrow shipping lane, less than a thousand kilometres, between the Indonesian islands and Malaysian peninsula. It is less than 700 km from Nicobar.

2. The UN Convention on Law of the Sea (UNCLOS) defines an EEZ as extending two hundred nautical miles from the shore, within which the coastal state has the right to explore and undertake commercial ventures (to the exclusion of others). It also enjoins on the state the responsibility to conserve and manage both the living and the non-living resources in this zone.

3. India's Look East Policy envisages cultivation of economic and strategic relationships with nations in South East Asia to bolster its standing as a regional power. Traditionally, India's foreign policy was more aligned towards South Asia.

4. Was a member of the IAS, and deputy commissioner of Nicobar Islands. The Institute for Defence Studies and Analyses (IDSA) commissioned him to write a book on the untapped strategic potential of A&N islands.

5. *Andaman and Nicobar Islands: India's Untapped Strategic Assets*, Sanat Kaul, Pentagon Press in association with Institute of Defence Studies and Analyses, 2015.

6. A Franciscan friar and missionary explorer who travelled to India, via the land route, and probably touched base on these islands en route to Ceylon (now Sri Lanka), Sumatra, Java, Borneo before reaching the South China coast. He wrote a very popular account of his travels.

7. Was a Venetian merchant who visited East India, the Indies, and the land beyond the Indies and Malaccas. He left a brief description of them in Italian for the 'profitable instruction of merchants and all other travellers for their better direction and knowledge of these countries'.

8. A naval surveyor and lieutenant with the Bombay marines. His report on the Islands to the governor general in council in 1789 was received favourably and led to the establishment of the British settlement. The headquarters of A&N Islands, Port Blair, is named after him.

9. One of the first British settlements in the islands where a sawmill was established for facilitating trade in timber. It now houses a Forest Museum.

10. An island in the Malay Archipelago was the headquarters of Straits Settlements, a loose confederation of British colonies that included

Penang, Malacca and Singapore. It was also a penal settlement which drew convicts from all the British colonies – from Straits, Burma, India and Ceylon.

11. A British surgeon, who was appointed as the first superintendent of the penal colony at Andamans. Very ruthless in his approach and method, he hanged eighty-one convicts when they tried to escape. Retired as the surgeon general in the Indian Medical Service.

12. The Wahabi movement was an Islamic revivalist movement which offered the most serious and well-planned challenge to British authority in India from 1830s to 1860s. Earlier, it took up arms against Ranjit Singh's reign in Punjab as well.

13. One of the most famous Irishmen of his times, and a prominent member of the Conservative Party from Dublin, he was the viceroy of India from January 1869 till his assassination in 1872.

14. 'The Andaman Island Penal Colony: Race, Class, Criminality and the British Empire', C. Anderson, *International Review of Social History*, 2018,

15. The Anglo Manipur War between the British forces and the commander-in-chief of Manipur Army, Tikendrajit Singh, who resisted the British interference in the internal affairs of the state.

16. 'Oral History of Freedom Struggle with Special Reference to Ex-Andaman Freedom Fighters (1921–27)', P.K. Srivastava, Indian Council of Historical Research, 1992.

17. This is drawn from 'Survivors of Our Hell' by Cathy Scott-Clark and Adrian Levy's column in *The Guardian* of 23 June 2001.

18. 'Oral History of Freedom Struggle with Special Reference to Ex-Andaman Freedom Fighters (1921–27)', P.K. Srivastava, Indian Council of Historical Research, 1992.

19. The Indian Jails Committee was established in 1919 to suggest measures for prison reforms and was headed by Sir Alexander Cardew. The committee had been set up in the wake on a series of newspaper reports across India about the sordid conditions in Indian jails.

20. The Malabar Rebellion from August 1921 to 1922 started as a resistance against the British colonial rule in that region. It has been called a 'peasant revolt' for it was triggered by new tenancy laws, which favoured the landlord over the tiller. However, there was a communal angle as well, as most of the tenants were Mapilah Muslims, and the landlords were Namboodiri Brahmins.

21. Under the colonial legislation, some social and ethnic communities were classified as 'addicted to systematic commission of non bailable offences', and adult males were expected to report to the nearest police station once a week. The Act was repealed in 1949.

22. A Protestant Christian church organization which is organized on the lines of an army consisting of soldiers, officers, and adherents, collectively called Salvationists, with the mission of providing 'physical and spiritual' relief to the poor, the destitute and the hungry.

23. In reply to a Parliamentary question, the state-wise break-up of the 585 political prisoners was given: needless to say, the overwhelming majority (398) were from Bengal, followed by Punjab with a figure of 95.

24. *Andaman and Nicobar Islands under Japanese Occupation during WWII*, T.R. Sareen, Bio-Green, 2018.

25. According to Puranic cosmology, the world is divided into seven concentric island continents of which Jambudwip stands for the territory occupied by the Bharatas as well as the archipelagos in the seas and oceans around this land.

26. A nation of 1192 islands in the Indian Ocean it is one of the most geographically dispersed sovereign states with some atolls across the equator, making it a country in both the hemispheres.

27. A group of seven atolls comprising sixty islands in the Indian Ocean, including the US military base of Diego Garcia. The original inhabitants of Diego Garcia, a Bourbonnais Creole speaking people, were expelled from the islands in 1971. Mauritius has often expressed its claims over these islands.

28. Is a log book written in ancient Greek (Koine) which describes the navigation and trading routes from Roman and Egyptian ports to Horn of Africa, Persian Gulf, Arabian Sea and the Indian Ocean.

29. Tamil maritime empire which held its sway for over a sixteen hundred years (300 BCE to 1279 CE) in the Indian Ocean littoral. Its influence extended to present-day Indonesia, Cambodia, Vietnam and Malaysia. The peak of the empire was reached in the year 1030 under Rajendra Chola.

30. Was the ruler of Mysore from 1782 to 1799. He put up a formidable challenge to the British East India Company and expanded his kingdom to include some islands that were proximate to the Canara district.

31. Muslim kingdom based out of the present-day Kannur district of Kerala. The king was called Ali Raja and the queen Arakkal Beevi.

32. The language draws from Prakrit and Sinhala languages.
33. Also known as Dwip Bhasha, it is a dialect of Malayalam.
34. An IAS officer of the 1964 batch, he was the administrator of Lakshadweep Islands, and moved the headquarters to Kavaratti. His book on the islands is a comprehensive account of the administrative history of the islands.

14. From Subjects to Citizens – Sikkim Joins India

1. States whose defence and external affairs were under the protection of the British Empire. They were states with specific limits on their sovereignty, especially with regard to relationships with foreign powers and their external boundary.
2. A concept which was unique to Sikkim, and the Constitution had to be amended to accommodate this arrangement.
3. A consultative body of the Indian princes in which they discussed issues of common and mutual interest, especially their rights and privileges with respect to the British Crown and their key representatives like the viceroy and the provincial governors and lieutenant governors.
4. King of England and Emperor of India from 1910–1936. It was under his term that the statute of Westminster was drawn.
5. Was the foremost leader of the mass movement which wanted the immediate merger of Sikkim with India as the majority population of Nepalis were disempowered because the elections were not on the basis of universal adult franchise.
6. 'Sikkim Story: Protection to Absorption', N. Ram, *Social Scientist*, vol. 3, no. 2, 1974.
7. An ICS officer of the 1909 batch, he became an outstanding jurist, administrator and diplomat. He was the Constitutional Adviser to the Constituent Assembly. He foresaw no legal difficulty in the Sikkim merger with India.
8. It was backed by the Chogyal, and supported the 'status quo' of having denominational representation in the Sikkim Legislative Assembly.
9. Founded in 1962 by Kazi Lhendup Dorjee with the objective of merging Sikkim with India by the coming together of the Swatantra Dal, Rajya Praja Sammelan and the dissidents of Sikkim state congress and Sikkim National Party.

10. He was charged with sedition in 1972 after he wrote 'there can be no king without people, but there are countries without a king. As such, the Chogyal and his coterie must see the writings on the wall, and give democracy to the people of Sikkim, or else a day will come when the Chogyal will have to hand power to a strange successor'. He had been legally adopted as a son by the Kazi and Kazini, but they were soon estranged.

11. Hope Cooke was eighteen when she met Palden Thondup Namgyal at the Windermere Hotel in Darjeeling. Their fairy tale romance and marriage were covered by such prominent American magazines like the *National Geographic*, *New Yorker* and *Life*. She was given the title of Gyalmo (queen consort).

12. The first, and eminently readable, chronicle of how Sikkim became the twenty-second state of the country. It was a counter narrative to the story of 'voluntary and willful' accession to India.

13. Gives the perspective of an administrator on the developments in Sikkim in those critical years. It is also the story of three powerful women (Prime Minister Indira Gandhi, Gyalmo Hope Cooke and Kazini Eliza Maria Dorjee) and their narrative on Sikkim.

14. Narrates the story of Dhondup, the last Chogyal, his high-profile marriage to Hope Cooke, and their failed attempts at garnering international support for the independence of their landlocked Himalayan kingdom.

15. An insider's view on what led to the ouster of Chogyal from Sikkim, as well as an account for the fledgling democracy movement and struggle for reforms led by Kazi Lhendup Dorjee.

16. An Indian civil servant and diplomat. He was India's foreign secretary when the Protectorate of Sikkim was merged with India.

17. Was the first chief minister of Sikkim (1975–79) after Sikkim's union with Indian. Prior to this, he had led the movement for universal adult franchise and democratic reforms in Sikkim. This author had the privilege of knowing him and the Kazini Eliza Maria Dorjee as they had settled in Kalimpong where the author was posted as the SDO in 1987–88.

15. Delhi, New Delhi, NCT and NCR

1. All the three names have been used to describe India, and a fuller description of these terms can be seen in the first chapter. The British

wanted to name the two dominions as Hindustan and Pakistan, but the Constituent Assembly stated quite clearly: India, that is Bharat. However, several PSUs in India are named after Hindustan: the HAL, HMT, HZL, for instance. The India operations of Unilever are called Hindustan Unilever and one of the leading English newspapers of New Delhi is called *Hindustan Times*.

2. The Kuru kingdom was formed after the alliance/merger of the Bharata and Puru clans. The kingdom had economic, political and matrimonial ties with kings and tribes from the Himalayas to the Ratnakara (Arabian sea) – from Gandhara (modern-day Kandahar) to Kamrup in the North-east, Dwarka in the west, and Mallya in the south.

3. Ashokan edicts are a collection of thirty-odd inscriptions on pillars, boulders and cave walls carrying Emperor Ashoka's ideas about Dhamma (universal law) as propounded by Gautama, the Buddha. They were installed/carved at places where people were expected to congregate.

4. Written from left to right, the Brahmi script was developed in the Indus Valley region. Extensively used to propagate Buddhism in Prakrit (the local tongue). It is said that both Sanskrit and Dravidian languages evolved from the Brahmi script.

5. Suraj Kund is an ancient reservoir (literally Lake of the Sun) built by Suraj Pal of the Tomar dynasty. They were Suryavanshis (worshippers of the sun who claimed descent from Surya Deva). The Haryana Tourism Department conducts a marquee event, the Surajkund Arts and Crafts Mela, a fair which attracts over a million footfalls.

6. In popular discourse, this was built by Prithvi Raj Chauhan. However, several scholars believe that this was built by Anangpal Tomar, but (wrongly) attributed to Prithviraj by Abul Fazal in his *Ain-i-Akbari*.

7. The Afghan ruler from Ghor, who defeated Prithviraj in 1192, and laid the foundations of the Islamic Empire in India. Although some refer to his Persian origin, this seems doubtful as he was a staunch Sunni. As he had no children, he appointed his faithful slave Qutb-ud Din Aibak to succeed him, thereby laying the foundations of the Slave Dynasty.

8. Declared a UNESCO world heritage site in 1993.

9. He is the person who gave Delhi its name. The inscription in the Delhi Museum reads: 'In a country called Haryana, which is equivalent to Heaven on earth, the Tomars built a city called Dhillika.'

10. Was founded by Humayun on the banks of Yamuna in 1533 but Sher Shah razed it to the ground, and built his new capital Sher Shahi, also called the Purana Quila Fort.

11. There were twelve sovereign states of the Sikh confederacy, which rose in Punjab during the eighteenth century and considerably weakened the Mughal Empire prior to the complete breakdown after the invasion of Nadir Shah.

12. Fought between the EIC and the Holkars on one side, and the Peshwas and Scindias on the other. Scindias had to cede Rohtak, Gurgaon, Ganga–Jamuna Doab and the Delhi Agra region to the EIC.

13. The twelfth and the last Mughal emperor of India. Was exiled to Rangoon at the age of eighty-two where he died after five years.

14. Fellow of the Royal Asiatic Society of Great Britain and Ireland.

15. Lahore was made the capital of British Punjab after the Anglo Sikh War of 1849. With the establishment of Government College and Forman Christian College in 1864, it became an important centre of learning.

16. Organized on the lines of Mughal Durbars, the Proclamation was read out in English and Urdu and the viceroy presented each native chief with a gold medal and a banner that read 'Victoria, Empress of India, 1st January 1877.'

17. The Act provided for 'diarchy' or power sharing in the major provinces, as transferred subjects like 'local self-government, health, education and agriculture' were transferred to ministers who were responsible to the Provincial Council.

18. The Act expanded the electorate (from seven to thirty-five million), granted a large measure of autonomy to the provinces, and envisaged India as a federation of provinces with possible inclusion of the princely states. Bihar, Orissa and Sindh became new provinces, and Burma was separated from India.

19. Elected to the Constituent Assembly from Madras, he was also a member of the Negotiating Committee to deliberate with the Chamber of Princes on the integration of the princely states with Indian.

20. *Nehru and the Language Politics of India*, Robert D. King, OUP, 1997.

21. The cataclysmic event that marked the division of British India into the dominions of India and Pakistan. It led to 'ethnic cleansing' in both East and West Punjab. This has been documented by Ishtiaq Ahmed in his book

The Punjab Blooded, Partitioned and Cleansed: Unravelling the 1947 Tragedy through Secret British Reports and First-person Accounts.

22. A French demographer who works with the Centre for Policy Research and works on urban settlements, public spaces and geographies.

23. 'Patterns of Population Mobility in Delhi', Veronique Dupont, Institute of Economic Growth, 1995.

24. Article 239 deals with the administration of the UT of Delhi. Article 240 authorizes the President to make regulations for the peace, progress and good governance.

25. The first and the youngest chief minister of Delhi at thirty-four, Ch Brahm Prakash was a Gandhian freedom fighter and a Congress worker from Shakurpur village in north-west Delhi. He was also very active in the cooperative movement and was keenly engaged in co-op reform legislation.

26. The chief commissioner was Anand Pandit who enjoyed a good rapport with the then home minister, G.B. Pant. It is often said that none of the chief commissioner/LGs have had a smooth relationship with the chief ministers of Delhi.

27. Also known as Rajarshi, he was one of the most important Congress leaders of Delhi, but not in the same camp as Home Minister Pant and Prime Minister Nehru.

28. Held the important positions of chief minister of UP and home minster of India

29. Founder of the All-India Mahila Congress, also the first woman to become the chief minister of UP. Known for her forthright observations and clear thinking, she often held views that were different to those of Prime Minister Nehru.

30. A prominent BJP leader and sports administrator who became CEC in 1967.

31. Politically affiliated to the RSS and the BJP, he served as the CEC as well as mayor of Delhi, and later governor of Goa and Sikkim.

32. Often called the 'grand old man of Delhi politics', Jag Pravesh Chandra was an active leader of the Congress party.

33. Was asked to head the committee on Centre–state relations. The document is called the Sarkaria Commission Report.

34. The observations of this report have been quoted extensively by all the high court and Supreme Court judges looking into the issue of division of powers between the chief minister and the LG.
35. Special provision in case of failure of Constitutional machinery in the NCT of Delhi.
36. In 2016, the GNCTD was under the political control of the Aam Aadmi Party, with Arvind Kejriwal as the chief minister and Manish Sisodia as the deputy chief minister.

16. Regional Aspirations: Chhattisgarh, Uttarakhand and Jharkhand

1. UP was, and continues to be, the most populous state even after the formation of Uttarakhand. Its projected population for 2021 is 23 crore. The second most populous state is Maharashtra (12.44 crore) followed by Bihar (12.3 crore). MP is the fifth most populous state (8.45 crore).
2. 'Aranya' refers to forests: territories over which no battles were fought by kings. Dandakaranya was also the place where a project for rehabilitation of refugees from East Bengal was attempted.
3. The Kalachuris of Chedi ruled central India from seventh to thirteenth century. The capital city was Tripuri (present-day Tewar) near Jabalpur.
4. Known for their southern empire, and patronage to Kannada and Telugu languages, their rule extended from Narmada to Godavari. It is, therefore, quite likely that they were patrons of the local traditions of temple architecture as well as languages.
5. Scholar activist who filed a Public Interest Litigation (PIL) against human rights violations emerging from the Salwa Judum.
6. *The Burning Forest: India's War in Bastar*, Nandini Sundar, Juggernaut Books, 2016.
7. Region in the Northern Deccan Plateau with an average height of 600–700 meters. Inhabited by Gond tribals, most of whom live in Chhattisgarh, but also found in contiguous districts of MP, Orissa and Telangana.
8. Formed by the Congress dissidents J.B. Kriplani, P.C. Ghosh and T. Prakasam, it merged with the Socialist Party to form the Praja Socialist Party. In the first elections held in 1952, the Socialist Party got 10.59 and Praja Socialist Party got 5.59 per cent of the popular votes, way behind the Congress party which received 44.9 per cent.

9.   Shaukat Ali and Mohammad Ali published the *Hamdard* and *Comrade*,
     an Urdu and English weekly magazine, and were in the forefront of the
     Khilafat agitation. They were opposed to the British abolition of the
     'Khalifa' as the head of the state of Turkey. They worked very closely with
     Mahatma Gandhi in the Non-Cooperation movement, but Shaukat Ali
     later joined the All-India Muslim League.

10. Prominent Congress leader. Served as the premier of Central Provinces
     and Berar, and the first chief minister of Madhya Bharat. Was keen on a
     separate state, but in 1956, the SRC was in favour of 'large sized states'
     for better administrative and economic planning.

11. *Ravi Shankar Shukla: Life and Times*, S.R. Bakshi, Om Publications, 2001.

12. Subhas Bose was elected president of the Congress in this session held at
     Tripuri, near Jabalpur, in 1939.

13. Born in 1900, he completed his medical education, joined the Congress,
     and participated in the satyagrahas launched by Mahatma Gandhi. After
     Independence he joined the PSP, and campaigned for a separate state of
     Chhattisgarh.

14. Originally from Jalpaiguri in West Bengal, he was the founder of the
     CMM which worked with the contract and piece-rated workers. He also
     led a successful anti-liquor campaign, organized healthcare and education
     facilities for the workers.

15. Indian National Trade Union Congress.

16. All India Trade Union Congress.

17. Centre of Indian Trade Unions.

18. 'Chhattisgarh: Nationality Movement and the Oppressed', Ish N Mishra,
     Countercurrents.org, 19 October 2017.

19. Ibid.

20. Prominent journalist and Congress leader who was elected to the 4th,
     5th, 7th, 8th and 10th Lok Sabha.

21. A social welfare organization established in 1952 by the Rashtriya
     Swayamsevak Sangh (RSS) to focus on the welfare activities of the families
     of Scheduled Tribes in the remote parts of undivided MP. It was founded
     by Balasaheb Deshpande, and one of its objectives was to counter the
     appeal of the Christian missionary schools.

22. Was a powerful minister during the Emergency period under Indira
     Gandhi. Later he joined Jan Morcha, Janata Dal, Samajwadi Janata Dal,

Janata Dal (Rashtriya), the NCP and also the BJP for different lengths of time.

23. A martial race from Nepal: recruited to the armies – Nepal, India and the UK. Nepalis settled in India prefer to call themselves Gurkhas, as most are descendants of ex-servicemen. In the eighteenth century, Nepali kings occupied large areas of the present-day Kumaon and Garhwal.

24. The dynasty adopted Shah as the title during the Mughal rule to indicate their royal and independent status. Retained its independence even during the heydays of the Mughal empire.

25. Due to internal strife and infighting, the Chand kings were defeated by the Gurkhas in 1790. The British took these territories as per the Treaty of Sugauli under their control after the Anglo Nepalese War.

26. Also called Pahari Wilson or the Raja of Harsil by the locals, he amassed vast wealth and influence on account of the timber trade. However, to his credit, he introduced new crops like apple and rajma to the region, and also built roads and bridges. He was the muse for Rudyard Kipling's novel *The Man Who Would Be King*.

27. Dhandak was a form of protest/mass agitation in which the subjects directly approached the ruler for the resolution of their difficulties.

28. Established in 1916 to raise the issue of 'neglect of the region' and for raising national consciousness, prominent members included G.B. Pant, B.D. Pandey and Manoj Joshi.

29. Rose to prominence and fame on account of his refusal to fire on an unarmed assembly at Peshawar in 1930. He was sentenced for fourteen years but released after eleven in 1941 from where he went to Gandhi ji's ashram at Wardha. He became a member of the Communist Party in 1946. The Government of Uttarakhand now runs a tourism, entrepreneurship scheme in his name.

30. A 'British' construct to classify communities as martial and non-martial. Generally, all those regions from where the British got support in 1857 were classified as martial, and they received priority and preference in recruitment to the army.

31. The agency was created in 1901 to manage the relations of the Raj with the princely states within the territorial jurisdiction of British Punjab. In 1936, the hill states, including Tehri, were made part of the Punjab Hill States Agency. However, at the time of Independence, the two were merged again, and Tehri was part of Punjab States Agency.

32. P.C. Joshi was the first general secretary of the CPI from 1935-47. Although expelled from the party in December 1949 for advocating the need to work together with the Indian National Congress under the leadership of Nehru, he was reinducted in 1951 and became the editor of the party organ, *New Age*.

33. The chief minister of UP at the time of Independence, and Union home minister from 1955–61. Pant ensured that the National Academy of Administration was established in Mussoorie in 1960.

34. Originally from Pauri Garhwal, he was the chief minister of UP from November 1973 to November 1975. After the Emergency period, he established the Congress for Democracy with Jagjivan Ram and Nandini Sathpathy, and joined the Janata government as the minister for chemicals and fertilizers.

35. An activist from his student days, he was with the PSP from 1952 to 1963, before he joined the Congress party. He became chief minister of UP thrice, and the first chief minister of Uttarakhand. Also served as the Union external affairs, commerce and industries minster as well as the deputy chairman of the Planning Commission.

36. An MP for twenty-six years, he was also India's defence minister, deputy chairman of the Planning Commission as well as minister of state for home affairs.

37. Led to a sudden halt in transhumance, as well as export of sugar, cereals and grains from India and import of raw wool, pashm, yak tail, sheep, rock salt and medicinal herbs from Tibet.

38. Established in 1964 by a group of Sarvodaya activists under the leadership of Chandi Prasad Bhatt. The author visited the DGSM in 1987 and has kept in touch with Shri Bhatt since then.

39. From Lata village in Chamoli district, she was a grassroots activist and a community leader for rural women: the first person to literally 'hug' a tree thereby making it difficult for contractors to cut the trees.

40. Fallout of the Mandal Commission recommendations which mandated 27 per cent reservations for members of the OBC.

41. Between 1952 and 2000, the governor of a state could decide on the nomination of one or more members of the Anglo-Indian community to the State Assembly (Article 333).

42. SP–BSP: although both parties are bitterly opposed to each other, they are often bracketed together because of their clear caste affiliations. The

OBCs form the base of SP, while an overwhelming number of SCs and Muslims support BSP.

43. Served as the twelfth prime minster of India from 1 June 1996 to 21 April 1997.

44. Senior leader of the BJP, he played an important role in getting his party and the RSS to agree that smaller states were good for the country.

45. Also called Bhararisen. A town in Chamoli district which is right in the centre of the state – equidistant to the last outposts of Garhwal and Kumaon. It has now been declared the summer capital of the state and at least one session of the State Assembly (Vidhan Sabha) has been held there from 2012.

46. Historian, writer, intrepid traveller and chronicler of the movement. Taught at Kumaon University, and was a Nehru Memorial Fellow at the Centre for Contemporary Studies at Teen Murti in New Delhi.

47. *The Creation of a Region: Politics of Identity and Development in Uttarakhand*, Pampa Mukherjee, Routledge India, 2011.

48. The name finds reference in the early Hindu scriptures as the combined region of Kedarkhand (present-day Garhwal) and Manaskhand (the present-day Kumaon). It embraced a wide diversity of geographical, ethnic and cultural identities. Where most of Garhwal is dominated by rugged mountain ranges, steep slopes and deep valleys, many parts of Kumaon have a softer terrain, and an enchanting view of the high Himalayan peaks. The district in the foothills of Nainital, Udham Singh Nagar, is part of the plains, both culturally and geographically, and has settlers from West Punjab and East Bengal, besides the Tharu tribes. Uttarakhand is also home of different tribal communities with their distinct languages and traditions: the Bhotias, the Rajis and the Jaunsaris. Haridwar was the starting point of the pilgrims proceeding to Kedarkhand. Haridwar had been part of the canal system – it was part of Meerut Division till 1975, after which it came under the jurisdiction of Garhwal.

49. The author of this book joined the state of Uttaranchal on deputation on 2 January 2002, but was relieved from the state of Uttarakhand on 2 January 2007!

50. *Select Speeches and Writings of Jaipal Munda*, Ashwini Kumar Pankaj (ed.), P.K. Foundation, 2020.

51. The BJP was not keen to use terms like Jharkhand and Uttarakhand, for this went against the concept of Akhand Bharat (a Bharat which is indivisible and one integral whole). This resistance has now waned.

52. In his short span of twenty-four years, Birsa Munda spearheaded an armed movement for land rights, and against restriction on rights to collect forest produce in the Munda belt of Khunti, Tamar, Sarwada and Bandgaon. Though he became a Christian for a brief period, he renounced the religion and urged his people to follow their traditional faith.

53. A movement in the Chota Nagpur belt by Oraon tribals, against oppression of local landlords, and the complete neglect of their welfare by the British authorities.

54. Active student leader of St Columbus's College, Hazaribagh.

55. The Santhals 'self-pride and self-image' were deeply affected on learning that they were being recruited, not as combatants, but as 'coolies'.

56. 'Making of Jharkhand Identity and Culture', Vijay Prakash Sharma, https://www.academia.edu/40843191/Making_of_Jharkhand_Identity_and_Culture

57. A welfare organization devoted to the development of the region. Opened membership to non-tribals and worked towards intra tribal unity as well.

58. 'Making of Jharkhand Identity and Culture', Vijay Prakash Sharma, https://www.academia.edu/40843191/Making_of_Jharkhand_Identity_and_Culture

59. Vinodanand Jha belonged to Deogarh (which is now in Jharkhand) and was the chief minister of Bihar from 1961–63.

60. Headed the Marxist coordination committee and was elected to the Lok Sabha and Vidhan Sabha. Formed a tactical alliance with Mahato and Soren to press for Jharkhand state.

61. An advocate and a political activist, he established a social reform organization called the Kudmi Mahato or Shivaji Samaj. Mobilized all Kurmis in favour of Jharkhand.

62. Founder of the JMM, was chief minister of Jharkhand thrice, and currently a member of the Rajya Sabha. He was sentenced to life imprisonment on the charges of murder of his political aide, Shashinath Jha, but the conviction was overruled by the Delhi High Court.

17. Bande Utkal Janani

1. Poet, thespian, freedom fighter and a leading campaigner for the unification of Odisha, adoption of Odiya language, and a prominent member of the Utkal Sammelani.

2. Founded by Madhusudan Das in 1903, it continues to play an important role in promoting Odiya language amongst NRIs. It was in the forefront of getting Odiya the classical language status along with Sanskrit, Tamil, Telugu, Kannada and Malayalam.

3. Seven states in India, including Odisha have a state song/anthem. These include Tamil Nadu, Andhra Pradesh, Telangana, Karnataka, Assam and Bihar.

4. Was a part of Bombay Presidency till it became a separate state, along with Bihar and Orissa. This was a follow-up to the Report of the Indian Statutory Commission (Simon Commission). The Congress had recognized the linguistic identity of Sindhi in 1918.

5. Bengal Presidency, with Calcutta as the capital city, was the hub of the British Empire in India. At the height of its territorial jurisdiction, it included all of present-day Bangladesh, West Bengal, Assam, NEFA, Bihar and substantial parts of Orissa.

6. With its capital in Nagpur, Central Provinces covered the present-day MP, Chhattisgarh besides parts of Maharashtra, Bihar, Orissa.

7. Also called the Presidency of Fort St George, it covered the state of Tamil Nadu besides substantial parts of Andhra Pradesh, Kerala, Karnataka, Telangana and Orissa.

8. Thomas Edward Ravenshaw was the commissioner for Orissa in the British Raj. He was a well-known educationist, and together with his wife Mary Nee Symonds, he founded the Ravenshaw Collegiate in 1868. It is now a state university in Orissa.

9. Indian lawyer and social reformer who started the Utkal Sammelani. First Odiya to be member of the Imperial Legislative Council, and the first Odiya to sail abroad.

10. Also called Utkal Mani (Jewel of Odisha), he was an educationist, editor, columnist, political worker and Gandhian.

11. V.P. Menon was the first secretary to the ministry of states and was a confidante of Sardar Patel. He played a stellar role in the integration of Indian states. He also became the governor of Orissa.

12. Praja Mandals (Subjects' Forum) were organizations which sought constitutional reforms within the princely states, and later their merger with India.

13. Swaraj, or self-rule, was the Gandhian ideal in which he believed that people could govern themselves at all levels – panchayat in villages, municipalities in urban areas. Swaraj envisaged a minimalist government in which the role and functions of the state and central government were limited only to those matters that required pan-India coordination.

14. Literally 'holding firm to truth' is a Gandhian technique of non-violent resistance. The satyagrahi resists force through non-submission and non-cooperation. The technique was followed by Martin Luther King in the civil rights movement in the USA, and by Nelson Mandela in his struggle against the apartheid regime in South Africa.

15. British ethnographer and administrator and member of the ICS. He is remembered for his extensive study on the tribes and castes of Bengal Presidency, Central Provinces and Berar. He was the census commissioner for the 1901census, in which caste categories were used for the first time.

16. Literally 'gentleman', well-mannered person, the term was used for the Bengali intelligentsia who had access to education and were the new elite. Although technically an 'open social group', its core strength and membership came from the Brahmans, Baidyas and Kayasthas. However, poor and illiterate Brahmans and Kayasthas were excluded, even as government or corporate officials of all caste groups were part of the bhadralok imagination.

17. The Boundary Commission was established in 1931 to demarcate the boundaries of the (proposed) state of Orissa. B.C. Mukherjee of the ICS was the secretary to the commission which recommended that the proposed Orissa province should include Orissa Division, Anugul, Padampur and Khariar, besides the greater part of Ganjam district and the Vizagapatam Agency tracts.

18. Often referred to as the 'Utkal Byasa Kavi' (the Vyasa of Odisha), he played a leading role in establishing the distinct identity of Odiya language.

19. 'Jagannatha and Oriya Nationalism', G.N. Das, in *The Cult of Jagannatha and the Regional Tradition of Orissa*, A. Eschmann, H. Kulke and G.C. Tripathi (ed.), Manohar, 1978.

20. Legend has it that she was the 'most favoured devotee' of Lakshmi. Lakshmi went to the extent of cursing Balarama and Krishna for discriminating against women and untouchables.

21. Although technically a large zamindari, the ruler was called Maharaja. Krushna Chandra Gajapati was a leading architect of the unification of all the Odiya-speaking regions.

22. The first Congress premier of Odisha. He was also elected to the Constituent Assembly and became the governor of UP as well.

23. *Indian National Congress and Orissa, 1885–1936,* Purushottam Kar, Kitab Mahal, 1987.

24. Popularly known by the sobriquet 'Utkal Keshari', he started his political career as the chairman of the Ganjam District Board.

25. *Indian National Congress and Orissa, 1885–1936,* Purushottam Kar, Kitab Mahal, 1987.

26. Founded in 1936 under the auspices of the Communist Party of India, it sought the abolition of zamindari and regularization of tenancy.

18. Telangana: The Second State for Telugu Speakers

1. The demand for a separate state for Telangana was made on several occasions: they peaked in the years 1956, 1969,1972, 1985, 2001, 2009 and 2011.

2. Statement made by Rosa Parks 'history is always in the making; we just don't always recognize it. It's not old books and great men, it is often small things in a larger context.'

3. This was the first Subsidiary Alliance (policy initiated by Lord Wellesley) signed by the British under which the ruler of an allaying state was compelled to pay a subsidy for the maintenance of a British Army garrison and protection of their external boundary. It also institutionalized the system of a British resident, who ensured that the ruler was kept in check.

4. The three Lingams: Kaleshwaram, Srisailam and Draksharamam are located in Telangana, Rayalaseema and coastal Andhra.

5. An informal, non-binding agreement between two or more parties. The breach of this agreement can have political, but no legal implications.

6. Although nationalism and class struggle were fundamentally irreconcilable, Marx acknowledged the tactical alliances that had to be made by

mobilizing the oppressed linguistic and ethnic groups against the global forces of imperialism. The communist formulation of India was that it was a multilingual, mutlinational, mutli-ethnic state.

7. Communist Party of the Soviet Union was one of the most powerful ideological think tanks, which guided the 'strategic' direction to Communist Parties across the world. However, by mid-'60s, the Communist Party of China (CPC) and CPI (M) stopped accepting the directions of CPSU.

8. Communist Part of India was founded in 1925 in Kanpur by M.N. Roy, Charu Mazumdar and Abani Mookerjee.

9. Distinguished political scientist and ICSSR National Fellow with the Tata Institute of Social Sciences, Hyderabad.

10. 'The Telangana People's Movement: The Unfolding Political Culture', G. Hargopal, *Economic and Political Weekly*, vol. 45, no. 42, 2010.

11. Peasant mode of production refers to an agriculture cropping pattern in which the farmer is producing essential for consumption within the family, while in the market mode, the farmer is producing essentially for the market.

12. Actively engaged in politics from his student days, he became a minister at the age of thirty. Was opposed to the merger of Telangana with Andhra in 1965 itself. He became the chief minister of Andhra twice to assuage the feelings of the adherents of Telangana.

13. The informal name given to the Congress Working Committee, the supreme policymaking body in the Indian National Congress. Almost all decisions with regard to appointment of chief ministers and selection of candidates for different elections is done by the high command.

14. An agitation which sought a separate political entity for Andhra, minus the Telangana districts.

15. Mulki refers to the erstwhile permanent residents of the Nizam's territory of Hyderabad. As the education levels in Hyderabad were lower than those in Andhra, a special dispensation was allowed for them in government jobs and admissions to educational institutions.

16. Built his career as a trade union leader and rose to become the Union minister for labour. He was the chief minister of Andhra from October 1980 to February 1982.

17. 'The Telangana People's Movement: The Unfolding Political Culture', G. Hargopal, *Economic and Political Weekly*, vol. 45, no. 42, 2010.

18. Starting his political career with the Youth Congress, he joined the TDP and became the chief minister of united Andhra Pradesh from 1995 to 2004 after ousting his mentor and father-in-law, N.T. Rama Rao. At the peak of his political career, in 2000, Bill Clinton, the President of US and Tony Blair, the PM of UK, visited Hyderabad. He also became the first chief minister of the bifurcated Andhra Pradesh from 2014 to 2019. He is currently the leader of Opposition in the Andhra Assembly.

19. Leader of the TRS. It was his hunger strike which triggered the announcement of the Telangana state. Has been the CM since the formation of the state in 2014.

20. Left of centre coalition formed in 2004 with Sonia Gandhi of the INC as the chairperson. The Congress had 145 seats against 138 of the BJP. The other parties which extended support to UPA 1 were the CPI, CPM, SP, BSP and TRS.

21. Popularly known as YSR, he led a three-month long padyatra in 2003 of the state, and defeated Chandra Babu Naidu in 2004. He led his party to victory again in 2009, but was killed in a chopper accident on 2 September 2009.

22. Established in 1918 by the seventh Nizam of Hyderabad, it played a leading role in the movement for a separate Telangana.

23. A state university established in 1976, this university is located in Guntur district, and its faculty and students were opposed to the bifurcation of the state.

24. The TDP had demanded that Hyderabad may be made into a UT to serve as the capital of both Telangana and Hyderabad. However, given the Chandigarh experience, this did not find too many takers. Incidentally, Dr Ambedkar had proposed Hyderabad as the winter capital of India to ensure better integration between the north and the south.

BIBLIOGRAPHY

1. Maps and Milestones: The Marking of Internal Boundaries in India

'How 1976 Seat Freeze Has Altered Lok Sabha Representation', *The Times of India*, March 2019.

Adeney, Katharine. *Federalism and Ethnic Conflict Regulation in India and Pakistan.* Palgrave Macmillan US, 2016.

Ambedkar, Dr B.R. *Thoughts on Linguistic States.* Samyak Prakashan, 1955.

Asif, Manan Ahmed. 'The Loss of Hindustan: The Invention of India.' In *The Loss of Hindustan: The Invention of India*, by Manan Ahmed Asif. Harvard University Press, 2020.

Bangash, Yaqoob Khan. 'A Princely Affair: The Accession and Integration of the Princely States of Pakistan, 1947–1955.' In *A Princely Affair: The Accession and Integration of the Princely States of Pakistan, 1947–1955*, by Yaqoob Khan Bangash. Oxford University Press, 2015.

Barbara Ramusack, Richter, William L., and 'The Chamber and the Consultation: Changing Forms of Princely Association in India.' *The Journal of Asian Studies*, vol. 34, no. 3, 1975.

BBC. 'Tibet Profile.' *BBC*, 2019.

Bipan Chandra, Mridula Mukherjee, Aditya Mukherjee, K.N. Panikkar, Sucheta Mahajan. 'India's Struggle for Independence.' In *India's Struggle for Independence*, by Mridula Mukherjee, Aditya Mukherjee, K.N. Panikkar, Sucheta Mahajan, Bipan Chandra. Penguin Random House India, 2016.

Chirol, Valentine. 'Indian Unrest.' In *Indian Unrest*, by Valentine Chirol. Outlook Verlag Publication, 2018.

Cohen, Stephen, *The Idea of Pakistan*, Brookings Institution Press, 2004.

Clémentin-Ojha, Catherine. '"India, that is Bharat …": One Country, Two Names.' *South Asia Multidisciplinary Academic Journal*, 2014.

Dube, M.P. 'Regionalism in India: Some Critical Observations with Special Reference to Uttarakhand Movement.' *Indian Journal of Political Science*, 1995.

Gray, Francine Du Plessix. *The Fairy Tale that Turned Nightmare?* 8 March 1981. https://www.nytimes.com/1981/03/08/books/the-fairy-tale-that-turned-nightmare.html (accessed March 10, 2021).

India, Government of. *Report of the Backward Classes Commission*. Government Report, Government of India, 1980.

India, Government of. *Report of the States Reorganization Commission*. Government of India, 1955.

India, Survey of. *Handbook of Topography: Chapter XI – Geographical Maps.* Copyright, India: Government of India, 2009.

Khajuria, Sanjay, M. Saleem Pandit. *The Times of India.* December 2020. https://timesofindia.indiatimes.com/india/50-voter-turnout-in-4th-phase-of-ddc-polls-in-jammu-and-kashmir/articleshow/79613039.cms (accessed March 2021).

Marathe, Om, 'Explained: Sikkim, from Chogyal Rule to Indian State', *The Indian Express*, August 2019.

Mill, James, Horace Hayman Wilson. 'The History of British India.' *The History of British India*, by James Mill, XIII, vol. 9. Madden Publishing House, 1858.

Sarhadi, Ajit Singh. *Punjabi Suba: The Story of the Struggle.* U.C. Kapur, 1970.

Singh, Col. Gambhir. *India's Political Map or Bharat ke Rajnaitik Vibhag.* Survey Report, Government of India, 1952.

Sinha. *Hem Chandra Sen Gupta and Ors. vs The Speaker Of Legislative …* on 17 April 1956. AIR 1956 Cal 378, 60 CWN 555, 1956.

Tod, James, *Annals and Antiquities of Rajasthan: Or, 'The Central and Western Rajpoot States of India Asian Educational Services'*, H. Milford, Oxford University Press, 2001.

2. 1947: The First Map of Independent India

Abdullah, Sheikh. *The Blazing Chinar: Autobiography.* Pragun Publications, 2013.

Ahmed, Ishtiaq. *Jinnah: His Successes, Failures and Role in History.* Penguin Random House India, 2020.

Appleby, P.H. 'Some Thoughts on Decentralized Democracy.' *Indian Journal of Public Administration, 8*(4), 1962.

Apri, Claude. *1962 and the McMahon Line Saga.* Lancer, 2013.

Cambell-Johnson, Alan. *Mission with Mountbatten.* Atheneum, 1985.

Copland, I. 'The Princely States, the Muslim League, and the Partition of India in 1947.' *The International History Review, 13*(1), 1991.

Chester, L.P. *Borders and Conflict in South Asia: The Radcliffe Boundary Commission and the Partition of Punjab.* Manchester University Press, 2017.

Debroy, Bibek. 'An Area of Light.' *The Indian Express,* 20 September 2010.

Guha, Ramachandra, *India after Gandhi.* HarperCollins, 2007.

Edney, M.H. *Mapping an Empire: The Geographical Construction of British India, 1765–1843.* University of Chicago Press, 2009.

Jalal, A. *Self and Sovereignty: Individual and Community in South Asian Islam since 1850.* Routledge, 2002.

Hasan, M. 'Memories of a Fragmented Nation: Rewriting the Histories of India's Partition.' *Economic and Political Weekly,* 1998.

Krishan, Y. 'Mountbatten and the Partition of India.' *History, 68*(222), 1983.

Langworth, Richard M. *Churchill by Himself: The Definitive Collection of Quotations.* PublicAffairs, 2008.

Mahajan, Justice M.C. *Looking Back,* Har-Anand Publication (revised edition), 2018.

Masaldan, P.N. 'The Sphere of Provincial Government under the Government of India Act 1935.' *The Indian Journal of Political Science, 8*(3), 1947.

Menon, V.P. *The Story of the Integration of the Indian States.* Longmans, Green and Co, 1955.

Thorpe, Robert. *Cashmere Mismanagement.* Wyman Bros, 1968.

Qasim, Syed Mir. *My Life and Times.* South Asia Books, 1993.

3. Riyasat e Jammu wa Kashmir wa Ladakh wa Tibet ha

'Full Text of Document on Government's Rationale behind Removal of Special Status to J&K.' *The Hindu,* 6 August 2019.

'Implications of J&K Reorganization Act,' *The Telegraph,* 20 Maty 2020.

Agarwala, Jai Shankar, 'Article 370 of the Constitution: A Genesis.' *Economic and Political Weekly,* vol. 50, no. 16, 2015.

Anand, Adarsh Sein, 'Accession of Jammu and Kashmir State – Historical & Legal Perspective.' *Journal of the Indian Law Institute,* vol. 43, no. 4, 2001.

Anand, Adarsh Sein, 'Kashmir's Accession to India.' *Journal of the Indian Law Institute,* vol. 6, no. 1, 1964.

Abdullah, Mohammad, 'Kashmir, India and Pakistan.' *Foreign Affairs,* vol. 43, no. 3, 1965.

Ankit, Rakesh. '1948: The Crucial Year in the History of Jammu and Kashmir.' *Economic and Political Weekly,* vol. 45, no. 11, 2010.

Bal, S.S., 'British Interest in Creating the Dogra State of Jammu and Kashmir.' *Proceedings of the Indian History Congress,* vol. 29, 1967.

Dogra, P.C. *1947 Kashmir Invasion: Why Stalemate?* Manas Publication, 2020.

Ganguly, Sumit, 'Stalemate in the Valley: India, Pakistan, and the Crisis in Kashmir.' *Harvard International Review,* vol. 18, no. 3, 1996.

Ganguly, Sumit, and Kanti Bajpai. 'India and the Crisis in Kashmir.' *Asian Survey,* vol. 34, no. 5, 1994.

Habibullah, Wajahat. *My Kashmir: The Dying of the Light,* Penguin, 2014.

Indurthy, Rathnam, and Muhammad Haque, 'The Kashmir Conflict: Why It Defies Solution.' *International Journal on World Peace,* vol. 27, no. 1, 2010.

Jagota, S.P. 'Development of Constitutional Relations between Jammu and Kashmir and India, 1950–60.' *Journal of the Indian Law Institute,* vol. ?, no. 4, 1960.

Jamwal, Shailender Singh, 'Jammu & Kashmir State's Accession to the Indian Union: Role of the Prince and the People.' Proceedings of the Indian History Congress, vol. 57, 1996.

Jamwal, Shailendra Singh, 'J&K State's Accession to India: A Debate over Delay.' Proceedings of the Indian History Congress, vol. 59, 1998.

Kaul, Nitasha. 'On Loving and Losing Kashmir.' India International Centre Quarterly, vol. 37, no. 3/4, 2010.

Naidu, M.V. 'The Kashmir Dispute and India-Pakistan Relations: The Untold Story of Cold War Diplomacy.' Peace Research, vol. 32, no. 2, 2000.

Puri, Balraj. 'Jammu and Kashmir: The Issue of Regional Autonomy.' Economic and Political Weekly, vol. 43, no. 34, 2008.

Rasool, Irfan, 'Jammu and Kashmir: A Confederate within a Federal System.' Economic and Political Weekly, vol. 49, no. 4, 2014.

Sheikh, Tariq Ahmad. 'The Residency Question in The Princely State of Jammu and Kashmir.' Proceedings of the Indian History Congress, vol. 71, 2010.

Varshney, Ashutosh. 'India, Pakistan, and Kashmir: Antinomies of Nationalism.' Asian Survey, vol. 31, no. 11, 1991.

Verma, P.S. 'Jammu and Kashmir Politics: Religion, Region and Personality Symbiosis.' The Indian Journal of Political Science, vol. 48, no. 4, 1987.

Widmalm, Sten. 'The Rise and Fall of Democracy in Jammu and Kashmir.' Asian Survey, vol. 37, no. 11, 1997.

'Behind Removal of Special Status to J&K.' The Hindu, 16 August 2019.

4. The Nizam and His Firmans

Copland, Ian. 'Communalism' in Princely India: The Case of Hyderabad, 1930–1940.' Modern Asian Studies, 1988, 22(4).

Copland, Ian. 'The Princely States, the Muslim League, and the Partition of India in 1947.' The International History Review, vol. 13, no. 1, 1991.

Datla, Kavita Saraswathi. 'The Origins of Indirect Rule in India: Hyderabad and the British Imperial Order.' Law and History Review, vol. 33, no. 2, 2015.

Faruqui, M. 'At Empire's End: The Nizam, Hyderabad and Eighteenth-Century India.' Modern Asian Studies, 43(1), 2009.

Gondhalekar, Nandini, and Sanjoy Bhattacharya, 'The All India Hindu Mahasabha and the End of British Rule in India, 1939-1947.' *Social Scientist*, vol. 27, no. 7/8, 1999.

Indian States – Political Affairs (Int): Andhra Pradesh (1968–69), (File No.FSS 1/14), Foreign and Commonwealth Office Files – South Asia.

Kooiman, Dick. 'The Nizam's Last Victory: Hyderabad on Eve of Second World War.' *Economic and Political Weekly*, vol. 33, no. 12, 1998.

Kozlowski, Gregory C. 'Loyalty, Locality and Authority in Several Opinions (Fatwah) Delivered by the Mufti of the Jami'ah Niẓāmiyyah Madrasah, Hyderabad, India.' *Modern Asian Studies*, vol. 29, no. 4, 1995.

Leonard, K. 'Reassessing Indirect Rule in Hyderabad: Rule, Ruler, or Sons-in-Law of the State?' *Modern Asian Studies*, 37(2), 2003.

Meeneshwar Rao, G. 'Last Phase of Freedom Struggle in the Hyderabad State: A Case Study of the Telangana Region.' *Proceedings of the Indian History Congress*, vol. 52, 1991.

Purushotham, Sunil. 'Federating the Raj: Hyderabad, Sovereign Kingship, and Partition.' *Modern Asian Studies*, 54(1), 2020.

Purushotham, Sunil. 'Internal Violence: The "Police Action" in Hyderabad.' *Comparative Studies in Society and History*, vol. 57, no. 2, 2015.

Sherman, Taylor C. 'Migration, Citizenship and Belonging in Hyderabad (Deccan), 1946–1956.' *Modern Asian Studies*, vol. 45, no. 1, 2011.

Sherwani, H.K. 'The Evolution of the Legislature in Hyderabad.' *The Indian Journal of Political Science*, vol. 1, no. 4, 1940.

Talbot, Phillips, 'Kashmir and Hyderabad.' *World Politics*, vol. 1, no. 3, 1949.

5. India as a Republic!

Bal, S.S. 'Punjab after Independence (1947–1956).' In *Proceedings of the Indian History Congress*, vol. 46. Indian History Congress, January 1985.

Bamzai, S. 'The Failed Plot of the Deccan Princes'. *ORF Special Report*, 2017. https://www.orfonline.org/research/the-failed-plot-of-the-deccan-princes/

Divatia, H.V. *Linguistic Limits of Maha Gujarat*. Gujarat Research Society, 1948.

Ernst, W., B. Biswamoy Pati (Eds.). *India's Princely States: People, Princes and Colonialism, vol. 45*. Routledge, 2007.

Fortnightly Reports from Chief Commissioner Delhi, 1950. National Archives of India,

Digitized Public Records States.

Jhala, A.D. 'The Indian Princely States and Their Rulers.' *Oxford Research Encyclopedia of Asian History,* 2019.

Khan, Q., O.A. Khan, P. Minister, I. Khan, M.L. Ali, T. Rebellion and P. Purse. 'Early History.' *Population,* 1941.

Khanna, B. 'The Problem of Part C States.' *The Indian Journal of Political Science,* 14(4), 1953.

L.F.R.W. 'The Indian Dominion and the States.' *The World Today,* 5(1), 1949.

Mishra, D.P. *Revolt in Orissa: A Study of Talcher.* Atlantic Publishers, 1998.

Moore, R.J. 'The Transfer of Power: A Historiographical Survey.' *South Asia: Journal of South Asian Studies,* 9(1), 1986.

Moon, P. *Divide and Quit,* vol. 10. University of California Press, 1962.

Ramusack, B.N. *The Indian Princes and Their States.* Cambridge University Press, 2004.

Schwartzberg, Joseph E. *A Historical Atlas of South Asia.* University of Chicago Press, 1978.

Seshan, R. 'The Maratha State: Some Preliminary Considerations.' *Indian Historical Review,* 41(1), 2014.

Singh, T. *The British in India.* 1992.

Singh, M.P. 'Reorganization of States in India.' *Economic and Political Weekly,* 2008.

Vasishta, L.C. *Census of India, 1951. Vol. VIII: Punjab, PEPSU, Himachal Pradesh, Bilaspur and Delhi.* Part IB: Subsidiary Tables, 1953.

Zutshi, C. 'Re-visioning Princely States in South Asian Historiography: A Review.' *The Indian Economic and Social History Review,* 46(3).

6. The First Hindi Map of India

'How Uttar Pradesh Got Its Name.' *Hindustan Times,* 5 February 2018. https://www.hindustantimes.com/lucknow/how-uttar-pradesh-got-its-name/story-53gjNNUbmJ0b17HcKOcovL.html

'The Cambridge Shorter History of India.' Cambridge Encyclopaedia.

'UP Divas: How Uttar Pradesh Got Its Name.' *The Indian Express*, 24 January 2018. https://indianexpress.com/article/india/up-divas-how-uttar-pradesh-got-its-name-5037306/

'UP Diwas: Tracing History on How Uttar Pradesh Got Its Name.' India News, 24 January 2018. https://www.ndtv.com/india-news/up-diwas-tracing-history-on-how-uttar-pradesh-got-its-name-1804301

Ali, A. Yusuf. *The Making of India*, A&C Black, 1925.

Baker, David E. U. *Changing Political Leadership in an Indian Province: The Central Provinces and Berar, 1919–1939*. Oxford University Press, 1979.

Bandyopadhyay, Sekhara. *From Plassey to Partition: A History of Modern India*. Orient Longman, 2004.

Barton, William. 'The Indian Princes and Politics.' *Pacific Affairs*, vol. 17, no. 2, 1944.

Bashir, Yasir. 'Role of British Political Agent in the State of Bikaner.' *Proceedings of the Indian History Congress*, vol. 76, 2015.

Bayly, Christopher Alan. *Rulers, Townsmen, and Bazaars: North Indian Society in the Age of British Expansion, 1770–1870,* Cambridge University Press, 1983.

Brown, Judith Margaret. *Gandhi's Rise to Power, Indian Politics 1915–1922*, Cambridge University Press, 1972.

Copland, Ian. 'Integration'. *Key Concepts In Modern Indian Studies*. New York University Press, 2015.

Copland, Ian. 'The Princely States, the Muslim League, and the Partition of India in 1947.' *The International History Review*, vol. 13, no. 1, 1991.

Gokhale, Vijay. *The Long Game: How the Chinese Negotiate with India*. Penguin Random House India, 2021.

Hossain, Ishtiaq. 'Review of the Aftermath of Partition in South Asia by Gyanesh Kudasiya, Tan Tai Yong.' *Asian Journal of Social Science*, vol.33, no.3, 2005.

Kudasiya, Gyanesh. *Region, Nation, 'Heartland': Uttar Pradesh in India's Body Politic*. Sage Publication, 2006.

Kudasiya, Gyanesh and Tan Tai Yong. *The Aftermath of Partition in South Asia.* Routledge, 2002.

Markovits, Claude (eds.). *A History of Modern India: 1480–1950,* Anthem Press, 2004.

Mathew, George. 'Republic of India.' *Distribution of Powers and Responsibilities in Federal Countries,* McGill-Queen's UP, 2006.

Mcleod, John. 'The English Honours System in Princely India, 1925–1947.' *Journal of the Royal Asiatic Society,* vol. 4, no. 2, 1994.

Menon, V.P. *Integration of the Indian States,* Orient Blackswan, 2014

Mishra, Pankaj. 'The Problem.' *Seminar,* No. 450, February 1997.

Mishra, Jai Prakash. *Researches in Social Sciences,* Agam Kala, 1993.

Olson, James S. and Robert Shadle (eds.). *Historical Dictionary of the British Empire,* vol. 1. Greenwood Publishing Group, 1996.

Pachauri, S.K. 'Some Responses of the Princely States to the Freedom Movement and Popular Demands.' *Proceedings of the Indian History Congress,* vol. 62, 2001.

Panikkar, K.M. 'The Princes and India's Future.' *Foreign Affairs,* vol. 21, no. 3, 1943.

Pateriya, Raghaw Raman. *Provincial Legislatures and the National Movement.* Northern Book Centre, 1991.

Robins, Robert S. 'Political Elite Formation in Rural India: The Uttar Pradesh Panchayat Elections of 1949, 1956, and 1961.' *The Journal of Politics,* vol. 29, no. 4, 1967.

Rudolph, Lloyd I. and Susanne Hoeber Rudolph. 'Rajputana under British Paramount: The Failure of Indirect Rule.' *The Journal of Modern History,* vol. 38, no. 2, 1966.

Rudolph, Susanne Hoeber, et al. 'A Bureaucratic Lineage in Princely India: Elite Formation and Conflict in a Patrimonial System.' *The Journal of Asian Studies,* vol. 34, no. 3, 1975.

Sengupta, Hindol. *The Man Who Saved India.* Penguin Random House India, 2018.

Sen, Ronojoy. 'Players And Patrons.' *Nation at Play: A History of Sport in India,* Columbia UP, 2015.

Sharma, Phool Kumar. 'Integration of Princely States and the Reorganization of States in India.' *The Indian Journal of Political Science*, vol. 28, no. 4, 1967.

Singh, Ajit Kumar. 'The Demand for Division of Uttar Pradesh and Its Implications.' *Economic and Political Weekly*, vol. 51, no. 53, 2016.

Singh, Shashank. 'The Princely State of Gwalior and a bid to centralise the administrative machinery, 1860–1925.' Proceedings of the Indian History Congress, vol. 79, 2018.

Singh, Uma Shanker. 'The Politics of Mass Mobilisation: Eastern Uttar Pradesh, C. 1920–1940.' *Social Scientist*, vol. 43, no. 5/6, 2015.

Swami Sahajanand Saraswati Rachnawali. *Selected Works of Swami Sahajanand Saraswati*, Prakashan Sansthan, 2003.

Tomlinson, B.R. *The Indian National Congress and the Raj, 1929–1942: The Penultimate Phase*. Macmillan Press Ltd, 1976.

Vashishtha, V.K. 'Quit India Movement in the Mewar State.' *Proceedings of the Indian History Congress*, vol. 73, 2012.

Vashishtha, V.K. 'Role of Mahatma Gandhi in the Prajamandal Movement in the Princely States of Rajputana.' *Proceedings of the Indian History Congress*, vol. 78, 2017.

Yang, Anand A., Bazaar India: Markets, Society, and the Colonial State in Bihar. University of California Press, 1999.

7. The Andhra State and the SRC

'A Century of Political Fasting.' *Economic and Political Weekly*, vol. 44, no. 52, 2009.

'Delhi Felt Razakars, Communists a Threat to India.' *Deccan Chronicle*, 15 September 2018.

'New Book on Hyderabad's Invasion, 1948's Police Action.' *The Milli Gazette*, 4 February 2021.

Cohen, B. *Kingship and Colonialism in India's Deccan: 1850–1948*. Springer, 2007.

Gangadhara Rao, G. 'Hyderabad and the Bifurcation of Andhra Pradesh.' *Economic and Political Weekly*, vol. 48, no. 42, 2013.

Gautam, Pingle. 'The Historical Context of Andhra and Telangana, 1949–56.' *Economic and Political Weekly*, vol. 45, no. 8, 2010.

Gray, Hugh. 'The Demand for a Separate Telangana State in India.' *Asian Survey*, vol. 11, no. 5, 1971.

Gray, Hugh. 'The Failure of the Demand for a Separate Andhra State.' *Asian Survey*, vol.14, no. 4, 1974.

Graziosi, Andrea. 'India and the Soviet Model: The Linguistic State Reorganization and the Problem of Hindi.' *Harvard Ukrainian Studies*, vol. 35, no. 1/4, 2017.

Hancock, Mary. 'Review of Language, Emotion, and Politics in South India by Lisa Mitchell.' *The American Historical Review*, vol. 114, no. 5, 2009.

King, Robert D. *Nehru and the Language Politics of India*. Oxford University Press, 1997.

Keiko, Yamada. 'Origin and Historical Evolution of the Identity of Modern Telugus.' *Economic and Political Weekly*, vol. 45, no. 34, 2010.

Lacina, Bethany. 'Regional Interests, National Crisis.' *Rival Claims: Ethnic Violence and Territorial Autonomy Under Indian Federalism*, University of Michigan, 2017.

Madras Legislative Assembly Debates, Legislative Assembly.

Mehrotra, S.R. *Towards India's Freedom and Partition*. Vikas Publishing House, 1979.

Menon, V.P. *Integration of the Indian States*. Orient Blackswan, 2014.

Metcalf, Barbara D. and Thomas R. Metcalf. *A Concise History of India*. Cambridge University Press, 2006.

Moore, Robert E. 'Review of Language, Emotion, and Politics in South India: The Making of a Mother Tongue by Lisa Mitchell.' *Cultural Anthropology*, vol. 25, no. 1, 2010.

Murthy, C.K. 'Census of India, 1951: Hyderabad.' Hyderabad Superintendent of Census Operations, 1953.

Purushotham, Sunil. 'Internal Violence: The "Police Action" in Hyderabad.' *Comparative Studies in Society and History*, vol. 57, no. 2, 2015.

S.D.U. 'Indian Statesmanship and Communist Opportunism.' *The World Today*, vol. 11, no. 3, 1955.

Sherman, Taylor C. 'The Integration of the Princely State of Hyderabad and the Making of the Postcolonial State in India, 1948–56.' *Indian Economic and Social History Review,* 44 (4), 2007.

Siwach, J.R. 'Nehru and the Language Problem.' *The Indian Journal of Political Science,* vol. 48, no.2, 1987.

Weiner, Myron. 'Middle-Class Protectionism' *Sons of the Soil: Migration and Ethnic Conflict in India,* Princeton University Press, 1978.

Windmiller, Marshall. 'Linguistic Regionalism in India.' *Pacific Affairs,* vol. 27, no. 4, 1954,.

8. The Linguistic States of the South: Tamil Nadu, Karnataka and Kerala

'"Ekikarana" Movement: A Timeline." *Deccan Herald,* 31 October 2011. https://www.deccanherald.com/content/201500/ekikarana-movement-timeline.html

'The Role of Burgulla in Telangana.' The Hans India, 19 September 2013. https://www.thehansindia.com/posts/index/Opinion/2013-09-19/The-role-of-Burgula-in-Telangana/72201

Annadurai, C.N. *Carry on, but Remember! Selected Speeches of C.N. Annadurai in the Indian Parliament.* Thannatchi Pathippagam. Chennai, 2021.

Balan, J. 'The Possibilities and Discourse of Dakshin Pradesh, A Union State of Madras and Travancore-Cochin.' *Proceedings of Indian History Congress,* 2012.

Dev, A. 'Explained: The Demand for a Separate North Karnataka State.' The Quint, 28 July 2018. https://www.thequint.com/explainers/north-karnataka-bandh-for-separate-state

Devi, K.G. 'Telangana/s of Karnataka.' *Economic and Political Weekly,* 2007.

Gavaskar, M. 'Land, Language and Politics: Apropos 70th Kannada Sahitya Sammelan.' *Economic and Political Weekly,* 2003.

Ganeshan, V.B. 'The Story of Madras.' *The Hindu,* 24 October 2015. https://www.thehindu.com/books/literary-review/vb-ganesan-reviews-madras-tracing-the-growth-of-the-city-since-1639/article7796379.ece

Ghargi, A. 'Why Demand for Separate North Karnataka State?' HW News, 31 July 2018. https://hwnews.in/articles/explainers/demand-separate-north-karnataka-state/51537

Harrison, Selig S. *India: The Most Dangerous Decades*. Princeton University Press, 2016.

Jeffrey, R. 'Coalitions and Consequences: Learnership and Leadership in India, 1948–2008.' *The Indian Economy Sixty Years After Independence*. Palgrave Macmillan, 2008.

K.S.L. 'Aryan and Dravidian Metanarratives.' *Proceedings of the Indian History Congress*, 2016.

Kadekodi, G., R. Kanbur, V. Rao. 'Governance and the "Karnataka Model of Development".' *Economic and Political Weekly*, 2007.

Khajane, M. 'The Word Karnataka Has Existed Since 1336, Say Historians.' *The Hindu*, 10 November 2018. https://www.thehindu.com/news/national/karnataka/the-word-karnataka-has-existed-since-1336-say-historians/article25465678.ece

Kurien, C.T. 'Dynamics of Rural Transformation: A Case Study of Tamil Nadu.' *Economic and Political Weekly*, 1980.

Manor, E.R. *Broadening and Deepening Democracy: Political Innovation in Karnataka*. Routledge, 2009.

Nagaraj, P. 'When Karnataka Came to Be the Motherland.' News Karnataka, 9 May 2018. https://www.newskarnataka.com/features/when-karnataka-came-together-to-be-the-mother-land

Nair, J. 'Memories of Underdevelopment: Language and Its Identities in Contemporary Karnataka.' *Economic and Political Weekly*, 1996.

Nair, J. 'The "Composite" State and Its "Nation": Karnataka's Reunification Revisited.' *Economic and Political Weekly*, 2011.

Nair, T.S. 'The Non-Brahmin Movement and Dr T.M. Nair.' *Proceedings of the Indian History Congress*, vol. 43. Indian History Congress, January 1982.

Nijalingappa, S. *My Life and Politics*. Vision Books, 2007.

Niranjana, T. 'Reworking Masculinities: Rajkumar and the Kannada Public Sphere.' *Economic and Political Weekly*, 2000.

Pandian, J. 'Re-Ethnogenesis. The Quest for a Dravidian Identity among the Tamil of India.' *Anthropos*, 1998.

Perlin, F. 'State Formation Reconsidered: Part Two.' *Modern Asian Studies*, 1985.

Pillai, K.R. 'Politics of Kerala.' *The Indian Journal of Political Science*, 48(4), 1987.

Pinto, A. 'End of Dravidian Era in Tamil Nadu.' *Economic and Political Weekly*, 1999.

Rag, P. 'Indian Nationalism 1885–1905: An Overview.' *Social Scientist*, 1995.

Raghavan, E. and J. Manor. *Broadening and Deepening Democracy: Political Innovation in Karnataka*. Routledge India, 2012.

Raj, N. 'The Distribution of Social Justice by Rajarshi Krishnaraj Wodeyar IV.' *EPRA International Journal of Economic and Business Review*, 2015.

Ramanappa, M.N. *Outlines of South Indian History with Special Reference to Karnataka*. Vikas Publishing House, 1975.

Ramaswamy, V. 'Tamil Separatism and Cultural Negotiations: Gender Politics and Literature in Tamil Nadu.' *Social Scientist*, 1998.

Rao, M.K. 'Lines of Research in Karnatak History.' *Proceedings of the Indian History Congress*, vol. 23. Indian History Congress, January 1960.

Regani, S. *Highlights of the Freedom Movement in Andhra Pradesh*. Ministry of Cultural Affairs, Government of Andhra Pradesh, 1972.

Schwartz, S. 'Communism and the Indian Election.' *The American Scholar*, 1952.

Shea, T.J. 'Implementing Land Reform in India.' *Far Eastern Survey*, 25(1), 1956.

Special Election Correspondent. 'Travancore–Cochin Prepares for Elections.' *Economic Weekly*, 1954.

Subramanian, N. 'Political Formation of Cultures: The South Asian Experience.' *Economic and Political Weekly*, 2005.

Venkata, R.M.N. *Outlines of South Indian history: With Special reference to Karnataka*. Vikas Publishing House, 1975.

Venkatachalapathy, A.R. 'The "Classical" Language Issue.' *Economic and Politically Weekly*, 2009.

9. The Roy–Sinha proposals and the Boundaries of West Bengal

The Statesman Archives, 24 January 1956.

The Times of India Archives, 1953–1956.

'West Bengal–Bihar Merger.' *The Economic Weekly*, 24 March 1956.

'Bhupesh Gupta's Speech in Rajya Sabha.' *New Age*, 26 February 1956.

'Hiren Mukherjee's Speech in Parliament.' *New Age*, 29 April 1956.

Chatterji, Joya. 'The Fashioning of a Frontier: The Radcliffe Line and Bengal's Border Landscape, 1947-52.' *Modern Asian Studies*, vol. 33, no. 1, 1999.

Cons, Jason. 'Histories of Belonging(s): Narrating Territory, Possession, and Dispossession at the India-Bangladesh Border.' *Modern Asian Studies*, vol. 46, no. 3, 2012.

Dhavan, Rajeev. 'Treaties and People: Indian Reflections.' *Journal of the Indian Law Institute*, vol. 39, no. 1, 1997.

Feldman, Shelley. 'Bengali State and Nation Making Partition and Displacement Revisited.' *International Social Science Journal*, Unesco, 2003.

Ghosh, Arun. 'Bengal–Bihar Merger Movement of 1956.' *Karatoya*, vol. 10, March 2017.

Ghosh, Arun. 'Bengal-Bihar Merger Movement of 1956: A Glance of West Dinajpur – A District of West Bengal.' *Journal of History*, vol.10, North Bengal University.

Gupta, Bhupesh, 'The West Bengal Anti-Merger Movement.' *New Age*, 7 July 1956.

Judgement of Hon'ble Judge Sinha on Hem Chandra Sen Gupta Vs the Speaker of Legislative at AIR on 17 April 1956.

Memorandum Submitted to the States Reorganization Commission by Bihari Association, Patna, 1954.

Monmohan Chakrabarti. 'A Summary of the Changes in the Jurisdiction of Districts in Bengal, 1757–1916.' Revised and updated by Kumud Ranjan Biswas, West Bengal District Gazetteers, Department of Higher Education, Government of West Bengal, Calcutta, 1999.

Pant, Harsh V. 'India and Bangladesh: Will the Twain Ever Meet?' *Asian Survey*, vol. 47, no. 2, 2007.

Popkin, William D. 'Advisory Opinions in India.' *Journal of the Indian Law Institute*, vol. 4, no. 3, 1962.

Rajaraman, R. 'Secularism in Indian Politics: Theory and Practice.' *The Indian Journal of Political Science*, vol. 68, no. 2, 2007.

Report of the States Reorganization Commission, New Delhi, 1955.

Roy, Haimanti. 'Citizens of the Nation: In Partitioned Lives: Migrants, Refugees, Citizens in India and Pakistan, 1947–65.' Oxford Scholarship Online, 2013.

Sanyal, Romola. 'Urban Dislocations in Post-partition Calcutta.' *Transactions of the Institute of British Geographers*, vol.39 (1), 2014.

Sarkar, Shamita. 'The Role of the Communists in the Anti-Bengal – Bihar Merger Agitation.' *Proceedings of the Indian History Congress*, vol. 74, Indian History Congress, 2013.

Sen, Subhasis. '"Tin Bigha" – Where the People Live Their Daily Life Is Complicated.' *Proceedings of the Indian History Congress*, vol. 73, 2012.

The Bihar and West Bengal (Transfer of Territories) Bill, New Delhi, 1956.

Van Schendel, Willem. *'Stateless in South Asia: The Making of the India-Bangladesh Enclaves'*, The Journal of Asian Studies, vol. 61, no. 1, 2002.

10. Questions of Bi-lingualism

'Two Languages, Two Regions? Punjab's Communal Politics.' *The Economic Weekly*, 2 July 1960.

Ahluwalia, Manjit Singh. *Social, Cultural, and Economic History of Himachal Pradesh*. Indus Publishing Company, 1998.

Aneesh, A. 'Bloody Language: Clashes and Constructions of Linguistic Nationalism in India.' *Sociological Forum*, vol. 25, no. 1, 2010.

Bal, S.S. 'Punjab after Independence (1947–1956).' *Proceedings of the Indian History Congress*, vol. 46, 1985.

Bombwall, K.R. 'Sikh Identity, Akali Dal and Federal Polity.' *Economic and Political Weekly*, vol. 21, no. 20, 1986.

Brass, Paul R. *Language, Religion and Politics in North India*, Cambridge University Press, 1974.

Charak, S.D.S. *Himachal Pradesh*, Light & Life Publishers, 1978.

Datta, Nonica. *Violence, Martyrdom and Partition: A Daughter's Testimony*, Oxford University Press, 2009.

Gandhi, M.K. 'Gandhi's View on Language.' *Collected Works of Mahatma Gandhi*, Volume I (1884–1896); Volume II (1896–1897); Volume III (1898–1903); Volume IV (1903–1905); Volume V (1905–1906); Volume VI (1906–1907); Volume VII (June–December 1907); Volume VIII (January–August 1908); Volume IX (September 1908–November 1909). Publications Division, Ministry of Information and Broadcasting, Government of India, 1958; 1959; 1960; 1960; 1961; 1961; 1962; 1962; 1963.

Gosal, Gurdev Singh. 'Religious Composition of Punjab's Population Changes, 1951–61.' *The Economic Weekly*, 23d January 1965.

Gupta, Jyotirindra Das. *Language Conflict and National Development: Group Politics And National Language Policy in India*. Oxford University Press, 1970.

Habib, Irfan. 'Mahatma Gandhi and the National Question.' *Social Scientist*, vol. 47, nos. 1–2, 2019.

Harrison, Selig S. *India: The Most Dangerous Decades*. Princeton University Press, 2016.

India, Ministry of Home Affairs. 'Report of the States Reorganization Committee.' 1955.

Jaffrelot, Christophe. 'Caste and Politics.' *India International Centre Quarterly*, vol. 37, no. 2, 2010.

Jeffrey, Robin. 'Punjabi: The "Subliminal Charge".' *Economic and Political Weekly*, vol. 32, no. 9/10, 1997.

Joshi, Saran, *Indian State Haryana*, Kripal Pustak Kendra, 2016.

Kahol, Prakasha. *Hindus and the Punjab State*, Hindu Prachara Sabha, 1955.

King, Robert D. *Nehru and the Language Politics of India*. Oxford University Press, 1997.

Kumar, Ashutosh. 'Exploring the Demand for New States.' *Economic and Political Weekly*, vol. 45, no. 33, 2010.

Kumar, Pradeep. 'Sub-Nationalism in Indian Politics: Formation of a Haryanavi Identity.' *The Indian Journal of Political Science*, vol. 52, no. 1, 1991.

Malhotra, S.L. *Civil Disobedience to Quit India*. Publication Bureau, Panjab University, 1979.

Mittal, S.C. *Haryana: A Historical Perspective*, Atlantic Publishers & Distributors, 1986.

Mittoo, H.K. *Himachal Pradesh*, National Book Trust, India, 1978.

Nayar, Baldev Raj. *Minority Politics in the Punjab*, Princeton University Press, 1966.

Prakash, Ved. 'Punjab–PEPSU Merger.' *The Economic Weekly*, 10 November 1956.

Rai, Gulshan, *Formation of Haryana*, B.R. Publishing Corporation, 1987.

Sarangi, Asha. 'Ambedkar and the Linguistic States: A Case for Maharashtra.' *Economic and Political Weekly*, vol. 41, no. 2, 2006.

Sen, Geeti. 'Editorial: On Language and Identity.' *India International Centre Quarterly*, vol. 24, no. 2/3, 1997.

Shah, A.M., et al. 'A Heady Mix: Gujarati and Hindu Pride.' *Economic and Political Weekly*, vol. 43, no. 8, 2008.

Sharma, Arvind. 'Dr B.R. Ambedkar on the Aryan Invasion and the Emergence of the Caste System in India.' *Journal of the American Academy of Religion*, vol. 73, no. 3, 2005.

Sharma, Sadhu Ram. 'Dilemma of Punjab.' *The Economic Weekly*, 20 November 1955.

Singh, Ranbir and Anupama Arya. 'Nehru's Strategy of National Integration.' *The Indian Journal of Political Science*, vol. 67, no. 4, 2006.

Smith, Marian W. 'Social Structure in the Punjab.' *The Economic Weekly*, 21 November 1953.

Tejani, Shabnum. 'The Necessary Conditions for Democracy: B.R. Ambedkar on Nationalism, Minorities and Pakistan.' *Economic and Political Weekly*, vol. 48, no. 50, 2013.

Verma, V. *The Emergence of Himachal Pradesh: A Survey of Constitutional Developments.* Indus Publishing, 1995.

Weekly Notes. 'A Part of the Martin Burn Enterprise to Make India Industrially Self-Sufficient.' *The Economic Weekly*, 26 November 1955.

Weekly Notes. 'Punjab: Not the End.' *The Economic Weekly*, 4 July 1964.

Windmiller, Marshall. 'Linguistic Regionalism in India.' *Pacific Affairs*, vol. 27, no. 4, 1954,

Yadav, Kripal Chandra (ed.), *Haryana: Studies in History and Culture.* Kurukshetra University, 1968.

11. The End of Foreign Jurisdictions

Akhila, Yechury. 'Chandernagore: A "Glorious Chapter" in the History of Independence.' *Economic and Political Weekly,* vol. 50, no. 3, 2015.

Akhila, Yechury, 'Imagining India, Decolonizing "L'inde Française", C. 1947 – 1954.' *The Historical Journal,* vol. 58, no. 4, 2015.

B.E.H.F. 'Goa and the Indian Union: Background of the Recent Dispute.' *The World Today,* vol. 10, no. 12, 1954.

Couto, Francisco Cabral. *Remembering the Fall of Portuguese India in 1961.* Tribuna da Historia, 2006.

Das, Durga. *India: From Curzon to Nehru and After.* Rupa & Co., 2002.

Desouza, Peter Ronald. 'Politics of the Uniform Civil Code in India.' *Economic and Political Weekly,* vol. 50, no. 48, 2015.

E.B. 'The Salazar Regime and Goa.' *The World Today,* vol. 10, no. 9, 1954.

Fernandes, Aureliano. 'Political Transition in Post-Colonial Societies: Goa in Perspective.' *Lusotopie,* 7 (1).

Gopal, Sarvepalli. *Jawaharlal Nehru: A Biography,* vol. 3: 1956–1964. Harvard University Press, 1984.

Heimsath, Charles H. and Surjit Mansingh. *A Diplomatic History of Modern India,* Allied Publishers, 1971.

Joy, Varkey. 'The Significance of Mahe in Eighteenth-Century French India.' *Proceedings of the Indian History Congress,* vol. 58, 1997.

Luthera, Ved Prakash. 'Goa and the Portuguese Republic.' *The Indian Journal of Political Science,* vol. 17, no. 3, 1956.

Mendes, Sushila Sawant. 'Jawaharlal Nehru and the Liberation Struggle of Goa.' *Proceedings of the Indian History Congress,* vol. 67, 2007.

Moreira, Adriano. 'The Portuguese Overseas Provinces.' *Civilisations,* vol. 7, no. 2, 1957.

Newman, Robert S. 'Goa: The Transformation of an Indian Region.' *Pacific Affairs,* 1984, 57 (3).

Parobo, Parag D. 'Tristão Bragança Cunha and Nationalism in Colonial Goa: Mediating Difference and Essentializing Nationhood.' *Economic and Political Weekly*, vol. 50, no. 31, 2015.

Pöllath, Moritz. '"Far Away from the Atlantic...": Goa, West New Guinea and NATO's Out-of-Area Policy at Bandung 1955.' *Journal of Transatlantic Studies*, Vol. 11, No. 4, 2013.

Robert S. Newman. 'Goa: The Transformation of an Indian Region.' *Pacific Affairs*, vol. 57, no. 3, 1984.

Rotter, Andrew Jon. *Comrades at Odds: The United States and India, 1947–1964.* Cornell University Press, 2000.

Rubinoff, Arthur G. 'Goa's Attainment of Statehood.' *Asian Survey*, vol. 32, no. 5, 1992.

Rubinoff, Arthur G. 'Political Integration in Goa.' *Journal of Developing Societies*, vol. 11, no. 1, 1995.

Salazar, Oliveira. 'Goa and the Indian Union: The Portuguese View.' *Foreign Affairs*, vol. 34, no. 3, 1956.

Singhal, D.P. 'Goa: End of an Epoch.' *The Australian Quarterly*, vol. 34, no. 1, 1962.

12. The Frontiers of the North-east

Ahmed, Ishtiaq. *Jinnah: His Successes, Failures and Role in History.* Penguin Random House India, 2020.

Banerjee, Paula. 'Women, Violence and North-East India.' *Economic and Political Weekly*, vol. 49, no. 43/44, 2014.

Baruah, Lily Mazindor (ed.). *Lokopriya Gopinath Bordoloi: An Architect of Modern India.* Gyan Publishing House, 1993.

Baruah, Sanjib. 'Protective Discrimination and Crisis of Citizenship in North-East India.' *Economic and Political Weekly*, vol. 38, no. 17, 2003.

Baruah, Sanjib. 'Territoriality, Indigeneity and Rights in the North-East India.' *Economic and Political Weekly*, vol. 43, no. 12/13, 2008.

Bhattacharya, Alak. 'Tribal Politics of Tripura: A Study in Electoral Behaviour.' *The Indian Journal of Political Science*, vol. 68, no. 3, 2007.

Chakraborty, Anup Shekhar. 'Politics of Silencing: Echoes of the Margins from Mizoram.' *The Indian Journal of Political Science*, vol. 72, no. 2, 2011.

Das, Nava Kishor. 'Identity Politics and Social Exclusion in India's Northeast. a Critique of Nation-Building and Redistributive Justice.' *Anthropos*, vol. 104, no. 2, 2009.

Datta, Prabhat. 'Secessionist Movements in Northeast India.' *The Indian Journal of Political Science*, vol. 53, no. 4, 1992.

Datta, Prabhat Kumar and Panchali Sen. 'Governance in the Sixth Schedule Areas in India's Nort-East: Context, Content and Challenges.' *Indian Journal of Public Administration*, vol. 66 (2) 2020.

Ghosh, Biswajit. 'Ethnicity and Insurgency in Tripura.' *Sociological Bulletin*, vol. 52, no. 2, 2003.

Ghoshal, Anindita. 'Survival Question of East Bengal Refugees: The Case of Tripura (1946–71).' *Proceedings of the Indian History Congress*, vol. 71, 2010.

Ghoshal, Anindita, and Aparajita. 'The Altered State of Affairs: Hindu Refugees of India and Muslim Returnees in East Pakistan (1947–1977).' *Proceedings of the Indian History Congress*, vol. 76, 2015.

Gohain, Hiren. 'Ethnic Unrest in the North-East.' *Economic and Political Weekly*, vol. 32, no. 8, 1997.

Haokip, Thongkholal. 'Is There a Pan-North-East Identity and Solidarity?' *Economic and Political Weekly*, vol. 47, no. 36, 2012.

Hluna, J. V. and Tochhawng. 'The Mizo Uprising: Assam Assembly Debates on the Mizo Movement, 1966–1971.' Cambridge Scholars Publishing, 2012.

Jafa, Vijendra Singh. 'Insurgencies in Northeast India: Dimensions of Discord and Containment.' *Responding to Terrorism in South Asia*. RCSS Colombo and Manohar Publications, 2006.

Kikhi, Kedelizo. 'What Ails the North-East? Challenges and Responses', *Sociological Bulletin*, vol. 58, no. 3, 2009.

Mukherjee, Dilip. 'Assam Reorganization.' *Asian Survey*, vol., 9 (4), April 1969.

Nunthara, C. 'Grouping of Villages in Mizoram: Its Social and Economic Impact.' *Economic and Political Weekly*, vol. 16, no. 30, 1981.

Nunthara, C. 'Peace and Conflict in the "Frontier" Areas of North-east India.' *Sociological Bulletin*, vol. 54, no. 3, 2005.

Oinam, Bhagat. 'Patterns of Ethnic Conflict in the North-East: A Study on Manipur.' *Economic and Political Weekly*, vol. 38, no. 21, 2003.

Oinam, Bhagat. 'State of the States: Mapping of India's Northeast' East–West Center Working Papers, East–West Center, Washington, November 2008.

Prabhakara, M.S. 'Separatist Movements in the North-East: Rhetoric and Reality.' *Economic and Political Weekly*, vol. 42, no. 9, 2007.

Prabhakara, M.S. 'Is North-East India Landlocked?' *Economic and Political Weekly*, vol. 39, no. 42, 2004.

Rajagopalan, Swarna. 'Reading Maps, Seeking Directions, Peace Accords in Northeast India: Journey over Milestones.' East–West Center, 2008.

Ramunny, Murkot. 'Changing Face of Tripura.' *Economic and Political Weekly*, vol. 23, no. 37, 1988.

Roy, Sanjay K. 'Conflicting Nations in North-East India.' *Economic and Political Weekly*, vol. 40, no. 21, 2005.

Reuben Lyngdoh, C. and L.S. Gassah. 'Decades of Inter-Ethnic Tension.' *Economic and Political Weekly*, vol. 38, no. 48, 2003.

Saikia, Rajen. *Social and Economic History of Assam*. Manohar Publishers, 2002.

Saikia, Rajen. 'The Political Geography of Colonial and Post-Colonial Assam: Construction and Contestations.' *Proceedings of the Indian History Congress*, vol. 70, 2009–2010.

Samson, Kamei. 'The Zeliangrong Movement in North-East India: An Exegetical Study.' *Sociological Bulletin*, vol. 61, no. 2, 2012.

Samuel, John. 'Language and Nationality in North-East India.' *Economic and Political Weekly*, vol. 28, no. 3/4, 1993.

Sarmah, Bhupen. 'The Cauldron of Conflict: Politics of Peace, Governance and Development in India's North-East.' *Social Scientist*, vol. 44, no. 11/12, 2016.

Singh, B.P. 'North-East India: Demography, Culture and Identity Crisis.' *Modern Asian Studies*, vol. 21, no. 2, 1987.

Singh, N. Somorendro. 'Integration and Development in North-East India: An Assessment.' *The Indian Journal of Political Science*, vol. 67, no. 2, 2006.

Syiemlieh, David R. 'Sectional President's Address: Colonial Encounter and Christian Missions in Northeast India.' *Proceedings of the Indian History Congress*, vol. 73, 2012.

Venkata Rao, V. 'Northeast India: Problems and Prospects.' *The Indian Journal of Political Science*, vol. 36, no. 1, 1975.

Venkata Rao, V. 'Reorganization of Northeast India.' *The Indian Journal of Political Science*, vol. 33, no. 2, 1972.

Verghese, B.G. *India's Northeast Resurgent: Ethnicity, Insurgency, Governance, Development.* Konark Publishers, 1996.

13. Island Territories

Anderson, C. *New Histories of Andaman Islands: Landscape, Place and Identity in the Bay Of Bengal 1790–1920.'* Cambridge University Press, 2015.

Anderson, C. 'Colonization, Kidnap and Confinement in the Andamans Penal Colony 1771–1864.' *Journal of Historical Geography*, 2015.

Anderson, C. 'The Andaman Island Penal Colony : Race, Class, Criminality and the British Empire.' *International Review of Social History*, 2018.

Anderson, C. *The Indian Uprising of 1857–58: Prisons, Prisoners and Rebellion.* Anthem, 2007.

Dasgupta, J. *Red Sun over Black Water,* Manas Publications, 2002.

Kailash. 'From Penal Settlement to Capital Town : Human Ecological Aspect of the Rise and Growth of Port Blair.' *The Indian Journal of Social Work*, 1995, vol. 56, no.4.

Kailash. 'Peaceful Coexistence.' *Economic and Political Weekly*, 2000.

Koya, S.M. 'Matriliny and Malabar Muslims.' *Proceedings of the Indian History Congress*, vol. 40. Indian History Congress, January 1979.

Kaul, S. *Andaman and Nicobar Islands: India's Untapped Strategic Assets.* Pentagon Press in association with Institute of Defence Studies & Analyses, 2015.

Maddy, U.M. 'When Pakistan Claimed the Andaman and Nicobar Islands.' Live History India, 2021. livehistory.com/story/cover-story/when-pakistan-claimed-the-andaman-and-nicobar-islands

NITI Aayog. 'Transforming the Islands through Creativity and Innovation.' RSIS Monograph, *India-Asean Defence Relations*, 2019.

Sareen, T.R. *Andaman and Nicobar Islands under Japanese Occupation during WWII.* Bio-Green, 2018.

Sareen, T.R. *Sharing the Blame: Subhas Chandra Bose and the Japanese Occupation of the Andamans 1942–45.* S.S. Publishers, 2002.

Scott-Clark, Cathy and Adrian Levy. 'Survivors of Our Hell.' *The Guardian* 23 June 2001.

Sen, S. 'Contexts, Representation and the Colonized Convict :Maulana Thanesari in the Andaman Islands.' *Crime, History and Societies*, vol. 8, no. 2, 2004.

Sherman, T.C. 'From Hell to Paradise? Voluntary Transfer of Convicts to the Andaman Islands 1921–1940.' *Modern Asian Studies (43,2)*, 2009.

Srivastava, P. 'Resistance and Repression in India.' *Crime, History and Societies, 2013*.

Srivastava, P.K. 'Oral History of Freedom Struggle with Special Reference to Ex Andaman Freedom Fighters (1921–27).' *Indian Council of Historical Research*, 1992.

Vallangi, N. 'India's Abandoned Island of Colonial Horror.' *Smithsonian Magazine*, 8 May 2018. https://smithsonianmagzine.org

14. From Subjects to Citizens – Sikkim Joins India

'Sikkim.' *The International and Comparative Law Quarterly*, vol. 24, no. 4, 1975.

Amarjeet Singh, M. and Komal Sinha (eds), 'Democracy and ethnic politics in Sikkim.' *Identity, Contestation and Development in Northeast India*, Taylor & Francis, 2015.

Arora, Vibha. 'Assertive Identities, Indigeneity, and the Politics of Recognition as a Tribe: The Bhutias, the Lepchas and the Limbus of Sikkim.' *Sociological Bulletin*, vol. 56, no. 2, 2007.

Brass, Paul R. 'Review Article on Rulers of India.' *Economic Development and Cultural Change*, vol. 51, no. 2, 2003.

Chaudhuri, Sarit K. Sameera Maiti and Charisma K. Lepcha, *The Cultural Heritage Of Sikkim*. Routledge, 2018.

Chopra, Sanjeev. 'Keynote Address: Sikkim Requiem for a Himalayan Kingdom' *at* AKLF, Kolkata, 2016.

Das, B.S. *The Sikkim Saga*. Vikas Publishing House, 1983.

Datta-Ray, Sunanda K. *Smash and Grab: Annexation of Sikkim*, Westland, 2013.

Duff, Andrew. *Sikkim: Requiem for a Himalayan Kingdom*, Penguin Random House India, 2016.

Gupta, Ranjan. 'Sikkim: The Merger with India.' *Asian Survey*, vol. 15, no. 9, 1975.

Kohli, A. 'Can Democracies Accommodate Ethnic Nationalism? The Rise and Decline of Self-Determination Movements in India.' *Community Conflicts and the State in India*. Oxford University Press, 1998.

Lama, M.P. *Sikkim Human Development Report, 2001*. Social Science Press, 2001.

Levi, Werner. 'Bhutan and Sikkim: Two Buffer States.' *The World Today*, vol. 15, no. 12, 1959.

Little, K. 'From the Villages to the Cities – The Battlegrounds for Lepcha Protests.' *Transforming Cultures*, 5 (1), 2010.

Oinam, Bhagat. 'State of the States.' East-West Center, 2008.

Rai, D. 'Monarchy and Democracy in Sikkim and the Contribution of Kazi Lhendup Dorjee Khangsherpa.' *International Journal of Scientific and Research Publications*, vol.3 (9), 2013.

Ram, N. 'Sikkim Story: Protection to Absorption.' *Social Scientist*, vol. 3, no. 2, 1974.

Rock, Joseph F. 'Excerpts from a History of Sikkim.' *Anthropos*, vol. 48, no. 5/6, 1953.

Rose, Leo E. 'India and Sikkim: Redefining the Relationship.' *Pacific Affairs*, vol. 42, no. 1, 1969.

Sen, S.C. 'Sikkim – Where Feudalism Fights Democracy.' *Law and Politics in Africa, Asia and Latin America*, vol. 8, no. 3/4, 1975.

Sindhu, G.B.S. *Sikkim – Dawn of Democracy: The Truth Behind the Merger with India*, Penguin Viking, 2018.

Sinha, A.C. 'The Feudal Polity and Political Development in Sikkim.' *Indian Anthropologist*, vol. 3, no. 2, 1973.

15. Delhi, New Delhi, NCT and NCR

Ahluwalia, Sanjeev S. 'Has Democracy been Downgraded in Delhi?' Observer Research Foundation, 26 March 2021. https://www.orfonline.org/expert-speak/has-democracy-been-downgraded-in-delhi/

Ahmed, Ishtiaq. *The Punjab Blooded, Partitioned and Cleansed: Unravelling the 1947 Tragedy through Secret British Reports and First-person Accounts.* Rupa and Co., 2011.

Athar Ali, M. 'The Passing of Empire: The Mughal Case.' *Modern Asian Studies,* vol. 9, no. 3, 1975.

Bardiar, Nilendra, *Urban, Cultural, Economic and Social Transformation: History of New Delhi 1947–65,* Ruby Press & Co., 2014.

Blair, Sheila and Jonathan M. Bloom. *The Art and Architecture of Islam, 1250–1800.* Yale University Press, 1995.

Byron, Robert, *New Delhi: The Architectural Review.* Westminster, 1931.

Chandra, Moti. *Trade and Trade Routes in Ancient India.* Abhinav Publications, 1977.

Chandra, Satish. *History of Medieval India: 800–1700.* Orient Longman, 2007.

Dalrymple, William. *The Last Mughal: The Fall of a Dynasty – Delhi, 1857,* Random House, 2007.

Dupont, Veronique. 'Patterns of Population Mobility in Delhi.' Institute of Economic Growth, 1995.

Eaton, Richard M. *India in the Persianate Age.* Penguin Books, 2020.

Elliot, Henry Miers, John Dowson. *The History of India, as Told by Its Own Historians: The Muhammadan Period,* vol. 3. Trübner & Co., 1867.

Ettinghausen, Richard, Oleg Grabar, Marily Jenkins-Madina. *Islamic Art and Architecture: 650–1250.* Yale University Press, 2001.

Fanshawe, H.C. *Delhi – Past and Present.* J. Murray, 1902.

Faruqui, Munis D. 'The Forgotten Prince: Mirza Hakim and the Formation of the Mughal Empire in India.' *Journal of the Economic and Social History of the Orient,* vol. 48 no. 4, 2005.

Fraser, Lovat. *At Delhi (An Account of the Delhi Durbar, 1903).* Times of India Press and Thacker, 1903.

Gordon, S. *The New Cambridge History of India, II, 4: The Marathas 1600–1818.* Cambridge University Press, 1993.

Government of Delhi, NDMC Act (www.ndmc.gov.in).

Government of India, The Constitution (Sixty-Ninth Amendment) Act, 1991. The Constitution (Amendment) Acts, Constitution of India.

Habib, Irfan, *Atlas of the Mughal Empire: Political and Economic Maps*. Oxford University Press, 1982.

Harle, J.C. *The Art and Architecture of the Indian Subcontinent*. Yale University Press, 1994.

Hartcourt, A. *The New Guide to Delhi*. Victoria Press, 1873.

Hearn, Gordon Risley. *The Seven Cities of Delhi*, W. Thackwer & Co., 1906.

Jackson, Peter. *The Delhi Sultanate: A Political and Military History*. Cambridge University Press, 2003.

Johnson, David A. 'A British Empire for the Twentieth Century: The Inauguration of New Delhi, 1931.' *Urban History*, vol. 35, issue 3, December 2008.

Kapoor, Pramod, Malvika Singh, Rudrangshu Mukherjee. *New Delhi: Making of a Capital*. Lustre Press, 2009.

Khan, Mohd. Adul Wali, *Gold and Silver Coins of Sultans of Delhi*, Government of Andhra Pradesh, 1974.

Kumar, Pushpam. 'Assessment of Economic Drivers of Land Use Change in Urban Ecosystems of Delhi, India.' *AMBIO*, vol.38, no.1, 2009.

Kumar, Sunil. *The Emergence of the Delhi Sultanate*. Permanent Black, 2007.

Lal, Kishori Saran. 'History of the Khaljis (1290–1320).' *The Indian Press*, 1950.

Ludden, David. *India and South Asia: A Short History*. Oneworld, 2002.

Majumdar, R.C. and K.M. Munshi. *The Delhi Sultanate*. Bharatiya Vidya Bhavan, 1990.

Majumdar, R.C., H. Raychaudhuri and K. Datta. *An Advanced History of India: 2*. Macmillan, 1951.

McCrindle, J.W. *Ancient India as Described by Ptolemy*. Thacker, Spink, & Company, 1885.

Nath, Viswambhar, *Delhi before 1947: Urbanization, Urban Development, and Metropolitan Cities in India*. Concept Publishing Company, 2007.

Pothen, Nayantara. *Glittering Decades New Delhi in Love and War*. Penguin, 2012.

Prasanna, Alok. 'From "Trishanku" to a Puppet – How Modi Govt's GNCTD Bill Undermines Delhi Gov.' The Print, 27 March 2021. https:// vidhilegalpolicy.in/blog/from-trishanku-to-a-puppet-how-modi-govts-gnctd-bill-undermines-delhi-govt/

Raychaudhuri, H.C. *Political History of Ancient India: From the Accession of Parikshit to the Extinction of the Gupta Dynasty*. University of Calcutta, 1950.

Ridley, Jane. 'Edwin Lutyens, New Delhi, and the Architecture of Imperialism.' *Journal of Imperial and Commonwealth History*, vol. 26, issue 2, May 1998.

Sahoo, Niranjan. 'On Delhi, the Centre's Move Goes against the Spirit of Federalism.' Observer Research Foundation, 8 March 2021. https://www.orfonline.org/research/on-delhi-the-centres-move-goes-against-the-spirit-of-federalism/

Sahoo, Niranjan, 'Proposing a New Governance Structure for Delhi.' Observer Research Foundation, 1 April 2021. https://www.orfonline.org/research/proposing-a-new-governance-structure-for-delhi/

Saksena, Banarsi Prasad. 'The Khaljis: Alauddin Khalji.' *A Comprehensive History of India: The Delhi Sultanate (AD 1206–526)*. The Indian History Congress/People's Publishing House, 1970.

Sonne, Wolfgang. *Representing the State: Capital City Planning in the Early Twentieth Century*. Canberra, 2003.

Singh, Upinder. *The Discovery of Ancient India: Early Archaeologists and the Beginnings of Archaeology*. Permanent Black, 2004.

Singh, Upinder. *A History of Ancient and Early Medieval India from the Stone Age to the 12th Century*. Pearson, 2009.

Singh, Upinder. *A History of Ancient History*, Berghahn, 2006.

Srivastava, Ashirvadi Lal. *The Sultanate of Delhi, 711–1526 A D*. Shiva Lal Agarwala & Company, 1929.

Van Buitenen, J.A.B. and James L. Fitzgerald, *The Mahabharata, Volume 1: Book 1: The Book of the Beginning*. Chicago: University of Chicago Press, 1973.

Volwahsen, Andreas, *Imperial Delhi: The British Capital of the Indian Empire*. Prestel Publishing, 2003.

16. Regional Aspirations: Chhattisgarh, Uttarakhand and Jharkhand

Bakshi, S.R. *Ravi Shankar Shukla: Life and Times*. Om Publications, 2001.

Chadda, Maya. 'Integration through Internal Reorganization: Containing Ethnic Conflict in India.' *The Global Review of Ethno Politics*, vol. 2, September 2002.

Dietmar, Rothermund. 'Creating New States in India: Chhattisgarh, Jharkhand, Uttaranchal.' *ASIEN*, April 2001.

Dube, M.P. 'Regionalism in India: Some Critical Observations with Special Reference to Uttarakhand Movement.' *The Indian Journal of Political Science*, vol. 56, no. 1/4, 1995.

Environmental History Review, vol. 15, no. 3, 1991.

Guha, Ramachandra. *The Unquiet Woods: Ecological Change and Peasant Resistance in the Himalaya*. University of Berkely Press, 2000.

Guha, Ramachandra. 'Ideological Trends in Indian Environmentalism.' *Economic and Political Weekly*, vol. 23, no. 49, 1988.

Guha, Ramachandra and Madhav Gadgil. 'State Forestry and Social Conflict in British India.' *Past & Present*, no. 123, 1989.

Guha, Ramachandra. 'Scientific Forestry and Social Change in Uttarakhand.' *Economic and Political Weekly*, vol. 20, no. 45/47, 1985.

Guha, Ramachandra. 'The Prehistory of Community Forestry in India.' *Environmental History*, vol. 6, no. 2, 2001.

Gun, Punyabrata. 'Struggle and Create: My Days with Com. Shankar Guha Niyogi.' Countercurrent.org, January 2018.

Krishna, Daya. 'The New Tribal States: Can They Survive in the Modern World?' *Economic and Political Weekly*, vol. 35, no. 46, 2000.

International Affairs (Royal Institute of International Affairs 1944-). Vol. 90, no. 3, 2014.

Kumar, Dharmendra. 'Constitution of a Region: A Study of Chhattisgarh.' *Rethinking State Politics in India*. Routledge India, 2011.

Kumar, Kujur Rajat. 'Underdevelopment and Naxal Movement.' *Economic and Political Weekly*, vol. 41, no. 7, 2006.

Kumar, Kujur, Rajat. 'Left Extremism in India.' Institute of Peace and Conflict Studies, 2006.

Kumar, Sanjay. 'Creation of New States: Rationale and Implications.' *Economic and Political Weekly*, vol. 37, no. 36, 2002.

Linkenbach, Antje. 'Shaking the State by Making a (New) State? Fighting for Autonomy in the Central Himalaya (North India).' *Sociologus*, vol. 52, no. 1, 2002.

Mishra, Ish N., 'Chhattisgarh: Nationality Movement and the Oppressed.' Countercurrents.org, 19 October 2017.

Mukherjee, Pampa. 'The Creation of a Region: Politics of Identity and Development in Uttarakhand.' *Rethinking State Politics in India.* Routledge India, 2011.

Mukherjee, Siuli. 'Regionalism and Politics of Identity: A Story of Jharkhand.' *Heritage*, vol. II, 2015.

Munda, R.D. and Mullick S. Bosu. 'The Jharkhand Movement: Indigenous Peoples Struggle for Autonomy in India.' *IWGIA*, document 108, 2003.

Mawdsley, Emma. 'After Chipko: From Environment to Region in Uttaranchal.' *Journal of Peasant Studies*, 25(4), July 1998.

Mosley, Stephen. 'Common Ground: Integrating Social and Environmental History.' *Journal of Social History*, vol. 39, no. 3, 2006.

Nauriya, Anil. 'What Chhattisgarh Movement Means.' *Economic and Political Weekly*, vol. 26, no. 48, 1991.

Pankaj, Ashwini Kumar (ed.). *Select Speeches and Writings of Jaipal Munda.* P.K. Foundation, 2020.

Pathak, Shekhar, *The Chipko Movement: A People's History*, Permanent Black, 2020.

Rai, Anuradha. 'State Reorganization in India: Real -politicking or Electoral Politics.' *Indian Journal of Political Science*, October–December 2012.

Roy, A.K. 'Jharkhand: From Separation to Liberation.' *Economic and Political Weekly*, 7 October 2000.

Sen, Ilina. *Inside Chhattisgarh: A Political Memoir*, Penguin, 2015.

Sharma, Vijay Prakash. 'Making of Jharkhand Identity and Culture.' Making_of_Jharkhand_Identity_and_Culture:https://www.academia.edu/40843191/

Sundar, Nandini. *The Burning Forest: India's War in Bastar.* Juggernaut, 2016.

Sundar, Nandini. 'Insurgency, Counter Insurgency and Democracy in Central India.'

http://burawoy.berkeley.edu/Public%20Sociology,%20Live/Sundar/Insurgency,%20Counter-insurgency%20%26%20Democracy.pdf

The Indian Journal of Political Science. Vol. 74, no. 4, 2013.

Tillin, Louise. 'United in Diversity? Asymmetry in Indian Federalism.' *Publius*, vol. 37, no. 1, 2007.

Tillin, Louise. 'Questioning Borders: Social Movements, Political Parties and the Creation of New States in India.' *Pacific Affairs*, vol. 84, no. 1, 2011.

Tillin, Louise. 'Restructuring States, Restructuring Ethnicity: Looking across Disciplinary Boundaries at Federal Futures in India and Nepal.' *Modern Asian Studies*, vol. 49, no. 1, 2015.

Tillin, Louise. 'Statehood and the Politics of Intent.' *Economic and Political Weekly*, vol. 46, no. 20, 2011.

17. Bande Utkal Janani

Aquil, Raziuddinn and Partha Chatterjee (eds.). *History in the Vernacular.* Permanent Black, 2008.

Behera, Subhakanta. *Constitution of an Identity Discourse: Oriya Literature and the Jagannath Cult (1866–1936).* Munshiram Manoharlal Publishers, 2002.

Bihar and Orissa. 'Report on the Administration of the Territories Now Included in the Province of Bihar and Orissa.' JSTOR, 1912.

Das, G.N. 'Jagannatha and Oriya Nationalism.' *The Cult of Jagannatha and the Regional Tradition of Orissa.* Manohar Publishers, 1978.

Dash, S.C. 'States Reorganization Commission and Orissa.' *The Indian Journal of Political Science*, vol. 16, no. 4, 1955.

Kar, Purushottam, *Indian National Congress and Orissa (1885–1936).* Cuttack, 1987.

Mir, Farina. 'Imperial Policy, Provincial Practices: Colonial Language Policy in Nineteenth-Century India.' *Indian Economic and Social History Review*, vol. 43 (2), 2006.

Mishra, Kishore Chandra. 'Prajamandal Movements in the Feudatory States of Western Orissa.' *Proceedings of the Indian History Congress,* vol. 69, 2008.

Mishra, Laxmi Kanta. 'Social Formations in Early Historic Orissa.' *Proceedings of the Indian History Congress*, vol. 72, 2011.

Mishra, Pritipuspa. 'Beyond Powerlessness: Institutional Life of Vernacular in Making of Modern Orissa (1866–1931).' *The Indian Economic and Social History Review*, 48 (4), 2011.

Mishra, Pritipuspa. 'Odisha as Vernacular Homeland.' Cambridge Core (www. cambrdige.org/core).

Misra, Prasanna Kumar. 'H.K. Mahtab and the Merger of the Princely States of Orissa – An Introspection.' *Proceedings of the Indian History Congress*, vol. 50, 1989.

Mohanty, Prafulla Kumar, 'Ideas on the State formation in Ancient and Early Medieval Orissa – A Historiographical Analysis.' *Proceedings of the Indian History Congress*, vol. 68, 2007.

Nanda, Subrat K. 'Cultural Nationalism in a Multi-National Context: The Case of India.' *Sociological Bulletin*, vol.55 (1), 2006.

Padhy, S.C. 'Formation of Orissa Province and Role of Oriyas in Berhampur.' *Proceedings of the Indian History Congress*, vol. 66, 2005.

Padhy, S.C. 'Nationalism, National Movement and Peasants: A Historiographical Analysis in Case of Orissa.' *Proceedings of the Indian History Congress*, vol. 67, 2006.

Padhy, S.C. 'Indian National Movement and Individual Civil Disobedience Movement: A Study in Orissa Context.' *Indian History Congress*, vol.65 (2004).

Panda, Shishir Kumar. 'Process of Urbanization in Early Orissa.' *Proceedings of the Indian History Congress*, vol. 62, 2001.

Panda, Shishir Kumar. 'Sectional President's Address: Early State Formation in Orissa.' *Proceedings of the Indian History Congress*, vol. 70, 2009.

Pathy, Jaganath, 'Class Structure in Rural Orissa', *Sociological Bulletin*, vol. 30, no. 2, 1981.

Pati, Biswamoy. 'Independence and After: Orissa, 1946–52.' *Indian Historical Review*, vol.29 (1–2), 2002.

Pati, Biswamoy. 'Dialectics of Transition: Orissa, 1943–50.' *Economic and Political Weekly*, vol. 27, no. 7, 1992.

Pati, Biswamoy. 'Of Movements, Compromises and Retreats: Orissa, 1936–1939.' *Social Scientist*, vol. 20, no. 5/6, 1992.

Ramaswamy, Sumathi, *Passions of the Tongue: Language Devotion in Tamil India, 1891–1970*. University of California Press, 1997.

Roul, Kamalakanta and Bimal Kumar Raul. 'Cultural Component of Indian Nationalism: The Study of Odia Nationalism.' *Mainstream*, 14 August 2020.

Saha, Subrat Kumar and Mamata Dash, 'Expropriation of Land and Cultures: The Odisha Story and Beyond.' *Social Change*, vol.41 (2).

Saha, Suranjit K. 'Early State Formation in Tribal Areas of East-Central India.' *Economic and Political Weekly*, vol. 31, no. 13, 1996.

Sarangi, Asha (ed.). *Language and Politics in India*, Oxford, 2009.

Sharma, S.N. 'The Collector in 1960s.' *The Indian Journal of Public Administration*, vol.11 (3), 1965.

18. Telangana: The Second State for Telugu Speakers

'Telangana Demand.' *Economic and Political Weekly*, vol. 43, no. 46, 2008.

'The First Linguistic State – Andhra Pradesh – Was Born.' Sankalp India Found. (http://www.sankalpindia.net/book/first-linguistic-state-andhra-pradesh-was-born)

'The Role of Burgulla in Telangana.' The Hans India, 19 September 2013.

Hargopal, G. 'The Telangana People's Movement: The Unfolding Political Culture.' *Economic and Political Weekly*, vol. 45, no. 42, 2010.

Kannabiran, Kalpana, et al. 'On the Telangana Trail.' *Economic and Political Weekly*, vol. 45, no. 13, 2010.

Melkote, Rama S., et al. 'The Movement for Telangana: Myth and Reality.' *Economic and Political Weekly*, vol. 45, no. 2, 2010.

Pingle, Gautam. *The Formation and History of Telangana: A Collection of Nine Critical Essays*. Orient Blackswan, 2021.

Pingle, Gautam. *The Fall and Rise of Telangana*. Orient Blackswan, 2018.

Pingle, Gautam. 'Reddys, Kammas and Telangana.' *Economic and Political Weekly*, vol. 46, no. 36, 2011.

Pingle, Gautam. 'The Historical Context of Andhra and Telangana, 1949–56.' *Economic and Political Weekly*, vol. 45, no. 8, 2010.

Rao, C.H. Hanumantha. 'Srikrishna Committee on Telangana: Recommendations at Variance with the Analysis.' *Economic and Political Weekly*, vol. 46, no. 5, 2011.

Rao, C.H. Hanumantha. 'The New Telangana State: A Perspective for Inclusive and Sustainable Development.' *Economic and Political Weekly*, vol. 49, no. 9, 2014.

Rao, G. Gangadhara. 'Hyderabad and the Bifurcation of Andhra Pradesh.' *Economic and Political Weekly*, vol. 48, no. 42, 2013.

Sarojini, Regani. 'Highlights of the Freedom Movement in Andhra Pradesh.' Ministry of Cultural Affairs, Andhra Pradesh, 1972.

Srikanth, H. 'Construction and Consolidation of the Telangana Identity.' *Economic and Political Weekly*, vol. 48, no. 45/46, 2013.

Srinivasulu, K., et al. 'Srikrishna Committee: Thorough but Unviable.' *Economic and Political Weekly,* vol. 46, no. 10, 2011.

INDEX

ABOUT THE AUTHOR

Sanjeev Chopra superannuated as the director, Lal Bahadur Shastri National Academy of Administration, Mussoorie, after thirty-six years in the Indian Administrative Service. He has held the Hubert H. Humphrey Fellowship (Cornell); the Robert S. McNamara Fellowship (World Bank); and positions at Royal Asiatic Society, London; the Lakshmi Mittal and Family South Asia Institute (Harvard); and the USI New Delhi.

He lives with his better half, Rashmi, in Dehradun where they curate the Valley of Words, a literature and arts festival, in November every year.